T0300421

VARIORUM COLLECTED STUDIES SERIES

Commerce and Conquest
in the Mediterranean,
1100–1500

Dr David Abulafia

David Abulafia

Commerce and Conquest
in the Mediterranean,
1100–1500

Published by VARIORUM

Published by
Ashgate Publishing Limited
Wey Court East
Union Road
Farnham
Surrey, GU9 7PT
England

Ashgate Publishing Company
110 Cherry Street
Suite 3-1
Burlington
VT 05401-3818
USA

British Library Cataloguing in Publication Data

Abulafia, David
    Commerce and Conquest in the
    Mediterranean, 1100-1500. — (Variorum
    Collected Studies Series; CS410)
    I. Title II. Series
    909.09822

ISBN 978–0–8607–8377–0

The paper used in this publication meets the minimum requirements of
    American National Standard for Information Sciences
— Permanence of Paper for Printed Library Materials, ANSI Z39.48-1984.

Transfered to Digital Printing in 2010

MIX
Paper from
responsible sources
FSC® C004959

Printed and bound in Great Britain
by Printondemand-worldwide.com

COLLECTED STUDIES SERIES CS410

CONTENTS

vi

This book contains xiv + 343 pages

PUBLISHER'S NOTE

The articles in this volume, as in all others in the Collected Studies Series, have not been given a new, continuous pagination. In order to avoid confusion, and to facilitate their use where these same studies have been referred to elsewhere, the original pagination has been maintained wherever possible.

Each article has been given a Roman number in order of appearance, as listed in the Contents. This number is repeated on each page and quoted in the index entries.

PREFACE

I

The subject of this volume is trade and the flag. Did the merchants of the Italian maritime cities and of southern France lead the way in the conquest of the Mediterranean from the late eleventh century onwards? Or was the commercial expansion they led the consequence of political conquests in the Mediterranean, at the hands of the Normans and their successors in the central Mediterranean, and at the hands of the crusaders in the eastern Mediterranean? There has been a tendency to answer this question in fairly unequivocal terms; some have argued for the presence of Italian shipping (not just Venetian and Amalfitan, but Pisan and Genoese) in the Near East even before the First Crusade, with the result (it is maintained) that the crusade itself can no longer be seen as the start of the process of commercial penetration. Another approach, based again on observation of the early crusades, but easily extended also to Sicily and parts of north Africa, associates the clearing of the seas as much with the establishment of Latin kingdoms in the region as with the activities of the merchant fleets of Genoa, Pisa and Venice. Yet in most respects the distinction is a false one. Continued Latin rule was impossible without the support of western navies; but merchants who had previously possessed a nodding acquaintance with the markets of the Islamic world found their access much eased with the establishment of Latin rule in Acre (and, later, Famagusta) to the east, Palermo and Messina in mid-Mediterranean, and such ports as Ciutat de Mallorca and Valencia in the west.

Such ports functioned as jumping-off boards for immersion in the markets of the Islamic world and of eastern Christendom: from Acre access could be gained, directly or via intermediaries, to Aleppo, Damascus, Damietta, Alexandria, even on occasion Cairo; Palermo and Messina gave quick access to Mahdia, Tunis and the ports of Ifriqiyah; Catalan Mallorca became a way station and depot en route to Bougie and the Algerian coast (essays VII, X, XI). Consulates established by the Italians in these centres offered facilities not merely to native merchants of Pisa, Genoa and Venice, but to protected groups from many other cities who embarked on the often risky business of trading with the Muslims on Islamic soil (essays VI, X, XI, XIII). A mystery remains concerning the failure of Amalfi and the other south Italian ports to reap the benefits of these conquests, particularly since they had long been engaged in trade with Egypt and Byzantium. An attempt is made here to weigh up the arguments about the 'decline' of Amalfi and to place them in the context of developments in northern Italy (essay I).

The relationship between the success of the three major Italian cities and their smaller rivals or partners from Italy, Languedoc, Provence and (eventually) Catalonia deserves thought. It is argued here that by 1200 the lesser cities, such as Ancona, Narbonne, Messina, realised that the markets were still open to those who specialised in high quality goods to which the Big Three of Genoa, Pisa and Venice did not necessarily have access. The honey of Narbonne, the wine of Messina, as also the saffron of San Gimignano, had a good, in some cases unbeatable reputation on the Mediterranean markets, and on this basis the merchants of these and other lesser cities were able to create flourishing trade networks which historians have neglected in favour of Venice and Genoa (essays XI, XII, XIII, XIV). Yet the 'commercial revolution' is significant precisely because it extended rapidly beyond the Big Three cities to secondary centres (one of which was Florence, which of course did manage to catch up the leaders); it is precisely in this respect that the Mediterranean trade of this period differs funda-mentally from that of earlier Amalfitan and Venetian pioneers. It is not simply a question of the vastly enlarged scale of the cities' trade around 1200; it is also a question of the impact of this trade on the European hinterland, and it is argued here that the inability of Amalfi to serve that hinterland was a crucial factor in its failure to experience real take-off (essay I). Evidence for the Levant trade of Genoa, and also for some of the Tuscan cities, is tainted by the nineteenth-century Courtois forgeries; as late as 1989 Courtois charters were still on sale at Sotheby's in London, though the mistake was exposed in the British press partly with the help of a brief study printed here (essay XVI).

The kingdom of Sicily, and from 1282 two rival kingdoms of Sicily, sat astride the routes linking both the Tyrrhenian and the Adriatic to the eastern Mediterranean; at times the rulers of Sicily were able to exert such influence over the African ports opposite Sicily that they possessed command over the Sicilian straits (essay IV), and even conflict with the Almohads of Tunis ended amicably after a curious incident later remodelled in a *novella* of Giovanni Boccaccio (essay V). In the mid-fourteenth century the Genoese took care to regulate their relationship with the Queen of Naples and to police the entrance to the Adriatic, on the eve of one of the most damaging of their wars with Venice (essay XV). But those who established cordial ties with the rulers of Sicily stood to gain not merely access to the island's markets, rich in grain, and, until the late twelfth century, other products such as cotton, but also access to Tunis, a terminal point of the gold routes from Black Africa; striking is the presence of Florentines, Catalans, Pisans and others in the Sicilian-Tunisian grain trade by the end of the thirteenth century (essay VII).

What is visible here is that process of the takeover of Sicily's external trade by foreign merchants which underlies many of the studies contained in this book. While Messina functioned as the centre of a limited Levant trade, it was never able to compete on a large scale with Genoa or Venice; indeed, a major dimension to Messina's economy was the presence of large numbers of north Italian settlers in the port. At the risk of using a dangerous word, one could describe the city as a colony of the northern merchants (see essays I, XII). An important theme of this book is the impact of foreign trade on the economic structures of the areas penetrated by the Italian, Catalan and southern French merchants. This volume therefore opens with a discussion of the debate about the evolution of 'economic dualism' in medieval Italy, in which an attempt is made to establish a position distinct from either that of Henri Bresc or that of S.R. Epstein in their highly important, and greatly contrasted, books on late medieval Sicily published in 1986 and in 1992, and different also from that of John Day in his very stimulating studies of medieval Sardinia (essays I, II). In continuing to stress the role of trade, my own view retains some similarities to that of Bresc and Day; but it makes less emphatic claims for the damage done to the structure of the Sicilian and south Italian economy by the north Italian merchants, arguing that only Sardinia fits well into the model of a colonial economy. This picture is extended into the fifteenth century, taking mainland southern Italy, rather than Epstein and Bresc's Sicily, as the testing ground. In the late fifteenth century, foreign merchants dominated the fair of Salerno, and the undoubted efforts of the Aragonese king of Naples to stimulate economic recovery in southern Italy seem to have resulted most notably in an expansion of the export of raw materials (essay IX).

King Ferrante of Naples' courteous welcome to the exiled Jews of Spain and Sicily in 1492 serves as a reminder that the lengthy period handled in this book saw the transformation of the western and central Mediterranean into a region not just ruled by Christians, not just patrolled by Christian navies, but inhabited by an increasing proportion of Christians as compared to Jews and Muslims. The decline of *convivencia* in Sicily can be linked to the political and economic transformations mentioned already; the Norman conquest of Sicily ushered in not a golden period of harmony among Greeks, Latins, Jews, Muslims, but the gradual takeover of the cities and the land by immigrant Latins. By 1200 Islam was fully on the retreat in Sicily (essay III). The Jews remained as a testimony to the island's Islamic past, for their daily language long remained Arabic; at the time of the Aragonese invasion of Sicily they were still very well integrated into the economy and society of a small town such as Monte San Giuliano (now known as Erice), even though only a few years hence the Aragonese king would establish a true ghetto for the Jews of Palermo (essay VIII). The comfortable relations between Jews and Christians visible in the notarial acts of Erice serve as confirmation that it was often the rulers rather than their subjects who initiated the separation of Jews or Muslims from the surrounding society.

II

This volume is divided into two broad sections, one dealing with the kingdom of Sicily or Naples in relation to northern Italy, north Africa and to some extent Catalonia. The emphasis here is on a north-south axis, and particularly on the debate about economic dualism. The first essay can be read as a general introduction to these problems. Likewise, in the second section essay X is intended to outline some of the problems then taken up in essay XI and in more detail in the remaining studies. Essay XII, on the Levant trade of a Sicilian city, could evidently have fitted in either section. However, there are other studies that I have deliberately excluded from this collection, particularly a series of articles on the political, religious and economic history of the Catalan kingdom of Majorca, mainly between 1276 and 1343, which appeared in the *Mediterranean Historical Review*, 5 and 6 (1990–1), in the acts of the thirteenth and fourteenth Congress of the History of the Crown of Aragon, in a *Festschrift* for my colleague C.N.L. Brooke, in a volume in memory of C.-E. Dufourcq, and elsewhere. These form the backbone of a separate study of the Majorcan kingdom and its trade under the title *A Mediterranean Emporium: the Catalan Kingdom of Majorca,* (Cambridge, 1994). Some new studies concerned with Frederick II could not be included as a result of delays in their original publication. I have also excluded a long study of 'Asia, Africa and the trade of medieval Europe', published in 1987 in the *Cambridge Economic History of Europe*, volume 2, second edition, at the kind invitation of Sir Michael Postan.

The articles collected here were written over a slightly longer time span than those in my earlier Variorum collection, *Italy, Sicily and the Mediterranean, 1100–1400* (1987). I have included a few short articles left out of that volume, which it later seemed to me had been cited often enough to warrant reprinting after all. I am most grateful once again to Dr John Smedley of Variorum for his advice, encouragement and efficiency; Anna Sapir Abulafia again heads the list of my colleagues who deserve thanks; special thanks are due also to Henri Bresc and Stephan Epstein for sharing ideas and agreeing to disagree with me. Giuseppe Galasso, James Powell, Francesco Giunta, Richard Vaughan, Cinzio Violante, Pietro Corrao, Trevor Dean, Chris Wickham, Ruggiero Romano, Benjamin Kedar, Avrom Udovitch, Gabriela Airaldi, Guy Romestan, Peter Edbury have been civilised and co-operative editors of the publications in which many of these articles first appeared, and in several cases hosted conferences and meetings in Naples, New York, Palermo, Jerusalem, Montpellier and Cardiff where these results could be presented.

D.S.H. ABULAFIA

Gonville and Caius College, Cambridge
December 1992

I

SOUTHERN ITALY, SICILY AND SARDINIA IN THE MEDIEVAL MEDITERRANEAN ECONOMY[1]

I

In many recent studies, the economic relations between the Italian south and neighbouring regions have been analysed from the point of view of the theory of economic dualism, and from that of unequal exchange. The publication in 1986 of Henri Bresc's monumental *Un monde méditerranéen* has served to confirm the tendency of historians of Sicily to argue on these lines;[2] however, other regions of the

---

[1] This is the first publication in English of a paper originally written in Italian and presented at the conference *Venezia e l'economia mondiale attorno al 1200* held at the Centro tedesco di studi veneziani in Venice in September 1987. An Italian version, entitled 'Il Mezzogiorno italiano in rapporto con i suoi vicini verso il 1200', appeared as the new preface to the Italian translation of my book *The Two Italies: economic relations between the Norman Kingdom of Sicily and the northern communes* (Cambridge, 1977), published as *Le Due Italie: relazioni economiche fra il Regno normanno di Sicilia e i comuni settentrionali*, with an introduction by Giuseppe Galasso and translation of the main text by Cosima Campagnolo (Naples, 1991). I am grateful to Dr S. R. Epstein for his stimulating ideas and comments; special thanks are also due to Giuseppe Galasso, Mario del Treppo and Henri Bresc for their comments at the formal *presentazione* of *Le Due Italie* by Guida Editore at the Maschio Angioino, Naples, in February 1992. In the light of their views and of the recent publication of S. R. Epstein's *An island for itself. Economic development and social change in late medieval Sicily* (Cambridge, 1992), the English version of this paper has been brought further up-to-date.

[2] H. Bresc, *Un monde méditérranéen: économie et société en Sicile, 1300-1450*, 2 vols. (École française de Rome/Accademia di Scienze e Arti di Palermo, Rome/Palermo, 1986); cf. now S. R. Epstein's *An island for itself*, which takes a very different view from Bresc's work. It will be apparent from this paper that my own deep admiration for both scholars' work does not mean I am convinced by the arguments of either.

Southern Italy, Sicily and Sardinia

Mezzogiorno too (as defined by the modern Cassa del Mezzogiorno) have been examined from what is essentially a dualistic perspective, most importantly Sardinia. In 1984 John Day, one of the leading specialists in Sardinian history, published a study of *La Sardegna e i suoi dominatori* in which he identified the imposition of a 'colonial' economic regime on the island during the period of Genoese and Pisan ascendancy.[3] In the two cases of Sicily and Sardinia we can observe several points in common. In the first place, these islands do not conform with the wider demographic patterns of continental Europe, for they remained lightly populated in the twelfth and thirteenth centuries; we even find deserted villages in Norman Sicily. Indeed, it is striking that one island, Sicily, possessing wide-ranging and important commercial contacts with the outside world, shows such similarity in this respect to the more closed, in a certain sense primitive, economy of twelfth-century Sardinia. But a second common factor is the way that the transformation of both the Sicilian and the Sardinian economy can be attributed to the presence on the islands of Tuscan, Ligurian, Provençal and Catalan businessmen, anxious to exploit the grain resources of both islands, as well as pastoral products and other raw materials. Another common feature is the dating of these transformations, which can be identified in germ in the twelfth century, but which become amplified and confirmed in the thirteenth and fourteenth centuries. To understand the evolution of a dualistic economy in late medieval Italy, the years around 1200 are thus of special importance. In its classic form, this theory takes as its starting point the contrast between a northern Italy that was undergoing rapid 'industrialisation' (in the sense that this term can be applied to the textile and metal industries of medieval Europe), while the south retained its predominant interest in the export not of finished goods but of foodstuffs and raw materials. It remains a subject of debate how far local industry in Sicily or southern Italy was able to satisfy domestic demand; but in the case of Sardinia it is clear that 'industrial' output was minimal, so that even pots and pans were often imported from northern Italy. A final point to stress is that the relationship between north and south Italy relied not simply on commercial exchanges; the twelfth and thirteenth centuries were a period of mass migration from Liguria, Tuscany, ultimately Catalonia, into the towns and countryside of southern Italy; the result was the transformation of Muslim-Greek Sicily into a decisively Latin Christian, Italian-speaking island which was, by the time of the Vespers, quite clearly a part of the western Christian

---

[3] J. Day, 'La Sardegna e i suoi dominatori dal secolo XI al secolo XIV', in J. Day, B. Anatra, L. Scaraffia, *La Sardegna medioevale e moderna* (Storia d'Italia UTET, ed. G. Galasso, Turin, 1984), 3-186; reprinted separately as a single volume under the title *La Sardegna sotto la dominazione pisano-genovese* (Turin, 1986).

Southern Italy, Sicily and Sardinia

world. In Sardinia, the result was rather different: we see the emergence of towns, notably Sassari, Alghero, Cagliari, as well as the abandonment of the Greek rite in favour of that of Rome. In several ways, the islands were being 'italianised' in the twelfth and thirteenth centuries after centuries of physical, cultural, even commercial isolation from Italy. Not even the imposition of Catalan rule in both islands shattered all these links to the peninsula.

Historians of the medieval Italian economy have adopted a similar line on the question of north-south relations; the argument is well represented in the work of Gino Luzzatto, Philip Jones, Mario del Treppo, Giuseppe Galasso and Carlo Cipolla.[4] This consensus provided a framework for my own study of the relations between the Norman kingdom of Sicily and the Genoese, Pisans and Venetians, published in 1977.[5] Henri Bresc takes on board my arguments and lays stress on the way that I demonstrate the shift in Sicily from links to the trade of the Islamic world, mediated by the Jewish 'Geniza merchants' based in Cairo and Tunisia, to trade dominated by Italian entrepreneurs, to the extent that even links between Africa and Sicily increasingly fell into their hands - a tendency confirmed in the thirteenth century, to judge from several later studies of Sicily's role in trade with the Maghrib.[6] For

---

[4] For an analysis (often rather hostile) of the literature concerning dualism in medieval Italy see Epstein, *An island for itself*, 2-16; P. Jones, *Economia e società nell'Italia medievale* (Turin, 1980); M. del Treppo, *I mercanti catalani e l'espansione della Corona d'Aragona nel secolo XV* (Naples, 1972); M. del Treppo and A. Leone, *Amalfi medioevale* (Naples, 1977); G. Galasso, *Mezzogiorno medievale e moderno* (Turin, 1975), and other works by the same author; J. Yver, *Le commerce et les marchands dans l'Italie méridionale au XIIIe et XIVe siècle* (Paris, 1903).

[5] Abulafia, *Two Italies* and *Le Due Italie*. See also the papers by G. Pistarino in the *Atti delle giornate normanno-sveve: Società, potere e popolo nell'età di Ruggero II* (Bari, 1979); *Potere, società e popolo nell'età dei due Guglielmi* (Bari, 1981), and the works of such scholars as Illuminato Peri and V. D'Alessandro in Sicily.

[6] See on this my studies 'Asia, Africa and the trade of medieval Europe', *Cambridge Economic History of Europe*, vol. 2, *Trade and Industry in the Middle Ages*, second edition, ed. E. Miller, M. M. Postan and C. Postan (Cambridge, 1987), 402-73; 'Catalan merchants and the western Mediterranean, 1236-1300: studies in the notarial acts of Barcelona and Sicily', *Viator: medieval and Renaissance studies*, 16 (1985), 209-42, repr. in my *Italy, Sicily and the Mediterranean, 1100-1400* (London, 1987); 'A Tyrrhenian Triangle: Tuscany, Sicily, Tunis, 1277-1300', *Studi di storia economica toscana in memoria di Federigo Melis*, ed. C. Violante (Biblioteca del Bollettino Storico Pisano, Collana storica, 33, Pisa, 1987), 53-75, reprinted below.

Southern Italy, Sicily and Sardinia

Bresc, the late Norman period initiates a first phase of economic dualism, confirmed and deepened after the cataclysm of the Sicilian Vespers.[7] During the twelfth century, Sicily falls between an Islamic world characterised by the use of gold, by a high level of consumption of oriental goods, by the production within the island of 'oriental' textiles, especially silk, and, on the other hand, the Italian commercial world, characterised by the use of silver, by the export of Flemish and north Italian cloths, by the growing demand for raw materials and foodstuffs: Sicilian grain, cotton and skins.[8] In the fourteenth and fifteenth centuries these trends culminate in the emergence of a 'blocked' economy, based on a grain monoculture, with as its purpose the provision of grain to Genoa, Tuscany, Barcelona.[9] There were indeed initiatives to diversify agricultural production, to return to the diversified production visible in Islamic Sicily, but they were not influential enough to change the fixed, dependent, peripheral character of the Sicilian economy. Such initiatives are already visible in the twelfth century, as the Norman rulers try to draw settlers into depopulated areas of the island; in the thirteenth century we can see Frederick II encouraging Jewish settlers from Africa to cultivate indigo, henna and other products of Arab agriculture; there were several attempts to regenerate sugar production, and, while Frederick II's attempt failed, by the fifteenth century sugar had at last become a significant Sicilian export.[10] In the last analysis, however, the ability of the foreign merchants to mould the Sicilian economy is seen by Bresc as decisive; kings and great landlords were merely rowing against the current.

The intention here is to re-examine these arguments about economic dualism in medieval Italy, primarily by turning aside from the detailed discussion of Sicilian trade with Genoa and other north Italian ports offered in *The Two Italies*, and by stressing instead aspects of the problem which the book ignored. In addition, the publication not merely of Bresc's great work, but of an attempted debunking of the Bresc thesis (not to mention the ideas of Jones, Abulafia and many others) by Stephan

---

[7] Bresc, *Monde méditérranéan*, vol. 1, 16.

[8] Abulafia, *Two Italies*, 281-2; *Due Italie*, 369-71.

[9] Bresc, *Monde méditerranéen*, vol. 1, 3, 21, etc.

[10] On Frederick II's economic policy, see my 'Lo Stato e la vita economica nel Regno di Sicilia sotto Federico II', in *Federico II e il mondo mediterraneo*, ed. P. Toubert and A. Paravicini Bagliani (Palermo, 1992), 289-311; also my *Frederick II. A medieval emperor* (London/New York, 1988), 214-25, 320-39.

Southern Italy, Sicily and Sardinia

Epstein makes it essential to review the state of the debate. The publication of *The Two Italies* occurred at a time when the debate was relatively dormant; in a period of fifteen years it has come to dominate scholarly conferences, returning, in an age of renewed interest in the relations between the richer and poorer areas of modern Europe, to a central position in Italian historiography.[11] Here, attention will focus on the role of the south Italian cities, notably Amalfi, and the question why they seem to have been unable to compete with the Genoese and the Venetians in the battle for control of Mediterranean markets. In addition, stress will be laid on the Sardinian case, for it is arguable that some of the evidence for the evolution of a dualistic north-south relationship suits the Sardinian case better (or even better) than the Sicilian or south Italian. Sardinia, after all, was virgin territory, with no identifiable history of close links to the economy of the Islamic world; the Islamic background complicates and at times confuses the case for Sicilian dualism.

At this stage it would be helpful to draw some distinctions between Bresc's dualistic concept and my own.[12] It is obviously hazardous to attribute to the twelfth and early thirteenth centuries, and especially to the arrival of Latin rulers, all the blame for the 'blocked' or 'underdeveloped' character of the late medieval Sicilian economy, as seen by Bresc. In the sixteenth and seventeenth centuries important factors were also at work which strengthened the character of the Sicilian economy as that of a grain-producing, 'dependent' economy; important here is the history of social relations in Sicily, between the landlords of the great *latifondi* and the Sicilian peasantry. The dualism of the Norman and Hohenstaufen period is identifiable at another level: it concerns the interests of the merchants, the commercial development of the cities of Sicily and southern Italy, the re-orientation of the south away from Islam and towards northern Italy and Catalonia; it concerns too the 'northernisation' of Sicily in demographic and cultural terms. These changes did not necessarily, arguably could not, determine permanently and irretrievably the character of the Sicilian economy. But the economy of northern Italy, and, later, Barcelona or Mallorca, was moulded by the

---

[11] See, for instance: *Il Mezzogiorno medievale nella storiografia del secondo dopoguerra: risultati e prospettive. Atti del IV Convegno Nazionale dell'Associazione dei medioevalisti italiani, Università di Calabria, 12-16 giugno 1982*, ed. P. De Leo (Soveria Mannelli, 1985).

[12] As well as *The Two Italies*, my articles collected here and in *Italy, Sicily and the Mediterranean* often address this theme, e.g. 'Southern Italy and the Florentine economy, 1265-1370', *Economic History Review*, 2nd ser., 33 (1981), 377-88.

Southern Italy, Sicily and Sardinia

contacts that were established with southern Italy and the Italian islands. Without grain supplies from these regions the provision of basic supplies to the population of rapidly expanding industrial and commercial centres would have been exceptionally difficult. From Sicily, Apulia and Sardinia wheat reached Genoa, Florence and Barcelona, which had far surpassed the capacity of their regions to feed the urban population. Seen in these terms, the dualism of medieval Italy was not simply a core/periphery relationship of the form suggested by Bresc, Aymard and others. It was a relationship that served the interests of the north Italian cities, but it is not being suggested here that the door had yet been closed to the possibility of further diversification and renewed expansion in the southern economies. Indeed, Epstein insists that the period after the Black Death saw an intensification of regional specialisation in Sicily, as elsewhere in western Europe, and that the role of foreign trade in moulding Sicily's economy has been exaggerated.[13] But in a sense that is not the point as far as the dualism described here is concerned. It is the significance of the grain exports to those who received the grain, rather than to those who produced it, which is being stressed here.

A helpful approach to the question can be found in an observation by Richard Britnell about the comparative strengths of the Italian and English economies in the late Middle Ages.[14] The possibility of increasing the quality and quantity of agricultural output in a northern Italy that lacked extensive fertile areas should not be exaggerated. Sicily and Apulia, by the standards of the time, were the fertile areas, while the north had to support an impossibly dense urban population from limited resources. Seen from this point of view, it is the south that appears to be the wealthy region, rarely experiencing famines or long-term crises in production; in the north, the only avenue that was open to avoid perpetual shortages was diversification into commercial and industrial activities.[15] In this respect it is important to avoid the excessively free use of terms such as 'underdeveloped' in descriptions of the southern economy during the Middle Ages; such terms are applicable to the modern industrial economy, but are laden with values that do not belong in the medieval sphere. What is being used here is a value-neutral concept of dualism. Moreover, it is essential not to portray the contrast

---

[13] Epstein, *An island for itself*, 268-313.

[14] R. H. Britnell, 'England and northern Italy in the early fourteenth century: the economic contrasts', *Transactions of the Royal Historical Society*, ser. 5, 39 (1989), 167-83.

[15] Abulafia, 'Southern Italy', 388.

in black and white extremes. There was a strong internal market for locally-produced textiles in Sicily and in Campania; only in the case of Sardinia do we see an almost total lack of industrial initiatives before the arrival of the north Italians.

Jones has insisted on the need to extend the identification of a dualistic relationship between north and south Italy further, for the term 'dualism' can also be used profitably to describe the system of relations between town and country within the more restricted area of northern Italy itself.[16] Cities obtained from their contadi, and from the contadi of their neighbours, the primary products and the wheat needed to sustain the population and local industry. Cities gave priority to urban over rural needs, ensuring regular, reasonably cheap supplies to the city and placing the interests of their own inhabitants, especially those involved in industrial or commercial enterprises, including the artisans themselves, ahead of those of the rural labour force. In a certain sense, Sardinia itself was the contado of Genoa and Pisa; confirmation can be found in the role of institutions such as the Opera di Santa Maria (Pisa Cathedral) in the exploitation of the Sardinian lands.[17] But also on the mainland there are clear examples of dualistic relationships between regions in close proximity to one another: the presence of Tuscan grain merchants in the Maremma, with bases at Grosseto and Corneto, indicates the importance of the food producing lands of Etruria to the growing cities concentrated further north in Tuscia: by 1200, Florentines and Pisans were present at Corneto in large numbers, as were merchants from elsewhere in Italy, such as Gaeta.[18] This only serves to underline the great importance for the north Italian cities, especially Genoa, Florence and Venice, of easy access to sources of staple foodstuffs, whether in central Italy, Apulia, the Italian islands or, ultimately, in the Crimea and Morocco.

A second fundamental problem arises from the use of the term 'Italy' to describe Lombardy, mainland southern Italy, Sicily and Sardinia. The term is, arguably, applicable because, from about 1100 onwards, the merchants of the northern communes began to create an integrated commercial network binding these regions together, and because the plentiful immigration into the south and Sardinia brought the

---

[16] Jones, *Economia e società*, 205-6, 214-15; cf. my introduction to *Italy, Sicily and the Mediterranean*, 1-3.

[17] F. Artizzu, *L'Opera di S. Maria di Pisa e la Sardegna* (Padua, 1974).

Southern Italy, Sicily and Sardinia

language and religion of north and central Italy to these areas. In Sicily the transformation was perhaps more complete; in Sardinia the Italians were more confined to their own towns and fortresses. The bonding of Sardinia to medieval Italy was the result of Genoese and Pisan penetration of the island. But the concept of 'Italy' remains one of questionable value in this period, all the same, the more so when the role of the Catalans and other non-Italians in the exploitation of the islands is taken into account: their involvement in the creation of governmental institutions, in the process of settlement of town and country, in the large-scale export of Sicilian and Sardinian wheat and of Sardinian salt and silver.[19] Moreover, only because of lack of space have some other regions which are not now regarded as 'Italian' been excluded from this discussion, despite their subjection to strong influence by Pisan, Genoese and Venetian merchants: the history of Pisan and Genoese colonisation of Corsica is still little known, despite important similarities with the Sardinian case; and the history of the Dalmatian towns has much in common with that of the Apulian cities facing them across the Adriatic.[20]

II

The problem of Amalfi forms part of the larger problem of Italian dualism: here is a city that apparently lost its commercial vitality in the face of Genoese, Pisan, even Venetian competition, a city which seems to demonstrate the transition of southern Italy from a precocious centre of western European economic rebirth to a region characterised by a passive economy dominated by foreign interests, 'une économie bloquée'. In the late Middle Ages the Amalfitans looked back with pride on their first steps in maritime trade, and regarded themselves as pioneers in the exploitation of the great *pelagus*, the Mediterranean Sea. Such memories serve as a reminder that, at least after the earthquake of 1343, Amalfi had become a small town, with abandoned dockyards and empty workshops; however, this powerful image of decline has been increasingly questioned - it is even doubtful whether the 1343 earthquake was quite as

---

[18] D. Abulafia, 'Corneto-Tarquinia and the Italian mercantile republics: the earliest evidence', *Papers of the British School at Rome*, 42 (1974), 224-34; repr. in *Italy, Sicily and the Mediterranean*.

[19] So, at least, Epstein insists: *An island for itself*, 8-9.

[20] Further work on Corsica by Jean-A. Cancellieri will, it is to be hoped, amplify greatly our understanding of its relationship to Italy.

Southern Italy, Sicily and Sardinia

dramatic as Petrarch (writing under the influence of classical models) believed.[21]

There are two main ways of explaining the changes visible at Amalfi. The first interpretation concentrates on political factors, such as the Norman Conquest in the eleventh century and the final subjection of the city to Roger II in 1131, or the increasing hostility of the Byzantine emperors to the Amalfitans visible in the imperial chrysobulls of 992 and of 1082 onwards. Armand Citarella speaks of a decline as early as the eleventh century, following transformations in north Africa, which was at this point the battleground of Fatimid caliphs, Zirid emirs, Berber tribes, Arab invaders (the Banu Hillal). These events are argued to have shut off the Amalfitans from their famous role as providers of oriental and African goods to Italian consumers, and are said to have opened the way to Genoese and Pisan incursions into Islamic territory.[22] Thus the

---

[21] The bibliography on Amalfi is vast; its size reflects, paradoxically, the enormity of the puzzle alongside the poverty of the sources. The key arguments about its trade may be found in the following works. A. Citarella, *Il commercio di Amalfi nell'alto medioevo* (Salerno, 1977), gathers together the articles of this scholar and contains a detailed bibliography up to 1977. More popular is G. Imperato, *Amalfi e il suo commercio* (Salerno, 1980). Fundamental is M. del Treppo and A. Leone, *Amalfi medioevale* (Naples, 1977), the first half of which, by Mario del Treppo, may also be found in *Amalfi nel Medioevo: convegno internazionale, 14-16 giugno 1973* (Salerno, 1977), 17-175, which also contains important studies by Grierson, Pistarino, Giunta and others. Also very important are: R. H. Bautier, 'La marine d'Amalfi dans le trafic méditérranéen du XIVe siècle. A propos du transport du sel de Sardaigne', *Bulletin philologique et historique du Comité des travaux historiques* (1958-59), 181-94 (incorrect details of which appear in Citarella's bibliography); C. Cahen, 'Un texte peu connu relatif au commerce oriental d'Amalfi au Xe siècle', *Archivio storico per le provincie napoletane*, 34 (1955), 61-7; M. Camera, *Memorie storico-diplomatiche dell'antica città e ducato di Amalfi* (2 vols., Salerno, 1876-81; repr. Salerno, 1972); G. Coniglio, 'Amalfi e il suo commercio nel medioevo', *Nuova rivista storica*, 18/19 (1944-5), 100-14; B. Figliuolo, 'Amalfi e il Levante', *I comuni italiani nel Regno crociato di Gerusalemme*, ed. G. Airaldi and B. Z. Kedar (Collana di Fonti e Studi, Genoa, 1986), 573-664; G. Galasso, 'Il commercio amalfitano nel periodo normanno', *Studi in onore di R. Filangieri* (2 vols., Naples, 1959), vol. 1, 81-103; B. Kreutz, 'The ecology of maritime success: the puzzling case of Amalfi', *Mediterranean Historical Review*, 3 (1988), 103-13; E. Pontieri, 'La crisi di Amalfi medievale', *Studi sulla repubblica di Amalfi* (Salerno, 1935), repr. in E. Pontieri, *Tra i Normanni nell'Italia medievale* (2nd ed., Naples, 1964); also other contributions to *Studi sulla repubblica di Amalfi* (Salerno, 1935); H. M. Willard, *Abbot Desiderius of Montecassino and the ties between Montecassino and Amalfi in the eleventh century* (Miscellanea Cassinese, 37, Montecassino, 1973).

Southern Italy, Sicily and Sardinia

celebrated Italian raid on Mahdia in 1087 was the work of the Pisans and Genoese; the Amalfitans appear too, but only as a small group of exiles from the city. Other scholars, however, have looked at the evidence of the agreements between Amalfi and other Mediterranean cities up to the Angevin period, and have insisted on the survival in Amalfi of limited but very precious autonomy, visible, for example, in the accord with Genoa of 1302; Amalfi's subjection to the Normans is then seen as far from catastrophic.[22]

The approach adopted by the Neapolitan historian Ernesto Pontieri reveals a subtle change in the direction of the debate. The changing fortunes of the city are seen as a by-product of a broader transformation in the system of relationships right across the Mediterranean at the time of the early crusades, the period when the opening of the sea-routes by the aggressive fleets of Genoa, Pisa and Venice led to the creation of new bases in the Holy Land, in Byzantium, as also in Sicily and in Sardinia.[24] Vincenzo d'Alessandro has utilised the evidence for the Genoese and Pisan penetration of the Norman Kingdom of Sicily to relate the arrival of these groups in the *Regno* to the withdrawal of the Amalfitans from leadership in maritime trade.[25] It is certainly significant that Frederick Barbarossa was to promise the Pisans that he would grant them Gaeta, a lively centre of sea trade, if his plan to conquer the *Regno* succeeded with Pisan help. In other words, there is real evidence that the north Italian towns sought to dominate (but not necessarily to suffocate) the trade of ancient rivals whose commercial influence remained potent.[26]

An important characteristic of recent explanations of the fortunes of Amalfi is the reluctance to see the changes in Amalfi's trade as signs of simple 'decline'. Already signalled in a study by Coniglio, published in the 1940's, and then by Bautier, this approach has culminated in the fundamental reassessment by Mario del Treppo and Alfonso Leone,

---

[22] Citarella, *Commercio di Amalfi*, studies I-III.

[23] Pistarino, 'Genova e Amalfi', 320-3.

[24] Pontieri, 'Crisi di Amalfi'.

[25] V. D'Alessandro, 'Amalfi in età normanna', *Istituzioni civili e organizzazione ecclesiastica nello stato medievale amalfitano. Atti del Congresso internazionale di studi amalfitani, Amalfi 3-5 luglio 1981* (Amalfi, 1986), vol. 1, 33-52.

[26] *Two Italies*, 124-6; *Due Italie*, 182-5.

Southern Italy, Sicily and Sardinia

which has established a new orthodoxy on the question. Amalfi did not decline, but it changed. In the commercial arena, we do not see a total withdrawal but a reorientation, from long-distance trade linking Italy to the eastern Mediterranean, to land trade within Italy, or at best sea-trade within the Tyrrhenian Sea, serving the needs of the *Regno* by bonding Campania to Apulia, Catalonia and Sicily.[27] In Bautier's work we can observe the participation of the Amalfitans in the export trade in salt out of Cagliari, in southern Sardinia, towards the late fourteenth-century Kingdom of Naples; this was at a time when the Genoese were being obliged to steer clear of Cagliari. The point is that Amalfi was making its profits out of strictly Tyrrhenian trade. There was a long-standing interest in the Sicilian grain trade, well documented around the time of the Sicilian Vespers, which was clearly a blow to Amalfi's trade through Sicily and on to Africa. It is thus important not to be misled by the fine words of ibn Hawqal in the tenth century on the importance of Amalfi as a port and as a centre for the purchase of luxury cloths, or by the words of Benjamin of Tudela in the twelfth century on the almost total dependence of the Amalfitans on the sea.[28] For del Treppo, the characterisation of Amalfi as a city inhabited almost exclusively by merchants is a distortion of a far more complex reality. This was a 'city without merchants' not in the sense that merchants were absent from it, but in the sense that Amalfi lacked native merchants entirely committed to business without interest in other types of investment. Gradually, as competition became more acute, the Amalfitan patriciate dedicated itself more and more to the exploitation of the soil, for example viticulture and orchards, which were, interestingly enough, mentioned casually by Benjamin of Tudela.

Del Treppo's work has generated widespread agreement about the chronology of Amalfitan trade, based on the awareness that the trans-Mediterranean trade that may have characterised early medieval Amalfi cannot be taken as a measuring stick to judge the success of other, very different, types of business enterprise, possibly more limited in geographical range but possibly also more intensively the focus of investment. A document of 1105 deserves further examination in this context. It consists of an agreement between Sergio Zinzicapra, a member of an Amalfitan family at this point rising rapidly up the social scale, and the Amalfitan patrician Gregorio, on the one hand, and the *popolare* Costantino Castagnola on the other.[29] Castagnola's boat was to

---

[27] Coniglio, 'Amalfi e il suo commercio'; Bautier, 'Marine d'Amalfi'; del Treppo and Leone, *Amalfi medioevale.*

[28] *The itinerary of Benjamin of Tudela*, ed. M. N. Adler (London, 1907), 9, 76.

Southern Italy, Sicily and Sardinia

travel to Sicily, there to load sixty *cantari* of wool, and then to travel to *Rabennam*, which is generally assumed to signify Ravenna but which may be a corruption, or misreading, of the name Ravello, the neighbour and partner in trade of Amalfi. Whether the voyage was Adriatic-bound or confined to a return trip within the Tyrrhenian Sea, it is clear that the capacity of this boat was quite small, only about 80 *botti* according to del Treppo, who, like other recent historians of Amalfi, believes that Amalfitan ships of this era were still quite modest in size. Only in the late thirteenth century and in the fourteenth century does one see large ships of Amalfi piled high with grain, salt and other bulky goods. It does seem, whether or not this boat was bound for Ravenna, that Amalfitans traded actively in the Adriatic under the eyes of their Venetian rivals, for the Amalfitans formed an important part of the population of Durazzo in the late eleventh century; however, as will be seen, much of this trade was probably fed by Amalfitan merchants based in the cities of Apulia, rather than by direct voyages from Campania to Albania. It is likely that direct voyages to Sicily from Amalfi were, however, frequent and unremarkable: in 1200 the Amalfitan Costantino Balba, a *popolare*, was in Sicily with his son Urso; and a little earlier Hugo Falcandus mentioned the wealthy Amalfitan quarter of Palermo, which may have traced its origins back to Islamic times.[30]

What was an Amalfitan? Not necessarily, it seems, a native-born inhabitant of the Costa Amalfitana. As early as the eleventh century we have unequivocal evidence for an Amalfitan diaspora, which was to grow significantly in size by the thirteenth century. One case, already cited, is the Amalfitan colony at Durazzo, which Anna Comnena mentions.[31] At the same period we find at Bari, just opposite Durazzo, an *imperialis patricius* named *Iohannes qui dicitur grecus, filius Stefani, qui et Rabella dicitur, qui fuit de Tramunte de Amalfi* (1099).[32] Despite the hint here of links to the Byzantine world, we are on the verge of a new epoch in Amalfi's history. The old era of ibn Hawqal's opulent city, the richest in

---

[29] R. Filangieri di Candida, *Codice diplomatico amalfitano* (2 vols., Naples, 1917; Trani, 1951), vol. 2, 304; del Treppo and Leone, *Amalfi medioevale*, 196; Imperato, *Amalfi*, 241-2.

[30] Filangieri, *Codice diplomatico*, vol. 1, 474; del Treppo and Leone, *Amalfi medioevale*, 132.

[31] Anna Comnena, *Alexiad*, Book 6, cap. 1, section 1.

[32] Imperato, *Amalfi*, 191; B. Figliuolo has been working on a study of the Amalfitans outside Amalfi.

Southern Italy, Sicily and Sardinia

Longobardia, the most noble and illustrious, the most frequented and the richest, is giving way to a second phase in Amalfitan history in which clear distinctions need to be maintained between Amalfi and its small neighbours on the one hand (Ravello, Scala, Maiori, Minori, Atrani, Cetara and so on), and the great diaspora of Amalfitans, Ravellesi and other subjects of the ancient duchy of Amalfi, now scattered far beyond its boundaries. A privilege granted in the reign of King Tancred of Sicily to the Amalfitans of Naples in 1191 indicates clearly that many Amalfitan bankers and merchants had installed themselves in Naples, which was arguably a boom city at this time.[33] After 1200, too, Amalfitans and, above all, Ravellesi, are to be found in the Campanian and Apulian cities, where they formed a specialised élite of merchants, with major interests both in the traffic in local goods, such as grain and oil, and in that in luxury goods that arrived by sea. But what is noticeable about this luxury trade is the ever-decreasing role of the Amalfitans themselves in the transport of spices, drugs, dyes and fine cloths across the seas; this commerce was now dominated by the Genoese, Pisans and Venetians who had become such a significant force in the kingdom's trade.

It is worth examining a few cases of Amalfitan penetration into southern Italy. A patrician of Ravello, Giovanni San Salvatore, was living at Termoli on the Adriatic in 1153, and he was still there in 1175, when he acquired an orchard in the suburbs of the town.[34] At Giovinazzo there were Amalfitans from 1215 at least, and a Ravellese from as early as 1184. In the interior of southern Italy, there was a substantial colony of Amalfitans at Benevento, and they had the benefit of a papal privilege from Lucius III in 1184.[35] The pope, at the request of the Ravellesi, Scalesi and other Amalfitans, confirmed the ancient customs of the community established in what was in fact a papal enclave entirely surrounded by the lands of the Sicilian kingdom.[36] It is not necessary to list all the groups of Amalfitans known to have existed in other south Italian towns, such as Capua, Barletta, Taranto. D'Alessandro is right to

---

[33] R. Filangieri, 'Note al *Privilegium Libertatis* concesso dai Napoletani agli Amalfitani nel 1190', *Papers of the British School at Rome*, 24 (1956) [= *Studies in Italian history presented to Miss E. M. Jamison*, ed. P. Grierson and J. B. Ward-Perkins], 116.

[34] Imperato, *Amalfi*, 229-30.

[35] Imperato, *Amalfi*, 231.

[36] Imperato, *Amalfi*, 173.

Southern Italy, Sicily and Sardinia

state that the Amalfitan diaspora was in large measure a phenomenon of the thirteenth century, but it is also important to stress that what is visible then is the further expansion of smaller *Malfitanie* which had already been in existence in the twelfth century, especially in the Campanian hinterland and on the Apulian coast. Thus already in the Norman period the Amalfitans had a pre-eminent role in supplying the internal market, and they did not lose this role until, at the earliest, the large-scale penetration of Florentine financiers into the Angevin kingdom of Naples around 1300. In fact, under Frederick II and Charles I, the leaders of the Amalfitan diaspora acquired new functions; the role of the Amalfitan patriciate in the administration of the Hohenstaufen and Angevin state has been stressed by Norbert Kamp and by Henri Bresc; the fortunes of families such as the Rufolo and the Aconzaiaco was founded not, or not only, on trade or on exploitation of the soil, but also on royal service, on the mainland and in Sicily. For Bresc, the Sicilian Vespers was in some respects the Waterloo of the Amalfitan administrators of Sicily.[37] Indeed, as has been suggested, the blow may have been a double one, since trade between Sicily and Campania, long an interest of Amalfi's businessmen, was rendered impossible during the War of the Vespers and the later Angevin invasions of Aragonese Sicily.

What the north Italian republics resented was not so much the presence of the Amalfitans in the internal trade of the *Regno*, which arguably fed their own trade network, but the involvement of the Amalfitans in long-distance trade beyond the *Regno*. The Genoese, Pisans and Venetians had two basic options here. One possibility was the creation of formal agreements between the northern republics and the city of Amalfi; this occurred, for instance, in 1126 (between Amalfi and Pisa) and in 1302 (between Amalfi and Genoa).[38] The Pisans and the Genoese sought to tie the Amalfitan distribution network within the *Regno* to the more extensive network of Ligurian and Tuscan trade in Egypt, Byzantium and north Africa. In the treaties with Pisa and Genoa,

---

[37] H. Bresc, '1282: classes sociales et révolution nationale', *La società mediterranea all'epoca del Vespro. XI Congresso di Storia della Corona d'Aragona/VII Centenario del Vespro Siciliano* (4 vols., Palermo 1983), vol. 2, 241-58; repr. in H. Bresc, *Politique et société en Sicile, XIIe-XVe siècles* (Aldershot, 1990); N. Kamp, 'Von Kämmerer zu Sekreten: Wirtschaftsreformen und Finanzverwaltung im staufischen Königreich Sizilien', *Probleme um Friedrich II.*, ed. J. Fleckenstein (Sigmaringen, 1974); Abulafia, *Frederick II*, 418, 421, 425. See also Boccaccio, *Decameron*, Day 2, story 4, for a eulogy of the Rufolo family and of the Costa Amalfitana.

[38] Abulafia, *Two Italies*, 59-60; *Due Italie*, 108-9 (for Pisa); Pistarino, 'Genova e Amalfi', 320-3.

Southern Italy, Sicily and Sardinia

the Amalfitans were offered reciprocal rights so that they could trade in both cities free of the taxes and other restrictions normally imposed on foreigners. The advantage for the north Italians of access, on the backs of the Amalfitans, to the small towns of the *Regno* cannot be underestimated. But political difficulties with the Norman kings rapidly convinced the Pisans that an agreement with Amalfi would not produce the hoped-for results; they turned then to a more radical, alternative solution to the problem of Amalfitan competition: the destruction of the port in 1135 and 1137. During this period, when German armies sought to suffocate Roger's newly born kingdom, Pisa extended its ambitions still further and set out to acquire Salerno, which was very close to Amalfi and which was also a good point of access to the interior. What mattered most to the northerners was the opportunity to acquire a permanent base from which they would be able to penetrate into the interior of the *Regno*.[39]

There are signs of real competition between Amalfi and the north Italians in the privilege granted to the Amalfitans in 1190 by Guy of Lusignan during the siege of Acre. The king of Jerusalem granted the Amalfitans the same privileges as the Pisans, Venetians and Genoese: a court in Acre, with a viscount and consuls, tax exemptions on their goods and on their ships, large and small.[40] Other privileges received by this community in the Holy Land indicate the existence of a special Amalfitan cemetery at Acre and of tax exemptions in the county of Tripoli.[41] Indeed, the Amalfitan presence in Jerusalem antedates the First Crusade, even if Jerusalem itself was not a very important commercial centre: an Amalfitan hospice formed the core of the future Order of St John of Jerusalem, the Knights Hospitallers to be; a legend tells of Amalfitans who were inside the city at the time of the crusader siege and who, on being ordered to throw stones at the starving crusaders, witnessed their miraculous transformation in mid-air into loaves of bread. These Amalfitans were there to service the needs of the Benedictine community: they were the financial agents of Montecassino.[42] As for the privilege of 1190, it forms part of a series of donations made when the Christian army was desperate for any help

---

[39] Abulafia, *Two Italies*, 60-2; *Due Italie*, 109-11.

[40] Figliuolo, 'Amalfi e il Levante', 656-62.

[41] Figliuolo, 'Amalfi e il Levante', 616-21.

[42] For the role of the Amalfitans in the emergence of the Order of St John (the later Knights of Malta), see J. Riley-Smith, *The Knights of St John in Jerusalem and Cyprus, 1050-1310* (London, 1967), 36-7; R. Hiestand, 'Die Anfänge der Johanniter', *Die*

Southern Italy, Sicily and Sardinia

from any quarter, and required all possible aid from Italian ships of whatever origin, as from the Provençaux and Catalans, who benefited similarly in 1187. The aim was the recovery of the lost kingdom of Jerusalem, and the presence of Amalfitans in Syria around 1200 does not offer better proof of intensive maritime trade between Amalfi and Syria than the miracle of the stones that turned into bread. There are few documentary references to Amalfitans in the east after about 1100; the Amalfitan convent on Mount Athos is, once again, a sign of the links between Montecassino, Amalfi and, in this case, Byzantium.[43] The one Levant trader from the area around Amalfi whose career is well documented in the mid-twelfth century is Solomon of Salerno, who traded intensively to Egypt around 1160; but his career provides proof of the commercial vitality of his adopted city, Genoa, rather than of his home town, with which his contacts were at best sparse.[44] In the Byzantine Empire, the Amalfitans became, in fact, decreasingly privileged; the chrysobull of 1082 obliged them to pay a fine to the churches of Venice, and subsequently their quarter in Constantinople was reduced in size, to make room for their rivals.[45] On the other hand, it is possible that the explanation for this loss of territory is simply that their Constantinople trade was already contracting, and that their quarter in the capital was partly unoccupied. Yet, as Roman citizens who had become Norman subjects, the Amalfitans were no longer in the good graces of the emperor.

In other words, the Amalfitan Levant trade simply does not present to view that massive, rapid expansion that we see with Venice, Genoa and Pisa, even if, in earlier times, in the age of Liutprand of Cremona and ibn Hawqal, the Amalfitans had been the only serious

---

geistlichen Ritterorden Europas, ed. J. Fleckenstein (Sigmaringen, 1980), 33-47; B. Figliuolo, 'Amalfi e il Levante', 592.

[43] For links to Montecassino, see especially Willard, *Abbot Desiderius.*

[44] Abulafia, *Two Italies*, 237-54; *Due Italie*, 316-35. Unfortunately he is still often described in studies of Genoese merchants as a Jew. There is simply no evidence for this; not even his name suggests as much. Cf. O. R. Constable, 'Genoa and Spain in the twelfth and thirteenth centuries: notarial evidence for a shift in patterns of trade', *Journal of European Economic History*, 19 (1990), 635-56.

[45] R-J. Lilie, *Handel und Politik zwischen dem byzantinischen Reich und die italienischen Kommunen Venedig, Pisa und Genua in der Epoche der Komnenen und Angeloi (1081-1204)* (Amsterdam, 1984), 9-14.

rivals to Venice on these routes. Now, a very important factor in this failure to take off, or rather in the different manner of taking off, was the much greater distance separating the south Italian cities from the new centres of demand north of the Alps, which were beginning to supply the Genoese, Venetians and other 'Lombards' with textiles and silver in exchange for the produce of the Orient. While the Amalfitans became masters of the precious internal market of the *Regno*, Genoa sought to create extensive, extended markets as far away as Champagne and Flanders, with the help of Piacenzan bankers and other colleagues; meanwhile Venice sought to penetrate German markets, which was in some respects a greater challenge. In this sense, the developments in Amalfi are not simply part of the history of the Mediterranean; a commercial revolution which now took in the continent of Europe left Amalfi on the outer edge of the new, rapidly expanding western economy.

III

It is important to ask whether the experience of Amalfi was unique, whether Amalfi enjoyed the sort of primacy that, say, Venice enjoyed in its own region, and was atypical of the south Italian towns. The other southern towns have been examined less closely, but it is necessary to see now whether it is possible to speak of a general commercial contraction in the area. Further studies of Gaeta, the Tyrrhenian centre perhaps most similar to Amalfi, are much needed; Patricia Skinner's new examination of early medieval Gaeta reveals a complex patchwork of jurisdictions and brings to light the activities of the city élite, especially as landowners and political leaders.[46] The general image seems not far removed from that provided in del Treppo's analysis of Amalfi. The Gaetans, perhaps even more than the Amalfitans, retained a visible profile in the trade of the Tyrrhenian for several centuries; they remained important in the inter-regional trade in oil and grain. Striking, in fact, is the contrast between the small number of Amalfitans who are mentioned in the Genoese notarial acts around 1200, and the much larger number of Gaetans, either visitors to Genoa or colleagues of Genoese in trading stations such as the Sardinian ports and Corneto-Tarquinia.[47] Thus Coniglio's argument about the continued

---

[46] Pending the publication of Dr Skinner's work in the series of Cambridge Studies in Medieval Life and Thought, see M. Merores, *Gaeta im frühen Mittelalter* (Gotha, 1911); but both deal with an earlier period than is outlined here.

Southern Italy, Sicily and Sardinia

vitality of Amalfitan trade under the Normans and Hohenstaufen is applicable, to an ever higher degree, to Gaeta; the Gaetans competed with the Amalfitans and the Roman merchants in supplying Rome; but, as with Amalfi, relations with the north Italian cities became a factor of prime importance in the commercial development of the city. The Pisans and Genoese permitted Gaeta a specialised role as a regional transporter of objects of middle or low value, such as oil, but they were not prepared to permit Gaeta to have access to the lucrative long-distance trade routes to the east.

The similarities with Amalfi are visible again in the case of Bari and Barletta, both of which were analysed by the Russian historian M. L. Abramson.[48] She distinguishes between two groups of patricians in the Apulian cities: those who concentrated on maritime commerce, and who used types of commercial contract familiar in northern Italy; and those who were influential as city officials - the *baiuli*, the catapans, the judges. This distinction does, however, seem rather artificial, because (as Abramson admits) positions in the city administration enlarged the opportunities available to participate in the city's economic life. Abramson notes an impressive capacity on the part of the patricians of Bari and Barletta to preserve their position in city society; there seems to be a contrast here with the greater social mobility visible in Amalfi. She argues that the growing tax burden of the thirteenth-century royal governments had a depressing effect on commercial activity, and resulted in a shift away from investment in trade, towards investment in land. Such a picture lacks the subtle shading of that painted by del Treppo and Leone; but, as at Amalfi and Gaeta, trade did continue after the catastrophes of the twelfth century: the revolt of the Lombard prince, Grimoald; the invasion of Apulia by Manuel Komnenos; the almost total destruction of treacherous Bari by William I of Sicily. The indications are that Bari quite gradually lost its role in long distance trade even before its catastrophe; the era of the expedition to Myra and of the seizure of the bones of St Nicholas was over by the mid-twelfth century, and, once again, it was regional trade that became the source of mercantile wealth. Thus, around 1200, there is good evidence for trade between Bari and Dubrovnik (Ragusa), based on long-standing

---

[47] Abulafia, 'Corneto-Tarquinia'; on preparing the index for *Italy, Sicily and the Mediterranean* I realised how often I had mentioned Gaetans in my work.

[48] M. L. Abramson, 'Krupnye goroda Apulii v XII-XIII vv. (na materiale Bari i Barletty' ('The major cities of Apulia in the twelfth and thirteenth centuries, according to sources from Bari and Barletta'), *Srednye Veka*, 48 (1985), 47-70, with a brief Italian summary, 405-6.

Southern Italy, Sicily and Sardinia

commercial agreements including reciprocal tax exemption. In addition, Molfetta, Termoli and other maritime towns of the southern Adriatic were involved at this period in trade with Dubrovnik, while for several years the Sicilian king extended his protection to the Ragusans themselves.[49]

The final example of a southern city with a lively trade is rather different in character. Messina grew enormously after the Norman conquest and the creation of the sea routes linking Pisa and Genoa to the Levant.[50] But Messina is also of special interest, because it was, in a sense, refounded by Italian settlers - by immigrants from Amalfi, Pisa, Genoa, Lucca and so on, who transformed a predominantly Greek city into the active centre of Latin, Italian trade celebrated in Boccaccio's tale of the pot of basil. It was a specially privileged city, exempt from the greater part of the *commercium* tax, according to King William I's privilege of 1160.[51] Like Amalfi, Messina lacked an extensive contado suitable for grain production, but could export local wines, salted pork and other specialised products of the region. The interests of the Messina patriciate in the production of, and trade in, wine are documented in the late thirteenth century, when Messina's wine trade extended as far as Acre.[52]

A clear picture of the mixture of communities to be found in Messina by the early thirteenth century can be obtained from a Messinese document of April 1239. Giovanni Chipulla and Donna Rosa, daughter of the late Roberto of Lucca, possess a warehouse in common in the new suburb of Messina, next door to the property of an Amalfitan, of a Ravellese (who, however, has died), and to the *ruga Pisanorum*, the

---

[49] D. Abulafia, 'Dalmatian Ragusa and the Norman Kingdom of Sicily', *Slavonic and East European Review*, 54 (1976), 412-28, repr. in *Italy, Sicily and the Mediterranean*.

[50] For Messina, see C. Trasselli, *I privilegi di Messina e di Trapani, 1160-1355* (Palermo, 1949); E. Pispisa, *Messina nel Trecento: politica, economia, società* (Messina, 1980); D. Abulafia, 'The merchants of Messina: Levant trade and domestic economy', *Papers of the British School at Rome*, 54 (1986), 196-212, reprinted below.

[51] C. Giardina, *Capitoli e privilegi di Messina* (Palermo, 1937), 15-16; Trasselli, *Privilegi*, 13-16; Abulafia, *Two Italies*, 116-18; *Due Italie*, 173-5. See also Boccaccio, *Decameron*, Day 4, story 5.

[52] M. Alibrandi, 'Messinesi in Levante nel Medioevo', *Archivio storico siciliano*, ser. 3, 21/2 (1971-2), 97-110; Abulafia, 'Merchants of Messina', 199-212.

Southern Italy, Sicily and Sardinia

street, or more likely quarter, of the Pisans, which is documented, along with a 'street of Florentines', in the late Norman period.[53] Along the trade routes, we find Messinesi as consuls of the Sicilian fonduk in Tunis, after the Sicilian Vespers; there were Messinesi who were active in the trade of Cyprus around 1300; there were others who built ties to the king of Cilician Armenia, in 1331.[54] The Levant trade of the Sicilians was, in the first place, the Levant trade of Messina. By contrast with Amalfi and Bari, Messina seems to be a city undergoing rapid expansion, but its interests were shaped by those of the Genoese, Pisans, Florentines and Catalans who came as visiting merchants or who settled permanently in the town. The Messinesi were able to take part in long distance trade, alongside the Pisans and the Genoese, for two basic reasons: many inhabitants of Messina were also citizens, or descendants of citizens, of the Ligurian and Tuscan towns; and Messina derived its special success not from trade in all commodities, though it was an entrepôt through which all seemed to flow, but from trade in local products, such as wine and fruit, in demand elsewhere in the Mediterranean. Despite their need to buy in substantial quantities of Sicilian or south Italian grain, the Messinesi were not in competition with the Genoese, Pisans or Venetians in the great Levant trade in spices and oriental silks. The Messinesi, like the Amalfitans and the Baresi, were also active in supplying the internal market in Sicily and Calabria; in the latter region they already possessed major interests in raw silk, way back in the Byzantine period, as well as handling Calabrian grain and minerals.[55] Indeed, for S. R. Epstein, Messina's local trade, above all its trade with Calabria, provides the basic explanation for the city's success and importance; he greatly plays down the role of long distance trade and dismisses too readily the view in *The Two Italies* of Messina as a Norman phenomenon and a phenomenon of

---

[53] L. R. Ménager, *Les actes latins de S. Maria de Messina (1103-1250)*, (Palermo, 1963), 150-8. For the Pisans and other Tuscans in late twelfth-century Messina, see my 'Pisan commercial colonies and consulates in twelfth-century Sicily', *English Historical Review*, 93 (1978), 68-81, reprinted below. For the 'rua Florentinorum' see R. Pirri, *Sicilia sacra* (Palermo, 1733), 1288; this street, mentioned in 1193, contained property of the Count of Paternò, granted that year to the Cistercians of Messina.

[54] G. La Mantia, *Codice diplomatico dei re aragonesi Pietro I, Giacomo, Federico II, Pietro II e Ludovico, dalla rivoluzione siciliana del 1282 sino al 1355*, vol. 1 (1282-1290) (Palermo, 1917), 299-306, indicating that the Sicilian consul in Tunis must in fact be Messinese; C. Trasselli, 'Sugli europei in Armenia. A proposito di un privilegio trecentesco e di una novella del Boccaccio', *Archivio storico italiano*, 122 (1964), 471-91; Abulafia, 'Merchants of Messina', 211.

[55] Abulafia, *Two Italies*, 42-4; *Due Italie*, 89-91.

Southern Italy, Sicily and Sardinia

the Crusades, on the grounds that it suggests Messina was a more active participant in long-distance trade than was the case.[56] In fact, that is not being suggested; Messina's long-distance trade reflects the needs and interests of those, from Genoa, Pisa, Provence, Barcelona and elsewhere, who passed through the city. Its own merchant community did not achieve the high profile of the inhabitants of another re-settled entrepôt, conquered for Christendom much later, the City of Mallorca.

The disappearance of the indigenous merchants, especially the Muslims, is noticeable in the Sicilian case. Even the Greeks of Messina seem rather insignificant in those trade records that survive from the thirteenth century. The Muslims were the victims of active persecution, however: it is striking that, while ibn Jubayr and Hugo Falcandus portray the Muslims as the largest group of merchants in Palermo, they had simply ceased to exist by the mid-thirteenth century, when only very occasional Muslim traders can be found spending any length of time in the city. The process whereby the Latins inserted themselves alongside the Muslims into the supply system within Sicily itself can perhaps be seen in an Arabic act of around 1150 which describes a voyage along the north coast of Sicily made by Muslim merchants financed by the Latin Sir William, who may have been Genoese.[57] In the same period, the island was undergoing a reorientation of its business links, as the Jewish merchants based in Egypt and Tunisia, known from the famous Cairo Genizah documents, became a less potent force in trans-Mediterranean trade; a new commercial force emerged in their place inside Egypt, the Muslim *karimi* merchants, who enjoyed direct access both to the Ayyubid court and to the Venetian, Genoese and Pisan merchants visiting Alexandria and Damietta in search of spices. Sicily lost its traditional role as a point of exchange where Muslim merchants could bring the spices westerners required; the westerners now freely penetrated into the Middle East to obtain what they wanted.[58] At the same time, the ever-growing demand for grain in the cities of northern Italy, Provence, Catalonia helped transform extensive areas of Sicily and Apulia into large farms concentrating on the cultivation of wheat for export, as in the case of the lands of Monreale Cathedral.[59] For Henri

---

[56] Epstein, *An island for itself*, 243-5; cf. *Two Italies*, 42 and *Due Italie*, 90.

[57] S. Cusa, *I diplomi greci e arabi di Sicilia* (2 vols., Palermo, 1860-2), vol. 2, 502-4, 719; G. Trovato, *Sopravvivenze arabe in Sicilia: documenti arabo-siculi del periodo normanno* (Monreale, 1949), 73-6.

[58] Abulafia, 'Asia, Africa and the trade of medieval Europe', 437-43.

Southern Italy, Sicily and Sardinia

Bresc, indeed, Sicily was taking the route towards the 'monoculture' typical of the thirteenth, fourteenth and fifteenth centuries. It is still difficult to calculate what proportion of grain was exported from the island and what proportion was reserved for domestic consumption in the Sicilian towns, such as the swollen Palermo of the thirteenth century. It is arguable that internal demand was no less important than external in transforming the west and south-east of Sicily into an area of monoculture; on the other hand, some of the doubts raised by Epstein about the scale of exports are derived from fifteenth-century evidence, and they are also based in some measure on his heavily revised population estimates for the island.[60] Most would agree that around 1200 specialised 'Arab' agriculture was waning, as the Monreale evidence very clearly shows, and that efforts in the thirteenth century, notably by Frederick II, to restore cultivation of indigo, henna and sugar are interesting because they failed.

This brings the argument back to the theme of economic dualism in medieval Italy. Even if the Amalfitans, Gaetans, Messinesi and so on continued to live off trade in some measure in the thirteenth century, as well as other economic activities, it is clear that the Genoese and other northern merchants were gradually acquiring easy access to the most urgently needed agricultural products, notably the grain they needed to feed their fellow-citizens and the cotton and skins they required for the nascent industries of Lombardy and Tuscany. Nonetheless, it would clearly be absurd to speak of real control of the productive capacity of the south by the northerners, around 1200. Frederick II and others reacted against the northern presence; the emperor denied the Genoese their tax exemptions, from 1220 onwards, and he closed the Sicilian ports to Italian exporters when there was the chance of making a fat profit for the royal court out of grain supplies for a famished north Africa.[61] Yet the economy was being gradually reshaped under pressure from the northerners. The north Italian merchants gained what they needed at a good price, and came to control the movement of Sicilian wheat in all directions. Frederick II notwithstanding, the Genoese, Florentines and, later, the Catalans managed the export trade in Sicilian wheat towards Africa by the late thirteenth century. Despite the lasting presence of the Amalfitans and Gaetans, as also of the Messinesi, in trade beyond the

---

[59] H. Bercher, A. Courteaux, J. Mouton, 'Une abbaye latine dans la société musulmane: Monreale au XIIe siècle', *Annales: Économies, sociétés, civilisations*, 34 (1979), 525-47.

[60] Epstein, *An island for itself*, 270-87.

Southern Italy, Sicily and Sardinia

Regno, the real initiative had passed by 1200 to the Genoese, Tuscans and Venetians and, within the wider framework of Mediterranean trade, the role of the southerners would henceforth be a secondary one.

IV

The case of Sardinia appears to provide an extreme example of Italian economic dualism. The closed economy of the period of the early Judges, up to the twelfth century, was radically transformed by the Pisans and Genoese, who were masters not merely of the island's trade but, before the Aragonese invasion of 1323, also of its political life.[62] The attempts by Pisa and Genoa to obtain wide control over the island, in the face of each other's ambitions, resulted in an almost continuous conflict between the two republics throughout the twelfth century. Even at the start of the century Genoese and Pisans were competing for lands (*donnicalie* or *domos*, in Sardinian usage) in the territory of the Judge of Cagliari, in Gallura in the far north, and in Logudoro in the north-east. A document of 19 May 1108 is especially revealing: the Judge of Cagliari, Mariano-Torchitorio, donates to the cathedral of San Lorenzo in Genoa lands in southern Sardinia. But Mariano also endowed the Pisans with lands; while around Sassari, in the north, the canons of the cathedral of Santa Maria in Pisa were insisting in about 1115 that the monastery of San Michele di Plaiano was dependent on Pisa Cathedral.[63] Both Pisan and Genoese penetration into Sardinia was guided by the churches of the two republics, as, indeed, was sometimes the case in the eastern Mediterranean colonies too. And in fact there were rivalries between churches which sought to gain lands for colonisation in the island: the monks of Montecassino came to settle, aided by the naval power of nearby Gaeta; the Victorines of Marseilles took charge of the church of San Saturnino at Cagliari, and of its twenty dependencies, from 1119 onwards, following a grant by Judge Mariano-Torchitorio.[64] The

---

[61] Abulafia, 'Lo stato e la vita economica'.

[62] Day, *La Sardegna sotto la dominazione pisano-genovese*, 53-9, 180-6; and, more generally, P. Mugoni, *Economia e società nella Sardegna medievale* (Oristano, 1985). Dr Rosalind Brown Jensen is preparing a detailed study of northern Sardinia using Genoese and Pisan sources, based on her doctoral thesis *Social development and economic dependence: northern Sardinia, c.1100-1300* (Cambridge University, 1985).

[63] G. Pistarino, 'Genova e la Sardegna nel secolo XII', *La Sardegna nel mondo mediterraneo. Atti del primo convegno internazionale di studi geografici-storici*, vol. 2, *Gli aspetti storici*, ed. M. Brigaglia (Sassari, 1981), 45-50.

Southern Italy, Sicily and Sardinia

Cassinesi and the Victorines were engaged in a wider struggle too, led by the pope, for the suppression of the Greek practices which dominated the Sardinian church until the late eleventh century, and for the integration of Sardinia into the increasingly centralised Reform Church.

From 1128 onwards there are clear signs of a lively Genoese commercial presence in Sardinia, with merchants buying salt, skins and, increasingly, cheap wheat; the search for silver, which was to prove so lucrative to the Catalans, took off more slowly. In the twelfth century there still existed a limited trade in Sard slaves and servants.[65] The Pisans, too, made substantial strides forward, obtaining tax exemptions in north-western Sardinia and the promise of protection of their persons and property in the celebrated 'Logudoro Privilege' or 'Carta consolare pisana' of the 1080s:

> ci nulli imperatore ci lu aet potestare istum locu de non aptat comiatu de levarclis toloneum in placitu; de non occidere Pisanu ingratis...[66]

Sardinia appears regularly as a commercial destination in the notarial acts of Giovanni Scriba of Genoa, dating from the period December 1154 to August 1164. There are fourteen surviving acts for Sardinian trade, as against 84 for Sicily and 73 for north Africa.[67] On the other hand, it is evident that many a ship bound for Africa, Sicily or indeed Spain passed through Sardinian waters during its voyage; later notarial acts from Savona, of the start of the thirteenth century, give some idea of the tour of western Mediterranean ports, Sardinian as well as African, that trading voyages might involve. What is striking about the investments in Sardinian trade is their low average level, compared to investments in Syria or Sicily: in 1160-1 about £50 of Genoese money was invested in the average expedition to Sardinia, as against an average of £80 in Sicily and of £300 in Syria.[68] What this difference reflects is

---

[64] Pistarino, 'Genova e la Sardegna', 50; F. Artizzu et al., *Studi sui Vittorini in Sardegna* (Padua, 1963).

[65] Pistarino, 'Genova e la Sardegna', 53-6.

[66] There are several editions of this document; I have used that of C. Dionisotti and C. Grayson in *Early Italian Texts* (2nd ed., Oxford, 1965), 14-17, which is based on one edited by S. Debenedetti, *Atti del R. Accademia di Scienze di Torino*, 61 (1926), 66-79.

[67] Abulafia, *Two Italies*, 99, and *Due Italie*, 153; Pistarino, 'Genova e la Sardegna', 64-65.

the low price of Sardinian products, such as the grain of Oristano or the salt of Cagliari, compared to the high price of eastern luxury goods; in addition, transport costs between Sardinia and Genoa were much lower than those between Acre or Alexandria and Genoa. As John Day has noted, the low prices charged in Sardinia for goods sought by north Italian merchants, particularly grain, only served to intensify commercial penetration of Sardinia by Ligurian and Tuscan merchants, and stimulated attempts to acquire direct dominion over extensive lands where labour costs were low and where surpluses appear to have been reasonably plentiful.[69] Sardinia became the true hinterland of Genoa, for it had no hinterland worthy of the name in Liguria. It is significant that great Genoese families such as the Doria built power bases on the island; the Dorias, whose lands were in the north, managed to preserve their autonomy in the castles of the Logudoro, though tales of their foundation of Alghero in about 1102 are now viewed with some scepticism.[70] The Genoese also beat their way to the doors of the Judges' palaces; they provided credit and political support for Judge Barisone of Arborea, in the centre of the island, at a time when Genoa and Pisa were pressing their claims to dominion over the whole of Sardinia at the court of Pope Alexander III and his bitter rival Frederick Barbarossa. The Genoese told the emperor in no uncertain terms: *Sardinea nostra est et non Pisanorum*; to which the Pisans equally confidently replied: *Sardinea nostra erat primo et nunc rectiori iure nostram dicimus esse.*[71]

The rewards for Genoa's success in establishing control over Logudoro and in gaining influence in Arborea are visible in the expansion of Genoese trade with Sardinia, recorded in the acts of the Genoese notary Oberto Scriba de Mercato. We find ten contracts for Sardinian trade between September 1182 and January 1183, as against 35

---

[68] Abulafia, *Two Italies*, 113, 119, and *Due Italie*, 169, 176: £73 in 1160, £33 in 1161 - however, the evidence is slim. More useful is perhaps the evidence from 1191: 30 contracts with an average level of £39.50.

[69] Day, *La Sardegna sotto la dominazione pisano-genovese*, 38-53, 181.

[70] For Alghero, see F. Bertino, *Notizie e Ipotesi su un borgo sardo-ligure del basso medioevo: l'Alghero dei Doria*, vol. 1 (Alghero, 1989); Brown, *Social development*, 126-38.

[71] *Annali Genovesi di Caffaro e de'suoi continuatori*, ed. L. T. Belgrano and C. Imperiale di Sant'Angelo (5 vols., Rome, 1890-1920), vol. 1, 170-5; Pistarino, 'Genova e la Sardegna', 94-5; F. Artizzu, *La Sardegna pisana e genovese* (Sassari, 1985), 96-101; Day, *La Sardegna sotto la dominazione pisano-genovese*, 164.

Southern Italy, Sicily and Sardinia

contracts for north Africa and Alexandria, and 25 for Sicily.[72] In the Spring and summer of 1184 Sicily is recorded in ten contracts, Sardinia in nine and Corsica seven.[73] From January 1190 to August 1190 (with a break in the sequence in June) there survive 35 Sardinian contracts, which is second only to Sicily (41 contracts) and higher than Corneto (21) or Syria (20).[74] The acts of the notary Guglielmo Cassinese of 1191 present 52 contracts for Sardinia, 42 for Syria, 40 for Sicily, 21 for Naples and an impressive 113 for the Maghrib.[75] It stands to reason that the data from contracts can only suggest in a very approximate way the relative importance of the destinations the documents mention; but it is also evident that by 1200 contacts between Genoa and Sardinia were intense and regular, that they attracted not just the investments of the élite of wealthy patricians but also small investments by *popolani* - by widows, priests, artisans. From this point of view Guglielmo Cassinese's cartulary is especially useful and significant; his clientèle was generally less grand than Giovanni Scriba's customers thirty years earlier, and it is evident that Sardinian trade, to which lower risks were attached than the Levant trade, and in which return journeys could be achieved quickly, was a much more attractive proposition for those with £5 or £10 to spare than the long-distance expeditions to the east, dominated by the city's élite. Evidence from Pisa is much patchier, but material published by Artizzu suggests a very similar picture of trade links between Sardinia and its other mistress.[76]

---

[72] Abulafia, *Two Italies*, 158, and *Due Italie*, 222, (these figures are only for September and October 1182); Pistarino, 'Genova e la Sardegna', 94-5; E. Bach, *La Cité de Gênes au XIIe siècle* (Copenhagen, 1955), Appendix of unnumbered pages, under 1182.

[73] Abulafia, *Two Italies*, 161 and *Due Italie*, 225; Pistarino, 'Genova e la Sardegna', 106-7.

[74] Pistarino, 'Genova e la Sardegna', 107, though the figures in *Two Italies*, 174, 177, and *Due Italie*, 242, 245 are higher - the result of the different ways of calculating totals in what are often ambiguous texts.

[75] Pistarino, 'Genova e la Sardegna'; cf. *Two Italies*, 182, and *Due Italie*, 251, for the total value of the surviving contracts: £2947 for Sardinia, £8785 for Syria, £7816 for Sicily, but a mere £23 recorded for Corsica, which perhaps, because of proximity, was thought not generally to need the extra guarantee of a written contract.

[76] F. Artizzu, *Documenti inediti relativi ai rapporti economici fra la Sardegna e Pisa nel Medioevo* (2 vols., Padua, 1961-2).

Southern Italy, Sicily and Sardinia

What is significant about the Genoese and Pisan documentation is the very low level of participation in international trade out of Sardinia on the part of the Sards themselves, whether *maiorales* (nobles) or local merchants. The overseas links of the Sardinian nobility mainly consisted of marriage ties to Pisan or Genoese girls, as a way of strengthening bonds between a judgeship and one of the maritime republics. Thus Gunnaru, the son of Costantino, judge of Torres, 'fuit acumandadu... a sos dictos mercantes' of Pisa in 1127, taken to Pisa, and married there to a daughter of the Pisan Embriaco family.[77] A rare case of involvement by the Sardinian nobility in trade comes from the early thirteenth-century Genoese cartulary of Lanfranco, where the judge of Logudoro is seen selling wool in Genoa, by means of a Sardinian factor; but this document is significant precisely because it is atypical.[78]

However, Sardinia did not lack a merchant community by 1200. It was simply a community of foreign settlers and visitors. The most important example is that of Sassari, where there was only a small Sard settlement, but where the north Italians were busy creating a regional focus for north-western Sardinian trade. Sassari, and its out-port of Porto Torres, became the flashpoint of Pisan-Genoese rivalry in the Judgeship of Torres; but the thirteenth century saw, nevertheless, the rapid physical expansion of the town and the gradual formation of an autonomous government modelled on the northern commune, a process strengthened by the continual arrival of new settlers from the mainland.[79]

A further factor of significance in the consolidation of north Italian power was the Genoese capture of Bonifacio (Bonifaziu), atop its great rock on the southern tip of Corsica, in 1195, after a brief struggle with the Pisans. Bonifacio rapidly became the headquarters of a commercial network that linked Bosa, in western Sardinia, Alghero, in Logudoro, Sassari and other lesser centres: Bonifacio was the redistribution point for imports from and exports to the mainland.[80]

---

[77] Brown, *Social development*, 50-51, 77.

[78] Information about this document is owed to Dr Brown Jensen.

[79] *Gli Statuti Sassaresi. Economia, società, istituzioni a Sassari nel Medioevo e nell'età moderna. Atti del convegno di studi, Sassari, 12-14 maggio 1983*, ed. A. Mattone and M. Tangheroni (Cagliari, 1986). See especially the articles by J. Day, 'Sassari e il Logudoro nell'economia mediterranea nei secoli XI-XV' (37-44) and by M. Tangheroni, 'Nascita e affermazione di una città: Sassari dal XII al XIV secolo' (45-63).

[80] Brown, *Social development*, 156-206.

Southern Italy, Sicily and Sardinia

Bonifacio was already the target of Genoese trade in 1201 and 1202. Indeed, trade contracts for Bonifacio often speak explicitly of the link between Bonifacio and Corsica, specifying voyages *ad portum Bonifacium et inde in Sardineam.* A Genoese debtor promised in September 1203 to pay back a loan *postquam fuerint ad Bonifacium et a Bonifacio portare merces in Sardineam in lignis armatis sicut alii mercatores faciunt.*[81] The population of Bonifacio contained a high proportion of Sards, so that it became more obviously a Sardinian than a Corsican town. Guantino Zanche, a Sard, obtained a house in Bonifacio before 1239, and became a full citizen of the town. While other inhabitants of Bonifacio, of Genoese descent, traded directly to Genoa itself, Guantino Zanche restricted himself to local trade in the straits between Corsica and Sardinia.[82] But even this secondary trade network was largely dominated by Ligurians and their descendants, feeding into the main trade pipeline that linked Genoa to Sardinia by way of Bonifacio.

Thus in Sardinia we can see both the foundation and settlement of towns, dominated by the north Italians, and the exploitation of the countryside, increasingly dominated by the great churches of Pisa, Genoa and also Marseilles. For Day, this identified Sardinia as a truly 'colonial' economy, whose exploitation was based on unequal exchange, producing vast profits for the merchants and proprietors who worked together to extract cheap foodstuffs and raw materials from the island. Wheat, for Day, is 'la vera derrata coloniale... rivolta al mercato cittadino e internazionale'.[83] In addition, there were other attractions: the pastoral sector was important, producing then as now the justly famous *pecorino* cheeses; salt was the target of Gaetans, Victorines and, later, Catalans.[84] The presence of the northerners in the commercial life of the island, when set alongside their powerful role in the political life of Sardinia and alongside the success of the ecclesiastical proprietors in acquiring

---

[81] Brown, *Social development*, 164.

[82] Brown, *Social development*, 166.

[83] Day, 'Sassari e il Logudoro', 46.

[84] For the Catalan salt trade in fourteenth-century Sardinia, see C. Manca, *Aspetti dell'espansione economica catalano-aragonese nel Mediterraneo occidentale. Il commercio internazionale del sale* (Milan, 1966); for the Catalan grain trade see M. Tangheroni, *Aspetti del commercio dei cereali nei Paesi della Corona d'Aragona, 1. La Sardegna* (Pisa, 1981); for the Catalan silver exports see M. Tangheroni, *La città*

Southern Italy, Sicily and Sardinia

extensive estates, had dramatic effects on the Sardinian economy. The closed economy of the eleventh century was transformed into one that depended directly on the interest and advantage of Pisa and Genoa. While the conflict for control of the island continued, without really decisive results, right up to and beyond its invasion by a third force, the Crown of Aragon, in the fourteenth century, the Genoese and Pisans did manage to obtain a degree of influence on this island which far surpassed the level of control they achieved in Sicily, Syria or elsewhere. Such ambitions were not lacking, as the conquest of Syracuse around 1200 reveals. But even in Corsica, where the Pisans had more success in holding off Genoese competitors, there appears to be no comparison in the extent of penetration, in the completeness of the takeover. Indeed, it could be argued that the struggle between Pisa and Genoa for control of Sardinia, for deeper and deeper penetration into Sardinia and for mastery of both town and country, was all the more intense because each republic was consumed by jealousy at the other side's successes. This generated a drive to conquer and settle Sardinia not just for the exploitation of its resources, but also to ensure that the rival republic would not be able to use Sardinia as a strategic base from which to control the western Mediterranean. (Interestingly, the Pisans attacked Mallorca and Ibiza, to the west of Sardinia, in 1113-15, with the support of a Sard contingent; control of both the Balearics and of Corsica-Sardinia would arguably have made them masters of the entire sea.) Thus the war for the control of the Mediterranean trade routes had as a by-product the colonisation of an island that, up to the eleventh century, had been largely ignored except as a nest of pirates and as a source of slaves. Then, in the twelfth century, Pisa and Genoa, with the prompting of ecclesiastical landlords who had received major land grants in Sardinia, began to appreciate that the island's natural resources might have invaluable uses in meeting their need for food and raw materials.

V

It is now possible to see more clearly the differences between the experience of the *Regno* and that of Sardinia. In both cases, and especially in the instances of the two islands of Sicily and Sardinia, we can observe regions of low population at a time when, above all in northern Italy, the population was growing in leaps and bounds. In both islands the possibility of maintaining regular annual exports of foodstuffs

---

dell'argento. Iglesias dalle origini alla fine del Medioevo (Naples, 1985), and J. Day, *The Medieval Market Economy* (Oxford, 1986).

Southern Italy, Sicily and Sardinia

and raw materials would have to depend, though in differing ways, on the colonisation of these regions by mainlanders, whether landowners, merchants or peasants. In the Sardinian case we are looking at a society that is undergoing gradual commercialisation as a result of outside impulses, but one which retains throughout the Middle Ages many of the characteristics of a very lightly commercialised society, of Carolingian society fossilised. More or less the opposite is visible in the *Regno*. Here, in fact, the economy was already very diversified before the Norman conquest and before the coming of the northern merchants; it was an economy tied, by way of Jewish and Muslim businessmen, to the distribution networks of the Islamic world. In Sardinia neither Muslim corsairs nor Greek monks left important traces in the island economy. There was a significant lack of export industries, and the Ligurian merchants imported items as basic as simple kitchenware to satisfy a fairly restricted level of local demand.

In contrast, in Sicily and in mainland southern Italy there still existed in the late Norman period some active industrial enterprises, such as the dye-works of Salerno, controlled by Jewish artisans, and the silk workshops that still persisted in parts of Sicily. But, as in Sardinia, the export of raw materials, with cotton in first place, though also wool, skins, raw silk, became the major form of involvement in the Italian textile industry of the twelfth century onwards. In other words, the 'Lombards' of the north were left to produce high-value finished textiles, destined to be sold to consumers such as the king of Sicily himself. Situated astride the central Mediterranean, benefiting from the trade in its agricultural goods, Sicily still presents itself to view in the twelfth and early thirteenth centuries as a rich island, or at any rate an island of rich proprietors. Yet even in the Norman and Hohenstaufen period, as the evidence of Monreale indicates, Sicily was undergoing transformation towards an economy of monoculture, concentrated heavily in the west and south-east on wheat production. The disappearance of the Muslims coincides with the abandonment of local rural specialities, such as sugar production and indigo cultivation; increasingly, we see large estates developing whose landlords aim to produce grain for consumption in Palermo, Messina, Naples, Genoa, Florence, Tunis and elsewhere. In the same period we see a contraction of cotton production, despite its undoubted importance in the Norman period; cotton then becomes a speciality of Malta and one or two other areas.

On the other hand, the evidence from Monreale and western Sicily has to be distinguished from that provided by the Val Demone, north-eastern Sicily, which was better suited to the production of wine and of swine (both products reflect the longstanding importance of the Greek population in this region); it was also an area where artisan production of textiles, including heavy carpet-like cloths, was important. Here the diversified economy of old Sicily survived; paradoxically, in this least of Muslim areas, some features of the economy, notably the role of artisan crafts, are more reminiscent of the pre-Norman economy than are western or south-eastern Sicily. This question of continuity is still an open one; an examination of (for instance) Malta might reveal that cotton was being cultivated there in the Norman period, by a Muslim peasantry, but evidence from the post-Black Death era suggests that cotton production acquired the status of a monoculture only in the late fourteenth and fifteenth centuries. A similar picture obtains for Sicilian sugar production, even though this item never acquired the importance in Sicily that cotton acquired in Malta.[85] In any case, in the late Middle Ages inter-regional trade within Sicily, accompanied by further regional specialisation, may have been more intense than has been supposed; Epstein's rejection of Bresc's colonial economy, and of Abulafian dualism, moves dangerously close to another form of dualism, created by the interaction between the Val Demone and the grain-producing Val di Noto and Val di Mazara. There is, however, a problem in knowing how much impact to attribute to the international demand for Sicilian grain; Epstein insists that in the fifteenth century it was rare for 15% or even 10% of the harvest to be taken outside the island, and he stresses the importance of the internal market for grain, which was dominated by the larger Sicilian cities.[86] At the roots of this disagreement is a deeper debate about the influence of international trade on the economic structures of a region. But there is no sense in denying that the trade in Sicilian grain and raw materials brought salvation as well as profit to the north Italian cities, and later on to Barcelona and Ciutat de Mallorca. Their own economies depended on regular, substantial, good quality, cheap supplies; Sicily, and also Apulia, could meet these needs, as could Sardinia.

The foreign merchants could not, however, succeed in their ambition of conquering key points in the *Regno*; Genoa's hopes of acquiring the grain-rich Val di Noto were dashed by Henry VI's breach of faith and by Frederick II's recovery of Syracuse. In one sense, then, the label 'colonial' fits Sardinia far better than Sicily, for in Sardinia

---

[85]These thoughts were prompted by the current research of Charles Dalli on the economy of late medieval Malta.

[86] Epstein, *An island for itself*, 275, arguing 'that in medieval Sicily the foreign grain trade never involved a proportion greater than fifteen per cent of domestic output, and that for most of the later Middle Ages this proportion was below ten per cent'.

Southern Italy, Sicily and Sardinia

effective political control was established, with the business interests of the Italian merchants very much in mind. The kings of Sicily proved adept at playing off one Italian republic against another; the Sardinian judges failed early at this game, and forfeited their autonomy to the Genoese and Pisans.

Into this varied picture mainland southern Italy must also be fitted. For a major distinction between the *Regno* and Sardinia is the continued vitality of the maritime cities of Campania and Apulia; this vitality was quite different in origin from that of Sassari, Alghero or Bonifacio, which were primarily created by and for Genoese and Pisan settlers who retained intimate links to their mother-city. Messina is in a few respects comparable, in view of its absorption of large numbers of north Italians. Amalfi, Bari and in some measure Messina were the centres of the internal trade of the *Regno*, by land and by sea; they linked the island of Sicily to the mainland. They had always lacked that ready access to the new markets of continental Europe which was assuredly of the greatest importance in the emergence of Genoa and Venice. But they also lost their own ancient primacy in the Levant trade. Genoese, Tuscans and Venetians aimed to serve a vast European market, stretching as far as Flanders; the Amalfitans and their colleagues were increasingly confined to the *Regno* and the waters around. In Sardinia, the northern merchants (and, later, the Catalans) were masters of the external and internal markets; in the *Regno*, only of the external one; but in both cases they acquired a virtually permanent pre-eminence.

II

L'origini del dualismo economico italiano

Nel suo *Un monde méditerranéen* Henri Bresc si dichiara interessato in primo luogo al Trecento e al Quattrocento; ma se gli storici del dodicesimo o tredicesimo secolo lo ignorassero rischierebbero di trascurare un argomento di primaria rilevanza per la storia della Sicilia normanna, sveva e angioina. Il Vespro figura come punto di riferimento centrale nello sviluppo della teoria di Bresc riguardo all'emergere di una «nazione siciliana»; ma, rimane evidente, il Vespro è un'espressione di una evoluzione lenta e lunga nella società siciliana, che comincia già nell'undicesimo secolo non forse con l'arrivo dei Normanni ma almeno con l'insediamento dei primi gruppi dei cosiddetti «Lombardi» venuti dalla Liguria e dal Mezzogiorno continentale.

Secondo punto di riferimento, collocato attorno al 1200, sarebbe la sparizione dalla Sicilia della tecnologia agraria del mondo arabo, con un ritorno ad un'economia monoculturale che, secondo Bresc, rimane tipico dell'economia siciliana anche dopo la rinascita dell'interesse alla produzione dello zucchero, dopo il 1400. L'economia «bloccata» della Sicilia, controllata da principi e baroni per i quali il solo obiettivo economico è quello di elevare i propri redditi a livelli imponenti, rimarrebbe ancorata ai caratteri acquisiti durante i secoli XIII e XIV.

Fattore di gran rilevanza è la presenza di mercanti stranieri, e, in particolare, dei Genovesi: questi mercanti integrano l'isola in una rete commerciale che si estendeva sulla Sicilia come in tutto il Mediterraneo, e sulle Fiandre e l'Inghilterra. Imponevano all'isola un ruolo specializzato di produzione di grano e di altri prodotti grezzi, mentre acquistavano un ruolo preminente nell'importazione dei prodotti industriali, in primo luogo i tessuti dell'Italia settentrionale, della Catalogna, delle Fiandre. A questo punto è il caso di chiedersi se si possa parlare di un programma deliberato, imposto all'isola da mercanti che possedevano una chiara visione dell'economia mediterranea e dei bisogni delle potenti città mercantili di Genova e Barcellona. O se i mercanti si avvantaggiassero, forse inconsapevolmente di cambiamenti interni nell'economia isolana, diretti dai nuovi dominatori latini e dagli immigrati che avevano compreso assai bene le possibilità commerciali nella produzione di ingenti quantità di grano.

A questo punto l'argomentazione di Bresc deve confrontarsi con due diverse ipotesi. Una si trova nel recentissimo lavoro di Stephan Epstein, che pubblicherà i risultati delle sue ricerche nella collana di monografie *Past and Present*.[1] Esaminando in primo luogo il Val Demone nel Trecento e nel Quattrocento, Epstein insiste sul fatto che Bresc ha sottovalutato le diversità interne dell'economia siciliana del tardo medioevo. La documentazione della Sicilia nord-orientale potrebbe offrire un quadro molto diverso dall'economia di monocultura, più tipica della Sicilia occidentale, illuminata dalle fonti notarili palermitane molto efficacemente spogliate da Bresc. Bresc non ha negato che nella Sicilia occidentale un'economia monoculturale fosse rappresentata in un modo più cospicuo che nel Val Demone. Questo non aveva mai perso il carattere, già evidente all'epoca della documentazione della Geniza del Cairo, di regione ad economia mista, di centro di produzione di tessuti pesanti, di seta e di vino. Per Epstein, la presenza nel Val Demone di queste industrie, insieme con la pastorizia e i vigneti, dimostra come sia importante integrare nell'analisi dell'economia siciliana del tardo medioevo la domanda interna di prodotti agrari e industriali siciliani. Non tutti portavano abiti di tessuti fiorentini o catalani; una forte percentuale del grano prodotto nell'isola si consumava nell'isola, ad esempio nelle grandi città. Palermo e non Genova sarebbe stata il

---

[1] *Market Structures and Economic Development in late medieval Sicily*, tesi di dottorato dell'Università di Cambridge, 1988, in corso di pubblicazione, Cambridge University Press.

maggiore mercato del grano prodotto nell'interno della Sicilia. È interessante rilevare come Bresc stesso abbia identificato un gruppo di ricchi mercanti indigeni che si inserirono nei ranghi inferiori dell'aristocrazia isolana. Questi mercanti discendevano in parte da mercanti e immigrati continentali: ma divenuti siciliani non acquisivano un ruolo internazionale, ad esempio nel commercio delle spezie orientali o nella navigazione verso le Fiandre. Solo Messina si trovava in concorrenza con i settentrionali nel commercio con il Levante, ma in forma relativamente modesta e attorno al 1300, con il ruolo specializzato di fornitore di vini.[2]

Possiamo confrontare queste due analisi dell'economia siciliana con l'esperienza sarda alla stessa epoca. Gli studi sull'economia sarda di John Day parlano, come quelli di Bresc, di un'economia «bloccata», di «dipendenza» e perfino di un'economia «sottosviluppata».[3] In confronto alla Sicilia, in Sardegna si trovava una piccolissima comunità indigena di mercanti sardi, e le città non giungevano alle dimensioni di Palermo e Catania. In particolare grandi regioni dell'isola passavano sotto il controllo delle città norditaliane o almeno delle famiglie e istituzioni preminenti di queste città — i Doria di Genova, l'Opera di Santa Maria di Pisa — e, più tardi, sotto il controllo dei Catalani. La mancanza di un singolo centro di governo, come esisteva in Sicilia (anche se debilitato dalle ribellioni e dai tentativi angioini d'impadronirsi dell'isola) ebbe l'esito, nel caso sardo, dell'instaurazione di un controllo straniero molto più forte. Mentre, fino ai due Martini, i re aragonesi della Sicilia non furono re d'Aragona ma rimasero indipendenti da Barcellona. Le regioni catalane della Sardegna ebbero dinastie aragonesi locali. In questo senso, la caratterizzazione della Sardegna da parte di Day come prima colonia dell'Europa controllata dagli interessi di Pisa, di Genova, della Catalogna, ha una qualche validità. Non vale la pena, però, di confrontarsi con gli storici che hanno giocato con il termine «colonia», presentando all'estremo gli insediamenti italiani nel regno crociato come «colonie in una colonia». È chiaro anche che, nel caso siciliano, il termine «coloniale» avrebbe un altro significato. Quello che Bresc ha descritto è un colonialismo attenuato, in un certo senso indiretto, con il quale i mercanti stranieri raggiungevano il loro primo obiettivo — l'accesso immediato al grano siciliano — avendo realizzato stretti legami con la corte reale e con i baroni autonomi, dalle terre dei quali il frumento veniva estratto.

La questione centrale è stabilire fino a che punto i mercanti italiani e catalani riuscirono a imporre in Sicilia un'economia adeguata ai loro bisogni specifici. È chiaro che questi mercanti vedevano nella Sicilia una fonte importante di profitti, non da realizzare solo attraverso l'approvvigionamento della città madre, ma anche con la possi-

---

[2] D. ABULAFIA, *The merchants of Messina: Levant trade and domestic economy*, in «Papers of the British School at Rome», LIV, 1986, pp. 196-212.
[3] J. DAY, *La Sardegna e i suoi dominatori dal secolo XI al secolo XIV*, in *La Sardegna medioevale e moderna*, nella Storia d'Italia UTET, diretta da G. Galasso, Torino, 1984. Rist. sotto il titolo *La Sardegna sotto la dominazione pisano-genovese*, Torino, 1987.

bilità di rifornire di grano tutti i luoghi del Mediterraneo dove la produzione cerealicola scarseggiava.

Il coinvolgimento dei mercanti stranieri nei traffici tra Sicilia e Maghrib prova la capacità dei mercanti latini di sostituirsi ai mercanti arabi e ebrei che, dai documenti della Geniza, prima del XIII secolo avevano un ruolo primario in tale commercio. Secondo Epstein, gli anni del Quattrocento in cui veniva importato il 10% o 15% del raccolto del frumento sono del tutto eccezionali: normalmente si può ipotizzare una cifra che giunge al massimo al 5%.

Naturalmente ciò che può essere rilevato nel quindicesimo secolo potrebbe essere diverso dall'esperienza del Duecento e del primo Trecento, un periodo di rapida crescita demografica dell'Europa continentale, anche se non della Sicilia. I mercanti stranieri cercavano il grano siciliano e sardo perché il prezzo era normalmente basso: secondo Bresc in ciò può osservarsi il fenomeno dello scambio ineguale. Anche il raddoppiamento del prezzo del grano tra l'acquisto a Palermo e l'arrivo a Pisa o Genova non era d'ostacolo alla commercializzazione, dal momento che la domanda internazionale, specie quella delle città, cresceva fino all'epoca della Peste Nera. A Firenze, città famosa per il livello molto alto dei prezzi, tra 1320 e 1330 si vendeva il frumento «ciciliano» ad un prezzo poco superiore rispetto al prezzo del grano «comunale»; pur non esagerando la qualità del grano siciliano bisogna tener presente che esso era adatto alla lunga conservazione e, quindi, ad esempio, utilissimo per l'approvvigionamento delle navi.

«Dipendente» o no, l'economia siciliana attorno al 1300 aveva un importante punto di forza. Le carestie tipiche di questo periodo nell'Europa continentale erano rare in Sicilia: nell'Italia settentrionale terre povere ed un'ingente domanda delle città avevano già creato le condizioni della crisi di approvvigionamento per la quale il grano siciliano, pugliese, sardo offrì una soluzione parziale. Come ha dimostrato De Boüard in un celebre saggio, prima del Vespro i sovrani siciliani potevano utilizzare il grano isolano per approvvigionare le città campane, in particolare la gigantesca Napoli, ed operavano un sofisticato sistema di controllo sulle carestie nell'Italia meridionale.[4] Con il Vespro, dalla dinastia angioina alla dinastia aragonese diminuirono le risorse e riserve frumentarie della Sicilia ed iniziò per la prima un'epoca di seria emergenza. In conseguenza del Vespro anche i produttori siciliani cercarono nuovi mercati: per lunghi anni i mercati napoletani e salernitani furono almeno ufficialmente chiusi. A questo punto la Catalogna avrebbe fornito il nuovo mercato necessario ai produttori siciliani. Importantissimo, in questo meccanismo, sarebbe stato il ruolo degli amalfitani, gruppo al quale Bresc ha dedicato osservazioni di grande interesse.

Il Vespro rappresenta in effetti una vittoria per gli ambienti mercantili internazionali ostili alla dinastia angioina, genovesi e catalani. Anche quando alla città-madre non mancava il frumento, essi conoscevano molto bene lo stato dei mercati internazio-

---

[4] M. DE BOUARD, *Problèmes de subsistances dans un état médiéval: le marché et le prix des céréales au royaume angevin de Sicile*, in «Annales», X, 1938.

nali e potevano, ad esempio, fare da fornitori di grano siciliano a Tunisi, Bisanzio, ecc. I genovesi non persero l'occasione di rifornirsi anche da altre fonti, come la Sardegna e la Maremma. A questo punto osserviamo forse una contraddizione nella tesi di Bresc. Secondo questi il Vespro occupa una posizione preminente nella trasformazione dell'economia della Sicilia. Eppure, non si possono trascurare gli indizi del fatto che il cambiamento da un'economia agricola specializzata verso un'economia monoculturale sarebbe avvenuto già un secolo prima del 1282.

Attorno al 1200, almeno sulle terre di Monreale, si osserva chiaramente la tendenza verso l'abbandono della specializzazione.[5] Nel 1239 Federico II tentava di introdurre in Sicilia nuove colture come l'indaco, l'henné e lo zucchero.[6] In altri termini, il monarca vedeva con chiarezza i cambiamenti della vita agraria del paese, e cercava di correggerli attraverso l'incentivo all'immigrazione di ebrei o cristiani esperti nella coltivazione di piante.

Il problema di fondo era di carattere politico: l'espulsione dei musulmani e il mancato successo dei normanni e degli svevi nei loro tentativi di attrarre immigrati latini dall'Europa continentale condusse a una popolazione sparsa, poco esposta alla generale crisi demografica, a una grande capacità teorica di produzione granaria ma all'impossibilità effettiva di coltivare tutti i terreni frumentari dell'isola. La politica di Federico II verso i mercanti norditaliani fu complicata dalla volontà di trarre benefici fiscali da un prodotto che si vendeva a basso prezzo; per soddisfare i bisogni finanziari del sovrano fu necessaria la creazione di stretti rapporti con acquirenti regolari. L'obiettivo più interessante era il mercato africano, dal momento che le ricorrenti carestie tunisine rendevano possibile la vendita del grano siciliano a prezzi elevatissimi come, ad esempio, avvenne nel 1239. Questa politica ridusse la dipendenza dai servizi offerti dai mercanti stranieri, come i genovesi e veneziani che erano, invece, alleati dei papi.

Tentiamo adesso di rovesciare la direzione consueta dell'analisi storica, mettendo in luce un'epoca più remota, quella normanna. Bresc tra XI e XII secolo osserva una trasformazione da una Sicilia dall'economia diversificata e complessa alla Sicilia tardomedievale della monocoltura, e aderisce alle mie affermazioni riguardo alla posizione della Sicilia, attorno al 1150, tra due mondi commerciali, quello della Geniza del Cairo, caratterizzato da un intenso commercio di oggetti di lusso e da pagamenti in oro, e quello dei mercanti italiani, che pagavano di solito o di preferenza in argento e che cominciavano ad importare nel Mediterraneo tessuti occidentali, prima lombardi e poi fiamminghi.[7] Ma in che senso la Sicilia del dodicesimo secolo gettava le fondamenta dell'economia «bloccata» del tardo medioevo?

---

[5] H. Bercher, A. Courteaux, J. Mouton, *Une abbaye latine dans la société musulmane: Monreale au XII siécle*, in «Annales», XXXIV, 1979, pp. 525-47.
[6] D. Abulafia, *Frederick II: a medieval emperor*, Londra-New York, 1988, pp. 335-6.
[7] D. Abulafia, *The Two Italies: economic relations between the Norman Kingdom of Sicily and the Northern Communes*, Cambridge, 1977; è in preparazione a Napoli un'edizione italiana riveduta.

Il primo punto è che il dualismo economico del dodicesimo secolo in effetti prende forma a partire dall'ascesa economica dei mercanti italiani, che sfruttavano le risorse della Sicilia e della Sardegna e non dalla dominazione dell'economia siciliana da parte degli italiani. L'idea delle «due Italie» è utile per l'analisi del dodicesimo secolo semplicemente come indicazione del fatto che certi aspetti dei rapporti fra Sicilia e nord-Italia, forse veramente «dualistici» trovano la loro origine nel rapporto fra il Regno ed i mercanti di Genova, Pisa e Venezia nell'epoca dei normanni. Sotto questi sovrani l'isola non perse le sue posizioni di regione prospera (cioè regione con dei proprietari prosperi — non parliamo naturalmente dei contadini) e di ambienti mercantili relativamente prosperi, in primo luogo i musulmani con i loro stretti nessi con il Maghrib. I genovesi e i veneziani non furono dominatori ma sfruttatori della ricchezza siciliana.

Bresc ritiene che gli amalfitani rimanessero in prima posizione fra i mercanti latini nella Sicilia. Egli adotta questa interpretazione con l'aiuto dell'eccellente studio di Mario del Treppo e Alfonso Leone, che insiste sulla continuità della vitalità di Amalfi nel commercio del Mediterraneo durante il dodicesimo e il tredicesimo secolo.[8] Di contro, tuttavia, manca ogni prova che gli amalfitani operassero più intensamente in Sicilia rispetto agli altri latini; possediamo, infatti, solo pochissimi contratti commerciali di provenienza amalfitana che parlano di commercio siciliano a quest'epoca. Manca, inoltre, la prova che gli amalfitani godessero di esenzioni fiscali in Sicilia analoghe ai privilegi concessi ai genovesi ed ai veneziani. I re normanni e svevi offrirono privilegi a quasi tutti i concorrenti di Amalfi, con eccezione delle altre città meridionali — Gaeta, Bari, Trani, ecc. La cosiddetta «ruga» degli amalfitani a Palermo potrebbe avere origine in età musulmana, quando gli amalfitani operavano come trasportatori di generi di lusso fra Oriente e Occidente. In effetti, le prove offerte da Bresc consistono in riferimenti agli ufficiali di origine amalfitana e sorrentina presenti alla Corte Reale sotto Federico II e Carlo I d'Angiò; e Bresc ha spiegato con estrema vivacità come il Vespro possa essere spiegato come rivolta antiamalfitana. Questi amalfitani, tuttavia non beneficiarono in modo tangibile la città-madre. Rimane possibile, invece che le carriere burocratiche derivarono la loro maggiore attrattiva dal crollo delle possibilità commerciali. Dal sacco del porto di Amalfi da parte dei pisani nel 1135 non derivò che la scomparsa del commercio di Amalfi, ma esso è indice di un secolo di serrata concorrenza fra mercanti meridionali e mercanti settentrionali.

Gli italiani del nord ricevettero enormi vantaggi dalla formazione di una rete commerciale che integrava i mercanti europei e mediterranei. Per gli amalfitani, al contrario, l'accesso ai centri della domanda, la Francia, la Renania e il Nord dell'Europa, rimaneva difficile. Genovesi, Pisani e Veneziani potevano beneficiare della posizione geografica delle loro città per penetrare nei domini dei principi occidentali, utilizzando i passi alpini e i porti provenzali o occitanici. In Champagne, i fattori degli italiani, per la maggior parte lombardi e piemontesi e dei fiamminghi — nel dodicesimo secolo

---

[8] M. DEL TREPPO, A. LEONE, *Amalfi medievale*, Napoli, 1977.

— compravano a buon prezzo tessuti delle Fiandre e della Francia che esportavano poi a Bisanzio nel regno crociato e in Egitto attraverso la Sicilia. L'assenza di mercanti di Amalfi, di Gaeta e di altre città meridionali colpisce chi scorra gli atti notarili relativi al commercio dei tessuti fiamminghi.

La capacità dei Genovesi e degli altri italiani di fornire alla Sicilia prodotti industriali dell'Europa continentale e di rifornire l'isola di spezie orientali, va messa a confronto con l'effettivo esercizio del potere politico da parte dei mercanti settentrionali in Sardegna prima del 1200. Mentre in Sicilia questi aspiravano all'acquisizione di feudi, in Sardegna i genovesi infeudavano lo stesso cosiddetto re Barisone, che diveniva vassallo del Comune di Genova.[9] Nel caso sardo, dunque si può parlare di vera e propria dominazione senza confronti.

In Sardegna i mercanti italiani cercavano grano, sale, prodotti della pastorizia, materie prime. Bresc insiste sul fatto che in Sicilia, nel XII secolo, il grano rimaneva meno importante del cotone; l'ascesa del frumento nel commercio internazionale sarebbe un fenomeno del Duecento. Il trattato fra Genova e Guglielmo I del 1156 parla molto delle esportazioni di cotone; ed è evidente che un secolo dopo non si trovava più nell'isola il cotone greggio che essa poteva fornire in età normanna. In altri termini, assistiamo qui agli ultimi riflessi di un'economia specializzata islamica che spariva attorno al 1200, con l'eccezione di regioni remote come Malta e Pantelleria, le stesse regioni che mantenevano la loro popolazione musulmana o almeno la lingua araba dopo la sparizione del mondo islamico siciliano.

F. Maurici ha ragione quando insiste sul fatto che Bresc ha sottovalutato le esportazioni di frumento, tentando così di mostrare che la Sicilia della metà del XII secolo era ancora parte del mondo commerciale della Geniza, orientato verso i mercati dell'Africa settentrionale e produttore di generi specializzati come il cotone.[10] Il trattato del 1156, in effetti, parla anche di frumento, e di pelli d'agnello. Nel documento, tuttavia, il riferimento centrale rimane concentrato sulla produzione di materie prime; le attività industriali sono concentrate nel Val Demone (e non si può negare che parliamo di una regione abbastanza grande, con città di una certa importanza). Carne salata, formaggio, grano, cotone greggio sono i prodotti esportati attorno al 1150; a questi si devono aggiungere generi di lusso riesportati, giunti dal mondo islamico e destinati, attraverso Palermo o Messina, ai consumatori continentali. Il commercio siciliano di esportazione facilitava la creazione di un sistema monetario basato sull'oro africano, ed era la fonte della ricchezza dei re normanni. Il re stesso era produttore di grano nelle terre del demanio regio; e, attraverso una burocrazia efficiente, possedeva i mezzi per imporre diritti fiscali sul frumento esportato da qualsiasi terra del Regno. Un cambiamento si può osservare fra XII e XIII secolo: prima del 1400 le terre regie furono per la maggior parte alienate e passarono nelle mani dell'aristocrazia siciliana. Le *tratte* divenivano la

---

[9] F. Artizzu, *La Sardegna pisana e genovese*, Sassari, 1985, pp. 96-103.
[10] In «Schede medievali», 14-15, 1988, pp. 44-48.

fonte più importante delle entrate fiscali, ma anche i proventi di queste si ridussero a causa delle numerose concessioni alle grandi famiglie feudali che — come ha mostrato Bresc — esportavano direttamente il prodotto dei loro feudi.

Si trova un'indicazione dei profitti derivanti dall'esportazione del grano già in età normanna, in un passo burlesco del cronista egiziano ibn al-Athir, che scriveva attorno al 1200, ma si riferiva all'epoca della Prima Crociata; questi parla del rifornimento dell'Africa da parte di Ruggero il Gran Conte.[11] Più significativi sono i dati forniti dalle *fatwa* di al-Mazari, degli anni '40 del XII secolo, da Idrisi, anche se questi utilizzava fonti già vecchie e soprattutto il trattato del 1156 già citato. Per gli Amalfitani la lana della Sicilia rappresentava un'ulteriore attrattiva: un contratto amalfitano del 1105 parla di lana siciliana, da esportare a *Rabennam*, un luogo normalmente considerato essere Ravenna, ma che più probabilmente è Ravello.[12]

La preminenza della Sicilia nella produzione del grano fu confermata dalla crisi agraria nell'Africa settentrionale, dal tardo XI secolo in poi. Quello che colpisce è che i norditaliani, e non i Siciliani o gli Amalfitani, sono ricordati come intermediari in questo commercio. Naturalmente la perdita delle fonti arabe può fornire un'immagine inesatta del commercio in quest'epoca. Al contrario il sorgere di comunità italiane in città africane come Tunisi e i vani tentativi di Federico II di controllare tale flusso commerciale degli italiani tra Sicilia e Africa mostrano che la dominazione italiana era una realtà. Gli italiani, e poi i Catalani, valutavano la Sicilia sia per se stessa sia come area di mediazione fra l'Italia e il mondo islamico.

La Sicilia aveva un ruolo assolutamente fondamentale nello sviluppo del commercio italiano e catalano. Affermare ciò non deve tuttavia suggerire che prima della Peste Nera italiani e catalani dominavano la vita economica dell'isola. Essi ottenevano dalla Sicilia ciò che cercavano e utilizzavano imponenti mezzi diplomatici per garantirsi l'accesso al grano ed alle materie prime dell'isola. Le origini del ruolo della Sicilia nel commercio dei norditaliani stanno nei bisogni alimentari dei comuni marittimi dell'Italia settentrionale e nella capacità dell'isola di soddisfare questi bisogni. Almeno fino al 1350 la dominazione economica dei settentrionali in Sicilia aveva un carattere molto diverso da quella esercitata sull'altra grande isola italiana.

---

[11] ABULAFIA, *Two Italies, cit.*, p. 40.
[12] DEL TREPPO, A. LEONE, *op. cit.*, pp. 65, 68, 129, 196.

III

THE END OF MUSLIM SICILY

THE KINGDOM OF SICILY has long been characterized as an island of tolerance; the harmonious coexis-
tence of Greek and Latin, Jew and Muslim is said to be
symbolized by the unashamed mixing of Byzantine, Romanesque, and Arabic styles in King Roger II's *Cappella Palatina*,
or by Frederick II's correspondence with Muslim scholars and
his patronage of Jewish translators.[1] Yet this is only to speak of
the royal court, and of the kingdom without its mainland half.
There, despite some settlement in the late Byzantine period,
few Muslims could be found until Frederick II emptied the island of Sicily of its Muslim rebels, resettling them at Lucera in
Apulia from the 1220s on. In any case, the fact that he had a
Muslim rebellion on his hands is revealing; for the *convivencia*
of Christian and Muslim on the island had broken down decades before his birth. Repeated outbreaks of violence in Palermo, in 1160/61, for instance, prove how fragile the peace
between communities was already under the Norman kings. At
first sight, then, the harmony attributed to the royal court
seems far removed from a grimmer social reality beyond the
palace walls. Yet the royal court is itself an indicator of the fundamental changes that were taking place in the religious and
ethnic composition of Sicily between about 1100 and 1300:
the Christianization of the island under the dual influence of

---

[1] See, e.g., D. C. Douglas, *The Norman Fate, 1100–1154* (London, 1976),
pp. 146–49, for an extreme statement of a positive view. Ernst Kitzinger has
tended to argue that the Palatine Chapel speaks for the symbiosis of Latin (even
Norman-French), Greek, and Arab. See, e.g., idem, *The Art of Byzantium and
the Medieval West* (Bloomington, 1976), pp. 290–313.

the Greek and Latin Churches; the arrival of large contingents of emigré mainlanders from Campania, Apulia, Liguria, Tuscany, and even from beyond the Alps; and the creation of a Romance language in Sicily, a young offshoot of mainland Italian dialects, first clearly revealed in a school of Sicilian court poets whose lack of inspiration is compensated by their influence on greater successors in Tuscany. In identifying these phenomena, it is possible also to identify the hand of the royal court, which did much to mold the new, Latinized Sicily of the thirteenth century. Perhaps a quarter of a million Muslims had lived on the island at the time of the Norman conquest, consisting of more than half the population (the rest largely Greek, with some Jews); about twenty thousand Saracens were deported to Lucera; and, even though a few lingered on in Sicily and its dependent islands, this 90 percent reduction in a century and a half raises the question of where most of the Muslims went and who came in their stead.

The transformation of Sicily can be approached from another direction—its economic relations with its Mediterranean neighbors and the effect these relations had on the composition and commercial function of the Sicilian cities. For just as the island itself was Latinized, so too were its trade routes. From the early twelfth century the Genoese, Pisans, and Venetians were able to establish trading bases in Palermo and Messina, partly to service their longer trade routes to Syria and Africa and partly to gain access to the grain, cotton, and other raw materials of the island.[2] One of the purposes of the Genoese-Sicilian treaty of 1156 was to assure the safety of Christian shipping bound through Messina for the Levant; but another purpose was to guarantee access to wheat, skins, and raw cotton produced on the island itself.[3] All this did not mean that

[2] David Abulafia, *The Two Italies: Economic Relations between the Norman Kingdom of Sicily and the Northern Communes* (Cambridge, England, 1977), pp. 90–8.

[3] Henri Bresc, *Un monde méditerranéen. Économie et société en Sicile, 1300–1450*, 2 vols. (Rome–Palermo, 1986), p. 16, sees cotton and even silk as the prime interest of the northern Italians in the twelfth century, giving way by about 1200 to wheat. This would fit well with studies of the western Sicilian

the northern Italians at once became the dominant commercial force on the island; but over a period of two hundred years they effected a gradual switch in Sicily's prime trading relations, away from North Africa and the Muslim world toward northern Italy and the Christian West. The trade between Sicily and North Africa, once in the hands of Muslims and Jews (as the Cairo Genizah texts make plain) now fell largely into the hands of merchants of Latin descent, many of whom were not even permanently domiciled in Sicily: Tuscan wine merchants furnished Tunis with its alcohol by 1300, but also carried many items that were not prohibited to Muslims.[4] Lines of communication linked Palermo to Champagne and Flanders.[5] And, whereas in the late twelfth century the majority of Palermo's merchants were still Muslim, by the late thirteenth century they were mainly Latin, and that probably means, in large measure, immigrants or descendants of recent immigrants.[6] A unique commercial contract from around 1160, drawn up in Arabic between Sicilian Muslims and a Latin named William, indicates that as early as the mid-twelfth century a Western merchant was providing loans to the Arabs of the island; the document speaks for the transition from Muslim and Jewish domination of the trade routes to Christian, even northern Italian, ascendancy.[7]

---

estates referred to *below*. The treaty of 1156 mentions both cotton and wheat, and it would be dangerous to hazard a guess as to their relative importance. But between the Norman conquest and the reign of Frederick II primary foodstuffs either gained a lead or increased an existing lead.

[4] David Abulafia, "A Tyrrhenian Triangle: Tuscany, Sicily, Tunis, 1276–1300," in *Studi di storia economica toscana nel Medioevo e nel Rinascimento in memoria di Federigo Melis*, ed. C. Violante (Pisa, 1987), pp. 53–75.

[5] Abulafia, *Two Italies*, pp. 95, 183, 263–64.

[6] Ibn Jubayr, *The Travels of Ibn Jubayr*, trans. R. J. C. Broadhurst (London, 1952), p. 348, says of the Muslims of Palermo: "In their own suburbs they live apart from the Christians. The markets are full of them, and they are the merchants of the place." Ibn Jubayr also says that the Muslims of Palermo maintained many mosques, but clearly some had been appropriated by the Christians, such as the Friday mosque that became the site of the cathedral or the mosque that is supposed to have formed the core of the buildings of the monastery of San Giovanni degli Eremiti.

[7] S. Cusa, *I diplomi greci e arabi di Sicilia*, 2 vols. (Palermo, 1860–1862), 2:502–4, 719; inaccurate translation in G. Trovato, *Sopravvivenze arabe in Si-*

So too in Messina. There, in the mid-thirteenth century, a Catalan settlement took root several decades before the Aragonese conquest of Sicily in 1282.[8] Boccaccio's story of the pot of basil portrays a group of Sangimignanesi resident in Messina;[9] and other, real, Tuscans are revealed in a document of 1239, describing the property of the daughter of a Lucchese merchant resident in the port. She owned a half-share in a warehouse in the new part of Messina; this property was surrounded by the possessions of an Amalfitan and of a citizen of Ravello, and it bordered on the street or quarter of the Pisans.[10] Over the generations, the inhabitants of the Sicilian cities lost their affiliations of origin, intermarried, and created a reasonably homogeneous, but primarily Latin, society. The Greek citizens of these towns played an insignificant role in their long-distance trade by 1300. There were very few Greeks involved in the

---

cilia: documenti arabo-siculi del periodo normanno (Monreale, 1949), pp. 73–76. The document appears to involve Muslims from Cefalù and Corleone and to speak of a sea voyage from Cefalù or another point to Messina and then back to Palermo. The money mentioned is perhaps Genoese. See David Abulafia, "The Crown and the Economy under Roger II and His Successors," *Dumbarton Oaks Papers* 37 (1983): 10, nn. 81–82, repr. in David Abulafia, *Italy, Sicily and the Mediterranean, 1100–1400* (London, 1987), chap. 1. Another Sicilian Muslim with business ties to the Latins in 1162 was "Caitus Bulcassem" (Qā'id Abu'l-Qāsim), surely a member of the Ḥammūdid dynasty that dominated the Sicilian Muslim community in the twelfth century, and maybe even the "leader and Lord" of the Muslims interviewed by Ibn Jubayr in 1185 (Abulafia, *Two Italies*, pp. 247–49; *Travels of Ibn Jubayr*, pp. 358–59). If the identification is correct, he was one of the wealthiest Muslims on the island, and a very rare example of a Muslim businessman who sent agents to Genoa. His Genoese contact, Solomon of Salerno, was himself a subject of the king of Sicily, domiciled in Genoa.

[8] Carme Batlle, "Les relacions entre Barcelona i Sicilia a la segona meitat del segle XIII," in *La società mediterranea all'epoca del Vespro: VII Centenario del Vespro Siciliano/XI Congresso della Corona d'Aragona, 1982, 2: Communicazioni* (Palermo, 1983), pp. 147–62; David Abulafia, "The Merchants of Messina: Levant Trade and Domestic Economy," *Papers of the British School at Rome* 54 (1986): 196–212.

[9] Giovanni Boccaccio *Decameron*, ed. Vittore Branca (Turin, 1984), pp. 526–32 (Giornata 4, Novella 5).

[10] L. R. Ménager, ed., *Les actes latins de S. Maria di Messina (1103–1250)* (Palermo, 1963), pp. 150–58.

trade of Messina with Cyprus around 1300, even though their knowledge of their ancestral language should have been an advantage. Instead we find such names as Pietro del fu Vitale "the Genoese," a citizen of Messina; or Oberto Manayra of Savona, a resident at Marsala; or Benvenuto of Pistoia, an inhabitant of Agrigento—the last two cities ancient centers of Muslim settlement.[11]

Nor were the new settlers all from the great trading centers of northern and southern Italy or, later, Catalonia. Naples, Amalfi, Gaeta, Florence, Pisa, Milan, and Barcelona are all represented, but so too are Assisi, Orvieto, Turin, and countless small inland settlements. A Bolognese appears resident at Cefalù as early as 1188; Piedmont and Liguria dispatched a substantial number of settlers, beginning at the end of the eleventh century with the colonization of parts of central and eastern Sicily. The special links between the family of Roger II's mother and Liguria help explain this phenomenon, for Adelaide was an Aleramico, a member of a great feudal family in the hinterland behind Savona, and not surprisingly the earliest settlers include such individuals as Obbertus of Savona or Gualterius de Garrexio, whose name refers to a small town near Savona.[12] Some small towns in those areas still preserve local dialects apparently of northwest Italian origin; Aidone, Nicosia, and Novara di Sicilia seem to be cases in point.[13] But the stream of immigrants from Piedmont was renewed in the fourteenth century, when the area round Corleone was resettled; this stream, if not continuous, never dried up completely, nor did it consist entirely of men of commerce. Under Frederick II Ghibelline refugees from Piacenza, Brescia, and elsewhere were reported, and even if the tales about them are unreliable, the

---

[11] Abulafia, "Merchants of Messina," p. 206.

[12] L. Villari, "Note sui comuni lombardi di Sicilia," *Archivio storico messinese* 58/9 (1957–1959): 155–62; C. A. Garufi, "Gli Aleramici e i Normanni in Sicilia e nelle Puglie," *Centenario della nascita di Michele Amari*, 2 vols. (Palermo, 1910), 1:47–83.

[13] Abulafia, "Crown and the Economy," pp. 11–13; G. Tropea, "Effetti di simbiosi linguistica nelle parlate gallo-italiche di Aidone, Nicosia e Novara di Sicilia," *Bollettino dell'Atlante linguistico italiano* 13/14 (1966): 3–5.

memory of such immigration may reveal an awareness of the transformations taking place in the Sicilian countryside around this time.[14]

The immigrants came to a lightly populated island; and, though many settled in towns, the Sicilian rulers eagerly encouraged the cultivation of unused or abandoned lands. Unfortunately, one effect of the presence of these "Lombardi" was the destruction of neighboring peasant communities. In the 1160s the Lombardi, under their leader Roger Sclavus, launched a series of pogroms among the Muslims, forcing them to flee westward to safer areas, where the population was still predominantly Arab. At times there was also new Muslim settlement in Sicily, particularly during the famines that struck North Africa in the middle of the twelfth century; but the Norman kings of Sicily, as rulers also of Mahdia and Tripoli on the African coast, encouraged these newcomers to return to their place of origin. The intention was to foster the economic recovery of Norman Africa, but there may also have been an awareness that further Muslim immigration would be violently opposed by the Greeks of Palermo and by the Latins and Greeks of eastern Sicily.[15] In any case, some of the African settlers in Sicily were Christians who had good reason to escape the persecutions of the Almohads.[16] By 1200 the Muslims were already concentrated mainly in the west of the island and on the high ground to the south and east of Palermo. As their num-

[14] Abulafia, "Crown and the economy," p. 12; H. Bresc, "La formazione del popolo siciliano," in *Tre Millenni di storia linguistica della Sicilia: Atti del Convegno della Società Italiana di Glottologia, Palermo, 1983* (Pisa, n.d.), pp. 243–66.

[15] David Abulafia, "The Norman Kingdom of Africa and the Norman Expeditions to Majorca and the Muslim Mediterranean," in *Anglo-Norman Studies 7: Proceedings of the Battle Conference, 1984*, ed. R. Allen Brown (Woodbridge, 1985), pp. 36–37, repr. in David Abulafia, *Italy, Sicily and the Mediterranean, 1100–1400* (London, 1987), chap. 12.

[16] Roger II appears to have encouraged Christian settlement in North Africa also. See Abulafia, "Norman Kingdom of Africa," p. 38. There is a late reflection of this in Joachim of Fiore's *Expositio in Apocalypsim*, pars iv, distinctio iv, in *Crusade and Mission: European Approaches toward the Muslims*, ed. Benjamin Z. Kedar (Princeton, 1984), p. 221.

bers declined so did the agricultural skills that they had brought with them from Africa. On the Monreale estates around 1200 specialized cultivation and crafts gave way to a more monotonous concentration on production of wheat. No doubt the interests of landlords in part accounted for this; but it is likely that skills were evaporating as the Muslim population declined in numbers.[17]

Yet the transformation of Sicily into a Christian island was also, paradoxically, the work of those whose culture was under threat. The Muslims either left the island for Africa or, later, Lucera; or they were slaughtered; or they converted—not necessarily *were* converted, but occasionally converted of their own accord. On the Monreale estates in western Sicily, around 1180, a new Christian generation of peasants emerges, with sons with names such as Philippos succeeding fathers with what are obviously Muslim names—Aḥmad, even Muḥammad.[18] Monreale is one area, however, where pressure to convert was probably strong; these lands also became a focus of opposition by Muslim rebels. Among the Muslim elite of Palermo a similar transition also occurs: ʿAbd ar-Rahmān, "Slave of the Merciful," a prominent civil servant, possibly becomes Christodoulos. At any rate, the Spanish Muslim visitor Ibn Jubayr insists that William II made extensive use of Muslims at court "who all, or nearly all, concealing their faith, yet hold firm to the Muslim divine law"—a point which confirms the refusal of the king to tolerate outward expressions of Islam at what was a decidedly Christian court.[19] In the country, though probably

[17] On this process, see the valuable article of H. Bercher, A. Courteaux, and J. Mouton, "Une abbaye latine dans la société musulmane: Monreale au XIIᵉ siècle," *Annales: Économies, Sociétés, Civilisations* 34 (1979): 525–47.

[18] These remarks are based mainly on a paper by Jeremy Johns at the symposium of the Society for the Promotion of Byzantine Studies, Oxford, 1984. See the tables and map in Bresc, "Formazione," indicating Muslim arrivals from as far as Persia and India in the Norman period—movement across vast spaces on a scale entirely typical of the medieval Muslim world.

[19] H. Bresc, "Mudejars des pays de la couronne d'Aragon et Sarrasins de la Sicile normande: le problème de l'acculturation," in *X Congreso de Historia de la Corona de Aragon, Zaragoza, 1979* (Saragossa, n.d.), p. 55; Kedar, *Crusade and Mission*, pp. 50–52; *Travels of Ibn Jubayr*, p. 340.

not at court, conversion to Greek orthodoxy seems more common than conversion to Roman Catholicism, and this may reflect the long-standing presence of Greek monks and priests in the Sicilian countryside. The Greek Church had long been more visible to the Sicilian peasantry, Christian or Muslim, than the Norman-dominated Latin Church. But it is important not to read too much into the evidence of personal names, either. As late as the mid-thirteenth century, Latin landlords sometimes gave their children Arabic or Greek names if they lived among Greek or Arabic speakers.[20] And, though the Norman rulers clearly encouraged conversion to Christianity, they offered few inducements to the peasants such as a lessening of their obligations; whether Muslims or Christians, their legal status remained much the same. In fact, Ibn Jubayr attributed unhealthy motives to the converts from Islam. He recounts how, "should a man show anger to his son or his wife, or a woman to her daughter, the one who is the object of displeasure may perversely throw himself into a church, and there be baptised and turn Christian. Then there will be for the father no way of approaching his son, or the mother her daughter." Some fathers escaped this threat by offering their pubescent daughters to visiting Muslims, who could take them abroad away from the temptation of apostasy.[21] The reference to conversions by Muslim women is particularly interesting; but the impetus to conversion came not only from the individual. It was said that if Ibn Ḥammūd, leader of the Muslims of Sicily, were to change faith, so would the entire Muslim community on the island.

Pressure to convert clearly came in waves. A revealing remark by Archbishop Romuald of Salerno indicates that Roger II became more enthusiastic about converting Jews and Muslims at the end of his life; secular matters occupied him less, and he made generous gifts to the new Christians.[22] Since, as has been

---

[20] Bresc, "Formazione," p. 249.

[21] *Travels of Ibn Jubayr*, pp. 359–60.

[22] Romuald of Salerno, *Rerum italicarum scriptores* ser. 2, 7:1 in *Chronicon*, ed. C. A. Garufi, p. 236: "Circa finem autem vite sue secularibus negociis ali-

END OF MUSLIM SICILY 111

seen, the peasantry did not apparently gain in economic status by conversion, and since Romuald's view is that of a courtier close to the king, it is quite likely that the primary emphasis lay on the conversion of Muslim and Jewish notables. Hence, indeed, his ire at the apostate Admiral Philip of Mahdia, who was executed at the end of Roger's reign. Roger had already made plain, in the *Assises* of Ariano, his detestation of those who abandoned the Catholic faith.[23]

At the royal court, then, the high Muslim officials were expected to pay more than mere lip service to Christianity, as early as Roger II's time. The Granadan pilgrim Ibn Jubayr described how the Muslim courtiers of William II were shielded by the hand of Allāh, so they could invisibly prostrate themselves in prayer at the prescribed times, even when the king was looking on:

> Another singular circumstance concerning these pages is that when in the presence of their Lord and the hour for prayer is at hand they will leave the chamber one by one that they might make their prayers. They sometimes do so in a place where the eye of the king might follow them, but Almighty and Glorious God conceals them. Thus they continue to labour in their purpose, covertly advising the Muslims in their unending struggle for the faith.[24]

Maybe King William had few illusions about what was going on; yet the assumption that Muslim pages would accept Christianity suggests a formalized hostility to Islam at court, and only the very greatest, notably Ibn Ḥammūd, managed to resist pressure to convert. It is impossible to say how long this community of Muslim *marranos* lasted; there survives nothing from

quantulum postpositis et ommissis, Judeos et Saracenos ad fidem Christi convertere modis laborabat, et conversis dona plurima et necessaria conferebat."

[23] Abulafia, "Norman Kingdom of Africa," p. 42, n. 84. On him and other courtiers of Muslim origin, see Dietlind Schack, *"Die Araber im Reich Rogers II."* (Inaugural-Dissertation, phil.-Fak., Free University of Berlin, 1969), pp. 142–50. Schack notes the words of the *assises*: "Apostantes a fide catholica penitus execramus, ultionibus insequimur, bonis omnibus spoliamus" (p. 149).

[24] *Travels Ibn Jubayr*, p. 343.

late medieval Sicily to compare with the later Qur'āns of the Valencian Moriscos. Such Muslims as appear in Sicily in the documentation of the fourteenth and fifteenth centuries were rare visitors from abroad, very few of whom managed to settle, or slaves. Evidence from personal names in modern Sicily suggests many Christianized descendants of Jews and Muslims still live on the island, but it is impossible to say whether a family such as Buscetta has Jewish, Muslim, or Christian Mozarabic antecedents.

Sicilian Islam was already under severe criticism from the Muslims of the twelfth-century Maghrib. The Sicilian Muslims were said to be lax in observance; but even to live under Christian rule was undesirable.[25] North African sages could hardly view with equanimity the presence of Muslims in the armies and navies of the Norman kings during the attack on Alexandria in 1174, or, later, with Frederick II during his crusade. The elite left; townspeople found their mosques converted into cathedrals and monasteries, notably in Palermo; in the countryside the structure of leadership disintegrated. This possibly helps explain the switch in cultivation away from specialized crops to the wheat that the Latin landlords, with an eye on the international or at least Sicilian urban food market, would tend to prefer. The disappearance of the Muslim aristocracy had particularly dire effects on the Muslims throughout Sicily. The Muslim traveler Ibn Jubayr recorded the demoralization of leading Sicilian coreligionists in his diary of 1184/85. He met the "leader and Lord of the Muslim community in this island," the *Qā'id* Abu'l-Qāsim ibn Ḥammūd, who was visiting Trapani and who was still feeling the effects of confiscation of part of his wealth and of gossip about his links with the Almohads. He had again been appointed to a post in the government, but was evidently aware that the king's favor was entirely conditioned on his good conduct; it was hardly an example of royal indifference to the religious tastes of the king's courtiers. In-

---

[25] For disapproval of trade with Christian-ruled Sicily in the verdicts of Islamic judges in North Africa, see H. R. Idris, *La Berbérie orientale sous les Zirides, X'–XII' siècles*, 2 vols. (Paris–Algiers, 1962), 2:666, where a *fatwa* of Al-Mazari is cited stating that Muslims may not go to lands conquered by the Infidel, however urgent their needs (e.g., to buy grain in times of famine).

deed he said to Ibn Jubayr, "I have wished to be sold [as a slave], I and my family, that perhaps the sale would free us from the state we are in and lead us to our dwelling in Muslim lands."[26] Hyperbole, perhaps, for Ibn Jubayr recalled seeing the magnificent palaces of Ibn Ḥammūd's relatives in Palermo, and later Frederick II was to grant the Genoese the palace of "Gaetus Bulcasim" in Trapani; but the Muslims of Sicily were fully aware that their future held no guarantees of prosperity.[27] And at Messina the civil servant ʿAbd al-Māssīḥ told Ibn Jubayr: "You can boldly display your faith in Islam. . . . But we must conceal our faith and, fearful of our lives, must adhere to the worship of God and the discharge of our religious duties in secret."[28]

A decade later the Muslims of western Sicily rose in open rebellion; their defiant leader Ibn ʿAbbād had even minted his own coins not long before 1220, probably at his stronghold of Entella. The last rebels were not flushed out until the 1240s.[29] It has been suggested that Islam survived in secret in the Sicilian countryside, just as it clearly did briefly at court, but the many Muslims who appear on the island from the 1280s on seem to be imported slaves, of whom more shortly.[30] Interestingly, the years around 1200 saw the appearance in Sicily of Islamic styles of pottery, made perhaps with royal encouragement. The so-called Gela ware, colored in yellow, green, and brown, was developed from twelfth-century Muslim Sicilian models, using a form of glazing as yet hardly known in Latin Europe. The origin of the potters, however, is uncertain.[31]

[26] *Travels of Ibn Jubayr*, pp. 358–59.

[27] The grant of the "domum que fuit Gaeti Bulcasimi" dates to 1200, a time when Frederick himself had no say in the government of Sicily (Abulafia, *Two Italies*, p. 250, n. 66).

[28] *Travels of Ibn Jubayr*, p. 342.

[29] On the coins, see F. D'Angelo, "La monetazione di Muhammad ibn 'Abbad emiro ribelle a Federico II di Sicilia," *Studi Magrebini* 7 (1975): 149–53. For other interesting perspectives, see Jeremy Johns, "Monte Guastanella: un insediamento musulmano nell'Agrigentino," *Sicilia Archeologica*, 16:33–51.

[30] See Bresc, "Mudejars," pp. 56–57; and for later slaves, see Verlinden's works mentioned below.

[31] David Abulafia, "The Pisan *bacini* and the Medieval Mediterranean Economy: A Historian's Viewpoint," *Papers in Italian Archaeology 4: The Cambridge*

What also survived was the Arabic language, but only in the most remote parts of the kingdom, particularly in the offshore territories of Malta and Pantelleria, where an unusual degree of cultural autonomy persisted.[32] Pantelleria acquired a special status in the thirteenth century as a Hohenstaufen-Hafsid condominium; here at least a Muslim population was able to survive relatively undisturbed. In essence, the island's Muslims possessed a special statute of autonomy, subject to Sicilian overlordship and the payment of half the revenues to the Hafsids.[33] The case of the decline of Islam on Malta is not typical of the rest of the *Regno*, but it is reasonably well documented for the reign of Frederick II.[34] Before then, the Maltese islands had experienced a Norman invasion in 1090 and a more definitive conquest in 1127, though at the end of the twelfth and start of the thirteenth centuries their rulers were Genoese counts whose loyalty to the Sicilian kings was spasmodic.[35] In

---

Conference, pt. 4, *Classical and Medieval Archæology*, British Archæological Reports, International Series 246, eds. C. Malone and S. Stoddart (Oxford, 1985), p. 293, repr. in David Abulafia, *Italy, Sicily and the Mediterranean, 1100–1400* (London, 1987), chap. 13.

[32] See A. T. Luttrell, "Approaches to Medieval Malta," in *Medieval Malta: Studies on Malta before the Knights*, ed. A. T. Luttrell (London, 1975), and other articles in the same volume. The only general history of Malta in the Middle Ages is A. Vella, *Storija ta'Malta* (Valletta, 1974), vol. 1, which is primarily concerned with political history and is written in Maltese.

[33] R. Brunschvig *La Berbérie orientale sous les Hafsides des origines à la fin du XVᵉ siècle*, 2 vols. (Paris, 1940–1947), 1:26; R. Brunschvig, "Note sur un traité conclu entre Tunis et l'empereur Frédéric II," *Revue tunisienne* (1932): 153–60, dates the agreement concerning Pantelleria to 1221; see also H. Bresc, "Pantelleria entre l'Islam et la Chrétienté," *Cahiers de Tunisie* 19 (1971): 105–27. In the late thirteenth century Leon de Lucera was governor of the island. Was he a Christian as Bresc (*Monde méditerranéen*, 2:622–23) assumes? Muslims remained responsible for the exercise of justice on the island at this time, and were still to be found there in the fifteenth century. By 1444 there were forty-three Jews on the island, active in cotton production, a presence which Bresc sees as a late example of a process visible in Sicily proper in the thirteenth century—the use of skilled Jewish agriculturalists and artisans to replace lost Arab manpower.

[34] For what follows, see Luttrell, "Approaches," pp. 34–40.

[35] David Abulafia, "Henry, Count of Malta and His Mediterranean Activities, 1203–1230," in Luttrell, *Medieval Malta*, pp. 104–25.

III

1175 Bishop Burchard of Strassburg said of Malta that it was
"a Sarracenis inhabitata, et est sub dominio regis Sicilie."[36]
Contrary to the wishful thinking of the island's modern inhabitants, it is hard to prove continuity in Christian observance on
Malta through the Middle Ages. For Luttrell, "Malta was never
really Norman;" it was after the Genoese counts were relieved
of the island around 1222 that the archipelago became integrated into the rest of the *Regno*.[37] The Muslim majority on
Malta was not immune from the treatment that had been meted
out to the Muslims of Sicily proper. Frederick II's Admiral of
the Fleet, Henry, Count of Malta, of Genoese origin, participated alongside his master in the siege of Celano, in the
Abruzzi. When Celano fell and was razed, its refugee population (all Christian) was gathered together by Henricus de
Morra, chief justiciar of the Sicilian kingdom. The *Celanenses*
arrived in Sicily, where the emperor decided they should be
sent on to settle Malta.[38] Ibn Khaldūn believed that Frederick
included the Maltese Muslims among the Saracens sent to settle
Lucera in Apulia, a statement which would date the expulsion
from Malta to approximately the same period as the settlement
by the *Celanenses*.[39] Evidence that a Muslim of Maltese descent
once lived at Lucera may be provided by a reference in 1301 to
a certain *Dallesium Maltesium* in the now-lost archives of the
Angevin kings of Naples.[40] The remote island was also used as
a prison for exiles, a medieval equivalent of the modern prison
on Asinara. It has even been suggested that the use of the term
malta to mean a prison, in the works of Dante and his contemporaries, originated during this period.[41] For Frederick Malta

[36] Luttrell, "Approaches," p. 32, citing *MGH*. SS. 21, 236.

[37] Ibid., pp. 32, 34.

[38] *Rerum italicarum scriptores*, in *Ryccardi de sancto Germano notarii Chronica*,
ed. C. A. Garufi, ser. 2, 7:2 (Bologna, 1938), pp. 112–13, but only in one
version of the text.

[39] M. Amari, *Biblioteca arabo-sicula, versione italiana*, 2 vols. (Turin–Rome,
1880–1881), 2:212–13. Ibn Khaldun says Frederick himself went to Malta to
expel the Muslims; this is a misconception.

[40] Luttrell, "Approaches," p. 37, n. 214.

[41] Ibid., p. 36, n. 206.

was a favorite source of falcons, while northern Italian merchants had an interest in its cotton.[42]

Around 1241 Frederick II received a report on conditions on Malta, at a time when he was working hard to maximize his revenues to help pay for his Italian wars. He learned that Malta had its own distinctive customs, but also that there were still plenty of Muslims on both Malta and Gozo. The existence of a majority of Christians may of course conceal a high rate of conversion from Islam to Christianity, though at least some of the Christians were likely *Celanenses*. The following statistics of the number of families on the two islands were offered to Frederick:

> Christians: 1250 (Malta, 1047 [emended by Luttrell from 47];
> Gozo, 203)
> Muslims: 836 (Malta, 681; Gozo, 155)
> Jews: 33 (Malta, 25; Gozo, 8).[43]

Apparently separate were eighty-four North African *servi*, possibly from Jerba, but also apparently Muslims. Yet the majority of Maltese Muslims were not newcomers who arrived after the expulsion of the old population to Lucera, but were *villani curie sarraceni* who paid the Crown one-quarter of what they produced, in kind, and who were apparently established peasant families whose obligations were defined by long usage.[44] Thus it is likely that here at least the deportations to Lu-

---

[42] Abulafia, "Henry, Count of Malta," p. 106; idem, *Frederick II: A Medieval Emperor* (London, 1988), pp. 267, 337.

[43] E. Winkelmann, *Acta imperii inedita sæculi XIII*, 2 vols. (Innsbruck, 1880–1885), 1:713–15; for the emendation by Luttrell of xlvii into mxlvii, see his "Approaches," pp. 38–40.

[44] Conversion from Islam might not have been enough to shake off the status of a *servus curie sarracenus*, a title that could as much be determined by descent as by religion. The exact process of change is invisible. Henri Bresc, "The *Secrezia* and the Royal Patrimony in Malta, 1240–1450," in Luttrell, *Medieval Malta*, p. 131, notes that the *servi* and *ancille* documented around 1241 were still seen in 1271 and were only granted complete liberty around 1372; he sees the incorporation of Malta into the royal demesne as part of a wider process of the creation of large *latifundia* which concentrated on the production of wheat. Cf. Bercher et al., "Une abbaye latine," pp. 536–37. But in fact he also shows

cera did not signal the end of Islam; nor, certainly, did they signal the end of a distinctively arabicized culture, which enveloped also the Christians of the islands, whether they were converted Muslims or new settlers, and which was characterized by the survival of Arabic speech.[45] In the late fifteenth century the Jews of Malta appear to have used a form of Arabic that was more or less identical to that of the island's Christians. It was, of course, written in Hebrew characters, just as the Christians adopted at some stage the Latin alphabet when writing Maltese Arabic.[46]

The use of Arabic did, however, continue in Sicily—not generally, but as the *koiné* of the Jews. There are noticeable differences between the economic and cultural standing of the Jews of Sicily and those of Spain. Among the Sicilian Jews, Arabic remained an everyday language until their expulsion at the end

---

that cotton was a particularly important local product in the late fourteenth and fifteenth centuries, and it is probable that cotton cultivation continued uninterrupted from Norman to Aragonese times. See Bresc, *"Secrezia,"* pp. 131–32. The year 1271 or a little earlier may also mark the virtual extinction of Islam in Malta, since a document of Charles I of Anjou mentions the possessions of the "quondam Sarracenorum de ipsis insulis ejectorum" (Bresc, *Monde méditerranéen*, 2:625). Malta had been a bone of contention in the struggle between Hohenstaufen and Angevins, with Genoese and Pisan interests also at work on the island. In 1267 Conradin of Hohenstaufen offered Malta to the Pisans in return for naval aid, but Manfred had already negotiated in 1257 with the heirs of Henry, count of Malta, for a return of much of Malta to the Genoese (see Luttrell, "Approaches," p. 40). Charles' joint crusade to Tunis with Louis IX in 1270 also highlighted the importance of the island. It may thus have seemed that the Maltese archipelago was strategically too valuable, and the inhabitants too untrustworthy, to permit the continued existence of a Muslim enclave there.

[45] The earliest document in Maltese is the fifteenth-century *cantilena* or lament of Pietro Caxaro. See Luttrell, "Approaches," pp. 66–67, for the text and translation. See also G. Wettinger and M. Fsadni, *Peter Caxaro's Cantilena: A Poem in Medieval Maltese* (Malta, 1968); Bresc, *Monde méditerranéen*, 2:626.

[46] G. Wettinger, *The Jews of Malta in the Late Middle Ages* (Valletta, 1984) is based on both Latin and Judeo-Arabic documents of late fifteenth-century Malta, and analyzes the material from both a historical and a linguistic perspective. The author's transcriptions into the Latin alphabet and his translations into Maltese are an object lesson to those who preserve a touching belief in the Punic rather than Arabic origins of the island's language.

of the fifteenth century, though in the late fifteenth century it was used more in the compilation of documents (in Hebrew characters) than in daily speech.[47] They gave their children Arabic as well as Hebrew names; yet they do not seem to have been socially or economically isolated from their Christian neighbors, at least in the smaller towns, until the mid-fourteenth century. Rabbi Abraham Abulafia, a Spanish Jew who traveled in Sicily, Greece, and the Holy Land in the late thirteenth century, mentioned the use of Arabic and Italian among the Jews, implying that Italian was the language of intercourse with Christians, while Arabic was the language of the Jewish community. There is an obvious comparison to be made with the later use of Castilian (*Ladino*) among the Jews of the Ottoman world as an archaic language confined to the Jews themselves:

Note that the Jews who live among the Ishmaelites speak Arabic like them; those who live among the Greeks speak Greek; those who inhabit Italy speak Italian, the Germans [*Ashkenazim*] speak German, the inhabitants of Turkish lands speak Turkish, and so on. But the great wonder is what happens among the Jews in all Sicily, who not only speak the local language or Greek, as do those who dwell there with them, but have preserved the Arabic tongue which they had learned in former times, when the Ishmaelites were dwelling there.[48]

[47] Bresc, *Monde méditerranéen*, 2:628; H. Bresc and S. D. Goitein, "Un inventaire dotal de juifs siciliens (1479)," *Mélanges d'histoire et d'archéologie de l'École française de Rome* 82 (1970): 903–17.

[48] Abraham b. Samuel Abulafia, *Ozar 'Eden ganuz*, extract edited by A. Neubauer in *Revue des études juives* 9 (1884): 149, from a MS in Oxford; also cited in C. Roth, *The History of the Jews of Italy* (Philadelphia, 1946), p. 82, without further identification. For the extraordinary career of Abraham Abulafia of Saragossa, see in particular the four-volume set of studies by Moshe Idel, of which the first part is *The Mystical Experience in Abraham Abulafia* (Albany, 1988). Abulafia visited southern Italy and Sicily, after an attempt in 1280 to convince the pope of his undoubtedly remarkable abilities, and is last heard of in 1291 on the island of Comino, off Malta. He appears to have been influenced by the view (reported in Nahmanides' disputation before King James I of Aragon) that the true Messiah would go to Rome and show himself to the pope.

In Erice, in the extreme west of Sicily, the Jews lived mixed together with Christians around 1300; the Jewish quarter [*rabato*] of the town evolved later, perhaps under the influence of a new wave of ill-feeling (of Spanish importation) toward the Jews.[49] A similar picture originally obtained in Mdina-Notabile, capital of Malta, and in Rabat, capital of Gozo, though in the latter case the Jews lived below the citadel and in the former they had a synagogue at the highest point of the citadel. In time they found themselves concentrated in particular areas of the two towns.[50] As elsewhere in the medieval Jewish world, the Jews of Sicily harnessed a borrowed language for their own use; they judaized it, and this, no less than their adherence to the dietary laws of *kashrut* and other observances, helped them retain their cohesion. Yet the range of occupations among the Jews of Erice seems comparable to that found among Christians. There are, certainly, several Jewish physicians, as in other parts of Sicily; the gold and silversmith's art, too, may have been a special Jewish interest, though in Palermo the silver bells of the Torah scrolls were on occasion actually made for the Jews by Christians.[51] They functioned as carpenters; they owned vineyards; they made improvement loans—but in the same way as their Christian neighbors.

The Jews of Sicily formed part of North African Jewry; some were in fact thirteenth-century settlers from Tunisia or nearby, invited by Frederick II to reintroduce date and indigo cultiva-

[49] David Abulafia, "The Jews of Erice (Monte San Giuliano) in Sicily, 1297–1304," *Zion* 51 (1986): 295–317 [in Hebrew; summary in English] and in the *Archivio storico per la Sicilia orientale* 1986 [in Italian]. See also various articles by E. Ashtor on the Sicilian Jews in his *The Jews and the Mediterranean Economy, 10th to 15th Centuries* (London, 1983).

[50] Wettinger, *Jews of Malta*. There has been much speculation about the possible influence of late medieval hostility to the Jews in Malta on Christopher Marlowe's play *The Jew of Malta*, but to little effect.

[51] G. Bresc-Bautier, *Artistes, patriciens et confrères: production et consommation de l'oeuvre d'art à Palerme et en Sicile occidentale (1348–1460)* (Rome, 1979), pp. 115–16. The example of the *rimonim* (bells) is very late—the end of the fifteenth century. Interestingly, the *rimonim* now preserved in the Cathedral Treasury in Palma de Mallorca are probably of Sicilian origin, brought to Majorca after the expulsion and expropriation of the Sicilian Jews.

tion. His invitation to the Jews of "Garbum" is usually understood to signify the Jews of the fertile island of Jerba, but more
probably it means the Jews of the Maghreb as a whole, for the
term "Garbum" was often used to describe the entire area between the Algarve or Andalusia and Cyrenaica: "Debent in eis
seminare alchanam et indicum et alia diversa semina que cres-
cunt in Garbo nec sunt in partibus Sicilie adhuc visa crescere."[52]
     The fact that Frederick was trying to restore the cultivation
of crops once produced on the island is of some significance.
The existence in late medieval Sicily of sugar plantations and of
other "exotic" products does not prove that Islamic agricultural
technology survived in Sicily, as it certainly did in Valencia;
again and again it was necessary to restore what had been lost,
in both know-how and labor reserves, after the destruction of
Sicilian Islam.[53] Evidence from the Monreale estates suggests a
sharp decline in the specialized agricultural skills practiced before 1200 by the Muslim peasantry of Sicily.[54] Frederick's recourse to North African Jews was a clever way to import Arab
technology without reimporting Muslim personnel; it was not
so much a policy favorable to the Jews as one unfavorable to
the Arabs.[55] (Equally, Frederick's statement in the *Constitutions
of Melfi* that the Jews and Saracens were "too greatly persecuted
at present" does not mean he was opposed to all persecution;
merely that, in accordance with the prescriptions of canon law,

[52] *Constitutiones regum utriusque Siciliæ mandante Friderico II Imperatore per
Petrum de Vinea Capuanum Prætorio Præfectum et Cancellarium . . . et Fragmen-
tum quod superest Regesti eiusdem Imperatoris Ann. 1239 & 1240*, ed. Cajetanus
Carcani (Naples, 1786), pp. 290–91 [this is the only effective edition of the
register]; cf. A. Watson, *Agricultural Innovation in the Early Islamic World*
(Cambridge, 1983) for the transplantation of eastern crops to Sicily and Spain;
and Bercher et al., "Une abbaye latine," for the break in continuity in western
Sicily.

[53] See the studies of the production of sugar and other Levantine commodities in late medieval Sicily by C. Trasselli, such as his *Storia dello zucchero siciliano*
(Caltanissetta, 1983), his *Siciliani fra quattrocento e cinquecento* (Messina,
1981), and more generally his *Mediterraneo e Sicilia all'inizio dell'epoca moderna
(Ricerche quattrocentesche)* (Cosenza, 1977).

[54] Bercher et al., "Une abbaye latine," pp. 525–47.

[55] Abulafia, *Frederick II*, pp. 335–36.

Frederick wished to curtail unjust and violent persecution.[56])
In any case, the Maghribi Jews had difficulties with the native
Jews of Palermo and had to be granted reserved use of a dilap-
idated synagogue.[57] Even so, all the Sicilian Jews looked to
North Africa for religious leadership and for a model liturgy.
Those few Jews who appeared at Frederick II's court were not
in fact Sicilians: Moses ben Solomon of Salerno was at least a
southern Italian, but the main figure, the translator Jacob
Anatoli, had reached the royal court via Provence, while his
relatives, the Ibn Tibbons, were Provençal Jews of Spanish descent.[58]

The same non-Sicilian origin had applied to a high proportion of the Greeks and Muslims at the court of Roger II a hundred years earlier. There were Calabrian Greeks such as the
Maleinoi, and probably some Sicilian Muslims and Greeks too,
but the non-Sicilian element carried the most weight, if not in
numbers, at least in influence. The Norman and Hohenstaufen
courts were accessible to talented administrators and men of
learning (often these were the same) from around the known
world, men in search of gold and honors. George of Antioch
had been born in Syria but became minister to North African
rulers before reaching the court of Roger II, and thus clearly
spoke Arabic as well as Greek; Philip of Mahdia, born a Muslim
in North Africa, had converted to Christianity in the hope of
achieving high office under Roger, but (as has been seen) was
executed by Roger in 1154 for backsliding. Countless Westerners were present too, of course, such as Thomas Brown who
later served under Henry II of England, Peter of Blois, and
Adelard of Bath. North African poets, disappointed at the re-
sponse to their verses in Mahdia and Tunis, offered flattery in
Arabic to Roger II in the hope of acquiring a wealthy and ap-
preciative patron; it is unlikely that Roger understood anything

[56] *Liber Augustalis* [various eds., 1475, 1568, 1786, etc.], I, tit. 28 (32);
Abulafia, *Frederick II*, p. 209.

[57] Carcani, *Registrum*, p. 290; Abulafia, *Frederick II*, p. 335.

[58] Ibid., pp. 255–57; C. Sirat, *A History of Jewish Philosophy in the Middle Ages*
(Cambridge, 1985), pp. 212–32.

they were saying.[59] But the real stars seem in this period to be the Muslim Idrīsī and the Greek Doxapatrios—both arriving from outside the kingdom, but both patronized partly at least for political reasons.

Idrīsī, a refugee prince from Morocco, was given the task of describing the produce and natural resources of each region of the world, and of making a great silver map of the world. The map was destroyed during the sacking of the royal palace by rioters in 1161; but his *Book of King Roger* still survives, a mixture of travelers' tales, of Arabic geography books, and of personal observation.[60] Its wealth of detail and reliability decrease somewhat the further north the coverage extends. Idrīsī had some awareness of the physical geography of northern Europe, and no doubt he did consult Western Europeans based at or visiting the royal court. But he seems not to make use of Latin or Greek sources; he is certainly happier with antiquated Arabic accounts of Europe than with up-to-date eyewitness testimony. This was not unusual in any twelfth-century writer; but it hardly suggests the syncretism lyrically attributed to the Sicilian court—an ability to cross cultural boundaries, to create an eclectic mix of the best or boldest ideas to be found in Greek, Latin, Arabic, and Hebrew sources. Nor, for that matter, did Idrīsī's book have any known influence on later writers at this or other European courts. Its future readership lay solely in the Arab world. For Muslim and Christian to exist side by side at court was not to observe and instruct one another.[61]

---

[59] For their works, see Amari, *Biblioteca arabo-sicula*. Modern studies of cultural life among the Muslims of Sicily include U. Rizzitano, *Storia e cultura nella Sicilia saracena* (Palermo, 1975); and M. Amari, *Storia dei Musulmani di Sicilia*, 2d rev. ed., 3 vols. (Catania, 1930–1939).

[60] See *L'Italia descritta nel "Libro del Re Ruggero" compilato da Edrisi*, eds. and trans. M. Amari and C. Schiaparelli (Rome, 1883), for the sections dealing with Italy and Sicily. See also *India and the Neighbouring territories in the Kitab Nuzhat al-Mushtaq fi'khtiraq al-'afaq*, trans. S. Maqbul Ahmad (Leiden, 1960); *Description de l'Afrique et de l'Espagne*, eds. and trans. R. Dozy and M. J. de Goeje (Leiden, 1886); and other studies of Idrīsī's comments on regions as remote as Finland. A new edition is in progress: *Opus geographicum, sive Liber ad eorum delectationem qui terras peragrare studeant*, eds. E. Cerulli et al. (Naples–Rome, 1971–).

[61] This agrees in some measure with N. Daniel, *The Arabs and Medieval Eu-*

So too among the Greeks: Neilos Doxapatrios's career had begun at the imperial court in Constantinople, though he may have been of Sicilian ancestry. His *History of the Five Patriarchates* laid heavy stress on the claims of jurisdiction of the patriarchs of Constantinople in Sicily and southern Italy. It was not, at first sight, the message Roger II might have expected, but in fact the work provided him with a useful stick with which to beat the pope.[62] In 1142/43 Roger was involved in one of the periodic rows with the papacy over his claim to exercise the legatine authority he had inherited from his father, and it is precisely at this time that we see the appearance of Doxapatrios's work, the renewal of diplomatic contact with Byzantium, and the portrayal of Roger II in the Martorana mosaic as a king crowned by Christ, receiving his power directly from heaven without papal mediation. Thus Doxapatrios's book has to be placed in the context of his uneasy relationship with a papacy insistent on its overlordship over the kingdom of Sicily; and of his occasional aspirations for a negotiated peace with Constantinople, in which even a renewed orthodox Sicilian church might be dangled as bait. Equally, the presence of distinguished Greek poets and rhetoricians, arriving at the Norman court from Constantinople or the Peloponnese, flattered Sicilian kings who wished to present their monarchy as comparable to that of Byzantium: indeed Roger was accused of wishing to secure from the one true Roman emperor recognition of the title of *basileus*, though more probably he was merely trying to secure acceptance of the plenitude of his authority as a territorial king.[63] But the real significance should

---

rope (London–Beirut, 1975), pp. 146–47, though he greatly overstates his case.

[62] The work on the five patriarchates appears in Migne, *Patrologia Græca*, 132: cols. 1083–1114. For Doxapatrios, see F. Giunta, *Bizantini e bizantinismo nella Sicilia normanna*, 2d ed. (Palermo, 1974), pp. 87–88.

[63] Joannes Cinnamus, *Epitome rerum ab Ioanne et Alexio Comnenis gestarum*, ed. A. Meinecke (Bonn, 1836); *The Deeds of John and Manuel Comnenus, by John Kinnamos*, trans. C. M. Brand (New York, 1976), p. 75, reports Roger's wish to gain recognition of his "equal plane of greatness" to the *basileus*, implying that Roger was placing impossible demands in the way of peace. But cf. the position implicit in W. Ullmann, "Rulership and the Law in the Middle Ages:

not be exaggerated; no firmly based local school of Greek literature was created. Just as again and again the mosaicists for the great churches had to be brought from Constantinople, so too the men of letters were lured thence by promises of pensions and patronage. It seems that even the great cycle at Monreale was the work of Byzantine mosaicists, and that the native Sicilian contribution consisted more of adaptation to Latin iconographical requirements than of real workmanship.

Finally, the much-acclaimed work of translation at the Sicilian court must be seen as a less glorious moment in Greco-Latin intellectual contact than is often supposed. Precisely because the court at Palermo was not a hive of Greek philosophers at home with Plato's texts and ideas, it proved necessary to render the Greek texts newly acquired from Constantinople into more familiar Latin. Plato's *Meno* and *Phaedo* and Ptolemy's *Almagest* were translated by or for William I's minister Henry Aristippus in the mid-twelfth century; the last of these was, in fact, to be retranslated under Frederick II. These works were being taken out of the Byzantine world into a cultural orbit in which classical Greek was not widely understood, despite the contemporary use of vernacular Greek in royal charters. Translation signifies, in this case, the removal of the text from its cultural context. The Sicilian court was not particularly interested in contemporary Byzantine scholarship; it wanted ancient texts for their philosophical content, not because they were important components in the syllabus of Constantinople.

In other words, the court as well as the country was being Latinized in the twelfth century. The eclecticism of Roger II's time—eclecticism in a slightly pejorative sense, given the lack of real contact between cultures—gave way to a heavy emphasis

The Case of Norman Sicily," *Acta Juridica* (1978), where Roger's place as practitioner of the theory of the king as "emperor in his own kingdom" is forcefully argued (a view explicitly propounded in the late thirteenth century commentaries on the laws of Roger II, William II and Frederick II). In other words, Roger aimed to secure recognition that neither the Greek ruler, nor the pope, nor the German king had any authority over one who was "*a Deo coronatus*"; and in that sense he would be the equal of the *basileus*, not in the whole world but within his kingdom.

on Latin culture, magnificently displayed in the rich neoclassical Latin of "Hugo Falcandus," the historian, at the end of the century.[64] There were, indeed, survivors of an earlier age. Admiral Eugenius, last of a family of Greek servants of state, continued to write elegant Greek poetry; but he too participated in the Latinization of court culture, by translating a Byzantine version of the Sibylline oracles into Latin.[65] The late twelfth century shows a significant expansion of Latin political influence at court: the Norman and southern Italian baronage gained a place in the government of the kingdom, placing further pressure on the Greek and Muslim remnants in the civil service. These Greeks and Muslims had been major patrons of Greek or Arabic culture, and as they disappeared the range of the court's cultural links contracted sharply. The same period sees the creation of close political and cultural bonds between the Sicilian and English courts, each harping on its Norman antecedents; this emphasis around 1180 was actually something new, and forms part of that process of Sicily's integration into the Latin world.[66]

This is not to deny the existence of a later revival in contact with the Muslim world under Frederick II; Frederick corresponded with leading Muslim scholars such as Ibn Sab'īn, and with Spanish Jewish philosophers as well. But he had no Muslim intellectuals permanently at court and few Greeks; the Saracens of Lucera were soldiers, not philosophers. Some of Frederick's closest advisers, such as the bureaucrat Uberto Fallamonaca, seem to have been of Muslim descent; but Frederick's main contact with Muslim culture was achieved either through correspondence, or through the mediation the Spanish-trained philosopher and astrologer Michael Scot, or

[64] *La Historia o Liber de Regno Sicilie e la Epistola ad Petrum Panormitane Ecclesie Thesaurarium*, ed. G. B. Siragusa (Rome, 1897).

[65] On Admiral Eugenius, see E. M. Jamison, *Admiral Eugenius of Sicily: His Life and Work* (London, 1957).

[66] E. M. Jamison, "The Sicilian-Norman Kingdom in the Mind of Anglo-Norman Contemporaries," *Proceedings of the British Academy*, 24 (1938); cf. R. H. C. Davis, *The Normans and Their Myth* (London, 1976).

through the translation work of Jews such as Jacob Anatoli.[67] Some of the cultural figures associated with him, such as the young prodigy Judah ha-Cohen and the mathematician Leonardo Fibonacci, met him only briefly and knew the emperor through correspondence rather than through close personal contact. Toledo was the great source of texts; and this side of the cultural life of Frederick's court was partly in a Spanish shadow.[68] It was their Spanish links and their understanding of Arabic as well as Western languages that brought the Ibn Tibbons and Judah ha-Cohen to Frederick's attention; but the Jews served increasingly as the channel of communication between the Sicilian court and the culture of Islam. No work symbolizes these links more than the Latin translation of Maimonides' *Guide for the Perplexed*, a great work of Jewish philosophy originally addressed (in Arabic) to philosophically minded Jews, but known too at Frederick's court through the efforts of Michael Scot and by the brilliant escapee from that court, Thomas Aquinas.[69] In any case the days of a Palermo-based court were long since over; Frederick's court was itinerant, and Naples rather than Palermo was the intellectual center of his Sicilian realm. Frederick's was really a hand-luggage court, whose main equipment consisted of manuscripts of works on zoology that the emperor carried on his Lombard campaigns, such as the Arabic treatise of the falconer Moamyn, which Frederick was studying during the siege of Faenza in 1240/41 and which Master Theodore of Antioch, Scot's successor, translated for him.[70]

[67] L. Thorndike, *Michael Scot* (London, 1965), pp. 32–39. Scot actually seems to have followed Frederick on his travels around Italy.

[68] For this view of Frederick's court, see Abulafia, *Frederick II*, esp. pp. 251–67. For the Greek men of letters, see M. B. Wellas, *Griechisches aus dem Umkreis Kaiser Friedrichs II* (Munich, 1983).

[69] Moses Maimonides, *The Guide for the Perplexed*, trans. M. Friedländer, 2d ed. (London, 1904).

[70] Abulafia, *Frederick II*, p. 268; C. H. Haskins, *Studies in the History of Mediaeval Science* (Cambridge, Mass., 1924), p. 318. An especially bleak view must be presented of Latin letters at Frederick's court. Haskins, *Studies in Mediaeval Culture* (Oxford, 1929), pp. 129–48, does not really prove that there was very much happening at any one time; many of his examples are from

Indeed, the cultural flavor of Frederick's court is in one very important way entirely Western: the appearance of a school of lyric poets writing imitations of the Provençal love-songs under the emperor's patronage in an Italian dialect signals an interesting shift. Not merely Provençal but German poetry may have inspired the *Scuola Siciliana*—Frederick's father is supposed to have been a *Minnesinger* as well as an emperor. Looking more closely at the authors of these poems, one sees striking similarities. Guido delle Colonne, Giacomo da Lentini, Rosso Rosso, Mazzeo di Ricco of Messina—again and again they are the ruler's intimates, judges, and notaries in the imperial civil service or prominent landlords, in all these cases inhabitants of eastern Sicily or the tip of Calabria. (Others, such as Rinaldo d'Aquino, are southern Italians.) They represent the new Latin (or Latinized) population of the area in the kingdom where Islam had always been weakest, and where Latin immigration had long been strongest.[71] Iacopo Mostacci is described both as a Messinese and as a Pisan, but this is no problem, since so many of Messina's inhabitants were of northern Italian origin by the early thirteenth century. Maybe the prominence of Messina in the *Scuola Siciliana* reflects accidents of manuscript survival, but in fact it seems that the bustling, prosperous port with its large settler population provided an ideal environment for the importation of European fashions—not merely fashions in textiles, but fashions in speech and literature. Just after 1200 the Provençal troubadour Peire Vidal certainly visited eastern Sicily, and composed poems in praise of the Genoese adventurers who had seized control of Malta and Syracuse.[72] But it was in

---

Frederick's youth or of cases where personal contact with the emperor was very limited. On this, see Abulafia, *Frederick II*, pp. 264–66.

[71] See B. Panvini, *La scuola poetica siciliana: le canzoni dei rimatori nativi di Sicilia* (Florence, 1955); and, for a valuable selection, F. Jensen, *The Poetry of the Sicilian School*, Garland Library of Medieval Literature, vol. A 22 (New York, 1986). For an overall interpretation, see Abulafia, *Frederick II*, pp. 270–79.

[72] Abulafia, "Henry, Count of Malta," pp. 113–14, repr. in David Abulafia, *Italy, Sicily and the Mediterranean, 1100–1400* (London, 1987), chap. 3, with additional nn. referring to later literature. See also J. Brincat, "Le poesie 'maltesi' di Peire Vidal." *Melita Historica* 7 (1976):65–89.

Italian that the Sicilian poets wrote, not in Provençal. They used an Italian that had been fused out of a mélange of southern Italian, Ligurian, and Tuscan dialects; and, though what survives is perhaps a literary rather than a spoken form of Italian, it still stands as testimony to the massive cultural and ethnic transformations that had taken place in Sicily between 1100 and 1250.

The repopulation of the cities by Italian immigrants, the settlement of eastern Sicily by Lombardi, and the expulsion or assimilation of the Muslims are one side to the Latinization of the island of Sicily. In lesser measure the same applies to parts of the southern Italian mainland; here it was the Greeks who were under immediate pressure, and there was also heavy immigration in the twelfth and thirteenth centuries, still revealed in the Franco-Provençal dialect of a tiny area of northern Apulia. In Calabria Greek gave way to Italian, and there were even some Provençal settlers there by the mid-fourteenth century. Arguably the survival of Greek Orthodoxy in southern Italy and Sicily was as much the work of the Albanian migrations of the fifteenth century as it was the result of tenacious traditionalism among the residue of Hellenophone Sicilians and Calabrians. The Muslim community of Lucera, founded by Frederick II, did not and was not intended to flourish as an outpost of Islamic culture in continental Europe. Frederick had transplanted about twenty thousand Muslims from Sicily to the northern parts of his kingdom in order to isolate them from the rest of the Muslim world, to ensure that the damaging links between the Saracen rebels in Sicily and their coreligionists in North Africa could not be duplicated. Lucera was too far away and its inhabitants were fully dependent on the favors of the emperor.[73] In fact Frederick declared that he was pleased that the Dominicans were prepared to work for the conversion of the Luceran Saracens, and (at least for a time) he may have expected the colony to become fully assimilated into the surrounding Christian society.[74] By 1233 some Luceran Muslims

[73] Abulafia, *Frederick II*, pp. 146–48, 252.
[74] See the discussion by James M. Powell in chap. 5. But for much of his

were familiar with Italian; in fact it is quite possible that Italian had been gaining ground among them even before they left Sicily.[75]

Although Frederick made extensive use of the royal castle at Lucera, he never made it into one of the cultural centers of his kingdom; perhaps he did live there surrounded by oriental ceramics, trumpeters, and dancing-girls (who doubled as concubines), but the men of Lucera were encouraged either to serve in the imperial bodyguard or to sow the fields around the town, for which purpose Frederick supplied plough-teams in 1239/40.[76] The emperor's idea was to bind the Saracen colony to the soil, "as was the case in the time of King William [II]"—to transform a settlement of restive, transplanted rebels into industrious peasants who could perform the same agricultural tasks as they had done when resident in Sicily, and who could help repopulate an area that, like other parts of the *Regno*, was lightly settled and therefore unable to realize its potential as a source of saleable foodstuffs. The Luceran Saracens became a *casus belli* when the popes began to declare the war against the Hohenstaufen a crusade: Innocent IV cited the Luceran Sara-

---

reign Frederick appears to have tolerated Islam at Lucera, as did his successors. He probably knew canon law well enough to resist the temptation to convert by force. He possibly assumed that the problem would take care of itself and that Islam in Lucera would be even less resilient than that close to Africa in Sicily. But embattled minorities can resist assimilation very fiercely. J. M. Martin's "La colonie sarrasine de Lucera et son environment: quelques réflexions," *Mediterraneo medievale; scritti in onore di Francesco Giunta*, 3 vols. (Soveria Mannelli, 1989), 2:795–811, appeared too recently to be discussed in the text, but deserves mention because of its extensive coverage of the literature.

[75] See J. L. A. Huillard-Bréholles, *Historia diplomatica Friderici secundi*, 12 vols. (Paris, 1852–1861), 4:452, for Italian speakers at Lucera. Powell suggests that the Luceran Saracens may have started to contaminate the local Christians with their beliefs.

[76] See David Whitehouse, "Ceramici e vetri medioevali provenienti dal Castello di Lucera," *Bollettino d'Arte* (1966): 171–78, for finds of Chinese celadon ware of the eleventh to thirteenth centuries. Clearly their main value was as curios and they could have arrived long after their manufacture—most probably via Egypt, where a delayed reaction to Chinese models led to the extensive imitation of Far Eastern pottery styles. For the Saracen farmers, see Carcani, *Registrum*, p. 307; Abulafia, *Frederick II*, pp. 334–35.

cens as proof that the hated Manfred was an ally of Islam.[77] But even Charles I of Anjou never fulfilled his promise to uproot the Luceran Saracens; it was left to his son Charles II to close down the Muslim colony in 1300, at a time when not merely the Muslims but the Jews of southern Italy were being subjected to calls for their conversion or expulsion. By the end of the thirteenth century the Muslim colony at Lucera had become an utter anomaly—a community that had lost touch with the Islamic world but had continued to resist attempts to integrate it into the Latin world, rebuffing visiting preachers and maintaining itself as an exclusively Islamic entity. Yet even after the re-Christianization of Lucera, there were still Muslim inhabitants scattered around Apulia, who complained to the royal court about their persecution and lack of protection, and were evidently caught in the theological and canon law vice that explicitly guaranteed the right of the Infidel to live unconverted under Christian rule, but used every method short of forced conversion to draw him into the Christian faith.[78]

After 1300 Islam had still not entirely vanished from Sicily and the south, for the expansion of the slave trade, in which the rising merchants of Catalonia and Majorca had a large stake, brought unknown numbers of unfree Muslims to Palermo,

[77] N. Housley, *The Italian Crusades: The Papal-Angevin Alliance and the Crusades against Christian Lay Powers* (Oxford, 1982), pp. 40, 62, 65, 243; and yet there were also Saracens of Lucera in the Angevin armies resisting Peter of Aragon after the Sicilian Vespers! See p. 158.

[78] J. Muldoon, *Popes, Lawyers and Infidels: the Church and the non-Christian World, 1250–1550* (Liverpool, 1979), pp. 1–28. For the fate of the expelled Saracens, see P. Egidi, *Codice diplomatico dei Saraceni di Lucera* (Naples, 1917), §166, 168, 241, 349, 350, 390, 450, where it is stated that the Christians of Apulia "multos graviter atque letaliter percusserunt et aliquos inhumane ac impie occiderunt." But the dominating flavor was one of relentless persecution of the Saracens, stopping just short of extermination. See P. Egidi, "La colonia saracena di Lucera e la sua distruzione." *Archivio storico per le province napoletane*, 36 (1911): 597–694; 37 (1912): 71–89, 664–96; 38 (1913): 115–44, 681–707; 39 (1914): 132–71, 697–766. Similar measures were also being adopted in the kingdom of Naples against the Jews. Financial considerations at a time of rising war costs may be one insalubrious motive; peace with the Aragonese was still a couple of years away. Cf. Housley, *Italian Crusades*, p. 243.

Trapani, and other centers.[79] In the period 1280 to 1310 there was an emphasis on the handling of Saracen slaves, but the slave markets were packed with Greek slaves over the next half-century, and by Tatar slaves between about 1360 and 1400. As in other areas of the western Mediterranean, the years after 1440 saw a return to African sources, by now primarily black African. Bresc warns against exaggerating the importance of the slave trade of late medieval Sicily, both in relation to the island's overall trade and as far as their numbers and functions are concerned.[80] It is probable that slaves never played the same part in the agricultural economy of Sicily that they played in contemporary Valencia, where slave gangs were set to work on the soil. They were either domestic slaves (including concubines) or they arrived in transit, awaiting sale in the slave markets of Palermo and elsewhere, before reexport, possibly back into the Muslim world. The Catalan slave handlers were middlemen who exploited the position of Sicily close to the slave sources in Cyrenaica, but who appear to have thought little about the religious affiliation of the purchaser. As for those slaves who remained in Sicily, it is unlikely that the unfree Muslims created their own religious communities, as the Christian unfree in North Africa had perhaps managed to do until the twelfth century;[81] many certainly converted to Christianity, and in the process could expect to gain their freedom, or at least gain the right to buy it. Among those who did not convert were Saracens of Lucera, sold as slaves in Sicily after the colony was disbanded by Charles II of Anjou.[82]

In Jewish households there was a special interest in Muslim slaves. The fourteenth-century kings of Sicily insisted that Jews

---

[79] C. Verlinden, *L'esclavage dans l'Europe médiévale*, vol. 2, *Italie, Colonies italiennes du Levant, Levant latin, Empire byzantin* (Ghent, 1977); C. Verlinden, "L'esclavage en Sicile au bas moyen âge," *Bulletin de l'Institut historique belge de Rome* 35 (1963).

[80] Bresc, *Monde méditerranéen*, 1:439–75.

[81] Ibid., 2:583, argues that "il n'y a pas de communauté, pas de lieu de culte: c'est un monde en survie précaire."

[82] Ibid., 2:582. It would be interesting to know how such Saracens reached Sicily, since the colony was dispersed during the War of the Vespers when southern Italy and Sicily had few trading links.

should not exercise power over Christians, but it remained permissible to own Muslim slaves. In addition, the use of circumcised Muslims may have made it possible for Jews to circumvent the complex religious laws concerning the handling of wine by non-Jews, since some rabbinic authorities allowed *kosher* wine to be poured by any circumcised person, not merely by a male Jew.[83] Thus as late as the fifteenth century there were some Muslims in Sicily, but virtually all were unfree and of non-Sicilian origin. Rare instances of Muslim merchants resident in Sicily come as little surprise: Asmectus (Aḥmad) Bursarius, a maker of bags and pouches, lived in Palermo with his wife Fatima from 1307 to 1309, and Saracens appear in the notarial acts of these years and as late as 1329 making oaths "tacto pane ad legem Muhamet" (swearing oaths in the Muslim fashion while holding bread). Salem de Messana, resident at Palermo, appears to have been the last prominent Muslim merchant; he died in 1345. After that, references to Muslims are very scarce; in 1402 a Muslim was functioning as headman (*raysi*—itself an Arabic word still in use in Sicily) in tunny-fisheries in western Sicily, but when the government of Sicily needed translators for Arab documents or embassies it had to turn to Jews, Muslim slaves, and Christians of Pantelleria.[84] It is striking, too, that Arabic left few marks on the Italian spoken in Sicily to compare with its impact on Castilian; about two hundred words of Arabic origin survive in Sicilian Italian, providing testimony to the reality of the cultural break between Islamic and Christian Sicily. There was thus no return of the Muslims to Sicily, such as occurred in late medieval Andalusia or indeed Castile proper, where the Muslim settlements in the major towns often contained new immigrants unconnected, it appears, with the original, expelled Moorish population.

Several dimensions to the Latinization of the Sicilian kingdom have been identified in this study. It has been seen that the cultural complexion of the court underwent significant changes between 1100 and 1250. The relative openness of Roger II had

[83] Abulafia, "Jews of Erice," p. 312. However, there was and is no consensus on this.
[84] Bresc, *Monde méditerranéen*, 2:582–84.

not resulted in the removal of existing cultural barriers; after him, interest in Greek and Arabic culture became more and more selective, with an emphasis on the acquisition of ancient texts preserved by Byzantines or Muslims rather than on the achievements of contemporary scholars outside the Latin orbit. Under Frederick II contact was restored, mainly by post, but the Sicilian court itself was heavily Latinized. These were developments in which the inhabitants of Sicily played little part. Their own cultural preferences can perhaps be gauged by the continuing interest in Byzantine-type icons even among the Latin citizens of Palermo as late as 1400; these icons were still being made, and demand for them was strong.[85] And in Messina and eastern Sicily the Greek language and liturgy survived beyond 1500, even if the number of Greek speakers continued to shrink rapidly. Thus on an island where the Greeks had— even under Norman rule—still constituted the vast majority of all Christians, they were now a minority, overtaken by the Latin settlers from further north. Italian became the *koiné* of nearly all the Sicilians.

In a famous passage in his book *The Leopard*, Giovanni di Lampedusa makes one of his characters remark that the Sicilians are "old, very old."[86] Some striking continuities are visible: the grain traffic of the Greco-Roman world, active again in the Middle Ages and the sixteenth century; the long sequence of foreign rulers, bewailed in the same passage by Lampedusa. But between 1100 and 1300 Sicily did change; it was renewed—in population, language, culture, and religion—in massive degree. When in 1282 the king of Aragon conquered the island he gained command, if not over a new country, at least over a new people.[87]

[85] Bresc-Bautier, *Artistes, patriciens et confrères*, p. 72.

[86] Giuseppe di Lampedusa, *The Leopard*, trans. A. Colquhoun (London, 1963), p. 145; D. Mack Smith, *Medieval Sicily, 800–1713* (London, 1969), p. xiii, uses this quotation as a starting-point for his analysis of Sicilian society.

[87] And indeed Bresc ("Formazione"; *Monde méditerranéen*, 2:*passim*) argues that by 1282 there had developed a consciousness of a Sicilian *populus*, revealed, for instance, in the attempt that year to replace King Charles of Anjou with a confederation of Sicilian communes.

L'Attività commerciale genovese nell'Africa normanna: la città di Tripoli

Sebbene l'informazione sulla struttura politica, e soprattutto economica, delle città africane sotto il governo dei Normanni sia molto scarsa
— perché il periodo di dominazione siciliana fu breve ed esposto a flut-
tuazioni di fortuna da regione a regione — il dibattito sulla situazione
economica dell'Africa settentrionale prima della conquista almohade non
è nuovo. Alle tribù arabe che percorsero l'Ifriqiya nell'undicesimo secolo,
i Banu Hillal ed i Banu Sulaym, sono state rimproverate, dal tempo di
Idrisi, il geografo andaluso di Ruggero II, la devastazione dell'Africa del
nord e la trasformazione del grande granaio dell'Impero romano, in una
regione retrograda, che dipendeva, almeno in parte, per l'approvvigionamento di derrate alimentari dall'estero — primieramente, senza dubbio,
dalla Sicilia, che fu durante il Medio Evo tanto ricca di frumento da ri-
fornirne gli abitanti del regno e quelli dei paesi vicini, come Pisa, Genova
e Tunisi. Nell'epoca sveva l'approvvigionamento di grano a Tunisi era già
un fattore fondamentale nelle relazioni politiche siciliane con questa regione dell'Africa [1]. È tuttavia percettibile che le città africane possedes-
sero le risorse per pagare il grano importato, ed infatti i principi di Tunisi
saldarono un tributo essenziale alla loro difesa, prezzo della pace lungo
la loro costa. C'erano altri nessi di primaria importanza politica ed economica tra il Regno normanno e l'Africa: i re siciliani mantennero la
tradizione arabo-sicula di coniare moneta d'oro, e la fonte principale per
questo metallo, dal punto di vista siciliano, era la via carovaniera che si

(*) Vorrei ringraziare il prof. R. C. Smail di Sidney Sussex College, Cambridge, che
ha letto questo articolo e la dott. Marina Scarlata dell'Università di Palermo, che ha
collaborato alla versione italiana.
(1) Vedi F. Giunta, « Sicilia e Tunisi nei sec. XIV e XV », in *Medioevo Mediterraneo*
(Palermo, 1954), pp. 138-140.

estendeva dal Sudan occidentale e dal regno di Ghana alle città dell'Ifriqiya, ove giungeva la via terrestre lungo l'Africa settentrionale e marittima attraverso il Mediterraneo. In aggiunta, i Normanni dovevano frenare l'attività estesa dei pirati arabi, a tutela delle coste meridionali ed orientali della Sicilia; allora i Normanni conquistarono gradualmente gli stretti maltesi, prima con l'acquisto di Malta e poi con la conquista di Gerbe, un vero nido di pirati, ed infine con il loro insediamento nel continente africano (²). Le celebri parole di Ugo Falcando affermano esplicitamente che non solamente motivi economici e militari, ma anche l'ambizione regia, condussero alla serie di vittorie normanne nell'Africa: re Ruggero « curabat ut non magis viribus quam prudentia et hostes contereret et regnum suum productis finibus ampliaret. Tripolim namque Barbarie, Affricam, Facsum, Capsiam aliasque quampluribus barbarorum civitates multis sibi laboribus ac periculis subiugavit »(³).

L'ampliamento dello stato normanno in Africa — o ugualmente in Romania — accrebbe solamente una diversità già esistente fra la Sicilia, di tradizione araba e greca, ed il Mezzogiorno d'Italia, di tradizione greca e longobarda; il regno non era, almeno nei suoi anni formativi, un'unità naturale, con un confine naturale, ed infatti i rapporti economici e, alle volte, politici, tra l'isola di Sicilia e l'Africa del nord erano stretti, già prima della conquista normanna. Per esempio le ceramiche d'Ifriqiya non differivano molto da quelle della Sicilia normanna.

Recentemente un orientalista inglese, il Dr. Michael Brett, ha rimproverato, non agli Arabi ma ai Normanni, il crollo economico dell'Africa settentrionale, ed ha tentato di dimostrare che i Banu Hillal non ridussero l'attività economica dell'Ifriqiya in condizione catastrofica, ma che la mole di traffico della regione forse si accrebbe. Dunque suggerisce il Brett, la devastazione raccontata da Idrisi e biasimata dagli Arabi fu portata dai Normanni che depredavano nell'Africa al pari degli Arabi:

« Is it not possible that Idrisi in his capacity as editor, writing shortly afterwards under the patronage of the Norman King responsible, should have made the Arabs the scapegoats for the devastation along the coast that the Norman themselves had caused and, in so doing, attributed to them widespread devastation inland that his own descriptions of individual localities do not bear out? » (⁴).

Si nota una contraddizione apparente fra alcuni elementi della re-

---

(2) L'importanza dello stretto maltese nella vita politica ed economica del Regno normanno-svevo è sottolineato da DAVID ABULAFIA, « Henry Count of Malta and his Mediterranean activities », in *Medieval Malta Studies*, a cura di Anthony Luttrell (Londra, British School at Rome, in corso di stampa).

(3) UGO FALCANDO, *Historia o Liber de regno Sicilie*, a cura di G. B. Siragusa, in *Fonti per la Storia d'Italia* (Roma 1887), pp. 5-6.

(4) MICHAEL BRETT, *Ifriqiya as a market for Saharan trade from the 10th. to the 12th. century A. D.*, in « Journal of African History », vol. X (1969), pp. 347-364, e in particolare p. 364.

lazione di Idrisi sull'Africa del nord e l'evidenza dei fatti sostenuta da altre fonti; di qui l'intenzione di far uso degli unici documenti di natura economica dell'Occidente latino che, nella stessa epoca di Idrisi, fanno riferimento alla città di Tripoli di Ponente, durante ed appena dopo il governo normanno, ed ai quali si possono aggiungere le limitate osservazioni di 'Ibn al-Atîr e di altri scrittori arabi o berberi.

La relazione di Idrisi non lusinga in tutto Ruggero, malgrado lo scrittore, forse, intendesse le sue parole come una dimostrazione della grande potenza del suo re. Dopo aver detto che Tripoli è un importante entrepôt commerciale, Idrisi continua:

« Avant l'époque actuelle, tous ses environs étaient extrêmement bien cultivés et couverts de plantations de figuiers, d'oliviers, de dattiers et de toute sorte d'arbres à fruits; mais les Arabes ont détruit cette prosperité, les habitants de la campagne ont été obligés de l'abandonner, les plantations ont été ravagées, les cours d'eau arrêtés. En 540 (1145) le grand roi Roger prit cette ville et fit périr ou reduisit en esclavage les habitants; il en est actuellement possesseur et elle fait partie de ses états. Le territoire de la ville de Tripoli est d'une fertilité incomparable en céréales, comme tout le monde sait » (5).

La presentazione è, dunque, di un doppio crollo politico ed economico, causati secondo Idrisi, tanto dagli Arabi quanto dai Normanni, e sappiamo che quest'epoca fu caratterizzata da una grande carestia, senza dubbio conseguenza diretta degli anni d'invasione e di conquista. Ma la presenza di negozianti genovesi a Tripoli verso la fine del periodo di dominazione normanna, può infatti suggerire, come spessissimo avviene nelle fonti arabe, che l'iperbole nasconda una verità meno forte. È vero che la presenza di commercianti stranieri in una regione impoverita può egualmente segnalare l'importazione di derrate alimentari essenziali, ma Idrisi parla di un crollo di attività commerciali in certe regioni dell'Africa (6), ed è possibile dimostrare invece che mercanti genovesi portarono a Tripoli nell'anno 1164, una quantità di rame e non prodotti alimentari (7).

I documenti genovesi che si riferiscono alla città normanna di Tripoli sono un gruppetto fra i 1300 atti (dei quali circa cento riguardano il commercio della Sicilia), che si trovano nel Cartolare di Giovanni Scriba, il registro notarile più antico che sopravvive a Genova, ed in Italia. Gli anni per i quali abbiamo notizia — da dicembre 1154 ad agosto 1164 — corrispondono, la più gran parte, al regno di Guglielmo I di Sicilia. Ma naturalmente, l'interesse genovese nell'Africa settentrionale non era nuovo, benché non sopravvivano contratti commerciali prima del 1154. Per esem-

---

(5) IDRISI, *Description de l'Afrique septentrionale et saharienne*, a cura di R. Dozy et J. de Goeje (Leiden, 1866), pp. 142-3.
(6) Ibid., p. 130, p. 137 (p. es.).
(7) M. CHIAUDANO, *Il Cartolare di Giovanni Scriba* (Torino-Roma 1935), II § 1245, pp. 219-220 (indicato, d'ora in poi, G. S.).

pio, la spedizione militare dei Genovesi e dei Pisani ad al-Mahdiyah nel 1087, alla quale i Normanni ricusarono di prender parte[8], mostra che le città tirreniche erano pronte parimenti ad aprire nuovi mercati attraverso la conquista, quantunque lo stabilimento del regno di Gerusalemme, con il loro aiuto, e gli stretti nessi col regno nascente di Sicilia, fornissero una fila di mercati lungo una via marittima un po' differente. Con tutto ciò, i contratti per gli anni 1154-64 ne comprendono parecchi per Tunisi e molti di più per il Maghreb (Bugia, Ceuta, ecc.)[9]. Ma quando Giovanni Scriba parla di *Tripuli*, come identificarla necessariamente con la Tripoli di Barberia, piuttosto che di Siria (e c'erano altre città dello stesso nome, in Grecia ed in Sicilia, ma non città marittime)? Non è possibile dubitare seriamente dell'identità africana della città. In primo luogo i contratti di Giovanni Scriba per la Terra Santa parlano sempre di *ultramare* come destinazione, e non di un porto specifico. In secondo luogo lo stabilimento principale genovese nella contea crociata di Tripoli (Siria) era fuori la città, a Gibelletto o Jubail, ed era lì che si prevedeva l'arrivo di navi genovesi; la città di Tripoli di Siria non aveva un fondaco genovese nel secolo decimosecondo, malgrado le promesse di Raimondo di S. Gilles all'epoca della conquista della contea[10]. Finalmente, un contratto del 1164 per commercio a «Tripoli» parla di un certo Xecha Bohahia de Tripoli e dei suoi scambi commerciali con la Sicilia[11]. La molteplicità dei suoi contratti con il regno normanno conferma la tesi che questa Tripoli fosse la Tripoli africana. Il suo nome, Xecha, Sceicco, vuol dire ' alto o vecchio signore '.

Il primo contratto interessante è un atto redatto il 6 giugno 1157 nel quale Albertone de Custode, Oberto Corso ed Enrico Fledemerio convennero di stabilire una *societas* composta di lib. 42 da parte dei primi due e di lib. 12 da parte di Enrico[12].

Cum omni ista societate debet ire laboratum Tripulim nominatus Enricus et inde quo voluerit per totam istam et sequentem estatem, e, di ritorno, Enrico deve dividere a metà il guadagno, secondo l'abitudine ordinaria. Enrico prese in più lib. 9 *de suo*. L'atto è cassato nel Registro e, a quanto pare, il notaio sarebbe stato più tardi richiesto di redigerne una versione piena, in forma di pergamena; in altri termini, il viaggio ebbe luogo[13]. Non si conosce abbastanza delle persone implicate nell'operazione. Enrico Fledemerio sembra genovese, perché c'è menzione di

---

(8) M. AMARI, *Storia dei Musulmani di Sicilia*, II ed. a cura di C. A. Nallino (Catania 1937-9), III, p. 170.

(9) Per Tunisi tutti gli anni 1155-64, esclusi il 1159 ed il 1161.

(10) J. RICHARD, *Le Comté de Tripoli sous la dynastie toulousaine (1102-1187)* (Parigi 1945), pp. 84-5.

(11) G. S., II § 1245, p. 219.

(12) G. S., I § 187, p. 99 (e tav. IV, p. 98 per la fotografia del foglio che contiene questo contratto).

(13) Su questo problema v. M. CHIAUDANO, *op. cit.*, I, pp. XXVIII-XXXII.

lui nelle note di Giovanni Scriba relative ad atti e lodi dei consoli dei placiti (1156) [14]; ed inoltre, si ritrova in un contratto dello stesso giorno, luogo e testi (con l'aggiunta di due soci nell'affare) del contratto per Tripoli, un atto registrato immediatamente sotto, nel quale riceve dalla moglie Iula lib. 12 *de dotibus* e di ritorno le dà lib. 25 *nomine antifacti* [15]. È una manovra per sistemare i suoi affari finanziari prima della spedizione oltremarina, e per assicurare un certo benessere alla moglie durante la sua lontananza o in caso di mancato ritorno. Abbiamo invece più notizie di Albertone de Custode, che il 28 luglio 1158, stabilisce con Alberto Clerico una *societas* di lib. 34 e 12 d., che Alberto deve portare a Messina, *et inde quo velit usque tres annos*; prende in aggiunta un pezzo di panno di S. Riquier, merci della Picardia, del valore di lib. 5. e 15 s. [16]. Il 25 settembre 1161 partecipa con lib. 80 e 3 s. ad una *societas* con destinazione generica *quo sibi* (il suo socio) *melius videbitur* [17]. Albertone appare negli ultimi fogli del Cartolare come testimone (1164) [18].

Benché non sia possibile dire che Albertone fosse un capitalista e un commerciante di alto rango, con interessi ricorrenti e grandi investimenti, aveva nondimeno legami internazionali con il Mediterraneo centrale e, forse, con l'Europa settentrionale o con i mercanti che si specializzavano nel commercio al nord. A causa della perdita di cartolari paralleli è difficile poter fare altro che congetture — anche se rimane la semplice coincidenza — ma il contratto per Messina, redatto quando è probabile che Enrico Fledemerio fosse ancora oltremare, suggerisce un interesse particolare verso il regno di Sicilia e le sue dipendenze. Quanto a Oberto Corso, è conosciuto in altri contratti, solamente come testimone [19].

Tripoli tornò in mano agli Arabi nell'anno dell'egira 553 (2 febbraio 1158-22 genn. 1159) con la più gran parte dell'Africa normanna, al Mahdiyah e Zawila escluse [20]; tuttavia l'interesse genovese continuò senza interruzione. È chiaro da un contratto genovese del 23 settembre 1160 che i mercanti andavano ancora in gran numero a Tripoli: Oberto Transasco deve prendere lib. 20 del suo, e lib. 46 del banchiere Baldo, e *laboratum ire Tripolim et quo iverit major pars mercatorum navis qua vadit* [21]; presumibilmente gli altri notai, adesso perduti, registrarono altri investimenti genovesi in questa spedizione. Nel 1164 troviamo due contratti per Tripoli, uno solamente per Tripoli, per niente altro che lib. 4 (con l'obbligazione di restituirne 5) [22], e quattro giorni più tardi (22 luglio

---

(14) G. S., II, p. 296.
(15) G. S., I § 188, pp. 99-100.
(16) G. S. I § 415, pp. 220-1.
(17) G. S., I § 913, p. 52.
(18) G. S., II § 1269, p. 229; § 1288, p. 237.
(19) G. S., I § 1163, p. 128; § 1188, p. 191.
(20) AMARI, *op. cit.*, III, pp. 483-4.
(21) G. S., I § 770, p. 414.
(22) G. S., II § 1238, p. 217.

1164) un secondo documento (²³) mostra visibilmente che i rapporti siciliani con Tripoli, almeno nella sfera economica, non erano stati grandemente danneggiati dagli avvenimenti del 1158: Baldezone Grasso riceve da Amico Çostro *cantara VI rami* che saranno portati a risico di Xecha Bohahia de Tripoli, ma che saranno venduti a Tripoli a risico di Amico:

et si Xecha sub sua lege (cioè l'Islam) *promiserit quod non habuerit de Sicilia nuncium vel litteras quod .XXXX. bisancii Roxaldini et .X. tripulati*(²⁴) *quos ipse Amicus ab eo acceperat missi sint fratri suo vel filio quod erat in Sicilia, eorum solucionem inde facere debeat et cartam accipere ab ipso Xecha in quam Amicum et omnes ianuenses quietos appellet de ipso debito.*

Poi stabiliscono la responsabilità in caso di mancanza o di eccesso di merci. Apparentemente si trova qui una connessione triangolare tra i mercanti genovesi, Xecha Bohahia a Tripoli ed i fattori di Xecha in Sicilia; ed è chiaro che il vincolo tra i genovesi e Xecha ha lontani precedenti. Roxaldino potrebbe essere un musulmano, siciliano o tripolitano, di nome Rascid-ad-din (possessore della fede) o Rukn-ad-din (colonna della fede). Amico e Baldezone sono conosciuti come testimoni di altri atti, ma raramente, e si sa che nel settembre 1163 quest'ultimo progettava d'inviare una nave a Tunisi(²⁵). Data l'evidenza del contratto per Tripoli, è possibile dire, forse, che Baldezone fosse versato nel commercio nell'Ifriqiya e in Barberia, avendo navigato come fattore, ed era da poco tornato da Tunisi, quando acconsentì ad andare a Tripoli. La presenza di rame mostra che le materie gregge portate a Tripoli non erano solamente alimentari, e nel Cartolare di Giovanni Scriba il rame è una derrata assai rara, anche se di primaria importanza nel commercio africano(²⁶). Il Nord Africa era quasi interamente tributario dell'Europa per l'acquisto di rame.

Il quadro generale è corroborato da un più grande numero di fonti arabiche, escluso un po' curiosamente Idrisi, perché scriveva senza dubbio prima che gli effetti del governo siciliano fossero visibili. Le fonti lodano la giustizia dei Normanni, e diffamano i Siciliani non come tiranni ma primieramente come infedeli. È vero che una fonte, 'At Tigani, suggerisce che l'attitudine benigna dei Normanni a Tripoli fu sviata, perché Giorgio d'Antiochia, « sorte de Francis Drake du Moyen Age » (²⁷), voleva ridurre la resistenza alla dominazione siciliana e la paura degli Africani

---

(23) G. S., II § 1245, pp. 219-220.

(24) Non si conoscono abbastanza queste monete africane da poterle singolarmente identificare.

(25) G. S., II § 1130, p. 163.

(26) L. DE MAS LATRIE, *Traités de Paix et de Commerce et Documents divers concernants les relations des Chrétiens avec les Arabes de l'Afrique Septentrionale au Moyen Age* (Paris 1866), t. I, p. 48. V. anche E. ASHTOR, *Les métaux précieux et la balance des payements du Proche-Orient à la basse epoque* (Paris, École Pratique des Hautes Études, 1971), cap. III, pp. 55-64 e passim.

(27) Nella bella frase di JOSHUA PRAWER, *Histoire du Royaume Latin de Jérusalem*, t. I (Parigi 1969), p. 367.

verso i Normanni ([28]); ma lo stesso cronista dice in aggiunta, che — come nelle altre città dell'Africa normanna —, ai Musulmani era data piena autorità nei loro affari religiosi e giudiziari ([29]), perché i Normanni erano essenzialmente una sovrastruttura militare e finanziaria. Incoraggiavano i fuggitivi a ritornare, ma sottoponevano Ebrei e Mussulmani al pagamento del testatico ([30]). Secondo Ibn Haldûn i Siciliani erano incoraggiati anch'essi a colonizzare Tripoli ([31]); ma non specifica la loro religione e — data la politica precedente nel regno di Sicilia e nel regno di Gerusalemme ([32]) — una colonizzazione cristiana è ben possibile; ma forse alcuni di questi « siciliani » erano i fuggitivi da Tripoli che, negli anni di guerra e di carestia, avevano preferito un signore infedele ad uno stomaco vuoto ([33]).

Gli altri luoghi dell'Africa continuavano ad affamarsi mentre Tripoli fioriva sotto il dominio dei Normanni ([34]). I re normanni, come i loro successori angioini, probabilmente possedevano un meccanismo capace di controllare l'approvvigionamento essenziale in tempo di carestia ([35]), e senza dubbio da questo trasse profitto anche Tripoli, mentre le altre città di Barberia dovevano 'far la coda' come i fratelli di Giuseppe in Egitto. Ibn 'al-Atîr dice espressamente che mercanti siciliani ed italiani frequentarono Tripoli e così aiutarono il ritorno alla prosperità della città:

« [Allor] s'avviarono bene le cose in questa città di Tripoli. I Siciliani ed i Rûm la frequentarono [per ragion de' commerci]; ond'essa prestamente ripopolossi e prosperò » ([36]).

Idrisi, a questo proposito, parla di rapporti commerciali tra Tripoli e Sciacca nella Sicilia meridionale ([37]); e Sciacca non poteva essere un caso unico. Una città ricca con un esteso commercio era un soprassoldo nella tasca del re siciliano. L'impulso verso lo sviluppo economico pare di ispirazione tanto ufficiale quanto privata, — in vista dell'incorporazione definitiva dell'Africa Normanna nel Regno, — un evento reso vano dalla

---

(28) M. AMARI, *Biblioteca Arabo-Sicula* (Torino-Roma 1880-1), traduzione II, pp. 60-61, testo pp. 388-9.

(29) 'At Tigani, B.A.S., II, p. 61, testo p. 389; cfr. 'Ibn 'abi Dînâr', B.A.S., II, pp. 295-6, testo p. 539.

(30) 'Ibn 'al-'Atir, B.A.S., I, p. 466, testo p. 289; 'An Nuwayrî, B.A.S., II, p. 158, testo p. 457; per il testatico (gizyah), 'Ibn Haldûn, B.A.S., II, p. 224, testo p. 499.

(31) 'Ibn Haldûn, *loc. cit.*

(32) Per la « colonizzazione » di natura economica vedi il privilegio di Ruggero I del 1094 per S. Bartolomeo di Lipari, in R. PIRRO, *Sicilia Sacra* (Palermo 1734), II, p. 772; d'interesse comparativo è J. PRAWER, *Colonisation Activities in the Latin Kingdom of Jerusalem*, in « Revue belge de philologie et d'histoire », t. 29, 1951, pp. 1063-1118.

(33) 'Ibn 'al-'Atir, B.A.S., I, p. 469, testo p. 292.

(34) M. AMARI, *Storia* cit., III, p. 417 « In breve (Tripoli) divenne prospera e ricca, mentre il rimanente della Barberia e gran parte dell'Asia anteriore sentian le dure strette della fame ».

(35) C. MINIERI RICCIO, *Saggio di Codice Diplomatico, formato sulle antiche scritture dell'Archivio di Stato di Napoli* (Napoli 1878-83), II, p. 286.

(36) B.A.S., I, p. 466, testo p. 290.

(37) B.A.S., I, pp. 77-8, testo p. 40.

conquista almohade. Un altro beneficio economico del governo normanno fu forse l'inclusione generale delle città africane nel trattato tra Guglielmo I e la Repubblica di Genova (1156-7) ([38]). La promessa *quod universi homines Ianue et illi qui sunt de districtu Ianue salvi et securi erunt et res eorum in terra vel mari dominii et potestatis eorum, exceptis galeatorum predonibus*, da parte del re Guglielmo, mentre non prevedeva un privilegio speciale per visitatori genovesi nell'Africa normanna, era un incentivo a commerciare a Tripoli, oltre il regno vero e proprio.

Senza dubbio l'esplorazione del grande archivio ebreo, la Genizah del Cairo, fornirà nuovi particolari economici, come per esempio la descrizione da parte di mercanti ebrei delle circostanze, economiche e politiche, nella costa della Barberia e dell'Ifriqiya durante il periodo di dominazione normanna. Uno studio sistematico di questo fondo da parte degli orientalisti sarebbe di gran valore se una critica profonda, negativa o positiva, sarà mai fatta dell'interpretazione del Brett ([39]). L'evidenza proposta qui non tocca necessariamente il suo argomento, perché si deve distinguere la razzia dalla conquista, e contrastare con l'evacuazione di una regione afflitta, la sua ripopolazione eventuale ed il recupero tentato dell'Africa normanna. Comunque, i limiti cronologici della sua generalizzazione sono ridotti, almeno per la regione africana direttamente sotto il governo siciliano; troviamo che i Normanni imposero una politica assai vantaggiosa con la loro dominazione e che, sulle loro orme, erano attivi, cautamente, i Genovesi in cerca del *proficuum, quod Deus dederit*.

---

(38) C. Imperiale di Sant'Angelo, *Codice Diplomatico della Repubblica di Genova*, (*Fonti per la Storia d'Italia*) (Roma 1936), I, pp. 338-42, v. in particolare p. 341.

(39) C'è solamente uno studio di documenti della Genizah relativi alla Sicilia: S. D. Goitein, *Sicily and Southern Italy in the Cairo Genizah Documents*, in « Archivio storico per la Sicilia orientale », vol. 67, 1971, pp. 9-33, in particolare p. 24 e seg.; v. anche il suo « opus magnum » *A Mediterranean Society: the Jewish Communities of the Arab world as portrayed in the Documents of the Cairo Geniza*, vol. I, *Economic Foundations* (Berkeley & Los Angeles 1967), passim.

The reputation of a Norman king in Angevin Naples

s not surprising to find that the city and rulers of
bles appear in the Decameron, for Boccaccio
s trained as a merchant in Naples. Sicily was also
ted by Florentine merchants and Boccaccio's
s of Sicilian history range from the near-present
k to the reign of the Norman King William II,
o died in 1189, a figure already associated with
od times' in Naples and Sicily. In one story
ccaccio describes members of William's family,
l and fictitious, and weaves romance around the
age of an African princess to Granada under this
g's guarantee of protection. This tale appears to
ive from real events in about 1180, when William
ured the safety of the daughter of an Almohad
er; in token of gratitude, and to gain other
crete advantages, the Almohads at last made
ace with the Sicilian king. Popular legends cir-
lating in southern Italy were clearly available to
occaccio, while writers of romance often located
titious events in Sicily, an exotic part of the Latin
orld.*

t is not difficult to explain the presence of
ories about Naples and Sicily in Boccaccio's
ecameron. Boccaccio, after all, was sent to
aples in his youth, in about 1328, and he
ained there as a merchant, working under
e wing of the great banking firm of the
ardi.[1] Not surprisingly his Neapolitan and
icilian stories retain that strongly mercan-
le streak which has conferred on the De-
ameron the modern epithet epopea mercantile

(Branca 1970:134–64; Scaglione 1973:579–
600). Many of the details are as true as we
could wish; the emphasis placed on Barletta as
a base for Florentine businessmen in Apulia;
the awareness of the horse-trade between
Perugia and Naples that permits the author
to introduce the Perugian Andreuccio to the
fleshpots of Naples (Decameron 9.10, 2.5). At
another level, Boccaccio shows an interest in
the recent history of the Neapolitan kingdom,
centred on the Sicilian Vespers and the
division of southern Italy from Sicily. He
writes of events both at the court of Charles
of Anjou, ruler of the mainland kingdom, and
at the court of his enemy Peter of Aragon,
conqueror of Charles' Sicilian territories; as
well he might – all Florentines, of whatever
political colour, recognised that Charles had
been champion of the Guelf cause, while
Peter of Aragon was identified in northern
Italy with the Ghibelline label (Decameron
2.6, 10.6, 10.7; compare 5.6). Certainly, the
idea that the Angevins of Naples were the
hereditary protectors of the Guelf legacy
meant much to the Florentines; in the fourteenth century King Robert's son Duke
Charles of Calabria came to regulate Florentine affairs; and, being ardent Guelfs, the
Florentines gained even readier access to
the markets of the kingdom of Naples than the
other northern merchants who flocked south
to buy grain and other raw materials
(Yver 1903:289–391). For a well-connected

Florentine there was no barrier between the merchant class and the Neapolitan nobility; Nicola Acciaiuoli was the most distinguished instance of a Florentine banker who gained positions at court – but any official of the banking firms could gain access to court, given the heavy dependence of the crown on loans by wealthy northerners.[2]

Boccaccio's close familiarity with the streets and citizens of Naples was demonstrated by Benedetto Croce in a memorable study of the story of Andreuccio of Perugia (1919:47–83; compare *Decameron* 2.5). The tale is located in real streets and around real land-marks; it is even possible, Croce suggests, that certain individuals known at court were introduced into the tale to add colour to Andreuccio's adventures. Perhaps such stories were part of a common stock of tales known at the Neapolitan court; or it may be that *il Boccaccio introducesse nella sua novella nomi e allusioni a persone ben conosciute a Napoli, in modo da far fiorire più volte il sorriso sulle labbra dei suoi ascoltatori e lettori napoletani.* Croce points to the existence of an Andrea da Perugia in the Angevin registers, as well as a *dompna Flora sicula* who, like Boccaccio's Fiordaliso, lived at Malpertugio in Naples. The Naples of the *Decameron* is, therefore, in essentials the Naples of the early fourteenth century. It was genuinely a city of tempters and temptresses.

Boccaccio, as a Florentine merchant, cannot be expected to have known the markets of Sicily proper as well as he knew those of Angevin Naples; Florentine support for the Angevins meant that the rôle of the Bardi, Peruzzi, Acciaiuoli and other Florentine bankers was much greater in Naples than in Sicily. Nevertheless, as Trasselli has shown (1956:188–9), there were Florentine bankers even in the enemy territories of Sicily. They were subject to controls, of course, and had to obtain a *carta securitatis* from the king before they could trade in the island without fear of expropriation. But the Aragonese kings of Sicily valued the presence of such persistent purchasers of their wheat and cotton as the Florentines; the Florentines, for their part, needed access both to the raw materials of Sicily and to the great centres of exchange within the island – points such as Palermo, Messina and Trapani that made Sicily the fulcrum of medieval trade routes. These three towns appear in the *Decameron*; and Boccaccio's description of the Palermo customs house appears accurate (*Decameron* 8.10). The existence of state warehouses can, however, be dated back to the reign of Frederick II (Kantorowicz 1931:283–5), so here Boccaccio had a hundred years of accumulated knowledge upon which to rely – there is, of course, no evidence that he himself visited Sicily. On a more general level, the impression he gives of a great Italian community of merchants, stretching in area from the Alps to Sicily, a flourishing and interdependent world of trade and finance, does not seem at all fanciful. The presence of large numbers of northerners in the markets of the south and the existence of an active group of native merchants in Sicily itself is amply confirmed by the evidence of the Palermo and Naples archives; the economic regions of Italy were increasingly learning to function together in a single large unit which, though riddled with variety, offered great opportunities for self-advancement and wealth.[3]

Boccaccio does not, however, confine his attention to recent events in Neapolitan and Sicilian history. Approval of the acts of Charles I of Anjou was, we learn, still a matter of contention among noble Florentines half a

:ury after his death (*Decameron* 10.7). His
s of Charles and his Aragonese rival Peter
ld be connected with any king; they have
obvious political or historical location. In
story (5.6), it is true, a number of historical
res appear, such as the Catalan admiral of
Sicilian fleet, Roger de Luria, and a real
orical monument in Palermo, the Cuba
ace, is also portrayed. Here too events
ounding the war of the Vespers are used
create difficulties for the lovers. Playing
h historical figures, on whatever legendary
is, is one thing; but using the details of
ividual historical events is quite another.
see Boccaccio handling historical material
nether or not he knows it to be such) we
st look at his stories of King William the
od of Sicily and southern Italy, stories
ced a century and a half before the Black
ath, in the Norman period of rule.

e association of King William II's reign
167–89) with good times was an ancient
e, dating to the reign of his cousin Frederick
. After William's death, royal power in
cily was seriously undermined by the dispute
hether the Norman royal bastard Tancred
d a better claim to the throne than
'illiam's aunt and uncle by marriage, Con-
ance and Emperor Henry VI of Hohen-
aufen. Henry's conquest of Sicily was
llowed by his early death and a long minor-
y during which German captains and native
obles eroded royal rights over land and
gislation. When in the 1220s Frederick
egan slowly to gather into his hands once
gain the ancient rights of his Norman pre-
ecessors, he took the reign of William II as
is principal point of comparison. Rights

held in his day were to be confirmed, on
presentation of documentary evidence (Dilcher 1975:796–7). There were several reasons
why William was chosen for this purpose. He
was the last Norman king in the legitimate
line of succession; he was popular in his own
lifetime; his father and predecessor William
I was accused, however unjustly, of lethargy
and misrule that his son ably ended; he had
sent impressively armed, though largely unsuccessful, expeditions to Alexandria, Thessalonika and Syria; he was noted for his piety,
evident in his support for Latin Syria and his
endowment of the great abbey of Monreale;
above all, by contrast with his father, he
maintained relatively cordial relations with
the feudal nobility.[4] Sicily was at the peak of
its wealth and prestige, and it is hardly
surprising that the reign of King William
retained its reputation as a golden age, in
Frederick II's legislation as in Neapolitan
legend. Dante, indeed, places William in the
higher circles of Paradise:

E quel che vedi nell' arco declivo
Guiglielmo fu, cui quella terra plora
che piange Carlo e Federigo vivo:
ora conosce come s'innamora
lo Ciel del giusto rege, ed al sembiante
del suo fulgore il fa vedere ancora. (*Paradiso* 20.61–6).

Boccaccio located two stories in "the reign of
good King Guiglielmo of Sicily". Both are
rich in what are intended to be historical
references. In one (5.7) we read of Genoese
galleys reaching Sicily from the Levant – a
common occurrence under the Normans, but
equally in the thirteenth and fourteenth
centuries. A certain Messer Currado is described as royal governor, either of Trapani or
of all Sicily; but no such figure or name
is known – indeed the name Conrad was

imported in the thirteenth century by the Hohenstaufen. It does not appear in the list of feudal tenants in southern Italy compiled for the Norman kings in the third quarter of the twelfth century and known as the *Catalogus baronum* (Jamison 1972). We read also of ambassadors sent to the pope by the king of Armenia, who travel through Sicily; but it was the post-Norman ruler of Sicily, Emperor Henry VI, who conferred a crown on the princes of Cilician Armenia. It is true that in the first years of the thirteenth century there was active correspondence between the popes and the Armenian kings (Maleczek 1971:13–25); but it would clearly be the height of folly to use Boccaccio as evidence for links between the Armenian princes and the papacy in the reign of King William. The story is, to be sure, a variation on a common motif, and its real value in a Norman context is to show how legend tended to accumulate around King William, even when his active rôle in such legend was minimal. Whence Boccaccio drew his story is, of course, impossible to say; that he was inspired to write it after living in Naples, where once King William had ruled, is obvious but not very helpful.

Attention must focus on the fourth tale of the fourth day of the *Decameron*. Here again William, *secondo, re di Cicilia, come i ciciliani vogliono*, appears; and here too we are provided with an unusual, because entirely mythical version of the Sicilian family tree. William is given two children, *l'un maschio e chiamato Ruggieri, e l'altro femina, chiamata Gostanza. Il quale Ruggieri, anzi che il padre morendo, lasciò un figliuolo nominato Gerbino.* Commentators on this story have grasped at this passage to suggest that here Boccaccio's tale "may be founded on fact, although possibly with a change of circumstances" (Lee 1909:135–6; compare Landau 1869: 116–7; Manni 1742:282–4). They have noted that this Ruggieri is probably Roger, eldest son of William I, who predeceased his father: he was accidentally killed in 1161 during a great uprising in Palermo. Admittedly other kings in the Norman line – Roger II and Tancred – had sons named Roger who predeceased them; but of the two Williams, only the first had a son Roger, or any sons at all. As for Gostanza, Constance mother to Frederick II was daughter to Roger II, and was born shortly after the king died in 1154. Boccaccio was certainly confused about Constance of Sicily's parentage; in *De claris mulieribus* (Boccaccio 1539:f. 76r) he once again makes her the daughter of William II, not Roger II – and this work, it is worth recalling, was dedicated to one of the Acciaiuoli ladies at the court of Queen Joanna of Naples. The complexities of Norman genealogy may not have been easy to unravel even in Neapolitan royal circles.

Giuseppe Billanovich was able to show that Boccaccio inserted some rough autograph notes on Norman genealogy in the margins of a text of Hugo Falcandus' Sicilian history (Billanovich 1953:21). This is evidence to confirm Boccaccio's strong interest in Norman Sicilian history, and to confirm his desire to unravel the profusion of Rogers and Williams into a clear line of succession. It is interesting to compare Giovanni Villani's own confused account of Norman history (Villani 4.24), where he makes Robert Guiscard grandfather, not uncle, of Roger II – Villani, like Boccaccio, had himself lived and worked as a banker in Naples (Luzzati 1971). However, Boccaccio corrected his error about Constance's genealogy in his later work *De casibus strium virorum*; there he states that *fuerat em Rogerio Regi primo filia cui nomen Conntia*. Either voluntarily or following a phecy that she would bring doom on her use she led the life of a nun (Boccaccio 20:f. 107v and Hall 1962:222; Boccaccio 44:254; compare Boccaccio 1539:f. 76r-v d 1963:240). As usual, Boccaccio could not sist the inclusion of a stirring story, or better ll two alternative stories, to add colour to s moral tales of historical figures. Boccaccio's uddle is even greater when we turn to erbino. No Gerbino appears in the royal le of descent; but it is true that Roger II's dest son Roger had a natural son named ancred, who displaced Constance's claim to e throne of Sicily and became king on illiam II's death in 1189. Prince Roger's ve for Tancred's mother was itself the bject of legend (Chalandon 1907b:425).

The tale turns, however, on Gerbino's love r the daughter of the king of Tunis, who ears of his exploits just as Gerbino hears of er beauty and charm. At this time, we are ld, Barbary was tributary to the king of icily. Now, tribute had been paid by the ulers of Tunis to Frederick II and Charles of njou, probably to guarantee Tunis against irate attack, rather than to indicate that unis was politically dependent upon Sicily Mas Latrie 1866:52). Earlier still, under Roger II, most of the north African coast from astern Algeria to Tripoli had been under Norman Sicilian control, though Tunis was probably the only large town not to be garrisoned by the Sicilians. Even then, it may well have paid protection money. The African empire of the Normans was intended to become a major source of wealth and of military strength, but in the event it proved ephemeral. In the first years of William I's

rule, from 1154 onwards, the fanatical Moroccan sect of the Almohads, or Unitarians, swept across Africa, extinguishing by 1160 the last remnants of Christian rule in North Africa. By the accession of William II, in 1167, there was no Norman town left in Africa (Wieruszowski 1962; Abulafia 1973: 395–402). The Almohads continued to look with hostility on Latin Christian rulers in Sicily as in Spain who dared exert lordship over the followers of Islam. The situation thus remained tense. Typically, however, it seems that trade between Tunisia and Sicily continued to flourish; the African towns bought wheat in exchange for gold from the southern Sahara, and possibly for textiles too. Commercially, relations between the Norman kingdom and its former African dependencies remained of necessity very close, if the African towns were to obtain adequate food supplies and the Norman kings adequate gold supplies.

Indeed, it is as a merchant that Gerbino charges a friend to dress and visit the court of Tunis with a message for his beloved princess; his agent gained access to her, *gioie da donne portandole, come i mercatanti fanno, a vedere*; and also, of course, brought a secret message from Gerbino. However, sudden problems arose.

Ardendo d'una parte la giovane e d'altra il Gerbino, avvenne che il re di Tunisi la maritò al re di Granata: di che ella fu crucciosa oltre modo, pensando che non solamente per lunga distanzia al amante s'allontanava, ma che quasi del tutto tolta gli era.

While Gerbino and his lady burned with mutual love, it befell that the king of Tunis gave her in marriage to the king of Granada, whereat she was wroth beyond measure, for that she was not only going into a country remote from her lover, but, as she deemed, was severed from him altogether.

It is true that a kingdom of Granada was only established in the 1230s (Watt 1965:111,

147–8), but in other respects we can for the moment suspend judgment about the validity of this account. Boccaccio goes on to relate that Gerbino felt deeply frustrated, and began to think of seizing the princess from the Spanish ruler. But further problems were to result.

> Il re de Tunisi, sentendo alcuna cosa di questo amore e del proponimento del Gerbino, e del suo valore e della potenzia dubitando, venendo il tempo che mandar ne la dovea, al re Guiglielmo mandò significando ciò che fare intendeva, e che, sicurato da lui che nè dal Gerbino nè da altri per lui in ciò impedito sarebbe, lo'ntendeva di fare.

Some rumour of Gerbino's love and of his intent reached the king of Tunis, who, knowing his prowess and power, took alarm, and as the time drew nigh for conveying the lady to Granada, sent word of his purpose to King Guiglielmo, and craved his assurance that it might be carried into effect without let or hindrance on the part of Gerbino, or anyone else.

The old king (*il re Guiglielmo che vecchio signore era*) sent his glove to the sultan of Tunis as pledge of his good faith, without apparently realising that Gerbino was the man involved. The sultan meanwhile fitted a ship to send his daughter to Granada; his daughter sent warning to Gerbino, who found himself torn between loyalty to his grandfather, who had given the sultan such assurances, and love for the sultan's daughter.

Gerbino chose love for his lady, fitted two ships at Messina, and stood guard off Sardinia, to await the sultan's vessel. Gerbino's galleys pounced on the ship bound for Spain, but the Saracen sailors barbarically put the sultan's daughter to death rather than surrender her to Gerbino. Gerbino returned, deep in grief, only to find that a Tunisian embassy had visited the king of Sicily and complained that faith had been broken. Gerbino was arrested and executed, for William preferred *avanti senza nepote rimanere che esser tenuto re senza fede.*

III

Though Gerbino may be fictional, William's honourable behaviour most certainly is not. It is in real events in the reign of William II – events, moreover, that turn on Sicilian relations with North Africa – that the historical background to Boccaccio's tale can be seen to lie. Naturally, the details, as they survive, have none of the tragic drama or even romantic flights that Boccaccio provides; but in many other respects the similarities are too striking to be coincidental. Had Boccaccio examined a south Italian chronicle such as the twelfth-century Montecassino anonymous he would, it is true, have found little to connect with the story of Gerbino: *1181: Dominus noster rex fecit treguam apud Panormum cum rege Maxamutorum usque ad decem annos, mense Augusti* – a laconic reference to a peace treaty with the Almohad ruler of north-west Africa (del Re 1845:470; also Mas Latrie 1866:152). This ruler was almost certainly Caliph Yusuf (Yusuf ibn Abd-al-Mumin or Abu Yaqub), for it is this figure, as will be seen, that the Arabic sources associate with a Sicilian truce (Amari 1880–1:185). Such a treaty was, admittedly, a breakthrough in the sense that relations between the Sicilian and Almohad rulers had been, at best, cool for the last twenty years. Another late twelfth-century source explains why the Almohads were prepared to make a truce with the Norman king (permanent treaties were, of course, ruled out by Muslim law, which only allowed temporary truces with princes of another faith). The second source is from Normandy, the chronicle of Robert of Torigny, abbot of Mont Saint-Michel, a work that shows strong though often uncritical dependence upon other English, Norman or continental chroni-

, This is part of his entry for 1179 or
):

Marroc, in cujus potestate est tota Affrica et etiam
aceni qui sunt in Hispania, mittebat filiam suam,
uidam rex Sarracenorum duceret eam in uxorem.
m stolus et galeae regis Sicilie invenerunt et
ixerunt ad dominum suum; unde rex letus
ficatus est cum patre ejus, illa reddita; et pater ejus
lidit regi Sicilie duas civitates, scilicet Affricam et
liam, quam Sarraceni abstulerant Willermo regi
ie, patri istius regis (Howlett 1889:285; also Mas
rie 1866:152).

re, as in Boccaccio's tale, we have a
acen ruler sending his daughter to another
islim ruler to be married; here again we
ve intervention by Sicilian ships, this time
ral ships. The princess is saved, not killed;
 is held hostage or protected by King
lliam – exactly which remains unclear;
od relations are established between the
rth African ruler and the Sicilian, but this
ne after rather than before the interrupted
yage. Such differences between recorded
t and Boccaccio's fancy iron out many
historical elements in the background
ccaccio provides: the idea that there was
ready a treaty relationship between Sicily
d the north African towns; the reference to
ranada, which disappears entirely (indeed,
e learn, rightly, that Almohad dominion
tually extended over southern Spain). And,
 course, Gerbino, not the princess, is the
rson we have to cast in the sea, for his
istence remains as thoroughly implausible
 ever. It is hard to believe Sicilian and south
alian chronicles would have ignored so
mpestuous a life; of surviving Norman
alian histories, only the Montecassino
nronicle is interested in the truce with the
lmohads, but the operative word is 'sur-
iving'. No doubt Robert of Mont Saint-
lichel had his own vanished sources, south

Italian chronicles or even *echt* Normans who
travelled from Latin Syria through Sicily
back to their homeland, and heard of these
events; and it is known that for earlier
Sicilian history he had available the chronicle
of William of Apulia (Howlett 1889:xv, xxv,
xxviii–xxix). There is thus ample reason to
suppose that Robert read later south Italian
chronicles too, though we have no knowledge
of their authors or scope.

Robert himself is not entirely to be trusted.
He says that two cities were returned to the
Sicilian king, 'Affrica' and 'Sibilia', by which
he means the trading centre of al-Mahdiyyah
and its suburb Zawila. No evidence exists that
these towns returned to Sicilian rule, other
than Robert's. Mas Latrie (1866:51–2) has
reasonably argued that the Almohad ruler
conferred on William not rule in al-Mahdiyyah, but the right to re-establish trade counters there and at Zawila. There had been
Sicilian commercial officers in al-Mahdiyyah
as long ago as 1117, but the Almohad conquest apparently chased them away (Wieruszowski 1962:18–20; compare Abulafia 1978:
69). The new trade counters, plus the offer of
peace, were certainly a valuable exchange
even for a Saracen princess. The Almohads
wanted more than the safe return of their
princess. They probably feared the growing
power of Saladin in Egypt and Mesopotamia,
knowing that they would not be considered
immune from attack by Saladin; they found
here common cause with King William, who –
at least in the 1180s – looked askance at Saladin's friendship with his enemy the Byzantine
Emperor. After the treaty with the Almohads,
then, if not in 1180/1, Sicily and North
Africa presented a common front against the
alliance of Saladin with the Greeks. William
took his truce with the Almohads seriously in

at least one respect, for when next he decided to wage war on Islam, in the winter of 1181/2, he attacked Majorca, which had remained in the hands of a pre-Almohad (Almoravid) dynasty; the Almohads had no particular preference between Christian and Almoravid, and, in the event, William's invasion came to nothing (Abulafia 1977a: 156–7; also Chalandon 1907b: 399–400).

The lack of reference in the Arabic sources to the events described by Robert of Torigny must be accounted for before Robert's own story is actually accepted. Ibn al-Athir, writing in the early thirteenth century, simply states that the Almohad caliph Yusuf arrived in May 1180 at Mahdia on the Tunisian coast; there the ambassador "of the king of the Franks, prince of Sicily" came to him to request an agreement (Amari 1880–1: 185). A ten-year truce was signed. A century later An-Nuwayri followed this account without embellishment (Amari 1880–1: 185). More fantastic, however, is a story presented in the 1220s by al-Marrakishi, himself an Almohad (Amari 1880–1: 131). He says that William of Sicily so greatly feared Caliph Yusuf's presence in Tunisia that he sent tribute voluntarily to him; and the caliph accepted this gift "on condition that he be paid each year a sum of money" – an apparent reversal of the real relationship identified by modern scholars such as Mas Latrie (1866: 52). Al-Marrakishi adds that on this or a subsequent occasion William sent Yusuf a precious stone called "the horse's hoof" owing to its amazing size; in the writer's own day it could be seen ornamenting the cover of a precious Koran. He may have confused the Sicilian kings and attributed to William II an object captured from William I after the fall of Mahdia, or sent for another reason

by Roger II; there is obviously no good reason to see in the existence of a gift a tributary relationship, except by self-delusion. The lack of reference to William's fleet and the princess might well be explained by embarrassment at the success of William's *coup* if indeed the king held her to ransom; or it might be explained by an established reluctance among the Almohads to think of the Christians as desirable allies, even when commercial or other considerations made them necessary allies (Amari 1938: 525–7; *Decameron* 1960b: 504). More useful is the information given by the Arabic sources about the identity of the African ruler who treated with William, and about the date of the events described; they are quite explicit in their statement that Yusuf arrived in Mahdia in 1180, whereas Robert of Torigny is consistently vague about dating events, and moves around rather than within calendar years. His 1179 or 1180 must probably be modified to late 1180; the Cassino Anonymous may either be a year out, or may be reporting the completion of negotiations that took several months to establish or to ratify (Amari 1938: 527n.).

How was this story transmitted to Boccaccio? He may himself have moulded the tale of Gerbino from historical sources known to him; he may have relied on popular legend. His historical sources certainly included the chronicle of Hugo Falcandus, who wrote a stylish but polemical account of the reign of William I and of the minority of William II (Billanovich 1953); however, Falcandus did not continue his history as far as 1180. There were, certainly, folk-songs circulating in southern Italy and Sicily from which he drew material – a point made evident in the tale that follows the story of Gerbino, that of the of basil, where the setting is Messina and re a popular song is actually cited ameron 4.5). Good King William no bt generated very many stories in the ury after he lived, and, as will be seen, king's name retains its appeal in Sicilian -lore. It is necessary to add that in the teenth century scholars thought they had tified Boccaccio's source, or at least a ted version of the tale of Gerbino, in the nymous *Novella di Cerbino in ottava rima*, ich some dated to the early fourteenth tury (*Novella di Cerbino* 1863). There is, vever, every sign that this poem is much er in date of composition than the *De-* *eron*, and that it is indeed based on the cameron. The only extra detail provided the poem is a name for the Tunisian ncess, Elena – a name that hardly carries viction in a Saracen. Moreover, the great seness of the prose version offered by ccaccio and its verse successor effectively les out the theory that the two accounts ay have had a single, lost ancestor (Lee 09:135–6; Passano 1868:92–4; Landau 69:117). The real ancestor of the *Novella* the *Decameron*; and the real ancestor of ccaccio's tale of Gerbino is a contorted, t recognisable, series of events – contorted w, when and by whom it is impossible to y; but the answer where is almost without ubt Naples.

V

roce warned of the dangers of transforming occaccio *da artista che esso era in un descrittore in uno storico* (1919:58). It would certainly e unwise to pretend that the tale of Gerbino as intended to be read as history, even as mbroidered history. For to say that it has its ancestry in real events is not to say that Boccaccio knew those events to be real; nor is understanding of the events enhanced by Boccaccio's version of them. But under- standing of Boccaccio's story is perhaps enhanced by an awareness of the balance between historical and fantastic elements in that story. Indeed, far from seeing a historical foundation for the tale of Gerbino, Branca has looked for affinities in French romances, pointing in particular to the tale of Huon of Bordeaux. However, this story does not speak of Sicily, though it does describe briefly a voyage from Saracen lands to the West which bears a remote resemblance to the voyage of the African princess known from history and from Boccaccio. Of course, there are stock motifs in the tale of Gerbino; Boccaccio or his own source has added much; and the very appeal of the story lay precisely in the similar- ity between the real events it mentions and the stuff of romance. Its suitability for re-telling does not detract from its ancestry in historical events, though the act of re-telling did in- volve the accretion of what were possibly standard frills.

That a vestigial popular history of King William circulated, orally or otherwise, does in the final analysis seem likely; and that, as far as it can be recovered, it bore a relationship to real events is impressive. No doubt there was a tendency to ascribe to William much that was either entirely fictitious or the attribute of another less loved historical figure: no Guelf would delight in tales favourable to Frederick of Hohenstaufen, but Good King William remained without taint. This notion of a popular history of certain Norman rulers seems to be corroborated by the survival of traditions in other parts of the Sicilian kingdom than Naples. In modern

Sicilian folk-tales William the Good is introduced, not surprisingly, as the founder of Monreale Cathedral, as a king guided to build his great abbey by a beatific vision: *mentri iddu era a caccia a Murriali cci fa veniri un gran sonnu e lu fici addurmisciri sutta un pedi di carrubba. Mentri dormi, si 'nsunnau a la Madonna,* ("while he was hunting at Monreale a great sleep came over him and he laid himself down to rest under a carob tree. While he slept the Madonna appeared to him"). He was guided to a treasure which he used to finance his new foundation (Pitrè 1875:35). The link between treasure and the crown is a common one in the modern legends of the Norman kings. William the Bad was accused of withdrawing gold coinage from circulation, out of greed, and replacing it by leather tokens; to test whether his edict had been obeyed, the king or his emissary went in disguise to the market, and sold a horse for money. He was paid in gold, not leather money; on asking the explanation, he was told that the gold came from the tombs of the dead – there was no other source. So he went away convinced that no living man had gold of his own (Pitrè 1875:23–34, for this and variants.) On the island of Malta, an integral part of the Norman realm from 1127, stories were told of Count Roger's invasion in 1090. The event itself was much exaggerated in significance – it became the moment of Christian liberation, when very likely it was rather less. But elements of truth there were. Unfortunately there is no guarantee that these legends, as opposed to their subject-matter, date back very far; they could have as many roots in the excited fantasies of such scholars as Fazello and Abela as in genuinely medieval folk-tales (Cassar Pullicino 1975: 96–103). By contrast, the tale of Gerbino can be regarded as an example of the legends that actually did circulate in the middle ages about the Norman kings, at least in polite Neapolitan circles. Can anything further be recovered of these legends from other sources?

The French romances of the late twelfth and thirteenth centuries sometimes mention Sicily and Apulia, and it has been argued that they draw on Sicilian or south Italian legends (Dunn 1960). The Arthurian tale of *Floriant and Florete*, composed in the mid-thirteenth century, places much of its action in Palermo, Monreale and at Mongibel, that is, Etna. But its geography is often weird: the island of Cyprus is placed between Naples and Rome (Williams 1947:6721–63; also Williams 1954: 85–92). Arguably this represents a confusion between Cyprus and Capri; but it is a confusion nonetheless. As H. A. Williams remarked, "one can hardly say that *Floriant* reflects current events. There is in the poem no hint or mention of specific occurrences" (1947:35). King Arthur was, however, popular in the south of Italy as early as the twelfth century, making a guest appearance in the mosaics of Otranto Cathedral. The exact relationship between *matière de Bretagne* and Sicily is hard to elucidate; it may be that Arthurian legends were brought south by the conquering Normans (McKeehan 1926:785–809, also Schlauch 1923; Jamison 1945). The popularity of Roland and Charlemagne, for all the evidence of Sicilian painted carts and puppet shows, cannot with certainty be dated to the middle ages, nor even to Ariosto. Here it was rather Spain and its traditions that acted on the imagination of the Sicilians.

Although the most famous medieval romantic cycles cannot be securely linked to Sicily, good claims can be made for the story of Guillaume de Palerne, or William of lermo. This romance first appeared in ench in about 1200 and enjoyed great pularity; it was translated into English and o Irish too (Michelant 1876; Skeat 1867; Rahilly 1949). It was originally prepared Countess Yolande of Hainaut, whose sband Hugh de St Pol possibly visited cily when he accompanied the French king crusade to the Holy Land; and the story ls of the son of a king of Sicily who was ved by a werewolf from assassination, and as reared as a foundling at the court of the oman emperor. Later Guillaume recovered s rights in Sicily and even gained the im-rial crown; while his wolf friend was re-aled to be a Spanish prince, evilly bewitched t of his own inheritance. The real parallels the tale are with folklore motifs rather than ith historical events, but arguments have een presented for the latter too (Dunn 960:123–31; also McKeehan 1926:785–09). It is true that King William III of icily was dispossessed of his throne, but under ery different circumstances to those des-ribed in the French romance; the use by the uthor of the name *Guillaume* need show no nore than a passing awareness of Norman dynastic history. It has also been argued that he author of *Guillaume de Palerne* presents icily as a tolerant 'multi-racial' society; thus figure appears called *Paien* (Dunn 1960:71). This was in fact an entirely neutral Christian name used in much of medieval Europe. More convincing is the evidence that the author knew the topography, if not the history, of Sicily very well – his description of the royal palace at Palermo does, for in-stance, seem based on reality. He may there-fore have accompanied the count of St Pol to the east, or have talked with him on the crusaders' return. In the end, however, such

an approach to *Guillaume* or to *Floriant* fails to detect the most patent motive for introducing Sicilian references into the French romances; the interest lies in the description of an exotic world to the South rather than in vague attempts to provide a recognisable historical and geographical framework. Moreover, the existence of a real setting for fabulous events should not be confused with the case of the tale of Gerbino, where real events provide material for fanciful elaboration on the theme of love that turns to disaster.

Boccaccio's Sicily is not the strange and re-mote world of the French romancers; it is not the closed, non-Italian, world of the Maltese storytellers. In the fourteenth century Naples and Sicily were entering the cultural milieu of France and Tuscany, prompted by Angevin lords, Florentine merchants and others; linguistically and economically, too, Naples and Sicily were more closely tied to the rest of Italy than they had ever perhaps been. Boccaccio's career, and his tale of Gerbino, are notable witnesses to the process by which the history and culture of southern Italy and Sicily became fused with that of the rest of the peninsula and of Europe.

Notes

* I should like to thank, for their comments on the literary side of this article, Stephen Bemrose, Françoise Bayliss-Smith, Victoria Rothschild, Ruth Morgan and Barry Windeatt.

[1] This article was written following the appearance of Gasparini (1974), a discussion of Neapolitan themes in the *Decameron* which fails to notice the significance of King William the Good; I have not been able to find C. Trasselli, *Le novelle siciliane del Decamerone*. Sicilia Regione. 23 gennaio 1953, the report of which by V. Branca (*Decameron* 1960a:504) is unclear. For Boccaccio's career in Naples, Léonard 1944 is now out of date; see rather Branca 1967:13–53.

V

[2] Davidsohn 1924:409–34. It is necessary to agree with Léonard (1954:293) that entry into the highest social circles was easy for Florentine bankers; thus there is good reason to suppose that the author of the *Decameron* played a part, however small, in the picnics and revels of the Neapolitan nobility, as well as being a keen member of any story-telling circle. For Nicola Acciaiuoli, see especially Léonard 1937; I am hoping to prepare an account of his business affairs myself.
[3] Abulafia 1977:5. The Naples archives, with the incomparable Angevin registers, were very largely destroyed by the Germans in 1943; some indication of relevant material can be gained from Davidsohn (1924) and Yver (1903). Work proceeds on the reconstitution of the registers from publications and transcriptions, but much is irreparably lost.
[4] William II has long been denied his biographer; La Lumia (1867) is no longer satisfactory; see Chalandon 1907b:305–426.

Literature

Abulafia, D. S. H. 1973. L'attività commerciale genovese nell' Africa normanna: la città di Tripoli. Atti del congresso internazionale di studi sulla Sicilia normanna: 395–402. Palermo.

Abulafia, D. S. H. 1977. The Two Italies: economic relations between the Norman kingdom of Sicily and the northern communes. Cambridge.

Abulafia, D. S. H. 1978. Pisan commercial colonies and consulates in twelfth-century Sicily. English historical review 93:68–81.

Amari, M. 1880–1. Biblioteca arabo-sicula, versione italiana. Folio edition. Roma.

Amari, M. 1938. Storia dei musulmani di Sicilia. Second edition, 3.2. Catania.

Billanovich, G. 1953. Il Petrarca, il Boccaccio, Zanobi da Strada e le tradizioni dei testi della *Cronaca* di Ugo Falcando e di alcune *Vite* di Pontefici. Rinascimento 4.

Boccaccio, G. 1520. De casibus illustrium virorum. Paris. See also Hall 1962.

Boccaccio, G. 1539. De claribus mulieribus. Bern. Also G. Guarino (transl.) 1963. Concerning famous women. New Brunswick.

Boccaccio, G. 1544. De casibus illustrium virorum. Augsburg.

Branca, V. (ed.) 1967. Tutte le opere di Giovanni Boccaccio, 1. Verona.

Branca, V. 1970. Boccaccio medievale. Third edition. Verona.

Cassar Pullicino, J. 1975. Norman legends in Malt: Medieval Malta: studies on Malta before th knights. Ed. A. T. Luttrell. London.

Chalandon, F. 1907a and b. Histoire de la dominatic normande en Italie et en Sicile. 2 vols. Paris.

Conrad, H., T. von der Lieck-Buyken and W. Wagn (eds.) 1974. Die Konstitutionen Friedrichs I Studien und Quellen zur Welt Kaiser Friedrichs I Köln.

Croce, B. 1919. La Novella di Andreuccio da Perugi Storie e leggende napoletane: 47–83. Bari.

Davidsohn, R. 1924. Geschichte von Florenz 4.: Berlin.

Decameron, by G. Boccaccio. V. Branca (ed.) 196(and b. Decameron. Second edition, 2 vols. Florenc

Dilcher, H. 1975. Die sizilische Gesetzgebung Kais Friedrichs II. Studien und Quellen zur We Kaiser Friedrichs II. Köln.

Dunn, C. W. 1960. The foundling and the werewolf: literary-historical study of Guillaume de Palern Toronto.

Gasparini, L. 1974. Echi di vita napoletana n Decamerone di Boccaccio. Napoli.

Guessard, F. and C. Grandmaison (eds.) 1860. Huc de Bordeaux, chanson de geste. Les anciens poètes (la France. Paris.

Hall, L. B. (ed.) 1962. De casibus illustrium virorur by G. Boccaccio. Facsimile of 1520 Paris editio with introduction. Gainesville, Florida.

Howlett, R. 1889. The Chronicle of Robert of Torigr abbot of the monastery of St Michael-in-peril-of-th sea. Chronicles of the reigns of Stephen, Henry I and Richard I. RS. London.

Jamison, E. M. 1945. The alliance of England ar Sicily in the second half of the twelfth century. Iı England and the Mediterranean tradition, studi in art, history and literature:20–32. London.

Jamison, E. M. 1972. Catalogus baronum. Fonti p la storia d'Italia. Roma.

Kantorowicz, E. H. 1931. Frederick the Secon 1194–1250. London.

La Lumia, I. 1867. Storia della Sicilia sotto Guglieln il Buono. Firenze.

Landau, M. 1869. Die Quellen des Decameron. Wie

Lee, A. C. 1909. The Decameron. Its sources ar analogues. London.

Léonard, E. G. 1937. Histoire de Jeanne Ier, 3. I Règne de Louis de Tarente. Monaco.

Léonard, E. G. 1944. Boccace et Naples. Paris.

Léonard, E. G. 1954. Les Angevins de Naplo Paris.

Luzzati, M. 1971. Giovanni Villani e la compagnia d Buonaccorsi. Roma.

eehan, I. P. 1926. Guillaume de Palerne: a
·dieval 'best seller'. Publications of the Modern
nguages Association of America 41:785–809.

czek, W. 1971. Ein unbekannter Brief König
os II. von Armenien an Papst Innocenz III.
϶mische historische Mitteilungen 13:13–25.

ni, D. M. 1742. Istoria del Decamerone di
₋ovanni Boccaccio. Firenze.

Latrie, L. de. 1866. Traités de paix et de com-
·erce et documents divers concernant les relations
·s Chrétiens avec les arabes de l'Afrique septen-
ionale au moyen âge. Paris.

·helant, H. (ed.) 1876. Guillaume de Palerne.
϶ciété des Anciens Textes Français. Paris.

·ella di Cerbino, 1863. Novella di Cerbino in
·tava rima di un anonimo antico. Scelta di
ıriosità letterarie inedite o rare del sec. XIII al
ϹIX, 25. Anonymous editor. Bologna.

·ahilly, C. (ed.) 1949. Eachtra Uilliam: an Irish
·ersion of William of Palerne. With translation.
Ϸublin.

·adiso. Dante Alighieri, Divina Commedia, ed. F.
Ϲhiappelli. 1965. Milano.

·sano, G. 1868. I novellieri italiani in verso indicati
descritti. Bologna.

·rè, G. (ed.) 1875. Fiabe, novelle e racconti popolari
iciliani, 4. Biblioteca delle tradizioni popolari
iciliane, 7. Palermo.

Re, G. (ed.) 1845. Cronisti e scrittori sincroni
·apoletani editi ed inediti, 1. Normanni. Napoli.

·aglione, A. D. 1973. Boccaccio, Chaucer and the
·mercantile ethic. In: The mediaeval world, ed. D.
·Daiches and A. Thorlby. Literature and western
·civilization 2:579–600. London.

·hlauch, M. 1923. Literary exchange between
Angevin England and Sicily. Romanic review
14:168–88.

·eat, W. (ed.) 1867. The Romance of William of
Palerne, otherwise known as William and the
Werwolf. Early English Text Society, extra series, 1.
London.

·rasselli, C. 1956. Nuovi documenti sui Peruzzi, Bardi
e Acciaiuoli in Sicilia. Economia e storia 3:179–95.

·/att, W. M. 1965. A History of Islamic Spain.
Edinburgh.

·/ieruszowski, H. 1962. The Norman kingdom of
Sicily and the crusades. In: A history of the crusades,
ed. K. M. Setton, 2:3–42. Philadelphia.

·Villiams, H. A. (ed.) 1947. Floriant et Florete.
University of Michigan publications, language and
literature, 23. Ann Arbor.

·Villiams, H. A. 1954. La Sicile et l'Italie méridionale
dans la littérature française au moyen âge. Bollettino del Centro di Studi Filologici e Linguistici
Siciliani 2:85–92.

Yver, G. 1903. Le commerce et les marchands dans
l'Italie méridionale au XIIIe et au XIVe siècle.
Paris.

Pisan commercial colonies and consulates in twelfth-century Sicily

IT is of some importance to know when the north Italian maritime communes began to establish permanent overseas agencies in Mediterranean ports. In the first place, it indicates where the commercial activity of the north Italian towns was most densely concentrated; and, in the second place, the major centres of Italian trade overseas themselves acted as bases from which Pisans, Genoese and Venetians ranged outwards to secondary destinations. A small number of primary focal points provided the north Italians with centres from which they could expand their trade into regions less readily accessible from the mother-city in northern Italy. Thus the merchants resident in Acre or Constantinople did not merely act as linkmen between northern Italy and middle eastern sources of supply, but they traded in their own right with ports in Anatolia and, when possible, in the Black Sea region. The north Italian colonies were not simply depots or way-stations; they were to a high degree self-sufficient economic units, full use of which was reserved to the citizens of an individual north Italian city and its dependencies or close allies.

The crystallization of these communities of merchants into units with their own permanent institutions was clearly an important moment in their development. The first institution of which there is normally a record is the church of the alien merchants; indeed Vsevolod Slessarev has suggested that up to the twelfth century churches functioned as warehouses, community halls, and of course as foci for a feeling of the special identity of particular groups of foreign merchants trading far from home.[1] Institutionally, a more important development is perhaps the appearance of commercial consuls appointed to oversee the welfare of a particular group of merchants, such as those from Genoa or Pisa or Venice. Such officers seem to have appeared in at least one overseas colony of north Italian merchants by 1189; there is no evidence how they were appointed, nor exactly who was appointed, and it is unclear whether they acted not merely as consular officials in the modern sense, but also as permanent ambassadors, as *ad hoc* officials able to present a

---

1. V. Slessarev, '*Ecclesiae Mercatorum* and the rise of Merchant Colonies', *Business History Review*, xli (1967), 177–97. For Genoese trade from overseas bases to more distant destinations, see G. I. Bratianu, *Recherches sur le commerce des Génois dans la mer Noire au XIIIe siècle* (Paris, 1929). Continuing work by M. Balard and G. Pistarino is illuminating the role of Pera, opposite Constantinople, and Caffa, in the Crimea, as centres of Genoese trade.

case at the royal or other courts. Intrinsically the second is likely to have been one of their functions; agents limited to the latter functions already existed in twelfth-century Africa, appointed by the Norman counts of Sicily, and they seem to have been the count's financial representatives rather than simply superintendents of the Sicilian merchants trading in north Africa.[1] A further possible function is a judicial one. In some Mediterranean kingdoms, north Italian merchants were obliged, as far as can be seen, to use the local courts; the Kingdom of Jerusalem provides an exceptional case in which Italian merchants were permitted courts of their own. But in Sicily north Italian consuls cannot have been concerned with anything more than the most petty disputes; major civil actions would be reserved for treatment back home in Pisa, Genoa or Venice, and criminal actions were placed under tight control by Roger II and his heirs.[2]

Norman Sicily in many ways provides the ideal starting-point for an investigation of overseas colonies of north Italian merchants. Given Norman control in Apulia as well as Sicily proper, neither Venetians nor Pisans nor Genoese could easily by-pass the kingdom of Sicily on the way to the east Mediterranean – a point made even more clearly after the ephemeral conquest of several African towns by Roger II, and after the repeated attempts of the Norman rulers to exercise some type of control in Dalmatia.[3] But Sicily did not simply impose itself on the north Italians. Its markets were full, its coinage stable, its wheat desirable; and the Sicilian navy was sufficiently strong to make a reality of royal promises to protect alien merchants. On the eve of the creation of the Kingdom of Sicily, Duke Roger II had expressly included merchants and other foreigners in his declaration of a land-peace throughout his realms; such pacific treatment could, it is true, be selective, as the Pisans were very soon to discover.[4] The peacefulness and productivity of

1. H. Wieruszowski, 'The Norman kingdom of Sicily and the Crusades', in her collection of essays, *Politics and Culture in Medieval Spain and Italy* (Rome, 1972), p. 23.

2. For the Kingdom of Jerusalem, J. Riley-Smith, 'Government in Latin Syria and the Commercial Privileges of Foreign Merchants', in D. Baker, ed., *Relations between East and West in the Middle Ages* (Edinburgh, 1973), pp. 109–32. Judicial powers over merchants in Pisa were exercised by *consules mercatorum*, whose office seems to have emerged from that of the *provisores*, officers with charge over actions brought by foreigners. See W. Heywood, *A History of Pisa, eleventh and twelfth centuries* (Cambridge, 1921), pp. 250–1, dating the creation of the *consules mercatorum* to the last quarter of the twelfth century. These *consules*, resident in Pisa, should not be confused with the consular officials described in this article, resident in Messina.

3. David Abulafia, 'L'Attività commerciale genovese nell'Africa normanna', *Atti del Congresso internazionale di studi sulla Sicilia normanna* (Palermo, 1973), pp. 395–402; David Abulafia, 'Dalmatian Ragusa and the Norman Kingdom of Sicily', *Slavonic and East European Review*, liv (1976), pp. 412–28.

4. E. M. Jamison, 'The Norman Administration of Apulia and Capua, more especially under Roger II and William I', *Papers of the British School at Rome*, vi (1913), 237–43, for the peace of Melfi (1129). For Pisan misfortunes, *cf. infra*. For the activities of the north Italian merchants in Sicily and southern Italy, see David Abulafia, *The Two Italies*:

Sicily and southern Italy encouraged the north Italians to make Messina and Palermo their bases from which to trade with north African, Spanish and, above all, eastern ports. Messina seems to have experienced rapid growth, and from 1116 there are signs of a large Genoese community there. That year Count Roger II conferred a privilege on Ogerio, κcύνσολος γένϲυας, and his brother Amico. In recognition of their past loyalty to him, Roger granted them a piece of waste-ground beyond the castle of Messina, ten cubits broad, stretching down to the beach. Here they were to rebuild an older ὁσπίτιον, a merchant hostel or sailors' rest; whether this means the enlargement of an existing building bordering on the waste-land, or a totally new building, is unclear. Ogerio and Amico were also to receive a pound of gold each per annum and freedom from the κομέρκιον up to a value of sixty ounces of gold, on exports and imports through Messina.[1] The κομέρκιϲν was probably at this stage a 10 per cent *ad valorem* tax, analogous to the Byzantine tax of the same name. It has often been assumed that this privilege was a grant to the whole Genoese community, under a resident consul who controlled the affairs of the Genoese in Messina. In that case, this would be the earliest evidence for the existence of a north Italian commercial consulate.[2] But all the signs are that this is in fact a personal favour granted to Amico, Ogerio and their own nominees. For Ogerio was not resident head of the Genoese community in Messina. He was almost certainly Ogerius Capra, consul of the commune of Genoa from 1114 to 1118; that is, he was a governing consul of the newly formed Genoese aristocratic commune.[3] It seems, too, from a document of 1127, that he had long-standing Sicilian interests. He appears as witness to an agreement drawn up between Roger II and the commune of Savona, in which the Genoese were involved as a third party; he seems to have been called in as an expert in Sicilian matters, though he was no longer consul of his home-city.[4] But dismissal of the idea of a commercial consulate does not involve dismissal of the evidence that there existed a Genoese hospice at Messina, and that its need for space

economic relations between the Norman Kingdom of Sicily and the northern communes (Cambridge, 1977).

1. The surviving Greek text of the grant was printed by S. Cusa, *I diplomi greci e arabi di Sicilia*, 2 vols. (Palermo, 1860–82), i. 359; *cf.* Abulafia, *The Two Italies*, pp. 62–4.

2. W. Heyd, *Histoire du Commerce du Levant*, 2 vols. (Leipzig, 1885–6), i. 182 n. and 123; E. Caspar, *Roger II. und die Gründung des normannisch-sicilischen Monarchie* (Innsbruck, 1904), p. 54.

3. A. Olivieri, 'Serie dei consoli del comune di Genova', *Atti della Società Ligure di Storia Patria*, i (1858), 233. *Cf.* A. Schaube, *Handelsgeschichte der Romanischen Völker des Mittelmeergebiets bis zum Ende der Kreuzzüge* (Munich–Berlin, 1906), pp. 464–5 n. He was consul again in 1123 – Olivieri, p. 240.

4. My own identification, from the original text of this diploma, A[rchivio di] S[tato,] S[avona], Registro a catena piccolo, fo. 6ʳ. The text given by G. Filippi, 'Patto di pace tra Ruggiero II Normanno e la Città di Savona', *Archivio storico per le provincie napoletane*, xiv (1889), 757, is defective.

was growing. With the conquest of the Holy Land, the quantity of Genoese ships travelling through Messina grew greatly; and Ogerio's friendship with Roger II suggests that Genoese trade in Sicily itself was also burgeoning. Acquisition of urban property continued. By 1194 the Genoese in Messina had a *fundicum* or warehouse, named after St John; and they were granted a palace there by Margarito of Brindisi, last Norman Admiral of the Fleet.[1] Evidence from the surviving Genoese commercial contracts confirms that trade in Sicily played a significant role in Genoese maritime commerce as a whole; and Sicily, like other centres of Genoese trade, was favoured with increasingly hefty investments of funds as capital reserves in Genoa rose to record heights.

The Venetians also had property in Sicily and southern Italy. The surviving church of St Mark in Bari may have been theirs; and in 1144 King Roger II granted them permission to rebuild an old Greek church in Palermo, as focus of the Venetian community there. Little is known about the importance of Palermo in Venetian trade; no commercial contracts from the twelfth century mention Palermo by name, though several refer to Messina. Whatever the scale of Venetian trade in Palermo, the community around the church of St Mark was a flourishing one. The permanence of the Venetian community in Palermo is suggested by the fact that Venetians were buried in Palermo at their own wish, in the cemetery of St Mark. From Palermo Venetian merchants ranged to Dalmatia and Gerba in north Africa, treating Palermo as their base and not Venice itself.[2] Though undoubtedly much smaller than the Venetian settlement in Constantinople, the Palermo colony shows the same tendency to act as a self-sufficient economic unit, open, it is true, to all Venetians, but with its own inner community of life members. The Norman kings welcomed the Venetians to Palermo, except during the period of their alliance with Manuel Komnenos in the late 1140s. Apart from Roger II's grant of the right to build a church, it is known that Roger II conferred on the Venetians the right to reduced payment of certain taxes, as did his successor William I. In 1175 William II halved the taxes Venetians were expected to

1. L. T. Belgrano, ed., *Annali Genovesi di Caffaro e de' suoi continuatori*, 5 vols. (Rome, 1890–1929), ii. 48 and n., 81 n., 132, 171; J. Huillard-Bréholles, *Historia diplomatica Frederici Secundi*, 5 vols. (Paris, 1859–61), i, i. 65. An analysis of Genoese trade, based on the evidence of the surviving commercial contracts, is provided in my book *The Two Italies, passim*.

2. F. Carabellese, *Bari* (Bergamo, 1909), pp. 85–86, identifies the Romanesque church of San Marco with the Venetian community, and provides illustrations. Charters relating to the Venetian community in Palermo were printed by C. A. Garufi, *I Documenti inediti dell'epoca normanna in Sicilia* (*Documenti per servire alla storia di Sicilia*, ser. 1, xviii, Palermo, 1899), §18 (Roger II's grant), §39, §60, §86; and T. Toeche, *Heinrich VI*. (*Jahrbücher der deutschen Geschichte*, Leipzig, 1867), p. 630 (Henry's confirmation of Roger's grant, 1197). For trade in Messina, the evidence of the commercial contracts is available in A. Lombardo, R. Morozzo della Rocca, eds., *Documenti del commercio veneziano nei secoli XI–XIII*, 2 vols. (Rome–Turin, 1940), i. §278–9, *etc*.

pay in Messina, Palermo and the rest of the island, but his charter of privilege gives no further details.[1] Genoa too benefited from special tax rights in 1156 and 1174, and here again it is Messina and Palermo that are given closest attention in the charter of privilege granted by the Norman ruler.[2]

In Messina, Pisans and Genoese had been at each other's throats as early as 1129; the Pisans secured something of a moral victory, since the townsmen of Messina supported them against the Genoese. But Duke Roger's intervention calmed the crisis.[3] In the 1130s the Pisans gave active support to Emperor Lothar's invasion of Norman Italy, but in 1137 they sailed away in high dudgeon when the German emperor refused them permission to pillage the wealthy city of Salerno which the Pisans and Germans had captured. A further reason for the quarrel with Lothar was the decision by Roger of Sicily to confiscate Pisan goods and money in Sicily; the Pisans had apparently continued to trade there while allied to Roger's mortal enemy Lothar.[4] Roger was no doubt happy to see the Pisans continue to arrive, not merely so that he could draw taxes from them, but so that he could hold a whole community hostage at a suitable moment in his war with Lothar. Confiscation of Pisan goods encouraged the Pisans to make their peace with Roger, but there are no signs the Pisans were granted tax exemptions as were other north Italians; the price the Pisans paid for being imperial allies was not exclusion from Sicilian markets, but higher, or rather normal, taxes, as compared to the taxes paid by the Venetians and Genoese. It seems likely that, had special privileges been conferred, the *Annales Pisani* would have mentioned this; and it is striking that the excellently preserved set of treaties in the Pisan archives contains no privilege granted by a Norman king of Sicily.

Others, however, with a claim to rule in Sicily and southern Italy did confer substantial privileges on Pisa. Frederick Barbarossa in 1162 promised the Pisans estates, quarters in cities and complete tax exemption, should they help him conquer the upstart kingdom established in Sicily and southern Italy in imperial lands and against the imperial interest. These promises were renewed verbatim by

1. Privilege of 1175: Archivio di Stato, Venice, Liber Blancus, fos. 272ᵛ–273ᵛ, Liber Pactorum i, fo. 84ᵛ and fo. 76ᵛ. Printed from the inferior Blancus text by G. L. F. Tafel, G. M. Thomas, *Urkunden zur älteren Handels- und Staatsgeschichte der Republik Venedig*, 2 vols. (*Fontes Rerum Austriacum*, sectio II, vol. xii, Vienna, 1856), i. §65; and by A. Zambler, F. Carabellese, *Le Relazioni commerciali fra la Puglia e la Repubblica di Venezia dal sec. X al XV*, 2 vols. (Trani, 1897–8), i. §1. For discussion of the relative merits of the Pactorum and Blancus texts, see my book *The Two Italies*, pp. 29, 143. Manuel Komnenos' alliance with Venice is chronicled by F. Chalandon, *Histoire de la Domination normande en Italie et en Sicile*, 2 vols. (Paris, 1907), ii. 137–45.

2. C. Imperiale di Sant' Angelo, ed., *Codice diplomatico della Repubblica di Genova*, 3 vols. (Rome, 1936–42), i. 338–41.

3. *Annali Genovesi*, i. 24.

4. M. Lupo Gentile, ed., *Gli Annales Pisani di Bernardo Maragone* (*Rerum Italicarum Scriptores*, ser. 2, vol. vi, part 2), p. 12.

Henry VI in 1191. On both occasions similar promises were made to the Genoese; but the promises made to the Pisans were far more generous than those made to the Genoese, whose reluctance to abandon their profitable arrangements with the Norman rulers cost them the fullest favours of the German Crown. The Pisans remained loyal to the principle of an alliance with the Hohenstaufen against the Normans. Yet it is not clear why this should have been so.[1]

In 1167 the Pisans realized that the chances of Barbarossa conquering Sicily had receded for the foreseeable future. They became anxious to re-establish peace with the king of Sicily, though it must be emphasized that their priority was safe access rather than tax-free access to Sicilian markets. In November of that year ambassadors were sent to the Sicilian court, but negotiations broke down, possibly because the Crown refused to settle claims arising from the seizure of Pisan goods at the time of the treaty between Pisa and Frederick.[2] In 1169 the Pisans tried again, sending Gerardo Cortevecchia, who was a consul, with Gerardo Barattule and Guidone Gallo; the king welcomed them and peace was made.[3] The terms are unclear, but at the very least the Pisans now had safe access to supplies of wheat and other raw materials – supplies that must have been especially valuable in the 1170s when Pisa was hit by serious famine.[4] Moreover, the burgeoning Pisan leather industry must have welcomed access to an island rich in hides; the Genoese had already gained preferential access to hides and to cotton in 1156, when William I reduced taxes on the export of these commodities. Pisa even more than Genoa was a centre for the import and processing of leather; for even Venetians came to Pisa for their leather, to judge from the inventory of the possessions of a Venetian merchant who died at Pisa in 1176.[5]

The Genoese archives contain thousands of commercial contracts that date to the twelfth century, bound together in the surviving notarial cartularies; Venice too offers several hundred loose charters, in the form of partnership contracts, loans and quittances. There are no Pisan records on this scale until 1263, the date of the earliest surviving cartularies[6]; but a handful of stray documents exists in the Archivio di Stato at Pisa and in the archive of the Pisan Charterhouse at Calci, bearing witness to active trade in Provence and

1. *Monumenta Germaniae Historica, Legum Sectio IV, Constitutiones et Acta Publica*, i. 282–7 (Pisa), i. 292–5 (Genoa); also *Cod. dipl. Gen.* i. 396–401 (Genoa).

2. *Ann. Pis.* p. 44; Abulafia, *The Two Italies*, p. 139.

3. *Ann. Pis.* p. 49.

4. *Ann. Pis.* pp. 59–60, 64.

5. For Pisan leather, see D. Herlihy, *Pisa in the Early Renaissance* (New Haven, 1958), pp. 134–45. The inventory of 1176 is preserved in the Biblioteca Marciana, Venice, MS. Lat. XIV-71 (coll. 2803), no. 8.

6. R. S. Lopez, 'The unexplored wealth of the Notarial Archives in Pisa and Lucca', *Mélanges Louis Halphen* (Paris, 1951), pp. 417–32, D. Herlihy, *op. cit.* 1–20.

Sardinia.[1] Sicily features more rarely in the Pisan charters; and those charters that mention Sicily differ from the Genoese and Venetian documents in a significant way. They are not commercial contracts, agreements in which one merchant licenses another to act on his behalf in overseas trade, carrying his funds or goods to Sicily or other destinations; rather are they documents that refer to visits to Sicily in the context of current litigation. Thus a document of 1169 survives in which a certain Uguiccio Boccone declares he is *paratus ire in itinere Sicilie* and appoints his relative Raffaione as his executor, commissioning him to sell half a house on his behalf. Uguiccio appears to be one of the Pisan party sent to Sicily in 1169 to negotiate with King William on behalf of the commune; the document is decidedly not a contract for trade overseas. Indeed, this document leaves an impression of 'unfinished business' – Uguiccio has been asked to leave Pisa before he has had time to sell half a house he had been hoping to place on the market; he is being sent south at a moment that is actually inconvenient to himself. Moreover, he is found appointing an agent to do business in Pisa – a reversal of the normal commercial contract, in which a sleeping partner might appoint an agent to do business on his behalf in Sicily or another overseas market. To judge from a later document concerning Uguiccio, he may have been a shipping contractor, who was asked to take the ambassadors south in a vessel he had fitted out, rather than a member of the official negotiating party.[2]

Given the lack of any great series to compare with the Genoese or Venetian trade contracts, the survival of a handful of documents such as that of Uguiccio Boccone cannot be passed by. Uguiccio's document seems to have been preserved because it was one of a series relating to law-suits conducted on behalf of Uguiccio and Raffaione, and provided evidence that Raffaione was Uguiccio's effective heir while Uguiccio was absent abroad. In a judicial act of September 1170 Uguiccio secured judgment against a recalcitrant debtor, so he had obviously returned from Sicily by late summer of 1170. A document of 1171 shows the tables being turned. Raffaione's wife, as representative of Uguiccio, is obliged to make a refund to one of Uguiccio's partners who provided naval equipment for a galley Uguiccio had fitted out, without paying his partner for the items he obtained. Uguiccio and Raffaione are on this occasion absent

1. Sardinia: A[rchivio della] C[ertosa di] C[alci] (near Pisa), 1182 dicembre 4; trade with uncertain destinations: A[rchivio di] S[tato,] P[isa], Diplomatico, Monastero degli Olivetani, 1170 agosto 16 (corta), 1180 ottobre 24 (corta), 1186 luglio 24 (corta). See also F. Artizzu, ed., *Documenti inediti relativi ai rapporti economici tra la Sardegna e Pisa nel Medioevo*, 2 vols. (Padua, 1961–2), i. §1–3. I should like to record my deep gratitude to the Superintendent of Monuments and Galleries for Pisa, who provided every conceivable facility for my visit to Calci, and to the Council of Gonville and Caius College for its donation from the Fellows' Research Expenses fund.

2. See Document I, *infra*. For Uguiccio as a shipping entrepreneur, see ASP, R. Acquisto Coletti, 1172 novembre 23 (corta).

from Pisa, and no doubt the deed of 1169, investing Raffaione as Uguiccio's trustee, was invoked in 1171 so that the case could be brought against Raffaione's wife as trustee for the trustee.[1] From these texts we have an interesting picture of a closely knit commercial and financial partnership between Uguiccio and Raffaione. As far as can be seen, we are dealing among members of the Pisan mercantile middle-class, men active in trade, but not the leaders of Pisan political life.

How great a rag-bag the surviving Pisan documents are is clear from a wide-ranging charter of 1189 that has not so far been fully exploited. Volpe noticed it in a nineteenth-century register of the Pisan documents that were preserved in the archive of the Pisan Charterhouse at Calci; and he seems only to have glanced at the register, since he cited this document in the Italian of the register rather than the Latin of the original.[2] He concentrated his attention, too, on one point: the evidence this text provides for the existence of a Pisan colony in Messina, with resident consuls; and this point was seized upon by later writers who had no ready access to the original, merely to Volpe's slightly cryptic quotation from the register in Italian.[3] Thus nobody noticed that Volpe's date of 9 October 1190 was in two respects erroneous. In the first place we have to make an adjustment for the Pisan dating, to arrive at a date of 9 October 1189 by our reckoning. Secondly, the passage quoted by Volpe was itself cited from an earlier document, this time dated 1190 Pisan-style, *i.e.* 1189, but to 12 September of that year. The original of the earlier charter is lost, but its text is summarized in the charter we have. The document of 12 September 1189 was drawn up *a Corrigia iudice et notario domini imperatoris rogatam apud messanam in hospitio consulum pisanorum messane*, in the presence of Enrico Muscerifa, Guido son of Pagano de Portamaris and Gerardo son of Sigerio. The wording of the 1189 document seems clear on one crucial point: that by 1189 there was a Pisan hospice at Messina as

---

1. ASP, Coletti, 1171 settembre 2 (corta), 1172 novembre 23 (corta), 1174 dicembre 29 (corta).

2. The register is ASP, Carte Lupi, Fonti I, Certosa, pp. 756–7. *Cf.* G. Volpe, *Studi sulle Istituzioni comunali a Pisa. Città e Contado, Consoli e Podestà secoli XII–XIII*, nuova edizione con una introduzione di Cinzio Violante (Florence, 1970), p. 233 n. Violante refers to Volpe's use of the registers rather than the original documents in Volpe, lxii. The eighteenth-century copy of the Certosa material in ASP (Misc. MSS. 67, made by Maggi) ends in 1122 and excludes the document printed below, no. II. An edition of the documents preserved in the Certosa at Calci is in course of publication: Silvio P. P. Scalfati, ed., *Carte dell' Archivio della Certosa di Calci*, ii. (1100–1150), (*Thesaurus Ecclesiarum Italiae*, VII, xviii, Rome, 1971). Vol. i is in course of preparation (*c.* 999–1099). See also C. Violante, 'Notizie sull' edizione delle Carte pisane dei secoli VIII–XII', *Mélanges de l'École Française de Rome, Moyen Âge-Temps Modernes*, lxxxv (1973), pp. 363–79. The late twelfth-century documents from the Certosa are still far from publication, and it has accordingly seemed fair to present a single, highly unusual charter of that period here, where it can be treated in a wider context.

3. P. Nardone, *Genova e Pisa nei loro rapporti commerciali col Mezzogiorno d'Italia* (Prato, 1923), p. 14 n., follows Volpe word for word.

well as the much older Genoese one, and that this hospice was operated by the 'consuls of the Pisans at Messina'. The repetition of the word 'messana' removes any very strong doubt that we have to deal here with resident Pisan consuls, consuls in the sense of overseas agents rather than governing consuls at Pisa itself.

This document provides further evidence that Messina had become a focus of Pisan trade in the Mediterranean, a base from which the Pisans radiated to other foreign ports. In its entirety, the charter stands witness to a complex set of commercial relationships whose existence has already been suggested by earlier Venetian texts concerning Constantinople and Palermo. The charter of 9 October was drawn up in Pisa, apparently the moment the contracting party from Sicily had arrived in the city. It was a statement by Odimundo di San Vito that he had paid Bartolomeo nephew of Pipindone, acting on Pipindone's behalf, 250 north African bezants, against a debt incurred at Montpellier in the form of £50 of Melgueil, received by Odimundo from Pipindone. This transaction was recorded by the notary Johannes scriptor Tortus de Massilia. Subsequently, the charter relates, Pipindone met Odimundo in Messina and arranged that Odimundo should pay Bartolomeo in Pisa, rather than himself in Sicily. This arrangement was recorded in a futher document, that drawn up in the hospice of the Pisan consuls at Messina. The Pisa charter then concludes with the usual description of the penalty that will be incurred if either side deny that payment has in fact been made.[1]

This document thus testifies to the movement of Pisan merchants, for such all the participants seem to be, in a triangle from Pisa to Provence, from Provence to Sicily and from Sicily to Pisa. This need not come as a surprise when compared to the rather older Genoese evidence for such triangular trading expeditions, bringing in Montpellier on the one hand and Sicily on the other.[2] Moreover, the Pisan charter predates by only eleven years the first native Provençal evidence for direct trade between the city of Marseilles and Sicily. It is true that from 1156 the Genoese had tried to persuade the Sicilian kings to exclude Provençal merchants from trade in

---

1. At this point it is worth suggesting how this charter reached the Certosa. The clue lies in the name of Odimundo di San Vito. The Certosa absorbed the property of the Pisan monastery of San Vito on the foundation of the former in 1366, and along with the property it seems to have acquired the San Vito documents. The connection between Odimundo and the monastery is, however, unclear. Possibly he left the monastery money and lands after his death, and this charter crept in alongside, but I have not noticed other references to Odimundo in the Certosa material; there are very few late twelfth-century documents in the Certosa that concern commercial activity, and this charter must be regarded as a stray. Other commercial evidence is in ACC, 1182 dicembre 4 (trade in Sardinia), while several charters refer to trade in Provence: ACC, 1174 luglio 30, 1175 aprile 20, 1175 marzo 14, 1175 marzo 17, 1175 giugno 7, 1175 luglio 11, 1176 marzo 29, 1176 dicembre 16, 1177 aprile 30.

2. For this, see Abulafia, *The Two Italies*, p. 229; cf. p. 268.

their kingdom, in the hope of channelling such trade through Genoa itself. But this did not mean that Genoese failed to trade between Provence and Sicily, nor that Provençaux failed to make use of Genoa as an intermediary between Sicily and their home-town. There are signs, however, that the Pisans connived with the merchants of Provence to carry their goods and even personnel to Sicily and far beyond to Syria.[1] There is thus no reason to take seriously the idea that Sicilian trade directly with Provence was restricted by Genoese interference, let alone by Provençal inactivity. As for the appearance of north African or Spanish gold in the deal between Odimundo and Bartolomeo, this can be explained in a number of ways. Such coins were probably available quite readily in Sicily itself, but it is no less possible that Odimundo visited Spain or the Maghrib at some stage in his trade tour. Once again, this would not have been an unusual fact. Documents from Savona from the early thirteenth century show ships sailing via Spain and North Africa to Sicily, often letting economic opportunity fill their sails and direct their rudder.[2] More attractive, perhaps, is the idea that the Sicilian kings restricted the export of their own coins, the remarkably stable gold tari, for there are very few signs of tari leaving Sicily for Genoa at this period; they are regularly kept on deposit in Sicily, for future use there. Thus the Pisans too may have found the best way to extract funds from Sicily was to convert their Sicilian gold into non-Sicilian coins that could without difficulty be exported. By analogy, the earliest commercial contract to survive from Marseilles shows two merchants in Messina receiving from two others the sum of $53\frac{1}{3}$ ounces of tari, and promising to repay their creditors in money of Marseilles once all four were in Provence again.[3]

The Pisan evidence for trade bases in Messina is strengthened by a further curious survival, a letter sent from Messina in 1198 by a Pisan merchant resident there, to a colleague in his mother-city. This is a letter from Alberto Celone in Messina to Baratterio Congiario in Pisa, in which Alberto asks Baratterio to pay a certain Villano for an *asbergum* or breastplate that Alberto had earlier sent him through a fourth individual.[4] Pisa was famous as a centre of production of iron goods, and it is possible that the breastplate was not sent from Messina to Pisa, but had been supplied in Pisa itself some time

1. L. Blancard, *Documents inédits sur le commerce de Marseille au Moyen Âge*, 2 vols. (Marseilles, 1884-5), i. 3-5, a letter of exchange drawn up at Messina on 15 Feb. 1200. For Provençal exclusion from long-distance trade, see H. E. Mayer, *Marseilles Levantehandel und ein akkonensisches Fälscheratelier des XIII. Jahrhunderts* (Tübingen, 1972), pp. 61-62.

2. ASS, Cartolare Martinus, fo. 38ʳ: 'ivit Buzeam et de Buzea Tunexim et de Tunice Mexinam'.

3. The idea that exports of tari were perhaps restricted is tentatively advanced; *cf.* my book *The Two Italies*, p. 267. *Cf.* Blancard, *loc. cit.*

4. See Document III *infra*.

before.[1] Whatever the details, Alberto Celone had now decided to foreclose, and was writing to inform Baratterio that his debt-collector was about to descend on him; there is a striking contrast between the almost unctuous charm of the early sentences, where Alberto protests his deep friendship for the debtor, and the dire threats of legal action that fill much of the letter. Whether Alberto received his due is unknown, but the survival of the letter of 1198 among the Pisan archives, composed almost entirely of public documents, implies that the letter was 'cited in evidence' in judicial proceedings. And the very fact that Alberto has decided to act through agents – one who brought the *asbergum* to Baratterio, one to claim repayment and, no doubt, a third to bring the letter to Pisa – suggests how permanent was his base in Messina. Alberto belongs to that elusive group of Pisan merchants resident overseas, whose names can only rarely be glimpsed alongside those of Venetians and Genoese in Sicily, Syria and Byzantium. Others there are too in Messina: Bonaccurso Unguenti has a house there, though he does not actually witness the sending of the letter. The church of S. Pietro in Caniccio seems to be the focus for the Pisan community in Messina.

The urge to establish exclusively Tuscan communities worked several ways. There are signs of fragmentation of the Tuscan merchants into smaller groups representing individual mother-cities. By 1193 there seems to have been a street of the Florentines at Messina; that year, Bartolomeo de Lucy, Count of Paterno, granted the Cistercians 'in rua Florentinorum domum meam soleratam, quae est ante domum Zacchi'.[2] This implies that the whole street was not in Florentine hands; it was not a street exclusive to Florentines, but a street favoured by them. Luccans too became more and more closely interested in Sicilian trade; in partnership with the Genoese, they sent northern woollens to Sicily and developed a sophisticated network of loans and deposits; and in 1197 Henry VI conferred on them and other 'men of Tuscany' the same trade rights in Sicily as the Pisans.[3] Indeed, by the end of the thirteenth century most communities of merchants trading in southern Italy and Sicily had their own consuls and their own bases in the major cities. Pisa was suspect in the eyes of the Angevin conquerors of the *Regno* because of its long-standing sympathy for the Hohenstaufen cause, and the

---

1. Herlihy, pp. 133, 143, 167.

2. R. Pirro, *Sicilia Sacra* (Palermo, 1733), p. 1288.

3. Preserved in a confirmation by Alexander IV: B. de la Roncière, ed., *Les Registres d'Alexandre IV* (*Bibliothèque des Écoles Françaises d'Athènes et de Rome*, Paris, 1902), i. 20–21: 'idem jus quod Pisani in tholoneo per omnes portus regni Sicilie obtinent' as well as 'idem jus ... in introitu et exitu quod habent Pisani.' Whether such rights were activated in the Pisan or Lucchese case is uncertain; the Genoese were unable to obtain from Henry VI confirmation of his promises of lands made in 1191, and the same may have held true for Henry's promises of tax exemptions to the Genoese, Pisans and Lucchesi.

Pisans suffered expulsion in 1267. In the long term it was not Pisans but other Tuscans – Sienese first, Florentines later – who came to dominate the economic life of southern Italy in the late thirteenth century, but the foundations were laid by the north Italian merchants who created the colonies of the Norman period.[1]

Appendix

Document 1
Archivio di Stato, Pisa, R. Acquisto Coletti, 1170 giugno 26 (corta).

In eterni dei nomine Amen. Scriptum pro futuris et modernis tempori-bus, ad memoriam habendam et retinendam, presentia bonorum hominum quorum nomina subtus legimus: Uguicio Boccone paratus ire in itinere Sicilie fecit usque ad suam reversionem in omnibus suis negotiis suum procuratorem Rafaionem cognatum suum, quatinus in omnibus agere et excipere et respondere possit sicut ipse potest. Et insuper dedit ei pote-statem vendendi medietatem domus sue, et possessionem inde tradendi et pretium recipiendi, et solvendi debita sua, et addidit atque ordinavit, ut si obierit sine alia legitima dispositione antequam reverteretur, habeat ipse Rafaione omnia bona sua tam mobilia quam immobilia, ad retinendum et dandum pro anima sua secundum quod ei placuerit. Et in tali ordine hec scribere rogavit me Uguicionem Notarium sacri palatii. Actum Pisis, in domo mea predicti Uguicionis. Presentia Amici quondam Amici, et Gualfredi quondam Lamfredi, atque Gratiani de Arcoata filii Alberti, qui ad hec interfuere rogati testes. Dominice incarnationis anno Millesimo Centesimo Septuagesimo, sexto kalendas Julii. Indictione secunda.

Ego Uguicio Notarius sacri Lateranensi palatii, hec rogatu istius Uguicionis Bocconis scripsi et complevi et dedi.

Document 11
Archivio della Certosa di Calci, 1190 ottobre 9.

In nomine dei eterni amen. Ex huius publici instrumenti serie omnibus clareat. Qua coram testibus subnotatis Odimunaus de sancto vito quondam Guidonis reddidit et solvit et dedit Bartholomeo nepoti Pipindonis filio quondam Baldicionis pro eodem Pipindone recipienti Bizanthios ducentos quinquaginta massemutinos aureos novos recti ponderis, quos de libris quinquaginta merguliensium et ramundigorum metadingis datis suis sibi Odimundo apud Montem Pessulanum ab eodem Pipindone in compagnia in emtica sua, renuntiavit et per breve ei dicendo misit, se habere inter capitale et lucrum. De qua societate Johannes scriptor tortus de massilia scriptum fecit. Et hos omnes Bizanthios ducentos quinquaginta eidem Bartholomeo pro suprascripto

---

1. For the late thirteenth and fourteenth centuries see G. Yver, *Le Commerce et les marchands dans l'Italie méridionale au XIIIe et au XIVe siècle* (Paris, 1903), especially pp. 228–9 (expulsion of the Pisans and subsequent return). Cf. also A. B. Hibbert, 'Catalan Consulates in the Thirteenth Century', *Camb. Hist. Journal*, ix (1949), 352–8.

Pipindone dedit, ex mandato quod ipse Pipindonus dedit ipsi Bartholomeo de ipsis ab eodem Odimundo petendis et recolligendis per cartam scriptam a Corrigia judice et notario domini imperatoris rogatam apud Messanam in hospitio consulum pisanorum Messane. Presentibus Henrico Muscerifa, et Guidone quondam Pagani de porta maris, et Gerardo quondam Sigerii, testibus ad ea rogatis. Anno dominice incarnationis Millesimo Centesimo Nonagesimo. Indictione septima. Pridie Idus septembris. Sicut in ipsa carta continetur. Et ipse Bartholomeus ex eo mandato et pro eo mandato predictos Bizanthios ducentos quinquaginta massemutinos aureos novos recti ponderis ab ipso Odimundo suscepit pro suprascripto Pipindone. Et cum suscepisset, promisit eidem Odimundo sub pena dupli stipulatione sollempni, quod predictus Pipindone hanc dationem et solutionem ab eo sibi pro ipso Pipindone factam, et susceptionem eorum a se factam, ratas et firmas semper habebit, et quod siquam ab eo de eis vel de suprascriptis libris quinquaginta metadingis habuerit brigam vel molestiam ipse Odimundus vel suus heres, suis expensis eum et heredes eius inter-disbrigabit et indempnes conservabit. Actum Pisis, in domo Guardie sancti viti. Presentibus Ughuicione quondam Carelli, et Fornario quondam Henrici, et Manfredo quondam Musche, rogatis testibus. Dominice vero Incarnationis anno Millesimo Centesimo Nonagesimo. Indictione octavo. Septimo Idus octubris.

Ego Ughicio nepos Gallici Judex et notarius domini imperatoris, prefatis interfui, et hac cartam rogatus a suprascriptis Odimundo et Bartholomeo inscripsi.

Verso: in faint hand:

Solutio Bizanthiorum ccl. massumutinorum novorum [*gap*] quam Odimundus de sancto vito fecit Bartholomeo pro pipindono.

Document III

Archivio di Stato, Pisa, R. Acquisto Roncioni 1199 marzo (corta).

In nomine eterni domini amen. Suo dilecto et amabili amico Baratterio Congiario plurimum diligendo. Albertus quondam Melonis de quiesa eius amicus intimus. Salutem et amoris plenitudinem. In vestra namque mente et memoria firmum constare credo qualiter vedere misi per Simundum Castaldi unum asbergum, cuius rei causa amicitiam vestram incessanter deprecor quatenus suprascriptum asbergum vel pretium dicti asbergi omni occasione post posita Villano quondam Johannis Barum latorem mea parabola atque mandato detis et persolvatis. Et totum illud et quicquid ullatenus inter ei dederitis tamquam interdatum et solutum inputabo et vos omnino liberum et quietum vocabo. Et si taliter omnia predicta ei dare nolueritis ut dictum est do eidem Villano plenam et liberam potestatem atque irrevocabile mandatum a vobis prefatum asbergum vel pretium dicti asbergi petendi et exigendi, et experiendi in curia et extra. Ad que omnia facienda ipsum Villanum meum certum nuntium facio et constituo, et procuratorem in rem suam. Insuper autem promitto ei presenti per sollempnem stipulationem ad penam dupli dicti asbergi quod totum illud et quicquid ullatenus ipse inter vobiscum fecerit se ut per firmum et ratum habebo et tenebo et contra non veniam per me nec per alium. Anno dominice Incarnationis Millesimo Centesimo

Nonagesimo nono. Indictione secunda. Septimodecimo kalendas aprilis. Et in tali ordine hec Rainerium quondam Bruni domini Imperatoris Henrici Judicem et notarium rogavit scribere. Actum Messane in domo Bonaccursi Unguenti et consortum, prope ecclesia sancti petri in caniccio. Presentibus Bonavincta quondam Ugonis et Benenato filio Rainonis, et Petro quondam Bernardi testibus ad hec rogatis:

Ego Rainerius quondam Bruni domini Imperatoris Henrici serenissimi Romanorum judex et notarius hec rogatus scripsi atque firmando complevi.

VII

A TYRRHENIAN TRIANGLE:
TUSCANY, SICILY, TUNIS, 1276-1300

There are two ways of seeing the intensive Tuscan penetration of Sicily during the late thirteenth century. Much attention has been paid to the role of Sicily and southern Italy as a source of grain and other primary products to the towns of northern and central Italy; the close Florentine links with the house of Anjou, and the massive exports of Sicilian grain to Pisa, Florence and other Tuscan towns, are easily identifiable in the sources [1]. Less attention has been paid to another form this penetration took: the management by Pisans and Florentines of the trade routes not merely between Sicily and their home territory, but between Sicily and other corners of the Mediterranean, most notably the coast of north Africa. It would be wrong to dismiss these activities as an undeveloped carrying-trade, out of which would eventually grow a more 'sophisticated' network — a veritable spider's web — centred on the mother-cities in Tuscany. In part this view may carry some weight, but the appearance of subsidiary trading networks whose hub lay not in Tuscany but across the sea can also be cited as evidence for highly developed trading activities, for a Tuscan take-over of the very corners of the Mediterranean. The Genoese of Bonifacio, in Corsica, or of Pera near the Black Sea, provide instances of the creation of flourishing local networks that fed the trade routes to the home city, but that were also flourishing in their own right — independently, it seems, of Genoa's specific demands [2]. A similar case, with important

---

[1] E.G. J. YVER, Le commerce et les marchands dans l'Italie méridionale au XIIIe et XIVe siècles (Paris, 1903); DAVID ABULAFIA, 'Southern Italy and the Florentine economy, 1265-1370', Economic History Review, ser. 2, XXXIII (1981), 377-88; V. D'ALESSANDRO, Politica e società nella Sicilia aragonese (Palermo, 1963).

[2] V. VITALE, 'Documenti sul castello di Bonifacio nel secolo XIII', Atti della Società Ligure di Storia Patria, n.s., i (1936), v (1940); J. HEERS, 'Un exemple de

modifications, can be made for Venice. The Tuscan towns, however, are of special interest. Unlike Genoa and Venice, they did not acquire important tracts of overseas territory — the Pisan defeat in Sardinia ended a long-fought struggle for hegemony on that island. And, whereas Pisa is sometimes regarded as being past its best after Meloria (1284), a new lead was gained by inland towns, especially Florence, whose commercial successes outdistanced those of the Pisans [3].

Pisa's naval defeat did not sap the strength of Tuscan communities overseas. The Tuscan carrying-trade to and from Sicily was manned not only by merchants based in Pisa and the Tuscan cities; a large community of permanent Tuscan settlers developed in the Sicilian towns, maintaining in various degrees links with visitors of common origin. Boccaccio relates in the *Decameron* how three merchants, whose father came from San Gimignano, and who were living in Messina, took into their employment the handsome young Pisan, Lorenzo, only to murder him because of his love for their sister [4]. Sicily was certainly a favoured destination of Sangimignanesi around 1250 and 1300, a base from which to sell their city's prized product of high-grade saffron [5]. The importance of the north Italian settlers in the wider process of the latinisation of Sicily, in its transformation from a Greek and (originally) Muslim land into one well-populated with Italian speakers of the Roman rite, cannot be under-estimated. The process has been illuminated for the fifteenth century in the fine work of G. Petralia [6]; the intention here is to look at the

colonisation médiévale: Bonifacio au XIIIe siècle', Anuario de estudios medievales, i (1964), 561-72; not to mention the studies by G.I. Bratianu, M. Balard and others of the Black Sea trade of Genoa.

[3] For the economic effects of Meloria, see DAVID HERLIHY, Pisa in the Renaissance: a study of urban growth (New Haven, 1958), 22, 44-5, 63, 107-8, 132-4, 172-5, 183.

[4] DECAMERON, Day 4, story 5.

[5] DAVID ABULAFIA, 'Crocuses and crusaders: San Gimignano, Pisa and the Kingdom of Jerusalem', Outremer: studies in the crusading Kingdom of Jerusalem presented to Joshua Prawer, ed. B.Z. Kedar, H.E. Mayer, R.C. Smail (Jerusalem, 1982), 227-43, especially 232. For later evidence, see R. ZENO, Documenti per la storia del diritto marittimo nei secoli XIII e XIV (Documenti e studi per la storia del commercio e del diritto commerciale italiano, vi, Turin, 1936), § 35, referring to «croco».

[6] GIUSEPPE PETRALIA, 'Ricerche prosopografiche sull'emigrazione delle famiglie

economic function of these communities just before 1300, and of other Tuscans passing through Sicily, in trade not with the mother-city but with the area much nearer Sicily that offered a rival market for the island's grain and foodstuffs: the coast of north Africa.

Emphasis will be laid, too, on the variety of Tuscans present in Sicily and north Africa: as well as Pisans and Florentines, Pistoiesi, Sangimignanesi, Lucchesi and others. Merchants from different towns occasionally, or perhaps generally, specialised in commodities closely linked to their mother-city's economic fortunes: the saffron of San Gimignano has been mentioned, but one could also cite the textiles, including silks, of Lucca. Lucca's close partnership with Genoa from the twelfth century onwards makes an interesting contrast to the links between other Tuscan cities and Pisa [7].

The inland towns needed a port, and they took their adoption of Pisa to the furthest lengths; their citizens, when overseas, declared themselves to be Pisans instead, and thereby benefited from the tax concessions earlier conferred on Pisa [8]. Pisa itself seems to have worried little about this impersonation. Presumably it brought Pisa greater economic strength and greater political influence; Tuscans overseas were often under the jurisdiction of the Pisan consul, and jurisdiction meant money — taxes levied within the fondaco, payments to notaries, even the expropriation of the goods of merchants who died overseas. A celebrated story recounted by Giovanni Villani suggests that under this smooth surface changes were taking place that deprived Pisa of its effec-

mercantili pisane in Sicilia dopo la conquista fiorentina del 1406', Bollettino Storico Pisano, 1 (1981), 37-93; 2 (1982), 229-70; GIUSEPPE PETRALIA, 'Mercanti e famiglie pisane in Sicilia nel XV secolo', Annuario dell'Istituto storico italiano per l'età moderna e contemporanea, XXXIII/XXXIV (1981/82), 167-296.

[7] DAVID ABULAFIA, The Two Italies: economic relations between the Norman Kingdom of Sicily and the northern communes (Cambridge, 1977), 256-61.

[8] ABULAFIA, 'Crocuses and crusaders', 234-9; for another example of this practice, mainly concerning Genoa and Ancona, see my article 'The Levant trade of Ancona and the Anconitan privileges in the Latin Kingdom of Jerusalem', in The Italian communes in the crusading Kingdom of Jerusalem (symposium of the Van Leer Jerusalem Foundation, May 1984), ed. G. Airaldi, B.Z. Kedar (Genoa, 1986). I would therefore qualify Herlihy's remarks (Pisa, 165) concerning limitation of access to some north African ports solely to Pisan merchants (e.g. in 1264): the term means merchants approved by the Pisans.

tive primacy; economic power was seized by other Tuscans, from Florence. At Tunis, we are told, the emir held the Pisans in the highest esteem as merchants, not realising that mingled among them were traders from elsewhere in Tuscany. One day he happened to notice, amid the dirty silver coins of Pisa, a dazzling piece of gold, a florin of Florence; he asked whence it came; the name of Florence was new to him; but he was deeply impressed, and saw clearly that the Pisans were not all he had supposed [9]. He was disillusioned with Pisa, but immediately recognized Florence's greater strength. Even so, the rulers of Tunis continued to make treaties with Pisa that were highly advantageous both to Pisan and to other Tuscan interests: the agreement of 1353, for instance, actually specifies that «whatever merchant of another nation may come with the Pisans in their ships, will have the same rights and duties as the Pisans»; and later it states that jurisdiction in cases between Pisans, including, presumably, flag-of-convenience Pisans, is to rest in the hands of the Pisan consul at Tunis [10].

II

Before it is possible to analyse the role of the Pisans in the trade network linking Sicily to Tunis and the Maghrib, it is necessary to ask how important Pisan and Tuscan merchants actually were in the trade of late thirteenth-century Sicily, as compared to the Genoese, Venetians and *regnicoli*. Grain, oil, wine and other primary products were in great demand in the Italian peninsula, not least in the largest cities such as Venice, Genoa and Naples, now much inflated in population; the Tuscans had many rivals [11]. Moreover, Pisa's difficulties with Charles of An-

[9] Giovanni Villani, Cronica, vi, cap. 54; L. de Mas Latrie, Traités de paix de commerce et documents divers concernant les relations des Chrétiens avec les Arabes de l'Afrique septentrionale au moyen âge (Paris, 1866), 131-3, with some sensible reservations; R.S. Lopez, 'Back to Gold, 1252', Economic History Review, ser. 2, iv (1956/7), 237-8.

[10] M. Amari, I diplomi arabi del R. Archivio fiorentino (Florence, 1863), 86-97 (1313); 98-111, and 303-8 (1353); André-E. Sayous, Le commerce des Européens à Tunis depuis XXIe siècle jusqu'à la fin du XVIe. Exposé et documents (Paris, 1929, 157-62 (1353).

[11] David Abulafia, 'Sul commercio del grano siciliano nel tardo Duecento',

jou deprived the merchants of Pisa itself of ready access to Sicily, though other Tuscans — Sienese and Florentine — fared very much better. Fortunately, Pisa was able to draw food supplies from Sardinia, much of which still lay under the city's control. The defeat of Charles of Anjou by the Sicilian rebels and by the Aragonese in 1282 restored Pisan access to Sicily, and the Pisans were exporting the island's grain within a year of the Vespers [12]; but the Vespers also boosted the economic influence of a new competitor in Sicilian waters, the Catalan merchants, who were already very active in north African trade as well [13]. And Pisan defeat by the Genoese also lay in the near future.

Some idea of the relative significance of merchants of different origins in Sicily's overseas trade can be gained from the *litterae responsales* of the Angevin court, issued in 1276-8, documents listing the export licences granted by the *portulani* of Sicily for specified amounts of grain to foreign and native merchants bound for a pre-arranged destination. It should be stressed that certain destinations, including for a time Pisa itself, were declared out of bounds; the Angevins attempted to coerce their Mediterranean rivals by a policy of economic boycott, though its real effect is unclear. Of course, the information given in the *litterae responsales* must be treated with care: it is unclear what quantities were exported without such specification, under separate agreements (such as the blanket agreements conferred on the Florentines a few decades later) or under no agreement at all (by smugglers, often with the connivance of local officials pocketing a bribe). Thus it cannot be assumed that the *litterae* provide a complete list of major exporters for the season they cover, though the Angevin government may have wished them to do so.

They represent the government's picture of licensed exports, and as any historian of taxation knows, reality is likely to have been somewhat different. The *responsales* of 24 July 1276 list the following export permits involving Tuscan shippers and merchants:

La società mediterranea all'epoca del Vespro: XI Congresso della Corona d'Aragona, Palermo-Erice-Trapani, 1982 (Palermo, 1983), ii.5-22.

[12] HERLIHY, Pisa, 85.

[13] DAVID ABULAFIA, 'Catalan merchants and the western Mediterranean, 1236-1300: studies in the notarial acts of Barcelona and Sicily', Viator, xvi (1985).

  i. 14 April 1276, from Trapani,
     for Bocco Tignesio, Bonello Fiorentino, Riccio
     Anselino, on the ship of Percivallo de Chavata,
     civis Messane
        .... 900 salme of wheat
        bound for Bougie

  ii. 23 April 1276, from Trapani,
     on the ship of Giacomo Buccacella and Berto Pisano
        .... 300 salme of wheat
        bound for Bougie

 iii. 6 May 1276, from Sciacca,
     on the ship of Grocco Pisano
        .... 700 salme of wheat
        bound for Bougie [14]

These quantities, totalling 1900 salme, formed part of a total of 4,000 salme that the court agreed could be exported to Bougie and north Africa. It is worth recalling that, following the Tunis crusade of 1270, Charles of Anjou had been able to rebuild commercial links between Sicily and north Africa [15]. By 1276 north Africa once again took a prominent place in Sicily's wheat exports: a further 20,000 salme of wheat and 10,000 salme of barley were approved for export to a variety of destinations including Africa, but excluding Pisa itself.

And yet, despite the ban on trade with Pisa itself, there was no ban on Pisan merchants trading between Sicily and Africa, as the following licences make very plain:

  iv. 25 April 1276, from Trapani,
     for Ugone de Barba, merchant of Pisa,
     on the ship of Antonio de Milio of Messina
        .... 300 salme of wheat
        bound for Bougie.

  v. 6 May 1276, from Sciacca,

---

[14] Nicola Nicolini, Codice diplomatico sui rapporti veneto-napoletani durante il regno di Carlo I d'Angiò (Regesta Chartarum Italiae, Rome, 1965), § 153, pp. 139-47, especially 141-2.

[15] G. Lesage, Marseille angevine. Recherches sur son évolution administrative, économique et urbaine de la victoire de Charles d'Anjou, à l'arrivée de Jeanne Ier (1264-1348) (Paris, 1950), 99.

for Pucchio Caniachio, merchant of Pisa,
on the *terida* of Pietro Torrente, Catalan,
.... 300 salme of wheat
bound for Bougie.

vi. 14 May 1276, from Girgenti,
for Gaddo Passarino, merchant of Pisa,
on the *terida* of Pisano de Plano, also of Pisa,
.... 200 salme of wheat
bound for Bougie.

vii. 20 May 1276, from Palermo,
for Rainerio Rosso, merchant of Pisa,
on the ship of Simone de Campo
.... 400 salme of wheat
bound for Bougie.

viii. 28 May 1276, from Girgenti,
for Sigerio de Barba, merchant of Pisa,
on the ship of Bartolomeo de Montemagno
.... 400 salme of wheat
bound for Bougie.

ix. 4 June 1276, from Licata,
for Daniele de Benedicto and Guido Carbone, Pisan
merchants, on Carbone's own boat
.... 250 salme of wheat
bound for Barbary [16].

Other Tuscan merchants exporting wheat that summer, according to the same document, included Filippo Fiorentino, taking 130 salme out of Sciacca, and Bonanno of Lucca, taking 120 salme out of Messina. Some other merchants for whom no identification is given may also be Tuscan; at any rate, it is clear that at least 4,000 out of the 24,000 salme cited here were to be exported by Tuscans to the markets of north Africa. It is evident, equally, that the Pisans and Tuscans possessed vigorous competitors; the *litterae* mention large numbers of King Charles' own subjects, merchants of Messina — whose role in Mediterranean traffic has wrongly been seen as entirely passive [17] — of Amalfi, and of the Provençal lands of the house of Anjou. Although the

[16] NICOLINI, Codice § 153, p. 143-4.
[17] E. PISPISA, Messina nel Trecento. Politica, economia, società (Messina, 1980).

citizens of Marseilles did not draw as much benefit from Angevin rule as did merchants from Florence and other Guelf cities, Marseilles received some privileges for trade in Sicily, and clearly acted on them [19]. It is worth adding too that Pisa's attempt to suppress by force the commerce of Amalfi, 140 years earlier, had been less successful than is sometimes supposed. We are faced with del Treppo's Amalfitans, still lively as late as the end of the thirteenth century, with strong interests in the Tyrrhenian trade circuits [19].

Licences to export wheat were expensive; Charles of Anjou's estimate of the value of his kingdom's prized asset was somewhat inflated, and a tax of 30 ounces of gold (such as he tried to levy) on 100 salme of wheat only discouraged purchasers. By August 1276 the Angevin court was obliged to lower the wheat tariff by a third in order to reduce market resistance; the court felt obliged also to permit grain sales to areas earlier under boycott, namely Pisa and Genoa [20]. A strict boycott was still enforced towards the lands of 'Paleologus', that is, the Emperor Michael VIII Palaiologos. So it is little surprise to find additional Tuscan and Genoese merchants in the *litterae responsales* of 1278 [21]. Some, no doubt, aimed to supply northern Italy with grain, but links to north Africa remained important too.

Evidence for the range of Tuscan commercial interests both in Sicily and in Africa is provided by a document of 28 March 1276 (1277 *stile pisano*), drawn up in Pisa partly in the vernacular. The Florentine Saraceno, son of Rustichello, now living at Pisa, forms a «compagniam, societatem et henticam», on his behalf and that of his sons, with Piero Bonacursi, Mainetto Guidi and Filippo Ubaldini of Florence (the last of whom was acting on behalf of his own sons Lapo and Baldino). Saraceno and his sons provided £ 11,367 11s 9d — a vast sum — while Mainetto contributed a mere £ 301 and Filippo £ 950. Funds were to be distributed among three bases: Palermo itself, where Rustichello was to operate; Tunis, where Filippo's son Lapo was to conduct business; and Pisa, where it seems Saraceno and the other principals would

---

[18] Lesage, Marseille angevine, 100-2.
[19] M. del Treppo, A. Leone, Amalfi medioevale (Biblioteca di studi meridionali, v, Naples, 1977).
[20] Nicolini, Codice § 155, p. 149-50.
[21] Nicolini, Codice § 217, p. 232-3.

remain [22]. Here we see not merely the intimate link between Pisa and Florence, but also that between Sicily and Africa on the one hand and Tuscany on the other. It can be safely assumed that Lapo in Tunis and Rustichello in Palermo also maintained contact, even, perhaps, worked in tandem.

It should perhaps be stressed that a second relatively short maritime route existed, linking Tunis and its neighbours to areas under the commercial domination of Tuscan merchants. As early as 1228 (1229 *stile pisano*) there is documentary evidence for the carriage of goods to and for between Cagliari and Tunis, in Pisan hands [23]; a document of 30 December 1286 (1287 *stile pisano*) brings to light a partnership between a Venetian, Tommaso Sanudo, and a Pisan, Betto Magnelli, «*actum Tunithi in fundaco pisanorum*», for trade with southern Sardinia [24]. Sardinia, like Sicily, was a producer of basic raw materials and (given the very substantial Pisan presence there) trade between Sardinia and north Africa can be assumed to have existed on a substantial scale. Much of what can be said here for trade within one 'Tyrrhenian triangle', from Tuscany to Sicily to Tunis, also applies *pari passu* to a second 'Tyrrhenian triangle', from Pisa to Sardinia to Tunis or its neighbours, though apparently on a smaller scale [25].

III

The range of evidence for Tuscan business in Tunis as well

[22] ROBERT DAVIDSOHN, Forschungen zur Geschichte von Florenz, III. Teil: XIII. und XIV. Jahrhundert. I. Regesten unedirter Urkunden zur Geschichte von Handel, Gewerbe und Zunftwessen; II. Die Schwarzen und die Weissen (Berlin, 1901), § 94, p. 28; Sayous, Commerce des Européens à Tunis, 55. See Appendix for an edition of the full text.

[23] F. ARTIZZU, Documenti inediti relativi ai rapporti economici fra la Sardegna e Pisa nel medioevo, 2 vols. (Padua, 1961, Pubblicazioni dell'Istituto di storia medioevale e moderna dell'Università degli Studi di Cagliari, i), i. § 5.

[24] ARTIZZU, i. § 20. For the notary Guillelmus quondam Raynerii Scorcialupi, see the discussion *infra* of Sicilian documents mentioning him. ARTIZZU, i. § 47 is an interesting document mentioning both Sicilian and Sardinian grain in the same breath.

[25] There are surprisingly few references to a grain trade between Sardinia and Africa in the excellent study by M. TANGHERONI, Aspetti del commercio dei cereali nei paesi della Corona d'Aragona, i. La Sardegna (Collana di studi italo-iberici, i, Pisa, 1981).

as in Palermo is greatly enlarged by the two surviving registers of the Palermitan notary Adamo de Citella, one of 1286-7, the other of 1298-9 [26]. An active community of Tuscan settlers and commercial visitors is revealed: a Sienese enters the employment of a Palermitan goldsmith, to prepare silk cloth on his behalf; a Pistoiese resident of Palermo rents a shop and two apartments from another Palermitan, in ruga Pisanorum Panormi, that is, in the Pisan quarter. A Florentine artisan takes an apprentice, the son of an ironsmith [27]. The representatives of a Florentine absent from Palermo, Faldo Bonusii de populo Sancti Jacobi ultra Arnum, make arrangements for the recovery of a runaway Saracen slave and of the goods she has stolen [28]. The involvement of foreign merchants in the slave trade has already been discussed at length by Verlinden; it is clear that Sicily drew large numbers of slaves from Cyrenaica, from the Mons Barcarum, and that the Tuscans were active alongside the Catalans in this traffic [29]. The picture that is presented is, then, that of a well-rooted community, containing both wealthy international merchants and more modest industrial workers. The Florentines, Pistoiesi and other inland Tuscans appear rather more often than the Pisans, but they, like the Pisans, are engaged in maritime trade, as well as providing services on land. Bartolomeo di Bonifazio of Pistoia hired a vessel from some merchants of Zara, in March 1287, to carry

[26] PIETRO BURGARELLA, Le imbreviature del notaio Adamo de Citella a Palermo (1° Registro: 1286-1287) (Fonti e studi del Corpus membranarum italicarum, ser. 3, Imbreviature matricole statuti e formulari notarili medievali, i, Rome, 1981); PIETRO GULOTTA, Le imbreviature del notaio Adamo de Citella a Palermo (2° Registro: 1298-9) (in the same series, vol. ii, Rome, 1982). In addition, a summary of the acts dating from 1286-7 was published by Burgarella in the Archivio storico della Sicilia orientale lxxv (1979), 435-553; the numbering of the documents is identical to that in the full edition. Several documents of commercial interest are also printed, though less accurately, in Zeno's Documenti (see note 5).
[27] BURGARELLA, § 66, § 327, § 384, cf. § 337; For the meaning of the term ruga in § 327, see David Jacoby, 'Crusader Acre in the thirteenth century: urban layout and topography', Studi medievali, ser. 3, xx (1979), 14-15.
[28] BURGARELLA, § 350.
[29] CH. VERLINDEN, L'esclavage dans l'Europe médiévale, ii. Italie, Colonies italiennes du Levant, Levant latin, Empire byzantin (Rijksuniversiteit te Gent, Werken uitgegeven door de Faculteit van de Letteren en Wijsbegeerte, clxvi, Ghent, 1977), 154, 156-7; identical is the discussion in his earlier article 'L'esclavage en Sicile au bas moyen âge', Bulletin de l'Institut historique belge de Rome, xxxv (1963), 31-2, 34.

VII

to Genoa all the wheat *quam dicta navis capere poterit et portare;*
thus neither he nor his Dalmatian backers is even sending the
wheat to their place of origin [30].

Some idea of the role of Tunis in the trading interests of the
Tuscans in Palermo can be gained from an examination of the
career of the Florentine financier Vanni (or Giovanni) Chyandono.
A document of 2 April 1287, recorded by Adamo de Citella, reveals
how far north his business interests extended. Vanni Chyandono
is seen assigning to a Roman merchant, Pietro Gavazario, 129
ounces of gold, promised to Gavazario by a Florentine partner,
Lando Buonsignori. This sum had its origin in a contract between
Lando Buonsignori and Chyandono's agent in Genoa, recorded by
the Genoese notary Parentino de Quinto; it was there specified
that the money would be paid in Palermo within fifteen days of
the arrival there of the ship *Squarchafica* (a very Genoese
name!) [31]. Whatever commodity was involved here — Sicilian
grain, perhaps — Vanni Chyandono certainly took a close interest
in another bulk item which was regularly ferried south to Tunis:
wine. On 17 May 1287 he bought all the red wine loaded on board
the ship of Leone de Vinders, a Genoese, now standing in the
port of Palermo [32]. The sellers were two merchants of Barcelona,
Guillem Fava and Pere de Bardols, but as will be seen in a moment this was not an unencumbered sale: the Catalans retained
certain interests. The wine, measuring 900 *mezarolae*, was to be
taken to the *fundico cabelle Tunisii*, the fondaco at Tunis; this
term probably indicates not the Pisan nor the Catalan warehouse,
but the state warehouse within the walls of Tunis proper [33]. A

---

[30] BURGARELLA, § 186; cf. § 326, § 341.

[31] BURGARELLA, § 226. It would be worth exploring the surviving acts of Parentino de Quinto, in the Archivio di Stato, Genoa, to find the corresponding document. Is the 'Banki Chyandonis' at Florence mentioned in this document the
Chyandono banking company, as Burgarella states, or a relative of Vanni called
Banki Chyandono, as I prefer to read the document?

[32] BURGARELLA, § 296; ZENO, § 8.

[33] Tunis and its port can be divided into three zones: La Goulette, the preferred harbour; outer Tunis, bordered by the harbour of Tunis itself, by canals
and by a line of walls; from there, through the Bab al-Bar, one reached the inner
city, about equal in physical extent to the outer one. The Christian merchants
were granted the right to operate fondachi in the outer city only. See R. BRUN-
SCHVIG, La Berbérie orientale sous les Hafsides des origines à la fin du XVe siècle

journey to Tunis presented special problems: the favourite harbour lay a little distance away at La Goulette (La Goletta), and
a ferry service carried goods from the wharves to the city proper [34]. These problems are reflected in the document, for, as far
as the harbour of La Goulette, the risk of loss was to be borne
two-thirds by Vanni Chyandono and one third by the two Catalans;
once the wine reached La Goulette, it would travel entirely at
Chyandono's risk. It is possible that past legal disputes had made
it advisable to specify in contracts at what point the merchandise
could be said to have completed its sea journey. Even so, the willingness of the Catalans to bear any part of the risk is striking.
The explanation lies in the fact that the Catalans received only
part of the payment due to them when the contract was drawn
up (244 ounces); the balance, paid at the rate of six besants per
mezarola of wine, was to be furnished only when the goods reached
their point of sale, Tunis.

In effect, therefore, Vanni Chyandono was entering into a form
of *societas* with the Catalans. He provided the labour and a small
proportion of the initial investment capital, represented by the
small part payment he made when the contract was drawn up;
the Catalans provided the remaining capital, in the form of the
wine. But any profit Vanni Chyandono could make by selling the
wine for more than six besants per measure was entirely his to
keep.

For whom was this wine intended? The quantity on board
ship seems large, and yet it is destined for a Muslim country,
where wine consumption should have been (theoretically at least)
very limited. But there were certainly large numbers of Christian
merchants who must have solaced themselves in wine; there were
groups of Christian mercenaries too, among whom demand was
no doubt unstinted. Native Christians were very few after the
Almohad invasions of the mid-twelfth century, and the Jews may
have preferred their own wine, in accordance with rabbinic law.
It is, however, hard to avoid the conclusion that there were enough
bibulous Muslims to keep wine-importers happy; even if consumption was much lower than in Christian Europe, production was

(Publications de l'Institut d'Études orientales d'Alger, viii, xi, Paris, 1940/1947),
i. 338-57.
[34] SAYOUS, Commerce des Européens à Tunis, 49.

probably very low indeed, and European wine served to bridge a gap between local supply and demand. Unfortunately the place of origin of this wine can only be surmised: Sicily itself is a good candidate, for the Jews and Christians of Erice (Monte San Giuliano) can be shown to have taken a strong interest in wine production around 1300 [35]. Liguria, Tuscany, Provence and Catalonia are also strong possibilities [36].

The agreement between Vanni Chyandono and the Catalans generated others, too. The Florentine had to negotiate with Leone de Vinders, the Genoese ship-owner, for the transport of the wine from Palermo to Tunis. Leone set a carriage fee of 300 gold dinars or 'doubloons' (*duplis aureis de miria et recti ponderis trecentis*), but also made Vanni a loan of 320 dinars at the same time, this sum to be paid within ten days of the ship's arrival at Tunis [37]. This arrangement too is more than it seems. We are not looking at two payments, one of 300 dinars and another of 320 dinars, each to be made in Tunis when the wine reaches its destination. Rather is Vanni Chyandono delaying payment of the 300 dinars owing to Leone de Vinders, by converting the price of passage into a financial advance. The additional twenty dinars, that is, the difference between the hire cost of the ship and the loan made by the Genoese, represent a fee for the loan. Such elaborate transactions were, of course, dictated in large measure by the desire to avoid accusations of usury.

Vanni Chyandono in fact used his own capital to make loans to compatriots. Money was not allowed to stand still. Lender and borrower were one. The diligent use of credit lubricated the wheels of commerce, making business smoother and faster to conduct. Thus Vanni entrusted Checco Bellotti of Florence with a loan of 161 ounces of gold, promising to repay Vanni's agent Gerardo Ugone in Tunis, within one month and five days, in besants of north Africa [38]. Checco in addition promised to guarantee against

---

[35] For the wine of Erice, see the register of the notary Giovanni Maiorana: ed. A. Sparti, Il registro del notaio ericino Giovanni Maiorana (1297-1300), 2 vols. (Palermo, 1982), and A. de Stefano, Il registro notarile di Giovanni Maiorana (1297-1300) (Memorie e documenti di storia siciliana, ser. 2, Documenti, ii, Palermo 1943). I am preparing a study of material from this register concerning Jewish wine-production in Erice.

[36] Herlihy attributes some Pisan exports to Tuscan vineyards: Pisa, 166.

[37] Burgarella, § 297; Zeno, § 9.

[38] Burgarella, § 298.

loss the wine already bought by Vanni for sale in Tunis; in other words, the loan to Checco incorporates an insurance policy, expressed most probably through a grant of very favourable terms of repayment. All this meant that Vanni Chyandono himself was free to remain behind in Palermo; his wine was under the protection of a Florentine guarantor; the ship-owner was aware that upon the safe arrival of his cargo depended his rapid receipt of payment for the passage; and in Tunis itself Vanni Chyandono possessed an agent, Gerardo Ugone, who would be able to manage the sale of the wine [39]. Nevertheless, it is striking how great was the concern of Vanni and his partners for the safety of the cargo. Such concern resulted not, in fact, from its being a prized vintage — as has been seen, not even its origin is specified — but from the presence of enemy fleets in the central Mediterranean during the summer of 1287. Only one day after the Chyandono contracts were drawn up, the Catalan merchant Jaume de Canuves asked Adamo de Citella to prepare a charter, noting the difficulties he had had in loading and exporting wheat *ob invasionem terre Auguste ad presens factam ab inimicis domini nostri regis et nostri* — that is to say, the Angevin attack on Aragonese Sicily that year [40].

Nor was Vanni Chyandono alone in his interest in wine exports from Sicily to Tunis. On 24 May 1287 Lapo Gumi received a loan of 108 ounces of gold from Simó de Pruners and Domenec de Uriol, acting on behalf of Pere de Pruners of Barcelona [41]. Thus the Catalan interest emerges once again alongside the Florentine. In other respects there are strong similarities to Vanni Chyandono's first wine contract. The money was to be repaid within ten days of the arrival at Tunis of the ship of Pere de Pruners, *S. Salvator*, and as guarantee Lapo Gumi offered 46 barrels of wine, containing 350 salme of wine according to the measure of Palermo. No use was to be made of the wine before Pere de Pruners had received satisfaction for the debt. It is thus clear that the sale cost of the wine was not to be used by Lapo Gumi

[39] BURGARELLA, § 303 extends the picture a little: Checco Bellotti of Florence receives 30 ounces of gold from Vanni Chyandono, under the instructions of a letter from Gerardo Ugone, and in return another Florentine, Ciprino Bonaguida, is to repay Gerardo in Tunis in besants: a sum of 630 besants is specified.
[40] BURGARELLA, § 300; cf. BURGARELLA, § 313.
[41] BURGARELLA, § 306; ZENO, § 10.

to repay Pere de Pruners: the money must be raised from another source. Among the witnesses to the act figures Checco Bellotti of Florence, fresh from the arrangement of his own contract with Vanni Chyandono.

IV

The partnership between Catalans and Florentines in the wine trade between Sicily and Tunis can in part be explained by the simple fact that inland Tuscans were in need of colleagues able to provide the ships they themselves did not normally possess. Similar partnerships, concerned with the transport of wheat, are identifiable in the second register of Adamo de Citella, from the very end of the thirteenth century. Here we can focus on the career of a shipping entrepreneur from Catalonia, Mateu Oliverdar or Oliverdarii (perhaps a member of the Alibert family); he was especially active in the international grain trade, and regularly conducted business with the Florentine bankers in Sicily [42]. For him, Tunis was one among a choice of possible trading destinations, and the decision to take cargoes there rather than to Genoa or Pisa was dictated by the needs and wishes of those who hired his services. On 24 September 1298 Guglielmo Cambi, representing the Bardi Bank, hired Mateu's ship *S. Franciscus*, acting through Gerardo Bonzuli, citizen of Palermo [43]. The vessel was to collect 2,500 salme of wheat — a large amount, perhaps all the grain the ship could carry — from one of the ports between Termini on the north coast of Sicily and Licata in the south. Thence it was to sail either to Tunis or to Genoa; and, as the Aragonese king of Sicily was still accumulating enemies in the western Mediterranean, the ship was to be properly armed and supplied with a large crew of 45 sailors and 15 servants. The cost of hiring the ship was to be three tari per salma if the vessel went only as far as Tunis, but four tari if it went to Genoa, to be paid in African or Genoese money as the case may be. Thus the cost of transport from Sicily to Tunis would be 250 ounces of gold.

---

[42] For other aspects of his career, see my study 'Catalan merchants and the western Mediterranean'.
[43] GULOTTA, 25; ZENO, 15 (Zeno: guarnimentis).

Just as Vanni Chyandono had sought to cover transport charges of 300 dinars by taking out a loan from a Genoese business partner, so too Mateu Oliverdar turned to a creditor for help in meeting his costs. For the carriage fee was not to be paid to him until he reached his destination; meanwhile he had to raise capital to hire sailors and fit out the S. Franciscus with all the balistis et aliis fornimentis expected by the Bardi. On 3 October 1298 a certain Naddo Rosso or Rubeo, a citizen of Palermo with a Florentine sound about his first name, lent Mateu 127½ dinars, to be carried at the Catalan shipper's own risk 'from the day that the said ship is loaded with the wheat of Guglielmo Cambi of the Company of the Bardi until thirteen days after the said ship shall have unloaded the cargo of wheat at Tunis on the present voyage that Mateu is about to make with the said ship from Sicily' [44]. Although the document makes plain Mateu's liability even if he does not sail to Tunis but to his alternative destination of Genoa, it seems likely that Tunis rather than Genoa had by now been settled upon as his preferred target. Ten days had elapsed since Mateu's agreement with the Bardi had been drafted, time in which encouraging news of prices and demand in Tunis may well have arrived.

Certainly the Bardi remained keen on exports to Tunis. On 22 October 1298 Gerardo Bonzuli of Palermo once again hired a ship on behalf of the Bardi (specifically, on behalf of Guglielmo Cambi and Guido Pepe). On this occasion it was Bernat Samider of Barcelona who agreed to convey 800 salme of wheat from the port of Licata to Tunis [45]. Once again, the ship was to be preparatam de marinariis bene armatis, and the fee of three tari per salma was payable in African besants on the ship's safe arrival.

During Autumn 1298 demand for grain in northern Italy, as well as in north Africa, seems to have been vigorous. In December 1298 the Bardi and other Florentines were hoping to export 19,000 salme of wheat from Apulia, and this may indicate shortages at home [46]. Further hints are provided by a document of 2 November 1298 in Adamo de Citella's register: Mateu Oliverdar's

---

[44] GULOTTA, 32; ZENO, 16.
[45] GULOTTA, 66; ZENO, 20.
[46] DAVIDSON, Register, § 309, p. 69.

ship *S. Franciscus* is described now as bound not for Tunis nor even Genoa, but for Pisa: it is thus apparent that the Bardi had decided to redirect its cargo through Porto Pisano to their home-town, or at least to one of the Arno cities [47].

The Bardi agent in Palermo, Guglielmo Cambi, was also active in the transfer of funds between Tunis and Sicily. On 19 January 1299 Cecco de Bonanno, a Pisan, declared before Adamo de Citella, in Cambi's presence, that he had received from Cambi 160 ounces of gold [48]. Behind this loan lay other transactions. Nardo Centummille, a Bardi agent in Tunis, had earlier received 2,960 besants in Tunis from Cecco's colleague and relative Bonavente de Bonanno, by way of an intermediary, Bundi di Canneto. This transaction had been recorded in Tunis by the Italian notary Lemmi (Guglielmo) Scorchialupi, commonly known as 'Fakini'. Nardo was under an obligation to repay Bonavente or his agent in Sicilian money, and so Cecco, acting on his relative's behalf, had requested settlement of the debt in Palermo by Nardo's associate Guglielmo Cambi. In essence, then, the document drawn up in Palermo is a quittance, marking the completion of a *cambium maritimum*; but it is also testimony to the smooth operation of financial services by the Bardi agents overseas. The Pisans were using Florentine facilities to transmit money rapidly and safely from one port to another. Who in this case bore the cost of the service is not, however, clear.

Further evidence for these banking services is provided by an act of 6 May 1299 in the same notarial register. Francesc de San Feliu de Guixols near Girona, is seen doing business with Guglielmo Cambi of the Bardi. Francesc de San Feliu is another regular client of Adamo de Citella, as indeed are most of the other figures mentioned in detail in this document. He receives 50 ounces of gold from Cambi, the agreed exchange value 912$\frac{1}{2}$ *milliarenses* of Tunis, entrusted by Pere Beltrami of Girona to Nardo Centummille of Florence, for repayment in Palermo [49]. Once again a notarial act of an Italian notary working in Tunis is cited; he is the same Guglielmo, or Lemmi, Scorchialupo who has appeared

---

[47] Gulotta, 91; Zeno, 22.
[48] Gulotta, 208; Zeno, 47.
[49] Gulotta, 385; Zeno, 100.

already. Adamo de Citella carefully provides a summary of the penalty clauses in Scorchialupi's act, because the parties to the new agreement in Palermo were afraid that Pere Beltrami, away in Tunis, might object to their settlement of the debt. And a Palermitan, Giacomo Guercio, was constituted guarantor in case Pere demanded indemnity. It is noteworthy that the Tunisian notarial act was dated 11 April, this one 6 May — only a brief period had elapsed, so the main aim of the transaction seems to have been to ensure the rapid transmission of working capital, rather than to deposit money with the Bardi in the hope of earning interest.

A brief word about the notary. He is known both from the references in Adamo de Citella's cartulary and from the document of 30 December 1286 concerning trade between Cagliari and Tunis, discussed earlier in this paper. There he appears as a Pisan notary working in Tunis: «Guillelmus quondam Raynerii Scorcialupi, imperiali auctoritate judex ordinarius atque notarius publicus»; while Adamo de Citella refers to him in similar words: «imperiali auctoritate iudicis ordinarii atque notarii puplici». The existence of a Pisan notary attached to the Pisan and Tuscan community in Tunis is only to be expected; less clear is the meaning of the phrase «puplici notarii dixerte» also applied to him by Adamo de Citella. Possibly «dixerte» is a corruption of «bixerte» and indicates that he also worked at Bizerta, which lies not far from Tunis.

Alongside the Bardi, the Peruzzi were also active in the grain trade between Sicily and Africa. A notarial act of 9 April 1299 refers once again to the links between Mateu Oliverdar and the great Florentine banks: the *S. Franciscus* has returned to Sicily from its voyage northwards, and is in port at Trapani; Mateu hires it out to Francesco Forcetti of Florence, an agent of the Peruzzi, who proposes to ferry grain from Sciacca, Girgenti, Licata or Eraclea to one of several possible destinations — Pisa, Genoa, Tripoli *de Barbaria*, Tunis or Gabes [50]. The quantity is once again 2,500 salme of wheat, defended now by 40 sailors and 12 *servitores*. Francesco Forcetti is bound to load the ship fully as soon as he has reached the port of collection in Sicily; and rates are fixed for the carriage of the cargo, as follows:

[50] GULOTTA, 346; ZENO, 90.

It is the *conductor* of the ship, the Florentine agent, who is to make the decision where to sail, once the grain has been loaded.

from:	to:	rate per salma:
Sciacca	Pisa	3 tari
Girgenti	Genoa	
Licata		
Eraclea	Pisa	3 ½ tari
	Genoa	
All ports	Tripoli	2 tari 15 grana
All ports	Tunis	2 tari 10 grana.

These documents concerning the Bardi and Peruzzi are of special interest because they date from an early period in the expansion of the Florentine banks to mastery over grain movements in the central Mediterranean. This is still the period when Lucchesi and Sienese bankers, not to mention Florentine rivals such as the Mozzi and Spini, vied for the pope's account and other positions of financial influence [51]. The fortunes of the 'Big Three', the Peruzzi, Bardi and Acciaiuoli, were built on several quite solid foundations: their striking ability to work together with one another; their links to the royal courts of Naples, France and England, as well as to the papacy; their role in the trade in wheat and in wool. Aragonese Sicily posed something of an embarrassment here. The Angevin allies of the Florentine bankers strongly discouraged trade between their merchant friends and the island of Sicily; the principle of operating an economic boycott, clearly enunciated in Charles of Anjou's *litterae responsales*, was not forgotten. In 1298 the Peruzzi found themselves forced to make their excuses to King Charles II of Naples, after the accidental arrival in Sicily of a storm-driven Catalan ship that had set out from Cyprus bearing their wares; it had been impounded by the Sicilians (now in conflict with their Aragonese brethren) and brought from Augusta to Messina. The Peruzzi prudently notified King Charles II that they would therefore have to send a mission to enemy territory, in the hope of retrieval [52]. Of course, they

---

[51] YVER, Commerce.

[52] S.L. PERUZZI, Storia del commercio e dei banchieri di Firenze (Firenze,

took care not to lay stress on their existing business in Aragonese Sicily, at Palermo and elsewhere.

The account books of the Peruzzi indicate that Tunis too remained an important base as late as the 1350's. There were 21 major creditors of the Tunis branch of the Peruzzi Bank in 1335[53]. In 1337 the Peruzzi representative at Tripoli was Giovanni Forzetti; it has been seen that a Francesco Forzetti was active in north Africa in 1299, with Tripoli as one possible destination for his cargo of grain[54]. The Acciaiuoli are the least well-documented of the major banks, but there is clear evidence of their involvement in the trade of Tunis; a quittance of 1329 mentions the export of leather, wool and skins from Tunis, and it is known that the Acciaiuoli had two representatives in Tunis in 1340, but three in Sicily and as many as nine in Naples[55].

Grain and wine: these were the two main imports. Gold, skins and wool: these were the main exports. It is clear from the documents examined here that Tuscan merchants maintained a strong interest in the high-quality gold currencies of north Africa. The pure gold of the southern Sahara attracted Florentine and other interest, as the move towards the production of gold currency in northern Italy gained pace[56]. In order to obtain that gold, the Florentines and their colleagues realised they could exploit the resources of ports very close to norh Africa: the grain stations of southern and western Sicily, at Sciacca, Girgenti and elsewhere. Although northern Italy had become increasingly dependent on southern wheat to make up shortfalls in its own production, the markets of Tunisia welcomed no less keenly the arrival

1868), 286 (giving 1331 for 1335); A. Sapori, ed., I libri di commercio dei Peruzzi (Milan, 1934), 9, with many further references to Tunis, *passim*; Sayous, Commerce des Européens à Tunis, 162-3.

[54] Peruzzi, 343-5; Sapori, 28; Sayous, 164.

[55] Sayous, Commerce des Européens à Tunis, 156-7; R. de Roover, 'The organization of trade', Cambridge Economic History of Europe, iii, Economic organization and policies in the Middle Ages (Cambridge, 1963), 86, Table ii, based ultimately on Archivio Ricasoli-Firidolfi, Florence, fondo Acciaiuoli, perg. 756 (già 798).

[56] Lopez, 'Back to Gold', 225-7; for the supplies themselves, N. Levtzion, Ancient Ghana and Mali (London, 1973), 124-52; also David Abulafia, 'Maometto e Carlomagno: le due aree monetarie dell'Italia medievale, dell'oro e dell'argento', Storia d'Italia, Annali, vi, Economia naturale, economia monetaria, ed. R. Romano, U. Tucci (Turin, 1983), 223-70.

of additional foodstuffs. Since the eleventh century, the region had come to depend increasingly on Sicilian wheat as its own agriculture declined; by the early fourteenth century the economic crisis of the north African towns had become even more acute [57]. And, as has been seen, drink as well as food came to Africa from Sicily.

Profits in gold drawn from this trade thus had a wider impact on the European economy, radiating far beyond the wheatfields and vineyards of Sicily. It was possible to maintain a vigorous trade in north Africa by selling European textiles for local skins, fibres and fruits, even (when there was a glut) for African grain. But the establishment of Tuscan mastery over the grain traffic between Sicily and Africa helped to adjust the balance of Italian trade in Africa in favour of Florence and its partners. That the Genoese and Catalans also participated in this trade, providing maritime services the inland Tuscan towns could not offer, is also apparent. But this was only to spread the profits more widely, and to make it possible for currencies based in part on African gold to be spread over a wider area too. The decline of the Sahara caravans by the late fourteenth century, and of demand for Sicilian foodstuffs after the population disaster engendered by the Black Death, meant that this trading network eventually lost its importance. The memory of African gold remained vivid and potent, but new methods, of far greater ambition and of dramatic consequence, were conceived for gaining access to it.

---

[57] YVES LACOSTE, Ibn Khaldun: the birth of history and the past of the third world (London, 1984; original edition, Paris, 1966), 79-91, buries some interesting ideas about the 'fourteenth-century crisis' in north Africa beneath a torrent of invective. For a more sober view, see BRUNSCHVIG, La Berbérie orientale, ii. 267; also LEVTZION, 152, for whom 'the fourteenth century was the period of greatest economic expansion' in the gold-producing regions: a much more positive picture than that painted by Lacoste in his bright red colours.

Archivio di Stato di Firenze, Dipl. S. Spirito, 28 Marzo 1277.

In eterni Dei nomine amen. Sit omnibus manifestum. Quod Saracinus quondam Rustichelli de Florentia et qui nunc habitat Pisis in Cappella sancti Pauli ad ortum pro Rustichello filio suo et pro aliis suis fratribus dicti Rustichelli fecit et contraxit et composuit compagniam et societatem et henticam cum Piero Bonaccursi et Maynecto Guidi et Filippo Hubaldini pro se et Lapo et Baldino filiis suprascripti Filippi de Florentia. In qua quidem societate et hentica suprascriptus Saracinus pro dictis filiis suis habet libras undecim milia trecentas sexaginta septem et solidos undecim et denarios nouem denariorum pisanorum capitale. Et suprascriptus Maynectus Guidi libras trecentas unam denariorum pisanorum capitale. Et suprascriptus Filippus Hubaldini pro se et dictis suis filiis libras noningentas quinquaginta denariorum pisanorum capitale. Et de qua hentica partem habent Pisis et partem in Panormo apud Chellum suprascriptum et partem Tunithi apud Lapum suprascriptum et partem habent ad recipiendum ut in carta concessionis [MS: confessionis] ab eisdem Saracino et Manecto et Filippo rogata hodie a me Iustiniano notario infrascripto continetur. Et quam henticam totam suprascripti Filippus et Pierus et Maynectus concessi fuerunt apud se habere et esse ut in suprascripta carta concessionis facte ab eisdem Saracino et Filippo et Maynecto continetur. Tractandam et procurandam ab eisdem Piero et Maynecto et Filippo usque ad redditum suprascripti Rustichelli filii suprascripti Saracini. Que quidem societas ordinata et composita est a suprascripto Saracino cum suprascriptis Piero Bonaccursi et Maynecto Guidi et Filippo Hubaldini ut infra continetur vulgariter:

> Al nomé di Dio et de la sua madre sancta Maria et di li sancti e sancte suoi et di guadagno di bono. Ordina et compone Saracino compagniam per Rustichello filio suo et per li suoi fratelli cum Piero Bonaccursi et Maynecto Guidi et Fili [sic, i.e. Filippo] Hubaldini et Lapo et Baldino fili del dicto Filippo. In questo modo. Che tucta et quanta moneta et mercatantia trouiamo del suo sia guidata et correcta in mercatantia per le soprascritte persone compagni. Riceuano in compagnia da fili di Saracino tucta la moneta che trouiamo del soprascritto Saracino a quanto prode. Cioe che Rustichello trara del prode che si fara le tre parte et piu si come tocasse per libre mille. Li altri compagni abia ilquanto [il qual *del.*] quanto prode in questo modo. Che Rustichello, Piero, Maynecto, Filippo et Lapo abiano et traghano iguale tanto luno quanto laltro. Et Baldino tragha et abia per meza parte di quello che trae luno del soprascritti magiori compagni. Et ordina che soprascritti Compagni laloro moneta chano di loro tegnano nela soprascritta compagnia et traghano del prode che si fa sopra lo quanto che decto, si come tocchera per libra et per soldo, si come Rustichello de libre mille che soprascritte sono traghera per se et suoi compagni de loro denaro per loro.

VII

Quam quidem societatem et henticam suprascripti Pierus et Maynectus et Filippus per sollempnem stipulationen conuenerunt et promiserunt suprascripto Saracino recipere pro dictis suis filiis saluare et guar-
dare et augere, et cum ea lucrari bona fide, sine fraude et eam eis renun-
tiare et dare et facere et reddere eis in [MS: intra] veram et puram rac-
tionem. Et si ita hec omnia et singula non fecerint et non obseruauerint
aut si contra factum uel uentum fuerint, penam dupli omnium predictorum et omnes expensas et dampna que intra fierint uel haberent ei recipienti pro dictis suis filiis dare et reseruare promiserunt. Obligando se
et eorum heredes et bona eidem Saracino recipere pro dictis suis filiis
ac eorum heredibus. Renuntiando omni iuri et auxilio et exceptionibus,
defensionibus et constitutionibus legi et usus et priuilegio fori omnique
alii auxilio. Sibi competentibus et competiturus contra predicta. Actum
Pisis in domo habitationis suprascripti Saracini que est heredum Jacobi
Parmisciani. Presentibus Guardi quondam Bentiuegne de Florentia et Ghe-
rarduccio quondam Guidonis de Florentia populi sancte felicitatis testibus ad hec rogatis. Dominice vero Incarnationis anno Millesimo Ducentesimo Septuagesimo septimo, Indictione decima, quinto kalendas Aprelis.

Ego Justinianus filius quondam Henrici de Vico Imperatoris dignita-
tis notarius. Hanc cartam a me rogatam. Rogatus, scripsi atque firmaui.

VIII

Una comunità ebraica della Sicilia occidentale: Erice 1298-1304*

La comunità ebraica di Erice o, per usare il toponimo medievale, di Monte San Giuliano, è più conosciuta per la sua presunta distruzione che per i suoi periodi di vitalità; nel 1392, essa condivise il destino delle *aljamas* di Barcellona, di Maiorca e di altri centri della Corona d'Aragona e venne violentemente distrutta nel corso di un tumulto ispirato da agitatori antisemiti di Spagna; ai suoi abitanti fu concessa la scelta fra la conversione e la morte. Sebbene vi sia stato un breve periodo di rinascita nel XV secolo, il 1392 segna una significativa rottura nell'esistenza della comunità [1].

Gli eventi del 1392, tuttavia, sono in stridente contrasto con il quadro che si può delineare per il primo '300; sembra infatti che a quella epoca gli ebrei ericini vivessero in pace insieme con i loro vicini cristiani; non c'è alcuna testimonianza di un *rabato* o di un quartiere ebraico – che si sviluppò solo in epoca successiva – e gli ebrei si dedicavano ad una vasta gamma di attività econo-

---

* Questo saggio è dedicato alla memoria del Professor Eliyahu Ashtor, dell'Hebrew University di Gerusalemme, non solo in considerazione dei suoi importanti studi sugli ebrei della Sicilia e della Spagna medievali, ma in segno di stima personale per uno studioso cui l'autore è stato sempre profondamente grato per il sostegno ed i consigli ricevuti. Una traduzione in ebraico del presente saggio apparirà sul numero LI di *Zion* (1986), 295-317. La presente traduzione italiana è opera del dott. Pietro Corrao.

[1] Sulla comunità nel tardo XIV e nel XV secolo, vedi G. Di Giovanni, *L'ebraismo della Sicilia ricercato ed esposto*, Palermo, 1748, p. 367-70; C. Roth, *The History of the Jews of Italy*, Philadelphia, 1946, p. 248. La maggiore collezione di documenti sul tema è il *Codice diplomatico dei giudei di Sicilia*, vol. I, parte I (*Documenti per servire alla storia di Sicilia* pubblicati a cura della Società Siciliana per la Storia Patria, serie I, Diplomatica, VI, Palermo, 1884).

miche paragonabile sotto tutti gli aspetti a quelle della maggioranza cristiana. Possiamo affermare tutto ciò grazie alla sopravvivenza a Trapani di un singolo registro notarile del notaio cristiano
ericino Giovanni Maiorana, contenente circa 150 documenti, dal
1 febbraio 1298 al 6 settembre 1304, molti dei quali riguardano o
menzionano degli ebrei [2]; scopo di questo lavoro è l'analisi in
profondità di tale materiale.

L'importanza del registro di Giovanni Maiorana per la storia
degli ebrei siciliani è notevolissima: se infatti, la *Genizah* del Cairo
getta luce preziosa sulle comunità ebraiche siciliane sopratutto per
i primi secoli del Medioevo, e i registri notarili di Palermo, Sciacca
di altri centri siciliani costituiscono fonti di grande valore per
l'ultimo secolo della loro storia, gli anni intorno al '300 sono
scarsamente documentati [3].

Sebbene negli atti notarili palermitani del tardo XIII secolo
compaiano alcuni riferimenti agli ebrei della città, l'interesse dei
documenti di Erice risiede nella loro relativa organicità e nel fatto
che si riferiscono ad un piccolo abitato situato a pochi chilometri
dalla costa ma – contrariamente al grande porto di Palermo –

---

[2] Conservato presso l'Archivio di Stato di Trapani, segnalato per la prima volta da A.
SALINAS, *Di un registro notarile di Giovanni Maiorana notajo di Monte San Giuliano nel
secolo XII*, Archivio Storico Siciliano, n. s. VIII (1883), pp. 435-62, che ne pubblicò nove
documenti; edito per la prima volta per intero, con una lunga introduzione da A. DE
STEFANO, *Il registro notarile di Giovanni Maiorana (1297-1300)* (Memorie e documenti di
storia siciliana, serie II, *Documenti*, II, Palermo, 1943); come lo stesso De Stefano rilevava,
le condizioni in cui venne effettuata la pubblicazione – si era in tempo di guerra – furono
causa di numerosi errori di stampa. Riedito da A. SPARTI, *Il registro del notaio ericino
Giovanni Maiorana (1297-1300)*, 2 volumi, Palermo, 1982 in una lussuosa pubblicazione
in occasione delle celebrazioni del VII centenario dei Vespri Siciliani; il e volume I contiene
l'edizione, il volume II la riproduzione fotografica integrale del manoscritto.

[3] S.D. GOITEIN, *Sicily and southern Italy in the Cairo Genizah documents*, "Archivio
Storico per la Sicilia Orientale", LXVII (1971), 9-33, e, per il XV secolo, gli importantissimi
studi di E. ASHTOR, basati su documenti notarili di Palermo, Sciacca ed altre località:
Palermitan Jewry in the Fifteenth Century, "Hebrew Union College Annual", L (1979),
219-51, ripubblicato in E. ASHTOR, *The Jews and the Mediterranean Economy, 10th-15th
centuries*, London, 1983; *La fin du Judaisme sicilien*, "Revue des études juives", CXLII
(1983), 323-47; vedi anche C. TRASSELLI, *Gli ebrei di Sicilia*, "Nuovi Quaderni del Meridio-
ne", VII (1969), in particolare le osservazioni a p. 47, ed il capitolo 'Gli ebrei di Sicilia'
nel volume *Siciliani fra Quattrocento e Cinquecento* (Messina, 1981), dello stesso autore,
p. 135-57.

relativamente lontano dalle grandi rotte del commercio internazionale. Solo un documento nel registro di Giovanni Maiorana riguarda il commercio marittimo ed i protagonisti dell'affare cui si riferisce sono dei cristiani catalani o maiorchini [4].

Erice era un centro abitato le cui principali risorse derivavano dalla agricoltura e gli ebrei, come pure i cristiani, concentravano i propri interessi sulla terra. Gli scoscesi campi attorno all'abitato risultano particolarmente adatti alla produzione di vino e di frutta: Erice è posta a più di 750 m sul livello del mare, su un monte che sorge ripido dalla pianura costiera della Sicilia occidentale e sovrasta il porto di Trapani; nei giorni più chiari, dal monte si può avvistare la costa africana. L'abitato, pur situato a soli 6 km da uno dei porti toccati dalle grandi rotte commerciali che legavano la Sicilia all'Africa, alla Sardegna, alla penisola iberica ed a Genova, era interessato solo marginalmente da questi traffici.

A causa della favorevole posizione, il sito di Erice fin dall'età preistorica fu sede di santuari e di abitati, tanto che il luogo conserva ancora importanti resti di mura megalitiche; fin dall'antichità la sua reputazione religiosa era notevolissima, ma la città acquisì il suo nome medievale al tempo della conquista normanna, quando si credette che Ruggero I, che aveva assediato il monte, fosse riuscito ad espugnarlo grazie all'intervento di un branco di cani feroci guidati da San Giuliano [5].

L'abitato conobbe una notevole crescita nel secolo XIII [6], profittando forse del ruolo di fornitore di prodotti agricoli del vicino porto marittimo, Trapani, e divenne luogo di residenza di immigrati provenienti da altre parti della Sicilia, dall'Italia meridionale e dal resto del Mediterraneo: Giovanni Maiorana registra infatti

---

[4] SPARTI, § 4, pp. 22-4; DE STEFANO, § IX, P. 13-16; i mercanti citati compaiono anche in atti notarili palermitani, cfr. D. ABULAFIA, *Catalan Merchants and the western Mediterranean: studies in the notarial acts of Barcelona and Sicily, 1236-1300*, "Viator, Medieval and Renaissance studies", XVI (1985), 209-42; *Sul commercio del grano siciliano nel tardo Duecento*, "XI Congresso della Corona d'Aragona: la società mediterranea all'epoca del Vespro", II (Palermo, 1983), 5-22.

[5] J.J. NORWICH, *The Normans in the South (1016-1130)* London, 1967, p. 253.

[6] I. PERI, Uomini, città e campagne in Sicilia dall'XI al XIII secolo, Bari, 1978, pp. 138-9.

degli abitanti cristiani provenienti da Amalfi, Napoli, Salerno, Pavia, dalla Puglia, dalla Calabria, dalla Toscana ed anche dalla Catalogna e da Narbona [7]. Fra XII e XIII secolo, d'altronde, l'intera Sicilia fu massicciamente popolata da immigranti provenienti dal continente che riempirono i vuoti lasciati dalla popolazione araba e berbera che andava diminuendo, ed i centri agricoli dell'interno, da Erice a Corleone, e Polizzi e Paternò furono interessati da tale fenomeno non meno dei grandi porti [8]. È interessante rilevare, tuttavia, come la maggior parte degli ebrei menzionati negli atti di Giovanni Maiorana portino nomi privi dell'indicazione dell'origine geografica; ciò potrebbe suggerire un più antico insediamento della popolazione ebraica rispetto a quello di buona parte della comunità cristiana. Probabilmente degli ebrei abitavano già ad Erice prima della conquista di Ruggero I, sotto il dominio musulmano.

Gli ebrei ericini, in ogni caso, portano nomi tipicamente arabi: *Bulfarachius*, ad esempio, che è chiaramente *Abu-l-Faraj*, e *Bussac*, o *Abu-Ishaq*, mentre anche il nome *Musa* – invece di *Mosse* – de Rubbisio riflette l'uso dell'arabo; è noto, d'altronde, che gli ebrei siciliani continuarono a parlare arabo fino al XV secolo, sebbene la popolazione musulmana fosse già scomparsa attorno alla metà del XIII secolo [9].

Parlate arabe sopravvisero tra i non ebrei in alcune aree isolate, come accadde a Malta, (accanto a più antichi elementi semitici, come si ritiene comunemente), ma in genere fu l'italiano importato dal continente a divenire il volgare dei siciliani [10]. Il giuramento-tipo degli ebrei siciliani del XIV secolo davanti ad una corte di giustizia, infatti, inizia in siciliano ma si conclude con l'esclamazione araba *"Alla, Alla, Uben, ubeni, lugleni"* reso dal Lagumina

---

[7] DE STEFANO, pp. XXXVI-XL.

[8] D. ABULAFIA, *The crown and the economy under Roger II and his successors*, "Dumbarton Oaks Papers", XXXVII (1983), 11-13.

[9] H. BRESC, S.D. GOITEIN, *Un inventaire dotal de juifs siciliens [1479]*, "Mélanges de l'École française de Rome", LXXXII (1970), p. 903-17, in particolare p. 905-6.

[10] ABULAFIA, *Crown and the economy*, 12; per Malta, vedi A.T. LUTTRELL, *Approaches to medieval Malta*, in A.T. LUTTRELL, ed., *Medieval Malta: studies on Malta before the Knights*, London, 1975, p. 66-7.

Una comunità ebraica

con "Dio, Dio, Fattore mio, timore mio" [11].

È stata avanzata l'ipotesi che gli ebrei di Erice non fossero ebrei in senso proprio, ma una particolare specie di *anusim*, musulmani "camuffati" da ebrei al fine di mantenere il diritto di risiedere in Sicilia, dato che, mentre gli ebrei erano stati lasciati liberi di rimanervi, i Musulmani erano stati obbligati ad emigrare o a convertirsi [12]; Giovanni Maiorana tuttavia non lascia dubbi sul fatto che gli ebrei di Erice agivano "per legem Moysi secundum ritum musaycum" o "iudaycum" [13]; molti di essi, inoltre, sia che avessero o no nomi arabi, avevano anche un nome ebraico che usavano comunemente: *Chayono*, probabilmente *Hayyim*, *Sybithen*, sicuramente *Shabbettai*, ed ancora *David*, *Nathan* ed il nome incontestabilmente ebraico di *Judas* o *Yehudah* [14]. Il *nusach* degli ebrei siciliani era con ogni probabilità strettamente legato ai riti nord-africani, e risulta evidente che le comunità ebraiche siciliane rimasero nell'ambito culturale e religioso dell'ebraismo magrebino fino alla loro estinzione alla fine del XV secolo [15]. Neanche l'immissione della Sicilia nell'area della Corona d'Aragona indusse tali comunità a perdere la propria identità magrebina, nonostante avesse fatto giungere dalla Catalogna *leader* ebrei quali Joseph Abinafia (attorno al 1400) [16].

La trasformazione della composizione sociale di Erice di cui si è detto rifletteva più generali cambiamenti politici ed economici verificatisi in tutta l'area del Mediterraneo occidentale, e nei quali

---

[11] *Codice diplomatico*, § LXXIV, p. 106.

[12] Da una lezione del Prof. I. Peri al Convegno internazionale di studio sull'urbanistica islamica in Sicilia, riferitami dal dott. J. Johns.

[13] Ad es. SPARTI, § p. 95; DE STEFANO, § 66, p. 119-20.

[14] Per molti di questi nomi, vedi i documenti citati nel presente lavoro; per Sybithen, vedi SPARTI, § 14, p. 28; DE STEFANO, § 14, p. 22; ma non posso condividere l'opinione di entrambi secondo la quale questa persona è una *iudea* e non un *iudeus*; in un documento del 1479, 'Xibiten' è un uomo: BRESC-GOITEIN, *Inventaire dotal*, p. 914.

[15] C. ROTH, *Jewish intellectual life in medieval Sicily*, "Jewish Quarterly Review", XLVII (1956-57), 317-53 in particolare p. 332-5, dove l'autore collega il *rito siciliano* pubblicato a Costantinopoli nel 1585 agli usi nordafricani.

[16] Sul quale vedi ASHTOR, *Palermitan Jewry*, 220; *Codice diplomatico* § CIX, CXVI, CXXIV, CXXX etc.; questi era probabilmente imparentato con l'Aaron Abinafia, o Ibn Yahya, attivo nei circoli della corte aragonese nel XIII secolo; la base delle sue attività era Siracusa, piuttosto che Palermo.

anche l'isolato centro montano rimase coinvolto. Nel 1282 il re d'Aragona Pietro III sbarcò a Trapani ed iniziò una rapida conquista della Sicilia, dalla quale espulse l'esercito del rivale Carlo d'Angiò [17]. La conquista dell'isola fu un momento di grande rilievo nel processo – lento e per molti versi casuale – dell'espansione catalano-aragonese nel Mediterraneo occidentale e centrale [18].

Mercanti ed artigiani catalani avevano cominciato a stanziarsi a Palermo, Messina ed in altre città siciliane già prima del 1282 [19], ma, mentre la conquista catalana di Maiorca, negli anni 20 del secolo XIII, aveva effettivamente stimolato nuovi insediamenti ebraici nelle Baleari, non sembra che, attorno al 1300, giungesse un gran numero di ebrei catalani ad insediarsi stabilmente in Sicilia [20]. È vero che a quell'epoca la presenza del mistico Abraham Abulafia, che si stabilì per un certo tempo nell'avamposto del regno siciliano – l'isola di Comino, vicino Malta – produsse molta eccitazione nelle città siciliane [21], ma, in generale, le giudecche siciliane mantennero un'identità abbastanza differente da quelle catalane, mancando in esse la presenza di quei grandi studiosi, funzionari governativi ed uomini d'affari benestanti che svolgevano un ruolo preminente in quelle dei territori iberici della Corona d'Aragona [22]. Probabilmente, tuttavia, fu proprio il basso profilo mantenuto dagli ebrei siciliani, come quelli di Erice, che li protesse da ogni violenza, fino a quando, nel XIV secolo, Federico III e la sua corte non importarono dalla Spagna una serie di misure antiebraiche indirizzate in parte contro gli ebrei benestanti o influenti; in un primo tempo, tuttavia, anche tali misure ebbero

---

[17] S. RUNCIMAN, *The Sicilian Vespers: a history of the Mediterranean World in the later thirteenth century*, Cambridge, 1958, p. 250.

[18] J.N.HILLGARTH, *The problem of a Catalan Mediterranean empire, 1229-1327* (English Historical Review, supplement no. VIII, London, 1975).

[19] ABULAFIA, *Catalan merchants*; C. BATTLE, *Les relacions entre Barcelona i Sicília a la segona meitat del segle XIII*, XI Congresso della Corona d'Aragona, II. 147-85.

[20] Per Maiorca, vedi G. ALOMAR, *Urbanismo regional en la edad media: las "Ordinacions" de Jaime II (1300) en el reino de Mallorca*, Barcelona, 1976, p. 16-19.

[21] G. SCHOLEM, *Major trends in Jewish mysticism*, New York, 1941, pp. 128, 379; S. BOWMAN, *Messianic expectations in the Peloponnesos*, "Hebrew Union College Annual", LII (1981), p. 195-6, per dati su piu ampi tumulti in Sicilia.

[22] ASHTOR, *Palermitan Jewry*, 219, 231.

scarsa applicazione in Sicilia. A quel tempo, inoltre, cominciava a svilupparsi nell'isola una grave crisi economica: i conflitti interni, seguiti dall'arrivo della Grande Peste nel 1347, condussero ad una forte depressione economica, e, come si vedrà, gli ebrei di Erice rimasero vittime non solamente di tali difficoltà, ma di un'ondata di sentimenti antiebraici in parte generati dall'immiserimento della maggioranza cristiana.

L'invasione aragonese del 1282, comunque, coinvolse gli ebrei ericini anche in un modo più diretto; Pietro d'Aragona aveva conquistato la Sicilia per affermare i diritti della moglie Costanza, della casa degli Hohenstaufen e, sebbene si fosse proposto di restaurare il "buongoverno" dei suoi predecessori svevi dopo anni di dura tassazione sotto Carlo d'Angiò, dovette anche raccogliere fondi per condurre la guerra contro gli angioini, che si prolungò anche dopo la sua morte, fino alla pace di Caltabellotta del 1302. L'impopolarità della guerra fra la nobiltà aragonese costrinse il sovrano a gravare sugli abitanti della Sicilia più pesantemente di quanto questi avessero sperato in un primo tempo.

Negli anni '90 del '200, Giacomo II d'Aragona tentò di risolvere i problemi finanziari posti da tale guerra accettando di scambiare la Sicilia con un territorio equivalente, la Sardegna, dove pensava che i suoi diritti potessero essere affermati più facilmente; ne conseguì che il suo luogotenente in Sicilia, il fratello minore Federico, agendo con il consenso del baronaggio siciliano, si schierò contro l'Aragona e venne incoronato quale sovrano indipendente dell'isola nel 1295. Per i successivi sette anni Federico dovette fare affidamento sulle risorse siciliane per finanziare la resistenza sia contro gli angioini di Napoli sia contro il fratello Giacomo [23]. È tale situazione a spiegare una serie di documenti registrati da Giovanni Maiorana, riguardanti le relazioni fra gli ebrei di Erice e la Corona siciliana.

Sia gli ebrei che i cristiani di Erice erano costituiti in *universitates* (un termine privo di significati accademici in questo contesto), una per ciascuna comunità; l'*universitas* siciliana ha analogie

---

[23] Per questi eventi, cfr. RUNCIMAN, 295-9; HILLGARTH, 29-32.

sia con la *gilda* sia con il Comune, ma, al contrario dei Comuni dell'Italia Settentrionale, era saldamente sottoposta al controllo regio. Testimonianze relative a Palermo ed a Malta indicano che il compito di maggior rilievo della *universitas* era di regolare affari economici locali, quali l'approvvigionamento granario, di organizzare la riscossione delle imposte generali e di nominare degli ufficiali che facessero all'occorrenza da mediatori fra la città e la corona [24]. Gli ebrei, normalmente, costituivano una propria *universitas*, ed una situazione simile si riscontra in altre città mediterranee come Marsiglia.

È proprio il primo documento del registro di Giovanni Maiorana a mostrarci all'opera l'*universitas* ebraica: il primo febbraio 1298 l'*universitas iudeorum terre Montis Sancti Iuliani* raduna i suoi membri "nel modo e nel luogo consueto, cioè la sinagoga degli ebrei di quella regione" per nominare due o tre collettori di imposte, in ottemperanza alle richieste della corte regia [25]; i testimoni di questo atto sono sia cristiani che ebrei: uno è Giovanni Maiorana, *iudex*, mentre fra gli ebrei più influenti compaiono Chilfa *faber* de David e Azaronus de Sydica, dei quali si dirà più avanti. La somma da raccogliere non è specificata, ma viene menzionata una pesante multa di 4 onze d'oro (da pagare alla corte) e di mezzo augustale (circa 1/8 di onza, da pagare al *baiulus* regio, il sovrintendente fiscale) a carico degli evasori.

I fondi raccolti dovevano essere utilizzati sia per scopi riguardanti la comunità sia estranei ad essa, ed è probabile che il documento si riferisca alla tassa annuale nota come *ghisia (Jizya)* o *agostale*, una sopravvivenza del periodo del dominio musulmano che continuò a gravare sugli ebrei anche dopo la conquista

---

[24] Palermo: P. BULGARELLA, ed., *Le imbreviature del notaio Adamo de Citella a Palermo (1° Registro; 1286-1287)* (Fonti e studi del Corpus membranarum italicarum, ser. 3, I, Roma, 1981), § 313, p. 190; Malta: H. BRESC, *The "Secrezia" and the royal patrimony in Malta: 1204-1450, in Medieval Malta*, ed. Luttrell, p. 126-51.

[25] SPARTI, § 1, p. 15-16; DE STEFANO, § 1, p. 3-5. DE STEFANO, p. LXXII e SALINAS, p. 449 si sorprendono di un riferimento ad una riunione in una chiesa dell'"università' ebraica (SPARTI § 43, p. 63; DE STEFANO, § 43, p. 72; SALINAS, § 4, p. 458), ma si tratta sicuramente di un errore dello scrivano: il notaio affermava che si riunirono nel modo consueto e la sua attenzione venne probabilmente sviata.

normanna. In ogni caso, la normale tassazione ad Erice era, attorno al 1370, di 15 onze d'oro per l'intera comunità; la tassa infatti non gravava sugli individui, ma era costituita da un unico versamento annuale, raccolto e pagato dall'*universitas* ebraica nel suo complesso [26].

La continua emergenza militare, però, non permetteva agli ebrei siciliani di sperare di evitare ulteriori richieste di imposte nel corso del 1298: il 21 giugno l'*universitas* ebraica di Erice si riuniva ancora per eleggere un collettore dei fondi necessari alla comunità ("*ad presens necessarias universitati predicte pro suis serviciis peragendis taxatis*") [27]; Sparti, come già De Stefano, nella sua edizione del registro di Maiorana suggerisce che lo scopo della raccolta fosse la costituzione di un fondo per un piano di manutenzione degli edifici comuni o per le elemosine, ma si può avanzare un'altra ipotesi. Ancora una volta, veniva specificato che gli evasori avrebbero dovuto pagare una multa alla corte ed al capitano di Erice, Eximen de Olit [28] e sembra che la corona stesse di fatto programmando di imporre una tassa di guerra dell'ammontare di 3 onze d'oro; il denaro doveva essere raccolto da un tale Busac (*Abu Ishaq*) Farchani Russi [29]. Nel frattempo, all'*universitas* cristiana veniva richiesto di esigere un tarì per famiglia (20 maggio 1298) e venivano nominati collettori Jacobus de Flamingo e Rogerius de Catalano [30]. L'esistenza di una tassa sui cristiani, che compare subito dopo quelle sugli ebrei, induce a pensare che l'ipotesi

---

[26] Di Giovanni, 370; cfr. L. Zunz, *Zur Geschichte und Literatur*, Berlin, 1845, p. 502-3, che spiega come la denominazione 'agostale' o 'agostaro' derivasse da una precedente esazione di un augustale (circa 1/4 di onza d'oro) a testa. La cifra di 15 onze si riferisce al tardo XIV secolo, ma sembra riflettere un uso più antico, dato che nel 1374 venne fatta richiesta al sovrano di ridurre l'esazione rispetto a questa entità: *Codice diplomatico,* § LXI, p. 88-9. Altre comunità pagavano somme molto diverse, e le dimensioni della popolazione ebrea presumibilmente erano il criterio per stimare l'esazione: Trapani pagava 45 onze. Sciacca 10, ma Randazzo solo 5 e Castroreale appena una (Zunz, p. 503).

[27] Sparti, § 21, p. 36-7; De Stefano, § 21, p. 35-5.

[28] Sul quale cfr. De Stefano, p. XLII.

[29] Il nome Busacca appare anche a Palermo, ed è reso da Ashtor come Abu Ishaq: *Palermitan Jewry,* p. 231; esso sopravvive ancora in Sicilia! Per il possibile significato, cfr. Ashtor, *Fin du Judaisme sicilien,* p. 345. Recentemente è stata resa nota l'esistenza in Sicilia di alcune comunità di 'marranos' analoghe a quelle scoperte in Portogallo.

[30] Sparti, § 23, p. 38-9; De Stefano, p. 36-7; Salinas, § 2, p. 456.

più probabile sia che si trattasse di una tassazione imposta dall'esterno alle comunità; entrambe le tasse dovevano gravare sui maschi di ciascuna comunità, ma la tassa sui cristiani era limitata alle famiglie nelle quali vi fosse un uomo "che potesse recarsi alla guardia dei passi delle dette montagne", mentre sembra che la tassa sugli ebrei gravasse su tutti gli *homines*; il manoscritto, però, in questo punto è danneggiato e parti del testo sono andate perdute.

Il 1298 fu certo un anno pesantissimo per i contribuenti siciliani; gli angioini di Napoli tentavano di stabilire una testa di ponte nella Sicilia orientale ed il traffico marittimo era preda della marineria nemica [31]. Una nuova ondata di richieste di denaro raggiunse Erice nell'autunno di quell'anno. Il 26 ottobre l'*universitas* cristiana dichiarava lealmente che avrebbe raccolto 87 onze e 10 tarì fra tutti gli uomini appartenenti alla comunità, per sostenere le spese necessarie al mantenimento di dieci cavalieri e di cento soldati a piedi che il sovrano le aveva richiesto [32] per tramite di un influente membro dell'*entourage* reale, Palmerio Abbate, fortemente radicato a Trapani [33].

Venne poi la volta degli ebrei: pochi giorni dopo, all'inizio di novembre, l'*universitas* ebraica eleggeva suo rappresentante Iudas *faber*, con il compito di presentarsi agli ufficiali regi, presumibilmente per concordare la misura della tassazione; successivamente, lo stesso fu incaricato della riscossione [34]. L'inizio del documento, con la sua datazione precisa, è andato perduto, ma l'atto successivo del registro, datato 7 novembre, indica che l'ammontare della somma venne rapidamente concordata: ad Eximen d'Olit, capitano di Erice, furono consegnate 4 onze d'oro, sufficienti al mantenimento di sei uomini nell'armata regia per un mese, a ragione di 20 tarì al mese per ciascun uomo (120 tarì, cioè 4 onze, complessivamente) [35]; sembra che questi uomini d'armi facessero parte del

---

[31] SALINAS, p. 441; più in generale, RUNCIMAN, p. 296.

[32] SPARTI, § 40, p. 60; 1; DE STEFANO, § 40, p. 67-9; SALINAS, § 3, p. 456-7.

[33] Sul quale cfr. DE STEFANO, p. XLV, dove Palmerio Abbate è chiamato "uno dei più grandi architetti dei Vespri siciliani".

[34] SPARTI, § 42, p. 62-3; DE STEFANO, § 42, p. 70-2.

[35] SPARTI, § 43, p. 63-4; DE STEFANO, , § 43, p. 72-3; SALINAS, § 4, p. 457-8. De Stefano, erroneamente, si riferisce ad un costo di 30 (e non 20) tarì al mese.

gruppo di cento armati a piedi e dieci cavalieri di cui si è detto.

Alcuni cristiani certamente servirono in armi personalmente, e fecero testamento in presenza di Giovanni Maiorana prima di raggiungere l'armata; non è specificato, invece, se i sei uomini mantenuti dagli ebrei fossero semplicemente pagati dall'*universitas* ebraica o fossero essi stessi dei membri di questa che servivano personalmente. È tuttavia probabile, per analogia con le esazioni della *jizyah* nei paesi musulmani, che gli ebrei non dovessero effettivamente servire in armi di persona.

Tutte queste cifre sono altamente significative: sulla loro base si può operare un cauto tentativo di determinare la proporzione fra comunità cristiana ed ebraica di Erice e di calcolare le dimensioni della seconda.

Cominciamo dai dati del 21 giugno e del 20 luglio. Il 21 giugno gli ebrei hanno l'obbligo di pagare 3 onze (90 tarì); il 20 luglio i cristiani devono un tarì per ogni famiglia con un uomo abile per il servizio di guardia. È ragionevole supporre che gli ebrei non fossero tassati in misura minore dei cristiani, ed in ogni caso, la *jizyah* fornisce prove credibili del fatto che il gravame fiscale degli ebrei fosse effettivamente più pesante. La tassa sugli ebrei, di 90 tarì, eguaglierebbe dunque le esazioni riscosse su 90 famiglie cristiane idonee al pagamento; la misura della tassa sugli ebrei maschi, come si è visto, forse su tutti gli ebrei maschi adulti, suggerisce che questi non fossero più di 90, o almeno che non vi fossero più di 90 famiglie ebree comprendenti degli uomini di condizione paragonabile a quella dei cristiani tassabili; se così non fosse stato, la tassa avrebbe gravato in misura minore sugli ebrei che sui cristiani, e ciò non è verosimile.

Possiamo adesso procedere con le tassazioni del 26 ottobre (87 onze e 10 tarì per i cristiani) e del 7 novembre (4 onze per gli ebrei). Adotteremo qui un presupposto diverso: supporremo che in questo caso il costo mensile per uomo armato non differisse in modo significativo sia che questo fosse mantenuto da ebrei che da cristiani; ciò può essere affermato con sicurezza, dal momento che la cifra che grava sugli ebrei, 20 tarì per uomo d'armi, è un divisore esatto della somma relativa alla tassa sui cristiani: 100 uomini a piedi costerebbero 66 onze e 20 tarì, sottraendo 20 onze per i 10 cavalieri e tralasciando pochi tarì per le spese dell'esazione, come effettivamente attestato dall'atto notarile; in altri termini, un cavaliere costerebbe 2 onze al mese, l'equivalente del costo di tre uomini a piedi; la somma pagata dalla comunità ebraica equivarrebbe dunque al costo di due cavalieri. Tale rapporto fra il costo di un cavaliere e quello di un uomo a piedi è pienamente accettabile, data la necessità di mantenere sia il cavaliere che il cavallo e il più alto costo dell'equipaggiamento. Come si è già visto, i sei uomini mantenuti dagli ebrei erano compresi nel totale dei 100 uomini a piedi e 10 cavalieri e, trasformando tali cifre in un totale teorico di 130 uomini al costo di 20 tarì per uomo, risulta che i sei uomini che la comunità ebraica doveva mantenere rappresentano solamente il 4,6% del totale. Questi calcoli portano alla conclusione che la popolazione ebrea tassabile costituisse solo il 4,5-5% della intera popolazione maschile tassabile di Erice e della relativa *terra*.

Nel 1374 Erice conta 838 *fuochi*; usando un coefficiente di 5,3 per *fuoco*, I. Peri calcola una popolazione totale di circa 4500 persone [36]. Dato che la Sicilia aveva sofferto gravemente per la peste e per i disordini interni, dobbiamo considerare la popolazione del 1374 assai inferiore a quella degli anni precedenti al peste, attorno al 1300; in altre aree d'Europa d'altronde, la popolazione medievale raggiunse il suo massimo proprio attorno a quegli anni. A metà del XVII secolo Erice era abitata da 7000 persone e si può supporre una cifra simile anche per il 1300 [37]; Carmelo Trasselli, d'altronde, insiste molto sull'impressionante declino della popolazione ericina nel corso del XIV secolo, almeno in termini relativi, osservando come, sulla base di una leva militare del 1283, subito dopo l'invasione aragonese, Trapani ed Erice risultino avere una popolazione di uguali dimensioni: la prima fornisce infatti 31 cavalieri e 70 uomini a piedi, la seconda, rispettivamente, 32 e 70 [38]. Si deve però sottolineare il fatto che le basi su cui si calcolarono

---

[36] I. PERI, *La Sicilia dopo il Vespro. Uomini, città e campagne, 1282-1376*, Bari, 1982, pp. 237, 242.

[37] DI GIOVANNI, p. 367.

[38] C. TRASSELLI, *I privilegi di Messina e di Trapani (1160-1355) con un'appendice sui consolati trapanesi nel sec. XV* (Studi di storia economica), Palermo, 1949, 83-8.

le diverse imposizioni potevano differire notevolmente, specie all'indomani dell'invasione, quando la corte probabilmente si basava su stime molto vecchie e molto approssimative della ricchezza e della popolazione delle città. Trapani, inoltre, fu forse leggermente favorita in segno di ricompensa per la buona accoglienza offerta al conquistatore al momento dello sbarco in Sicilia, e, di sicuro, la città si sviluppò molto rapidamente (nel 1374 contava 2608 *fuochi*, tre volte più di Erice), in conseguenza dell'enorme importanza che il porto acquisì nel commercio con l'Africa, la Sardegna e Maiorca.

Assumendo, per Erice, la cifra di 7000 abitanti come indicatore approssimativo, e supponendo che le famiglie ebree e cristiane avessero dimensioni simili, ricaviamo che una popolazione ebrea del 4,6% corrisponderebbe in termini assoluti a 322 persone. Sarebbe però avventato applicare una percentuale dedotta dalla tassazione dei maschi adulti all'intera popolazione; la popolazione ebrea potrebbe avere avuto un tasso di natalità più alto di quella cristiana, a causa del minor numero di celibi, di una maggiore longevità dovuta ad una maggiore cura dell'igiene, e di un diverso atteggiamento verso la famiglia e la procreazione. Si può supporre, inoltre, che una comunità ebraica più antica e più stabile avesse un tasso di nuzialità più alto rispetto ad una comunità cristiana ricca di immigrati recenti; infine, in alcune famiglie ebree di Erice, possiamo trovare anche quattro o cinque figli che sopravvivono fino alla maturità [39]. Tenendo conto della maggiore dimensione delle famiglie, avremmo dunque delle ragioni per estendere la misura della popolazione ebrea fino al 6%, cioè a 420 persone.

Anche se considerassimo la tassa per uomo per mese che gravava sugli ebrei effettivamente più elevata di quella imposta ai cristiani, e, conseguentemente la popolazione ebrea proporzionalmente più piccola, una cifra attorno alle 400 unità sembra accordarsi abbastanza bene con la stima di un massimo di 80 uomini abili calcolata sull'esazione del 21 giugno. Novanta uomini rappresentebrebbero il 4,6% di 1956,5 maschi adulti; applicando

[39] Cfr. SPARTI, § 14, p. 28; DE STEFANO, § 14, p. 22.

il coefficiente di Peri, 5,3, otterremmo una popolazione ebrea di più di 360 persone.

Tali cifre assolute devono essere considerate con la massima cautela; non sono disponibili infatti informazioni su molti fattori potenzialmente importanti: i *fuochi* o le famiglie esenti dalla tassa, gli obblighi gravanti sui poveri, sulle vedove e così via, mentre non è del tutto chiara la relazione fra le unità familiari considerate nelle tassazioni del tardo secolo XIII e i *fuochi* su cui si basano quelle del tardo XIV.

Una particolare riserva merita speciale attenzione: è addirittura possibile che la popolazione ebrea rappresentasse una porzione più vasta della popolazioné esistente all'interno delle mura cittadine di quanto ciascuna delle cifre citate suggerisca. Il termine applicato agli abitanti di Erice, *habitator terre Montis Sancti Iuliani*, si riferisce, naturalmente, non solo agli abitanti della città murata, ma anche agli abitanti dei campi circostanti; è tuttavia credibile che molti di coloro che vivevano all'interno delle mura lavorassero fuori di esse, impegnati in attività agricole come la viticoltura e che la popolazione rurale, scoraggiata dal terreno scosceso, fosse abbastanza ridotta. Può darsi, insomma, che alcuni *habitatores* vivessero fuori delle mura, ma in proporzione certo meno elevata che nelle città costiere. Possiamo infine supporre che gli ebrei preferissero vivere all'interno del centro abitato, per evitare fastidiosi spostamenti in occasione del *Sabbath*, e, d'altronde, non abbiamo indicazioni riguardo all'esistenza di una popolazione rurale ebrea.

In conclusione, la proporzione degli ebrei rispetto i cristiani all'interno delle mura doveva essere leggermente più alta della proporzione globale nell'intera *terra Sancti Iuliani*; non è però verosimile, in ogni caso, che raggiungesse il 10% del totale.

Le caratteristiche essenziali dell'*universitas iudeorum* che abbiamo delineatc vengono confermate da un documento, più tardo, dello stesso Giovanni Maiorana: l'11 aprile 1299 l'*universitas* si riuniva nella Sinagoga e nominava Saul de Challono e Chilfa de David suoi *prothos et syndicos generales*; in caso di necessità, questi sarebbero intervenuti presso la corte per difendere gli interessi degli ebrei di Erice. Il termine *prothus*, dal greco πρῶτος ("primo"), veniva usato anche dagli ebrei palermitani del XV secolo ed aveva il significato di "consigliere" della comunità [40].

Nel momento in cui le richieste fiscali si susseguivano numerose e pressanti, l'*universitas* si preoccupava dunque di chiamare due dei suoi membri piu attivi e probabilmente più agiati, a proteggere i propri interessi. Si vedrà di seguito come dal registro di Giovanni Maiorana si venga a sapere molto di più delle attività economiche di questi due ebrei.

II

Entrambe le *universitates* di Erice si servivano di Giovanni Maiorana come notaio ufficiale, e questi, nel 1298, divenne anche giudice cittadino; fortunatamente per lo storico, costretto a basarsi solo su un piccolo frammento di quella che deve essere stata una ben più vasta produzione documentaria, Maiorana registrava copie di documenti pubblici insieme ai documenti privati. Nell'Italia settentrionale, dove anche nelle piccole città il notariato si era sviluppato ai più alti livelli, atti pubblici e privati venivano affidati a registri diversi.

Per Giovanni Maiorana la redazione di atti privati di compravendita costituiva la regolare *routine*, e molti ebrei si servivano di lui come notaio sia per gli affari con altri ebrei sia per quelli con i cristiani.

Non era l'unico notaio della città, e fra gli altri colleghi, viene spesso menzionato nei suoi atti un *notarius Guillelmus de Gervasio*, ma di questi non ci è pervenuto alcun documento [41]; non

---

[40] SPARTI, § 66, p. 94-6; DE STEFANO, , § 66, p. 118-21; SALINAS, § 7, p. 460. Gli altri documenti in cui si eleggon dei rappresentanti, già citati, usano la stessa terminologia. ASHTOR, *Palermitan Jewry*, p. 241n; F. LIONTI, *Le magistrature presso gli Ebrei di Sicilia*, "Archivio Storico Siciliano", n.s., IX (1884), 328-71, in particolare p. 333-6; SALINAS, p. 450.

[41] SPARTI, § 14, p. 29; § 17, p. 33 etc. Fra gli altri notai presenti ad Erice, Carus de Sanguineo, Gilbertus de Dunayno, Bartholomeus de Mauro (p. 33), Guillelmus de Dimitro e Guillelmus de Scutera (Sparti, § 28, p. 45). De Stefano: pp. 24, 27, 29, 45-6.

abbiamo invece testimonianze di uno scriba ebreo che redigeva gli atti, sebbene uno o due esempi della Palermo del XV secolo rivelino che tale pratica non era sconosciuta nella Sicilia tardomedievale [42]. È d'altronde possibile che gli ebrei che usufruivano regolarmente dei servizi di Giovanni Maiorana fossero in un certo senso più "assimilati" di altri ebrei i cui nomi non hanno lasciato traccia documentaria, ma, in ogni caso, il tono generale degli atti del registro indica, come vedremo, che di norma ad Erice, tra ebrei e cristiani intercorrevano buone relazioni. Inoltre, gli ebrei che abitualmente erano clienti di Giovanni Maiorana erano i *leaders* della comunità, come Chilfa de David o il *phisicus* Maestro Iacob, e si rivolgevano a lui poiché, come notaio nominato dalla corte regia, Maiorana era il depositario dell'autorità e della correttezza giuridica richiesta dai più complessi contratti d'affari.

Chilfa de David è già stato menzionato quale rappresentante della comunità ebraica presso gli esattori fiscali regi. Le sue attività sono ben documentate nel registro: appare una prima volta come contraente il 9 febbraio 1298, quando acquista delle proprietà confinanti con la sua casa ad Erice [43]; in un'altra occasione i suoi affari si svolgono con un cristiano, Iunta di Calatafimi, che gli vende metà di una casa e metà di un appezzamento di terra condivisa con Ansaldus de Cartinuto e con la sorella di questi, Contissa. Immediatamente dopo tale acquisto, Iunta compra da questi ultimi la rimanente metà dei beni, acquisendo così la proprietà dell'intero appezzamento e della casa [44].

È significativo il fatto che, nell'enumerazione delle case confinanti con quella acquistata non figuri alcun proprietario dal nome ebraico: Chilfa viveva dunque circondato da vicini non ebrei, anche se, come vedremo, doveva sopportare la vicinanza di altri ebrei nello stesso edificio che abitava. Chilfa, d'altronde, non chiamava degli ebrei a fare da testimoni agli atti che stipulava e, il 24 ottobre del 1298, rivendeva la stessa casa a Bernardus Andree, catalano, che già possedeva una bottega contigua [45]; il 31 maggio

---

[42] ASHTOR. *Palermitan Jewry*, p. 249, atto del 1412.
[43] SPARTI, , § 4. p. 18-19; DE STEFANO, § 4, p. 7-8.
[44] SPARTI, § 5. p. 19; DE STEFANO, § 5, p. 9
[45] SPARTI. § 39. p. 59; DE STEFANO, § 39, p. 66.

1299, poi, il catalano figura come possessore di "botteghe", al plurale, nella stessa zona, tanto che è credibile che avesse trasformato il *casalinum* di Chilfa in un'altra bottega [46].

Bernardus Andree viene citato più volte come testimone, e doveva essere una figura di un certo rilievo nella città; si può supporre, in base ad esempi relativi a catalani in altre città siciliane, che un agiato mercante catalano commerciasse in tessuti ed altre merci pregiate [47].

Significativamente, gli altri vicini di Chilfa erano, come il mercante catalano, degli immigrati: Nicolaus Coci, di Trapani e Gentile de Scalense, forse di Scala nella penisola sorrentina [48].

Le proprietà di Chilfa si estendevano anche fuori delle mura: egli possedeva fra l'altro un appezzamento di terra incolta lungo la *via regia*, la principale strada che conduceva alla pianura, e, nel 1298, decise di destinarlo ad un uso produttivo. Nel tardo inverno di quell'anno, infatti, Chilfa stipulò con Bartholomeus di Catania, abitante di Erice, un contratto secondo il quale Bartholomeus avrebbe dovuto piantare degli alberi nel terreno, costruirvi dei muri e dei canali, e l'avrebbe coltivato e sorvegliato per quattro anni [49]. Durante il primo anno Chilfa avrebbe sostenuto le spese per la preparazione del terreno e per gli alberi, ma in seguito, fino alla fine dei quattro anni, ad affrontare le spese sarebbe stato Bartholomeus. Trascorso tale periodo, la terra sarebbe stata divisa fra i due contraenti, ma ogni eventuale negligenza da parte di Bartholomeus avrebbe comportato la restituzione a Chilfa della terra.

Il documento presenta, di fatto, la forma di un contratto di affitto benché siano presenti analogie con i contratti di mezzadria che si ritrovano per quell'epoca in tutta l'area mediterranea; ma, mentre il mezzadro doveva corrispondere al proprietario la metà del raccolto, nel nostro caso il lavoro sarebbe stato compensato

---

[46] Sparti, , § 76, p. 106; De Stefano, § 76, p. 136: 'Apothecas'.

[47] Abulafia, *Catalan merchants*.

[48] Sparti, § 4-5, pp. 18, 19; De Stefano, pp. 8, 9.

[49] Sparti, § 7, p. 20: 1; De Stefano, , § 7, p. 11-12.

con l'acquisizione di metà della terra [50]; nell'atto non è indicato chi avrebbe beneficiato del raccolto durante i quattro anni di validità dell'accordo, ma, dal momento che nel fondo dovevano essere piantati degli alberi, è possibile che semplicemente non si prevedesse che questi avrebbero dato dei frutti prima della fine del periodo stabilito.

Un contratto simile venne redatto il 14 luglio 1298 tra Chilfa ed il cristiano Gualterius de Chinchillo [51], ma, meno di un anno più tardi, Gualterius dichiarava che "*aliis serviciis impeditus*" – probabilmente lavorava altre terre per conto di qualcuno impegnato a prestare servizio in armi – era impossibilitato ad onorare i termini del contratto; Chilfa allora, amichevolmente, lo sollevava dai suoi obblighi, pagandogli, anche, per il lavoro svolto e per la cessione dei suoi diritti sulla terra, tre tarì e mezzo [52].

Il terreno in questione e quello ceduto a Bartholomeus erano probabilmente adiacenti, uno ai margini della *contrata critaciarum* e l'altro in *contrata Fons de Ficu* [53]. Appezzamenti vicini erano pure di proprietà di ebrei: Bulchayre *maniscalcus* da una parte, David *carpentarius* (che era pure vicino di Chilfa in città) da un'altra. Evidentemente si trattava di una zona di orti esterna alle mura, dove molti ebrei avevano investito nell'acquisto di terra, ma in ogni caso va sottolineato che la procedura adottata da Chilfa nella conduzione dei propri affari non era usata solo da ebrei e che anche i cristiani concludevano contratti simili per destinare le proprie terre ad usi produttivi [54].

Le proprietà di Chilfa gli procuravano dei problemi con i vicini: un altro ebreo di Erice, Nathan *faber* abitava la casa adiacente a quella di Chilfa ed usava, per raggiungerla, un passaggio in comune attraverso il terreno di Chilfa; preoccupato forse dal-

---

[50] Cfr. Ph Jones, *From manor to mezzadria: a Tuscan case-study in the medieval origins of modern agrarian society*, in N. Rubinstein, ed., *Florentine Studies: politics and society in Renaissance Florence*, London, 1968, 193-241.

[51] Sparti, § 22, p. 37-8; De Stefano, , § 22, p. 35-6.

[52] Sparti, § 72, p. 102; De Stefano, § 72, p. 129-30.

[53] La localizzazione ai confini di ciascuna *contrata* si deduce dall'enumerazione dei terreni circostanti, gli stessi in entrambi i casi.

[54] Ad es. Sparti, § 89, p. 119-20; De Stefano, § 89, p. 156-7.

l'acquisto da parte di questi di altre proprietà vicine, Nathan, il 5 marzo 1298, faceva registrare a Giovanni Maiorana un'ingiunzione che vietava a Chilfa di effettuare qualsiasi cambiamento nelle strutture esistenti [55]. Sei settimane più tardi venne raggiunto un accordo sulla questione, in presenza di Chilfa con la moglie Asira ed i tre figli, di Nathan con la moglie Syttinesi ed i loro cinque figli, e di una terza parte, David *carpenterius* con la moglie Milesa ed i quattro figli [56]; David era un altro vicino ed usava anch'egli il passaggio comune; risulta chiaro che le tre famiglie ebree abitavano un solo edificio o un gruppo di edifici disposti attorno ad un cortile centrale; tale costruzione era attorniata dalle case delle famiglie cristiane già menzionate.

L'accordo prevedeva che Chilfa avrebbe garantito l'accesso al passaggio comune ed avrebbe pure costruito un condotto sotterraneo per il drenaggio dell'acqua piovana e di altro genere fino alla strada (necessità evidente, dal momento che Erice, spesso immersa nella nebbia, ha un clima molto più umido della sottostante, assolata Trapani). In cambio, Nathan permetteva a Chilfa di operare alcuni cambiamenti nelle proprietà che questi aveva lungo il passaggio, ferma restando, naturalmente, la possibilità di usufruire dello stesso; testimoni dell'accordo, uno dei giudici cittadini e molti notabili di Erice, tutti cristiani.

Chilfa viene indicato come *faber*, un fabbro o, in genere un lavorante di metalli, come pure Nathan, ma questo aspetto delle sue attività non è testimoniato dai documenti [57]. La lavorazione dei metalli era un'attività importante di molte comunità ebraiche del Maghreb, ma è chiaro che Chilfa estendeva i suoi interessi finanziari molto al di là del suo mestiere [58] e degli investimenti lucrativi sul mercato della terra dovevano certamente essere vantaggiosi nel contesto di un piccolo centro agricolo.

---

[55] SPARTI, § 8, p. 21-2; DE STEFANO, § 8, p. 12-13.

[56] SPARTI, § 14, p. 28-9; DE STEFANO, § 14, p. 22-4.

[57] Cfr., ad es. l'intestazione in SPARTI, § 4, p. 18 e DE STEFANO, § 4, p. 7: "pro Chilfa iudeo fabro".

[58] Sui lavoratori dei metalli vedi N. GROSS, ed. *Economic history of the Jews*, New York-Jerusalem, 1975, p. 173-8; la partecipazione di ebrei siciliani ad attività minerarie (1327) è illustrata specificamente a p. 174.

Altro ebreo importante ad Erice era Saul de Challono, ed anch'egli trattava i suoi affari con altri ebrei davanti al notaio Giovanni Maiorana. Il 10 agosto 1298, con la moglie Cabile ed i tre figli, vendeva a Sadonus de Challono (o Callono) la metà di una "*domus solerate*", situata vicino alla casa con cortile del cristiano Hugo de Filechia [59]; in un secondo atto, Sadonus prometteva di pagare 2 onze e mezza entro il 15 di aprile dell'Indizione successiva (1299) per l'acquisto di tale proprietà (l'uso del calendario latino fra ebrei è naturalmente dovuto all'intervento di un notaio cristiano) [60]. Non viene indicato se i due Challono fossero parenti, mentre è stato già notato come *Challono* non sia altro che la corruzione latina dell'ebraico *Hayyim* [61].

Sadonus ricompare il primo marzo 1299, quando vende una mula nera ad un mulattiere cristiano per onze 2.11.5 [62], e qui non richiede sottolineare l'importanza del trasporto a dorso di mulo sui pendii del Monte S. Giuliano ed in generale in Sicilia.

Altri ebrei sono pure impegnati nel commercio di animali: il 31 maggio 1299 Abraham (Brachamus) de Sabbatini de Symono vende un mulo baio ad un cristiano del luogo [63] ed il 13 novembre 1303 Yehudah Ma'aluf (Iude Machalufi) di Mazara, allora residente ad Erice, scambia con Albertus de Nachono di Alcamo un cavallo con una casa nel centro abitato e onze 1.7.10 [64].

Oltre a Chilfa de David e Saul de Challono, altro personaggio influente nella comunità ebraica di Erice era Azaronus de Sydica, anch'egli, apparentemente, un fabbro di professione; nell'agosto del 1298 comprava parte del muro di una casa di un suo vicino, Luca di Lentini, che viveva anche a Corleone, nell'interno della Sicilia occidentale [65]; ad Azaronus veniva concesso di costruire

---

[59] SPARTI, § 25. p. 41-2; DE STEFANO, , § 25, p. 41-2.

[60] SPARTI, § 26. p. 42-3; DE STEFANO, 25, p. 42-3.

[61] Nel catalano di quest'epoca "ll" veniva pronunciata come 'yy'.

[62] SPARTI, § 62. p. 89-90; DE STEFANO, § 62, p. 111-2.

[63] SPARTI, § 77. p. 106-7; DE STEFANO, § 77, p. 137-8.

[64] SPARTI, § 139, p. 185-6; DE STEFANO, § 140, p. 245-6. Una seconda copia, corretta dello stesso documento venne poi registrata: SPARTI, § 139 bis, p. 186; DE STEFANO, § 140 bis, 246-7.

[65] SPARTI, § 27. p. 43-4; DE STEFANO, § 27, p. 43-4

accanto ed al di sopra del muro, ma sembra verosimile, dati gli altri suoi interessi, che Azaronus intendesse coltivare delle vigne sul lato del muro che fronteggiava la sua proprietà; possedeva infatti delle vigne ai margini dell'abitato, nella contrada detta "sottostante la fonte di S. Andrea", ed il 13 aprile 1300 vi comprava un vigneto da Iacobus de Gazarella e dalla moglie per due onze; in seguito, "*propter grata et accepta servicia*", restituiva a Iacobus la vigna, concludendo un contratto secondo il quale Iacobus avrebbe coltivato la vigna ed egli gli avrebbe corrisposto metà del prodotto fino all'inizio della XV indizione (autunno 1301)[66]. La carta del registro è danneggiata ed è impossibile ricostruire per intero i termini dell'accordo, sembra comunque che Iacobus sarebbe potuto rientrare in possesso della vigna rimborsando ad Azaronus le due onze ricevute; in caso contrario, l'atto lo afferma esplicitamente, Azaronus avrebbe tenuto il terreno in perpetuo. Siamo di fronte ad una combinazione fra investimento agricolo e prestito monetario, espresso attraverso una sorta di contratto ipotecario. Azaronus avrebbe ricevuto un interesse, ma in natura, non in denaro, e precisamente in uva e vino. La disponibilità di Azaronus ad essere pagato in natura riflette il particolare interesse di questi nei confronti del commercio vinicolo, testimoniato anche da un atto in cui, nella primavera del 1300 tale Gerardus gli prometteva 45 botti di vino nuovo (*musti*) proveniente dalle proprie vigne nei dintorni di Erice[67], ma anche qui l'inizio del documento è andato perduto e non sono disponibili dettagli sul prezzo del vino e sulle condizioni del contratto.

Gli interessi di Azaronus in campo vinicolo non sono affatto eccezionali fra gli ebrei di Erice: nel dicembre del 1299, ad esempio, un cristiano che aveva venduto a Brachamus de Sabbaono 100 botti di vino, riconosceva un debito residuo di 30 botti di vino rosso e di 15 di bianco[68].

Non sappiamo, naturalmente, se gli ebrei di Erice bevessero effettivamente il vino prodotto dai loro soci cristiani; E. Ashtor

---

[66] SPARTI, § 119-20, p. 152-3; DE STEFANO, § 119-20, p. 201-3.
[67] SPARTI, § 122, p. 155-6; DE STEFANO, § 123, p. 206-7.
[68] SPARTI, § 114, p. 148-9; DE STEFANO, § 114, p. 195-6.

afferma che a Palermo, nel XV secolo, gli ebrei bevevano vino e mangiavano del formaggio *non-kosher*, ma ad Erice le vigne di proprietà di ebrei erano abbastanza da soddisfare ampiamente la domanda degli stessi ebrei, e veniva considerata una pratica commerciale ammessa cedere in conduzione le vigne in sovrappiù a produttori non ebrei [69]. In ogni caso, era generalmente riconosciuto nell'Europa continentale che non ci fosse alcun impedimento a trattare in commercio del vino *non-kosher*, almeno per la vendita al dettaglio [70].

Azaronus continuò a commerciare vino per molti anni, come rivela un documento del 1304; l'involuto latino dell'atto consente diverse interpretazioni, delle quali la più verosimile sembra la seguente [71]: Bartholomeus de Baptizato – il cui nome potrebbe indicare una ascendenza ebrea – coltivava una vigna vicino Erice; come Iacobus de Gazarella, si era impegnato a fornire ad Azaronus una parte del prodotto, e, originariamente, intendeva cedergli il ricavato dalla vendita di una parte (presumibilmente la metà) del vino prodotto. Era stata concordata una somma di tre onze e 18 tarì, ma, essendo il mercato del vino ormai saturo, Bartholomeus potè ricavare solo la metà, o forse meno, di tale somma, vendendo il vino al prezzo di 3/4 di tarì a botte. Azaronus ammetteva allora di essersi impegnato a non chiedere la restituzione completa del debito; avrebbe dunque cancellato la somma rimanente dai suoi crediti (avrebbe cioè ignorato il resto del debito) se il prezzo del vino fosse sceso sotto la metà della somma che aveva anticipato, ma avrebbe ricevuto in cambio dal figlio di Bartholomeus, Raynaldus, del vino del valore della metà di tale somma, dopo la successiva vendemmia; se ancora una volta si fosse verificato un deficit nelle vendite, avrebbe poi atteso la vendemmia dell'anno ancora successivo [72].

---

[69] ASHTOR, *Palermitan Jewry*, p. 239-40; sebbene Obadiah di Bertinoro osservi con piacere che gli ebrei di Palermo non bevono vino 'non-kosher'.

[70] *Economic history of the Jews*, p. 132-3; J. KATZ, *Exclusiveness and Tolerance: studies in Jewish-Gentile relations in medieval and modern times*, Oxford, 1961, pp. 27-8, 40.

[71] SPARTI, § 140, p. 189-90; DE STEFANO, § 141, p. 251-2.

[72] Nell'edizione Sparti si legge "*Baronus etc. expectabit ad alium mensem Septembris quinte indictionis*", ma io leggo nel manoscritto "*Azaronus*" e non "*Baronus*" (cfr. la fotoriproduzione del foglio 80 del manoscritto); lo stesso errore appare nell'edizione di De Stefano.

Constatiamo dunque che ancora una volta, se necessario, i debiti vengono saldati in natura e non in denaro; inoltre, Azaronus sembra dimostrarsi sensibile alle esigenze del suo socio, non insistendo sugli obblighi contrattuali e sopportando la sua parte di perdite.

L'impressione generale che possiamo trarre dagli atti esaminati, è dunque che gli ebrei ericini contribuissero in modo significativo alla sussistenza economica della città con la loro politica di investimenti in agricoltura. La vigna, d'altronde, costituiva il cuore della vita economica di Erice: nel settembre 1298, ad esempio, Iudas *faber* pagava 22 tarì e mezzo a Iohannes Rogerii de Chinchillo per una vigna, che prometteva di restituirgli un anno dopo, non appena Iohannes gli avesse rimborsato il denaro [73]. Era un modo, per un abitante di Erice, bisognoso di denaro contante, di tentare di sopravvivere fino a tempi migliori.

Secondo l'accordo, Iudas avrebbe avuto diritto a ricevere l'uva della vendemia del 1299 anche se fosse già stato rimborsato del denaro: l'uva rappresentava infatti un interesse e dunque il suo diritto a percepirlo sarebbe rimasto immutato. È possibile, inoltre, che Iudas volesse assicurarsi che il vino prodotto nella vigna fosse *kosher*, prodotto cioè senza che dei cristiani vi intervenissero oltre quanto fosse consentito dalla legge religiosa.

Non si può non sottolineare, tuttavia, come anche i cristiani fossero interessati alla compravendita di vigneti: il notaio Matheus de Iuliano di Trapani, ad esempio, nell'agosto 1299 comprava parte di un vigneto da altri cristiani di Erice [74] e sembra che proprio gli abitanti di Trapani fossero particolarmente attivi in transazioni riguardanti le vigne: il 29 agosto 1299 un trapanese vendeva un vigneto, evidentemente di considerevoli dimensioni, per la grossa somma di 20 onze d'oro [75]. Trapani evidentemente dipendeva per una parte importante del suo approvvigionamento di vino dalla produzione delle pendici del Monte S. Giuliano, ed è pure probabile che del vino di Erice trovasse posto sulle navi genovesi e toscane

---

[73] Sparti, § 30, p. 49-50; De Stefano, § 30, p. 51-2.
[74] Sparti, § 89, p. 119-20; De Stefano, § 89, p. 156-7.
[75] Sparti, § 91, p. 121-2; De Stefano, § 91, p. 158-60.

che sorprendentemente, partendo da Trapani, trasportavano vino dalla Sicilia alla vicina Tunisi [76].

Sia ebrei che cristiani erano attivi nella valorizzazione di ogni tipo di terre attorno ad Erice, orti non meno che vigne, e vi lavoravano in stretta collaborazione. Bulchayra de Sydica, ebreo, ad esempio, assegnava un orto vuoto a Iohannes Nicolai de Neapoli – forse di discendenza peninsulare – ed a sua moglie [77].

Abbiamo già segnalato i molti fabbri della comunità ebraica di Erice, ma questa comprendeva anche almeno un medico che, come i fabbri, estendeva i suoi interessi ben oltre la sua professione. Esistono abbondanti testimonianze sull'esistenza di molti medici ebrei nella Sicilia tardomedievale, nonostante i tentativi – come quello del 1310 – di restringerne l'attività alla cura dei soli ebrei [78]: come mostra la carriera di Ioseph Abinafia attorno al 1400, perfino il re non teneva in gran conto tale legislazione [79].

Il medico di Erice era maestro Iacobus, noto anche come Iacobus Iude de Rumen: il 29 dicembre 1298 il cristiano Guillelmus de Gervasio, nel suo testamento, riconosceva un debito di due *augustales* con maestro Iacobus, *medico iudeo*, che lo aveva curato [80].

Iacobus era anche un proprietario terriero, ed il 20 aprile 1299 dispose che Riccardus de Caltavuturo lavorasse la sua terra "in parte piantata a vigna" nella contrada *Faldisseni* [81]; in base al contratto, Riccardus avrebbe dovuto lavorare per quattro anni, piantando altre viti, riparando i terrazzamenti e valorizzando la terra, mentre Iacobus gli avrebbe prestato 15 tarì "senza alcun profitto o usura" per sostenerne l'opera. Dopo quattro anni i diritti sulla terra sarebbero stati ripartiti fra i due ed a Riccardus sarebbe spettata una parte di 25 tarì.

Il 27 luglio 1299 Iacobus e la moglie Marzuca vendevano a

---

[76] DAVID ABULAFIA, *A Tyrrhenian Triangle: Tuscany, Sicily, Tunis, 1276-1300*, in *L'economia pisana e toscana nel medioevo*. (Società storica pisana, Pisa, in corso di stampa).

[77] SPARTI, § 102, p. 136; DE STEFANO, , § 102, p. 176-8.

[78] *Codice diplomatico*, § XXXIV, p. 31-5.

[79] *Codice diplomatico*, § CIX, CXVI, CXXIV, CXXX, CXLI, CLI, etc.

[80] SPARTI, § 49, p. 73; DE STEFANO, § 49, p. 87 and p. LXXV.

[81] SPARTI, § 68, p. 96-8; DE STEFANO, § 68, p. 122-4.

Iohannes de Ricio, cestaio due case adiacenti con un cortile per
sei onze d'oro, una piccola parte delle quali veniva versata in
contanti, mentre il resto sarebbe stato pagato a rate [82]. Sei onze
rappresentavano una grossa somma per gli standard di Erice, e
non soprende che l'acquirente di quella che sembra una proprietà
di notevoli dimensioni non fosse in grado di approntare una tale
cifra in contanti.

Iacobus, infine, non era il solo medico di Erice in quel periodo, dal momento che in un documento dell'*universtas* ebraica
compare anche un Aquatus *medicus*. Uno dei loro pazienti potrebbe essere stato Brachamus Ricius de Chalfono, che il 14 aprile
1299 redasse un codicillo al suo testamento registrandovi un prestito di onze 1.15, ottenuto dal figlio Helias (Eliyahu); Brachamus
aveva utilizzato tale somma per pagare delle cure mediche e per
altre spese essenziali ed il denaro doveva essere restituito a titolo
di legato testamentario, senza alcun interesse [83]. È interessante che
tale documento sia stato redatto in latino da un notaio cristiano
davanti a testimoni tutti cristiani eccetto due; uno degli ebrei,
Solimenus, era uno dei macellai della comunità.

Helyas de Russo, probabilmente, è una persona diversa dal-
l'Helyas figlio di Brachamus Ricius. Il 29 maggio 1303 Helyas
liberava il suo schiavo Musud, saraceno *"olim de genere sarracenorum araborum de Montibus Barcarum orto"* [84]. Questa espressione indica che lo schiavo veniva dalla penisola di Barca in Cire-
naica, che, come ha dimostrato Ch. Verlinden [85], era una fonte
importante degli schiavi che venivano venduti in Sicilia. Sebbene
dovesse essere liberato senza condizioni, *"secundum usum et con-
suetudinem civitatis Rome"*, Musud dovette pagare, a rate, sei onze

[82] SPARTI, § 80, p. 109-10; DE STEFANO, § 80, p. 141.
[83] SPARTI, § 67, p. 96; DE STEFANO, § 67, p. 121.
[84] SPARTI, § 138, p. 181-2; DE STEFANO, § 139, p. 239-40; SALINAS, § 9, p. 462.
[85] CH. VERLINDEN, *L'esclavage dans l'Europe médiévale*, II. *Italie, Colonies italiennes
du Levant, Levant latin, Empire byzantin* (Rijksuniversiteit te Gent, Werken uitgegeven
door de Faculteit van de Letteren en Wijsbegeerte, CLXVI), Gent, 1977, 154 (dove viene
discusso questo importante documento), 156-7; in larga misura identico è il testo del suo
articolo *L'esclavage en Sicile au bas moyen âge*, "Bulletin de l'Institut historique belge de
Rome", XXV (1963), 31-2, 34. Il Monte Barsteta, che fa parte del Monte Etna in Sicilia,
è un luogo differente.

per la sua libertà. Senza dubbio tale somma avrebbe contribuito all'acquisto, sui mercati di Trapani o di Palermo, di un buon rimpiazzo per lo schiavo perduto. Degli ebrei mercanti di schiavi, in questo periodo, possono essere identificati con certezza proprio in quest'ultima città [86]. Verlinden sostiene che Musud volesse convertirsi e che dunque il suo padrone ebreo fosse obbligato a liberarlo; ciò implicherebbe dunque che la legislazione contro il possesso di schiavi cristiani da parte di ebrei, rinnovata nel 1310, fosse strettamente osservata ad Erice già alcuni anni prima di questa data [87]. Verlinden tuttavia, rileva pure che pochi schiavi venivano emancipati senza che pagassero il proprio padrone.

Il possesso di schiavi nordafricani era d'altronde così diffuso in Sicilia, che l'esistenza ad Erice di un ebreo che tiene uno schiavo non desta certo sorpresa: schiavi musulmani circoincisi potevano essere considerati elementi preziosi nelle case ebree, specie per servire il vino a tavola.

Interessanti sono pure gli affari di Helyas de Russo nel campo delle proprietà cittadine; il sarto Iohannes de Actaviano, cristiano, riceveva da lui una casa ed una bottega, impegnandosi a pagargli due onze d'oro [88]; Helyas gli concedeva la proprietà "considerati i servizi che aveva ricevuto dal detto Iohannes e che sperava in futuro di ricevere"; una formula simile appare nel citato contratto tra Azaronus de Sydica e Iacobus de Gazarella relativo all'uso della vigna, ma qui la questione è più complessa. La casa in questione era stata di proprietà di Iohannes, ma era stata in seguito acquistata da Helyas; vicino ad essa era un vicolo, che già Helyas aveva comprato dallo stesso Iohannes, ed Helyas conservava i diritti su di esso anche quando la proprietà ritornava all'amico, nel dicembre 1299. Un documento successivo, tuttavia, dell'estate del 1300, indica che l'accordo era fallito, le due onze promesse da Iohannes non erano state pagate e l'intero affare era stato messo da parte [89]. Cosa fosse in effetti accaduto si può inferire da alcuni

---

[86] BURGARELLA, § 400, p. 239: Chackim di Messina, figlio di Shimaria, paga quattro onze per una schiava bianca. Cfr. KATZ, *Exclusiveness and Tolerance*, p. 41-3.

[87] VERLINDEN, p. 154 (del volume) e 32 (dell'articolo).

[88] SPARTI, § 113, p. 147-8; DE STEFANO, § 113, p. 193-5.

[89] SPARTI, § 132, p. 166-7; DE STEFANO, § 133, p. 223-4.

contratti riguardanti le vigne ericine, specie quelli in cui era coinvolto Azaronus.

Iohannes, sembra certo, aveva ipotecato la sua casa ad Helyas dietro un prestito di due onze, era stato lasciato in possesso dell'immobile o aveva potuto rientrarne in possesso, ed aveva fornito in cambio ad Helyas una rendita o servizi di qualche natura; successivamente, però, aveva mancato di onorare il debito ed aveva perso definitivamente la proprietà della casa.

Non si dovrebbe quindi sopravvalutare l'esistenza di buone relazioni personali fra i due che avevamo sottolineato prima, dato che l'affare si conclude in maniera piuttosto dura; e c'è anche di più: probabilmente questo episodio è la prima e l'unica testimonianza sicura dell'attività di un usuraio ebreo ad Erice, se non si considerano le più complesse forme di investimento agrario rilevate in precedenza.

III

Le attività economiche degli ebrei di Erice appaiono dunque, in generale, non differenti da quelle dei loro vicini cristiani: essi acquistano e valorizzano terreni, specie vigneti ed orti, vendono cavalli e muli, e, soprattutto, commerciano vino nuovo. La medicina doveva invece essere una specialità degli ebrei cui si rivolgevano anche i cristiani.

Non ci sono invece dati sulla partecipazione degli ebrei al commercio granario in questo periodo, mentre ad esso sono interessati molti cristiani del luogo [90], nè possediamo chiare testimonianze di un ruolo attivo nel commercio dei tessuti, certamente dominato da mercanti di origine straniera [91].

---

[90] SPARTI, § 142-3, p. 197-9; DE STEFANO, § 143-4, p. 257-60.
[91] Cfr. il dato per Palermo: BURGARELLA, passim.

184

Il registro di Giovanni Maiorana è, quasi letteralmente, pieno di buchi, ma da esso può essere ricavata l'immagine coerente di una comunità ebraica con un buon numero di artigiani interessati ad investire i loro capitali nelle terre di Monte S. Giuliano; una comunità modesta, come altre nella Sicilia tardomedievale, sia per le dimensioni, sia per la riuscita economica, che viveva in pace con la maggioranza cristiana, muro a muro, porta a porta, vigna accanto a vigna. L'unico segno di tensione che i documenti testimoniano è una disputa fra ebrei, quella sul passaggio di Chilfa. De Stefano, tuttavia, andava troppo oltre nel descrivere "il carattere quasi idilliaco" della vita degli ebrei ad Erice in quel periodo [92]. Certo, si può ritenere che gli investimenti degli ebrei in migliorie agrarie siano stati estremamente benefici per l'economia locale: le terre venivano messe a coltura, si incrementava la produzione di vino e di frutta, probabilmente per fornire mercati al di fuori di Erice, in primo luogo Trapani. Già nei primi anni del XIV secolo, tuttavia, il clima cominciava a mutare: re Federico di Sicilia cominciava a mostrare ostilità nei confronti degli ebrei.

Come si è già visto, nel 1310, il sovrano proibiva agli ebrei di possedere schiavi cristiani, di tenere uffici pubblici, di esercitare la professione medica [93]. Tale legislazione non era nuova, ma il 1310 segna il momento di un netto peggioramento del clima generale. Più minacciosa ancora era poi, probabilmente, la richiesta del re *"ut nullus christianus habeat familiaritatem assiduam cum Iudeis vel cum eis comedat"* [94], ed è evidente che per gli ebrei ericini la vita era diventata sempre più difficile già molto prima della crisi del 1392. Nell'aprile del 1374 la comunità non riusciva a raccogliere il denaro necessario per pagare il testatico (*jizyah*) dovuto alla Corona, e così il sovrano ne riduceva l'ammontare da quindici a sette onze e mezzo [95]. Tali difficoltà riflettono certamente un declino della popolazione negli anni di peste e di guerra del tardo XIV secolo e, dato che l'*universitas* ebraica veniva conside-

---

[92] De Stefano, p. LXV.
[93] *Codice diplomatico*, § XXXIV, p. 34.
[94] *Codice diplomatico*, § XXXIV, p. 34.
[95] *Codice diplomatico*, § LXI, p. 88-9.

rata collettivamente per il pagamento del testatico, una comunità più ridotta trovava il peso *pro capite* più difficile da sopportare.

Il 1374, inoltre, era per Erice un anno di carestia: gli ebrei chiesero esplicitamente la protezione reale nell'agosto di quell'anno, temendo che la plebe cristiana si rivoltasse contro di loro; essi venivano infatti accusati di incettare il grano e temevano che eventuali moti causati dalla carestia, se si fossero verificati, sarebbero degenerati in un *pogrom*.

Il sovrano confermava allora che gli ebrei del Monte S. Giuliano erano sotto la sua protezione quali *"servos nostre camere"* [96]. Nell'ottobre dello stesso anno veniva poi consentito agli ebrei di pagare in natura, in frumento, la *jizyah* dovuta sia per il 1374 che per l'anno successivo [97]. Data la ostilità locale, era senz'altro conveniente per gli ebrei immettere sul mercato tutto il grano che avevano accumulato.

Gli eventi del 1392, quando una folla di siciliani e stranieri si scagliò contro gli ebrei di Erice e impose loro la conversione sotto la minaccia delle armi, furono dunque la conclusione di un lungo periodo di crescenti difficoltà. Re Martino rimase irritato per il fatto che dei sudditi posti sotto la sua speciale protezione – fossero stati oggetto di una violenta aggressione, ma alla fine fu disposto persino a consentire che il vescovo di Mazara prendesse i convertiti a forza sotto la sua autorità, per estirpare alla radice le credenze blasfeme [98].

Una comunità ebraica ricomparve ad Erice nel XV secolo, quando gli ebrei del Monte, insieme a quelli di altre sedici comunità, chiesero ad Alfonso il Magnanimo la conferma dei propri privilegi. Alfonso, sempre pronto a vendere tali conferme a chiunque fosse in grado di pagarle, non disdegnò la richiesta [99].

---

[96] *Codice diplomatico*, § LXV, p. 95.
[97] *Codice diplomatico*, § LXVI, p. 96-7.
[98] *Codice diplomatico*, § XCI, p. 136.
[99] DI GIOVANNI, p. 369-70. Per le vedute di Alfonso in campo finanziario, cfr. A. RYDER, *The evolution of imperial government in Naples under Alfonso the Magnanimous*, in J. HALE, R. HIGHFIELD, B. SMALLEY, eds., *Europe in the late Middle Ages*, London, 1965, 332-57; A. RYDER, *Cloth and credit: Aragonese war finance in the mid-fifteenth century*, "War and Society" (University of New South Wales, Australia), II (1984), 1-21.

Nei 110 anni tra la conquista aragonese della Sicilia ed il *pogrom* del 1392 gli stretti legami che si erano stabiliti fra la Sicilia occidentale, in particolare attraverso il porto di Trapani, e la penisola iberica condussero dunque non solo all'immissione in Sicilia dei panni catalani, ma anche all'importazione dell'antisemitismo catalano. La comunità ebraica del Monte di Erice venne strappata all'isolamento e proiettata in un mondo ostile, quello che vedeva il declino delle *aljamas* catalane ed aragonesi, insieme alle quali gli ebrei ericini avrebbero duramente sofferto.

APPENDICE

Nomi ed occupazioni degli ebrei di Erice
citati da Giovanni Maiorana

Per chiarezza e brevità, tutti i riferimenti sono relativi all'edizione Sparti. L'abbreviazione f. indica *filius/filia* (i documenti non sempre specificano il sesso) Iug. indica *iugalis* (moglie).

Nome	Occupazione	Documento
A		
Magister Aquatus	medicus	21
Asira: *vedi Hasira*		
Asisa f. Chilfe		14,39
Azaronus de Sydica	faber	1, 21, 27, 32, 66, 117, 118, 119, 122, 140
B		
Baruc	coctonarius	21, 25, 26
Baruch de Sabbaono		14
Brachamus Ricius de Chalfono	faber	67
Brachamus de Sabbaono		42, 106, 114, 130, 136
Brachamus Sabbatini de Symono		77
Budaus	faber	26
Bulchayra	aurifex	25
Bulchayra de Sydica		1, 21, 42, 66, 101, 102
Bulfarachius de Solimeno		42
Bullara f. David		14
Busac Farchani Russi		21
Busac de Indulci		21
Busac f. Nathan		14

190

Addendum   5

*Non ebrei di possibile discendenza ebraica**

Alamannus de Moyse	103
Matheus Balbus [ebreo?]	42
Pandolfus de Moyse	68
Ricardus de Sydica [ebreo?]	1
Raynaldus de Baptizato	140
Sabbatinus de Vulpicta	77, 82, 142

* La selezione di questi nomi è stata effettuata in base ai seguenti criteri:
  a) la comparsa in un elenco di testimoni fra altri ebrei;
  b) nome apparentemente ebraico;
  c) possibile riferimento a padre o antenato battezzato.

IX

The Crown and the Economy under Ferrante I of Naples
(1458-94)

Ferrante I of Naples has suffered since his own time from a dual reputation. To Commynes he was one of an evil pair: 'never was any prince more bloody, wicked, inhuman, lascivious or gluttonous' than Ferrante's son Alfonso II, 'yet his father was even more dangerous, because no man knew when he was angry or pleased'. Since Machiavelli never mentions Ferrante in *Il Principe* it may be unfair to characterise him as a Prince before *The Prince*. But it is increasingly clear that the humanists at his court were beginning to articulate ideas of the relationship between political power and morality that have parallels with, even if they were not actually ancestral to, the ideas put forward by Machiavelli.[1] At the same time Ferrante's reign was a remarkable success story. He ruled for thirty-six years over a kingdom that his close neighbour the pope and many of his most powerful subjects wished to hand over to rival claimants whom his father Alfonso the Magnanimous had seen out of Italy once already. His repression of the barons earned him a fine reputation for brutality but also confirmed him in authority for long periods. Marriage alliances and vigorous military or diplomatic activity made him a pivotal figure in the politics of late fifteenth-century Italy. The lack of a modern biographer thus remains embarrassing testimony to the neglect of important southern dimensions to the history of Quattrocento Italy compared to the unweakened magnetism for historians of Venice, Florence and Siena in the selfsame period.[2]

A particular aspect of Ferrante's rule that has attracted some attention is his economic policy. His attempts to revive industry in Campania had a

---

[1] J. Bentley, *Politics and Culture in Renaissance Naples* (Princeton, 1987).

[2] The nearest to a biography is the collection of six studies by E. Pontieri, *Per la storia di Ferrante I d'Aragona Re di Napoli* (Naples, s.d.); there are good brief accounts of the reign in Bentley, pp. 23-34, and (more at second hand) in A. Atlas, *Music at the Aragonese Court of Naples* (Cambridge, 1985). At the other end of the spectrum there is the sensationalism of e.g. O. Prescott, *Princes of the Renaissance* (London, 1970), pp. 65-77, which labels him 'Ferrante, King of Villains'.

natural appeal for Italian political economists of the nineteenth century such as Ricca Salerno.[3] Moreover, alongside the evidence of privileges there exists the contemporary advice offered to the king's daughter Eleonora on how a prince could create wealth for himself by fostering the economic activities of his subjects. Although the princess went to live in Ferrara, it is surely right to see in Diomede Carafa's *De regis et boni principis officio* an assessment of economic conditions and opportunities in southern Italy.[4] Ferrante's liberality to merchants also needs to be considered in the light of the modern debate about the origins of southern 'underdevelopment'. The most recent work has concentrated on Sicily and Sardinia rather than the mainland Mezzogiorno, yet historians of Ferrante's Naples have insisted that the evidence reveals an export trade in raw materials and foodstuffs, and a dependence on foreign imported textiles.[5] What needs to be established in addition is whether by the late fifteenth century Ferrante and his court were aware of this imbalance or considered it a problem. In other words, how far were the privileges for foreign merchants, the efforts to stimulate a silk industry and so on, attempts to alleviate what were seen as economic problems, and how far were they motivated by a short-term desire to create sources of revenue that could pay for grandiose political schemes in the Italian peninsula? This question has added point since no one doubts that Ferrante's father Alfonso the Magnanimous was ruthless in finding new financial resources in Naples, Sicily and Spain, which were exploited in order to pay for his imperial dreams in Lombardy, Corsica, Africa, the Balkans and even Hungary.[6]

It is intended here to analyse four types of information about the economic 'health' of the *Regno* in Ferrante's time. First, there is the fictional world of the *Novellino* of Masuccio Salernitano, which presents a picture of the interaction of native and foreign merchants in the ports of Naples and Salerno, and shows a degree of awareness of the economic fluctuations that were affecting the trade of Naples and Salerno in the fifteenth century.[7] Then there is the idealised view of the role of the prince

---

[3] G. Ricca Salerno, *Storia delle dottrine finanziarie in Italia*, ed. S. Guccione (Padua, 1960), pp. 38-45.

[4] I have not had access to T. Persico, *Diomede Carafa: uomo di stato e scrittore del secolo XV* (Naples, 1899).

[5] H. Bresc, *Un monde méditerranéen: Économie et société en Sicile, 1300-1450*, 2 vols. (Rome and Palermo, 1986); J. Day, *La Sardegna sotto la dominazione pisano-genovese* (Turin, 1987; originally published as part of the U.T.E.T. *Storia d'Italia*); cf. the forthcoming critique by S.R. Epstein, *Sicily and its Markets, 1300-1500: Regional Development and Social Transformation* (Cambridge, 1991).

[6] On Alfonso's finances, see A. Ryder, *The Kingdom of Naples under Alfonso the Magnanimous: the Making of a Modern State* (Oxford, 1976); idem *Alfonso the Magnanimous, King of Aragon, Naples and Sicily, 1396-1458* (Oxford, 1990).

[7] Masuccio Salernitano, *Il Novellino*, ed. A. Mauro (Bari, 1940).

in the direction of economic life presented by Carafa.[8] Thirdly, the commercial privileges of Ferrante give some clue as to the ruler's aspirations, even if not all fulfilled; for war, with Florence and elsewhere, compromised these grants significantly.[9] Finally, there is the hard evidence of the commercial contracts from Salerno and Naples, particularly the contracts of the notary Petruccio Pisano.[10] The question remains acute how far the native merchants of the Mezzogiorno were really swamped by foreign competitors. The contracts help to answer this at least as far as long distance trade is concerned.

Imagination

Masuccio was a member of the Salernitan nobility. But his eyes were open both to courtly society and to the activities of all types of merchants. While he was clearly indebted to earlier writers of *novelle*, notably Boccaccio (who was also familiar with the commerce of Naples), we do have Masuccio's assurance that he heard his stories from traders of note.[11] Certainly, the society he portrays is one in which the Catalans and the Genoese hold a special place as men of wealth. At the start of the *Novellino* we are presented with a short tale of a greedy and accordingly very wealthy Genoese merchant who picked up a gold ducat that he saw under the nose of an unsuspecting poor tailor; when the tailor protested, Guardo Salusgio of Genoa argued that he alone could place the coin in the good

---

[8] I have used the Latin edition of 1668: *De regis et boni principis officio opusculum a Diomede Carafa primo Magdalunensium comite compositum* (Naples, 1668). Part of the Italian original was published by Petrucci, pp. 261-96; a new edition by F. Petrucci (author of the biography in *Dizionario biografico italiano*, xix, 524-30) is in preparation: see Bentley, p. 142n.

[9] Some previously unpublished privileges are printed in A. Silvestri, *Il commercio a Salerno nella seconda metà del Quattrocento* (Salerno, 1952), pp. 141-50.

[10] G. Coniglio, 'Mercanti forestieri a Napoli attraverso gli atti del Notaio Petruccio Pisano (1465-66)', *Samnium*, xxviii (1955), 78-85; Silvestri, *Commercio*, docs. i-cii, pp. 59-87; A. Sapori, 'La fiera di Salerno del 1478', *Bollettino dell'Archivio storico del Banco di Napoli*, viii (1954), 51-84, repr. as 'Una fiera in Italia alla fine del Quattrocento: la fiera di Salerno del 1478', in his *Studi di storia economica (secoli XIII-XIV-XV)*, 3rd edn., (Florence, 1967), pp. 443-74 – references in these notes are to the reprint. See also A. Grohmann, *Le fiere del Regno di Napoli in età aragonese* (Naples, 1969), especially pp. 225-34, 464-90. But the acts still need to be placed in a wider economic context, not merely of the *Regno* but of western Mediterranean trade as a whole. This is now possible thanks in part to the existence of good studies of the relations of the Catalan merchants with the Aragonese Kingdom of Naples: M. del Treppo, *I mercanti catalani e l'espansione della Corona d'Aragona nel secolo XV* (Naples, 1972); idem, 'Il re e il banchiere: strumenti e processi di razionalizzazione dello Stato aragonese di Napoli', in *Spazio, società, potere nell'Italia dei Comuni: Europa mediterranea, Quaderni*, i, ed. G. Rossetti (Naples, 1986), pp. 229-304; E. Ashtor, 'Catalan Cloth on the Late Medieval Mediterranean Markets', *Journal of European Economic History*, xvii (1988), 227-57.

[11] Masuccio, *Novella* XLVIII.

128

company to which it was rightly entitled.[12] In the *Novellino*, the Genoese form part of the fabric of a cosmopolitan Salernitan society in which, for instance, the governor of the city, who has *una certa infermità*, marries a beautiful Genoese damsel but is unable to consummate their marriage, with the predictable result that his wife looks elsewhere for pleasure.[13]

The second important group of merchants is the Catalans. They are treated with even more reserve than the Genoese:

> Nel tempo che tra Napoli e le castelle fieramente se guerriggiava, in Salerno più che in niun'altra parte del reame usavano mercanti d'ogne nazione; ove tra gli altri essendoci recapitato un richissimo catalano chiamato Piero Genefra, vi facia de gran trafichi e per mare e per terra, como de'mercanti è già usanza.[14]

He fell in love with the wife of an Amalfitan silversmith, named Cosmo; 'e ancora che da alcuni nostri salernitani, como a poco ne le loro faccende occupati, Cosmo fusse stato provisto che de prattiche e tratti catalani se guardasse', Cosmo paid no attention whatsoever. He was duped into helping his own wife elope aboard Genefra's ship; Masuccio comments acidly:

> Nondimeno giudico che'l poveretto sia in alcuna parte da escusare, atteso che le prattiche de'catalani in tali tempi non erano si note per lo nostro regno como sono ogge, quali sono in manera cognosciute e vintilate, che non solo chi vuole se ne sa e può guardare, ma offenderli con vergogna e danno, si come ogne dí le esperienze ce ne rendeno testimonio.[15]

The story apparently claims to refer to the period of Alfonso's contest with René of Anjou for the throne of Naples; that is, to a period when the Catalans had not yet established themselves as the leading commercial presence in Campania.

Elsewhere too Masuccio appears to look back on the early fifteenth century as a golden age of Salerno's prosperity. In *Novella* XII he begins:

> Negli anni che la nostra salernitana citá sotto l'imperio del glorioso pontifice Martino quinto si reggeva, in essa de grandissimi trafichi se faceano, e mercanti infiniti de continuo e d'ogni nazione vi concorreano: per la cui cagione venendoce ad abitare con tutte loro brigate de molti artesani forestieri.[16]

---

[12] Masuccio, *Prologo* to the *Novellino*.
[13] Masuccio, *Novella* XIII.
[14] Masuccio, *Novella* XL.
[15] Ibid.
[16] Masuccio, *Novella*, XII.

This passage refers back to the period when Joanna II had granted Salerno to the Colonna, from whom Alfonso the Magnanimous abstracted it, to hand it instead to their old rivals the Orsini. It is hard to say whether a decline in Salerno's prosperity might have occurred in the fifty or so years between the grant of Queen Joanna and Masuccio's *Novellino*. In 1474-78 Salerno had 856 assessable hearths, while La Cava had 1,000, Amalfi with Atrani 276, Maiori 235, Scala and Ravello 110 each, and Minori a mere 50.[17] Thus it was a notable regional centre, but greatly overshadowed by vast Naples; nor could the towns of what had once been a flourishing centre of international commerce rival in size the ports of northern Italy. This was true despite the marked contraction in population in Genoa and its rivals following the Black Death. It is known too that by 1400 much of the commercial business carried on by natives of the Campanian towns was restricted to the Tyrrhenian Sea: Amalfi briefly played a notable role in the salt trade with Sardinia and Gaeta traded as far east as Egypt, but Salerno itself had become an entrance gateway into the Mezzogiorno for foreign merchants, and its own merchants are rarely encountered outside the region by this period.[18]

Masuccio was aware of current political changes. In *Novella* XLVII he talks of how the 'rich and powerful city of Barcelona' returned to the fidelity it owed King John of Aragon at the time of the Catalan civil wars and the occupation by Louis XI of Perpignan. Masuccio moved in courtly circles, acting for a time as secretary to Roberto di Sanseverino, one of the leading figures in the kingdom, and a close adviser to King Ferrante. The stories themselves were dedicated to members of the royal house and to influential courtiers; thus Masuccio offers unctuous praise of the future King Alfonso II, an able military leader but a man of shameless brutality.[19] The stories are evidence, if not for the preponderance of foreign merchants in the trade of Salerno and Naples, at least for the reputation that the Genoese and Catalans had gained as somewhat unscrupulous merchants, whose hallmark was sophistry and trickery, both in business affairs (which aroused Masuccio's criticism) and in affairs of the heart (which aroused his wry admiration).

Idea

Diomede Carafa had no reason to extol the Angevin period in Naples. Born around 1406, he was always active in defence of Aragonese interests, and had even suffered exile from Naples in 1423. An accomplished soldier, he led or helped the armies of Alfonso I and Ferrante to key victories in the *Regno*, in Tuscany and even in north Africa. He was rewarded with the

---

[17] Silvestri, *Commercio*, pp. 40-47.
[18] M. del Treppo and A. Leone, *Amalfi medioevale* (Naples, 1977).
[19] Masuccio, *Novella* XLIV.

title and lands of the county of Maddaloni. In the 1470s he wrote a work on *I doveri del Principe* that has been described as 'more realistic in many ways than the sensational thought of Machiavelli', and less imbued with the preoccupations of the Italian humanists.[20] It is an intensely practical work, as is shown by the great amount of space it devotes to the management of the economy. Carafa was prepared to face the difficulties that arose when a choice had to be made between two policies, both in some sense evil; but the essence of this short book lies in the attempts to secure good governance not merely in order to obtain peace and freedom for the ruler to pursue his own objectives, but also so that the king's subjects can flourish. The sure result of a sound economic policy will be that the king's subjects are bonded to the ruler, and will contribute also to the greater wealth of the kingdom, which itself will provide the ruler with the funds he needs. The argument thus completes a full circle. Benign economic policies, mainly non-interventionist, bring wealth and peace, and free the ruler from the tiresome obligation to engage directly in trade and industry. Bentley remarks that 'Carafa developed stunning insights into the wealth of principalities', and suggests that he played a significant role in framing Ferrante's distinctive economic policy.[21] Perhaps it would be no exaggeration to describe him as an exponent of a rough-hewn sort of economic liberalism. His view was that when the prince has rich subjects he cannot possibly be poor.

The keynote of Carafa's approach to royal finance was the insistence that the ruler should maintain a sensible division between three types of expenditure: money needed for the defence of the realm; for the maintenance in its accustomed state of the royal family; and for the unpredictable emergency expenses that every ruler knew would arise, but few rulers bothered to anticipate.[22] This practical advice was one reason why the nineteenth-century political economist Ricca Salerno praised him in such resounding terms: 'eccetuati i migliori politici della repubblica fiorentina, non vi era in tutta l'Italia del medio evo uno scrittore, che intendesse al pari del Carafa l'ordine delle cose finanziarie'.[23] Carafa's astuteness is visible when he warns the ruler against heavy taxation and against manipulating the coinage – against, in other words, the sort of financial opportunism that Ferrante's father had ruthlessly practised in Italy, Sicily and Aragon. In a particularly strongly worded passage he states:

[20] Bentley, pp. 141-43; Ricca Salerno, pp. 38-39. For an older account of Carafa, see A. de Reumont, *The Carafas of Maddaloni: Naples under Spanish Dominion* (London, 1854), pp. 112-21.

[21] Bentley, p. 144.

[22] Carafa, pp. 53-54.

[23] Ricca Salerno, pp. 39-40.

Furthermore, we consider that those who steal other people's goods under cover of the word 'loan' deserve the strongest reproof. But similarly we should censure with equal severity those who, starting to feel the pinch, avoid the above method, and choose instead to sink themselves into the shadows of the treasury: from whose recesses they dig up obsolete and antiquated laws, statutes prised out with subtle ingenuity, like the most miserable of usurers . . . And straightaway you will see the Prince, without consulting anybody, dissipate and squander these precious monies – with no idea how much toil and misery on the part of his subjects brought them into his hands.[24]

There was a link between the economic health of the kingdom and the political order:

So it is no casual remark, when they say: Where one just rule flourishes, there the cities flower and the riches of the citizens grow. But where brute force reigns, there all concerns slide to ruin, and vanish forthwith.[25]

And later he expresses his economic theories in less than a dozen words: 'Neque enim Rex inops esse potest, cuius imperio ditissimi homines subjiciuntur.'[26]

Carafa insisted that the ruler should levy taxes on trade, saltworks and other potential assets not directly but by way of tax farmers.[27] The problem was that salaried officials tended to be careless, but those who had to maximise their own income as tax farmers would actually be more assiduous in collecting the king's dues; the king would in the end receive more funds, even allowing for the tax farmer's cut. In general, Carafa wanted royal intervention in the day-to-day operation of the economy to be reduced. It was undignified for the king actually to engage in commerce (an ancient tradition of the Sicilian and Aragonese rulers, of course).[28] But it was also certain that the king would make more profit from fostering the wealth of his subjects than from competing with them in business, since royal wealth was actually built upon the successful commerce of those subjects. For an essential difference still must be recognised to exist between the public and private domain. The ruler was being counselled not to stray into the latter domain. But this did not mean that he should leave mercantile affairs to look entirely after themselves. Carafa counselled government help to trade in two principal ways. The ruler should continue to provide ships for merchants, a practice already in force under Ferrante – as indeed under his predecessors on the throne of Naples and his precursors the kings of Aragon:

[24] Carafa, pp. 62-63.
[25] Ibid., p. 63
[26] Ibid., p. 79.
[27] Ibid., pp. 64-66.
[28] Ibid., p. 66.

And this has been the outstanding work of your most generous father these last years. At enormous expense he built a fleet of vessels – heavy transport ships and light craft – for one purpose, that they should be at the disposal of those who wanted to engage in trade. No other profit is extracted from them, than that the citizens can take to the sea and thereby either make their fortune, or increase it. Nor does he content himself solely with the provision of these ships (fitted, moreover, with all the necessary tackle); in addition, he entrusts to them the alum and wheat, and the other natural resources of his kingdom. The result of his activity is that, while in previous eras none except foreign merchants could be seen in our realms, now on the contrary you can find many native inhabitants devoting themselves to the business of buying and selling, and many ships ideally suited to that purpose; and more are built every day: to the extent that in the farthest reaches of east and west, our countrymen are there, ceaselessly trading.[29]

This insistence on the resurgence of native merchants is a striking claim to make, but Carafa is insisting at this point that he is writing from direct observation of Ferrante's policies. We are thus being presented with a view slightly at variance with Masuccio's image of a kingdom two of whose principal ports are swamped by Genoese and latterly Catalan businessmen. Carafa may not be saying that the foreign merchants have been pushed into second place, but his assertion that native merchants have established themselves as a significant economic force deserves to be tested.

Carafa pointed to Ferrante's role in the creation of native industries. His motive here was not simply to argue that the kingdom was less dependent on foreign merchants for the supply of essential goods, but also to demonstrate that royal patronage of a domestic textile industry would be a source of wealth to the crown and peace to the kingdom:

I hope it will not be long before it is easily apparent to everyone, how much that scheme, devised by your father for no purpose other than the advantage of his subjects, profited this kingdom. He acted likewise, again, in introducing the techniques of working wool. For when he realised the amount of gold being exported from the cities because of the scarcity of clothing, he at one stroke made them an interest-free loan of one hundred thousand gold pieces, so that they might have the means of getting started. Moreover, he never ceases, even at his own expense, exercising these same subjects in various skills, and in the conduct of magistracies or household management, each according to his own particular talent; and in all this it appears he has nothing else in mind, than to keep the vice of idleness from his peoples, and to increase individual inheritances.[30]

[29] Ibid., p. 77-78.
[30] Ibid., pp. 78-79.

Carafa apologises for this illuminating enough discourse on the usefulness of wealthy cities to princes, but in many senses it forms the empirical basis on which the rest of his argument about economic policy is built. Nor does the author confine himself to the urban economy. The prince should ensure that farmers have enough oxen for ploughing, 'ne agricultura deferatur', and similar care should be taken to protect the flocks of sheep which had become an especially important element in the economy under Ferrante's father.[31] All this meant that key economic activities should not have life squeezed from them by over-taxation; export taxes are seen as an obstacle to the maximisation of the kingdom's wealth, and so once again the idea is that the ruler can actually stimulate the production of resources, and thus his own income, by limiting his intervention in the productive cycle. Generosity to one's subjects was in any case a morally desirable act commendable for its own sake.

The vision of a prince who understands the relation between his own and his subjects' interests was taken further by Carafa in his discussion of the money supply. Carafa's main concern was that neither the ruler nor his subjects should play games with the coinage. He was clear on money's function: 'money is struck not for the profit of the prince, but for ease of buying and selling, and for the advantage of the people'.[32]

Carafa presents an interesting combination of practical and moralistic arguments in favour of his policies. On the one hand, the ruler should rule through love rather than fear; on the other hand, he must understand that in helping his subjects he helps himself: 'ubi vi agatur, ibi omnia in deterius ruere, ac celeriter euanescere.'[33] Carafa's prince is genuinely interested in the prosperity of his subjects, both for altruistic and for fiscal reasons. Above all, Carafa's observations were the product of experience. In some of these ideas Carafa was simply following a trend. The contemporary Neapolitan courtier and intellectual Giovanni Pontano, more aware than Carafa of recent debates among the Tuscan humanists, also portrays a liberal prince who will use his honesty and generosity to gain the respect of his subjects, and who will protect them from unjust imposts.[34] It would thus be wrong to assume that Carafa on his own moulded the economic outlook of the Aragonese dynasty at this period. It is now necessary to examine the application of these ideas – whether or not they originated with Carafa – to the government of Aragonese Naples.

Intention

Ferrante certainly adopted approaches to the economy that have much in

---

[31] Ibid., pp. 79-80.
[32] Ibid., pp. 84.
[33] Ibid., p. 63.
[34] Ricca Salerno, pp. 44-45; cf. Bentley, pp. 247-52 and *passim*.

common with those advocated by Carafa. His most famous initiative was the attempt to revive the silk industry.[35] But there were also vigorous efforts to stimulate internal trade by breaking down internal tariff barriers, mainly imposed by the powerful lords of the interior; Ferrante's assaults on the *diritti di passo* were frequent enough to indicate that the work could not be achieved all at once (he issued decrees in 1466, 1468, 1471).[36] By 1471 the king was indeed acting closely in accordance with Carafa's precepts, which were being penned at about the same time; on 20 January he attempted to abolish export taxes on raw materials, on bullion and on finished goods, stating that such taxes were not merely inconvenient to native and foreign merchants but were restraining the prosperity of the kingdom. Ferrante sees the complex export taxes as a disincentive to trade: he states that there would be many more exports if his subjects did not find existing taxation so vexatious.[37] It has to be said that the decree of January 1471 was not particularly effective; nevertheless, these comments come close enough to Carafa's views to suggest that there was, if not a direct influence from one to another, at least a common pool of ideas at court about the best way to stimulate economic life in the *Regno*. Some of these ideas certainly antedated Ferrante. Alfonso the Magnanimous had laid stress on the need to expand pastoral activities in the kingdom of Naples; the *mena delle pecore* is in many ways his creation, though even he was building in part on earlier Norman, Swabian, Angevin and even Spanish models.[38] On the other hand, the economic liberalism evinced by Carafa and Ferrante is generally absent from Alfonso's government of Naples, Sicily or Aragon.

More effective were individual grants of tax exemption to visiting merchants, such as those granted to the inhabitants of the Lipari islands by Alfonso and confirmed by Ferrante, or a privilege of 1461 to the inhabitants of Mazzara and privileges of 1467 and 1487 to the merchants of Dubrovnik.[39] The major foreign communities received privileges from Ferrante, who explained to the Genoese in 1480 that 'si aliter quam sic faceremus esset commercium in nostro regno prohibere et interdicere, quod in dampnum evidens puplicum privatum nostrorum cederet.'[40] The privilege begins with the remark that the ruler has ordained that all merchants of whatever nation who are present in the kingdom must be guaranteed the right to pursue their activities in safety; the motive that is

---

[35] Silvestri, *Commercio*, pp. 25-27.

[36] Ricca Salerno, p. 43.

[37] L. Bianchini, *Della storia delle finanze del regno di Napoli*, 3 vols. (Naples, 1834-35), ii, 72-73; Ricca Salerno, pp. 43-44n.

[38] Ryder, pp. 359-63; cf. J. Marino, *Pastoral Economies in the Kingdom of Naples* (Baltimore, 1988).

[39] Silvestri, *Commercio*, p. 13. For Dubrovnik, see M. Spremić, *Dubrovnik e gli Aragonesi (1442-1495)* (Palermo, 1986).

[40] Silvestri, *Commercio*, doc. I (iii), pp. 147-50.

cited is not in fact the good of these merchants, but 'pro bono puplico subditorum nostrorum et pro nostra nostreque Curie utilitate et comodo'. It is not perhaps easy to know how much can be made of any medieval *arenga*, but the striking emphasis on the good of Ferrante's subjects in a document in favour of the Genoese cannot be ignored; once again we seem to be in the mental world of Carafa and his peers.[41] Silvestri cites another revealing remark from a safe conduct issued to a Valencian merchant in 1488: the king must protect foreign merchants 'quippe cum ipsorum comitiva et negocia ad nostra vectigalia atque opes augendas plurimum pertinere videantur.'[42] It is in this light that should be understood the continuing generosity of the crown to alien merchants. True, they were encouraged to settle in Naples, being permitted the same tax reductions as Neapolitans if they took a Neapolitan wife or bought a residence in the city.[43] But – whatever Carafa may have implied in his remarks about the *transmarini* – it was privileges in their favour, rather than attempts to remove tariff barriers in the interior, that really produced results, both in fiscal and in political terms.

Thus in 1461 Ferrante was already trying to attract north European merchants to the *Regno*. In a grant of that year to Jean Duramont, consul of the French, Germans and English in the *Regno*, the consul's rights were confirmed over the merchants, artisans and all other 'gallicos seu francigenos, theotonicos seu alamagnos, anglicos etiam et scotos' who attended fairs in the kingdom.[44] This document should be placed alongside attempts to create a Neapolitan-managed trade route to England, though this met with only very limited success. Ferrante's willingness to look after the interest of the major Mediterranean maritime powers was more variable. The Florentines did well at the start of the reign, and saw many of their extensive rights of tax reduction, industrial monopoly and so on confirmed from 1459 onwards.[45] The Florentine banks responded, as they had done to earlier kings of Naples, with financial help in times of need, notably during the Turkish attack on Otranto (1480-81) and during the rebellion of the barons (1486). Even the quarrel between Ferrante and Florence in 1478-80 was no more than a large blip in a financial relationship that was too close to be destroyed by the official (and unfulfilled) sequestration of Florentine goods; it was Lorenzo de' Medici's good personal knowledge of Ferrante that made a rapid reconciliation possible, and that brought the Florentines to new

---

[41] For the Genoese bankers at Ferrante's court, see A. Silvestri, 'Sull'attività bancaria napoletana durante il periodo aragonese', *Bollettino dell'Archivio storico del Banco di Napoli*, ii (1952), 80-120; also del Treppo, 'Re e banchiere'.
[42] Silvestri, *Commercio*, p. 17.
[43] Ibid., p. 15.
[44] Ibid., doc. I (i), pp. 141-45.
[45] Pontieri, pp. 267-70.

strength in the *Regno*.[46] By 1483 Ferrante had decided to elevate Lorenzo to the office of Grand Chamberlain of the Kingdom of Naples, and to extend the rights of the Florentine merchants to such an extent that they came to form a virtual state within a state.[47]

The Florentines in Naples were by no means all Medicean in sympathy: the Strozzi exiles long possessed an important banking house in Naples and flourished undisturbed in 1478-80.[48] However, it was the close link between Naples' political interests in the Italian peninsula and the desire of Lorenzo's Florence to avoid a new pan-Italian conflict that guaranteed the ascendancy of Florentine businessmen at Naples in the last years of Ferrante's reign. Pontieri pointed out how the crown had actually tried to play off one group of foreigners against another, but in the end failed. He says: 'era un'utopia sperare che, imperante tale sistema, potessero fiorire quelle industrie nazionali (seta, lana, ferro, ecc.) che Ferrante, sfidando anzi tutta l'opposizione indigena, aveva pur tentato d'incrementare col palese scopo di sottrarre Napoli al monopolio dei mercati stranieri'; economic dependence on Florence developed into political dependence too.[49] It is thus interesting to see how in 1480 the king, in need of friends, was addressing the Genoese as a specially favoured nation.[50] There were certainly many powerful Genoese bankers in the kingdom alongside the Florentines, but the Florentines had the real pulling power. A letter of 20 March 1477 from Ferrante to Lorenzo de' Medici's bank in Naples stated that, in view of the king's debt of 964 ducats, 3 tari and 4 grana, the bank could export foodstuffs from the kingdom of a quantity sufficient to be liable for an equivalent sum in customs dues, from which the Medici Bank would then be exempt.[51] It was on such deals, linking the financial needs of the crown to the business interests of the Florentine merchants, that Florence had built its influence in the *Regno*.[52]

There is another example of Ferrante's intention of stimulating an

---

[46] On the Medici in Naples, see Silvestri, 'Attività bancaria', pp. 102-4.

[47] Pontieri, p. 269.

[48] Silvestri, 'Attività bancaria', pp. 99-101: del Treppo, 'Re e banchiere', pp. 233-40; R.A. Goldthwaite, *Private Wealth in Renaissance Florence: A Study of Four Families* (Princeton, 1968), pp. 26, 53-58, 238-39; of particular importance is *Il Giornale del Banco Strozzi a Napoli (1473)*, ed. A. Leone (Fonti e Documenti per la Storia del Mezzogiorno d'Italia, vii, Naples, 1981).

[49] Pontieri, p. 270.

[50] Silvestri, *Commercio*, doc. I (iii), pp. 147-50.

[51] Silvestri, 'Attività bancaria', p. 102.

[52] As was visible as early as the start of the fourteenth century: David Abulafia, 'Southern Italy and the Florentine Economy, 1265-1370', *Economic History Review*, ser. 2, xxxiii (1981), 377-88, repr. in idem, *Italy, Sicily and the Mediterranean, 1100-1400* (London, 1987), cap. VI; G. Yver, *Le commerce et les marchands dans l'Italie méridionale au XIIIe et au XIVe siècle* (Paris, 1903).

economic revival and at the same time of producing good fiscal returns: his policy towards the Jews. There is little reason to doubt that Ferrante's willing toleration of the Jews was prompted as much by financial motives as by dislike for the current fashion for persecuting Jews.[53] His encouragement of the Jews in fact aroused the ire of several Apulian towns, such as Bari and Trani. But by welcoming refugees from Spain, he and his father hoped to stimulate capital investment and to benefit from the know-how of exiles who were often highly experienced in the textile or metal industries. The large contingent of Syracusan Jews who arrived in Calabria at the end of Ferrante's reign were especially welcome because of their expertise in the indigo-dyeing industry.[54] Yet the monarchy was less happy about moneylending. It saw the Jews primarily as a specialist artisan force, and permitted at one stage a moratorium on debts to be proclaimed.[55] When a large influx of Spanish, Sicilian and Sardinian Jews arrived in 1492-93 (and of Portuguese in 1497) they were not turned away, but Ferrante and his successors were particularly keen to secure the services of the wealthy and cultured Isaac Abravanel: it was the elite of financiers and bankers who naturally appealed to them most. King Federigo, the last Aragonese ruler of Naples, even permitted the Jews to resume collection of debts, so long as he received half the proceeds.[56] Financial motives were never far from the surface. On the other hand, the obligation for Jews to wear a distinguishing mark was relaxed by Ferrante and by Federigo, and Jews (including new immigrants) were given the right to form communities, with synagogues, in the south Italian towns.[57] What appeared to Cecil Roth a good example of royal tolerance was in fact a deliberate attempt to ensure that the Jews of each city had a formal organisation which could compound legally for the payment of taxes to the crown.

The economic policies of Ferrante must in fact be placed in the context of a long history of similar initiatives. The abolition of tariff barriers on the passage of goods within the kingdom can be traced back to 1187, when King William II admitted that the problem of tax pirates in southern Italy had become so acute that the taxes due to the crown were not reaching him; he therefore abolished all such taxes.[58] Equally, attempts to revive

---

[53] But C. Roth, *The History of the Jews of Italy* (Philadelphia, 5706/1946), pp. 275-9, was as ever more optimistic.

[54] Roth, p. 278.

[55] Ibid., p. 277; Silvestri, *Commercio*, pp. 30-36, assembles some data on Jewish lending around 1490; but his vicious remarks on p. 34 are an unusual departure from the Italian norm.

[56] Roth, p. 281.

[57] Ibid, p. 276.

[58] David Abulafia, 'The Crown and the Economy under Roger II and his Successors', *Dumbarton Oaks Papers*, xxxvii (1983), 9, repr. in idem, *Italy, Sicily and the Mediterranean*, cap. I.

the cloth industry were far from new. These attempts should be divided into two classes: the creation of a specialist textile industry aiming to satisfy the needs of the royal court, such as the Norman silk workshops, and a genuine export oriented industry, which it does seem Ferrante aimed to create. The Jews had long been known in southern Italy as skilled dyers, and in some towns – notably Salerno – they exercised a dyeing monopoly as far back as the twelfth century;[59] and Frederick II had already looked abroad in the thirteenth century for Jewish cultivators of indigo.[60] Attempts to create a luxury woollen industry under Charles II and Robert the Wise may fall into the second category, but were unsuccessful, apparently among other reasons because the textile workers were suspected of heresy.[61] Moreover, in northern Italy the visible success of new or expanding silk industries would have suggested to any thoughtful Mediterranean ruler where industrial success might be sought; Genoa, previously lacking in any major industry other than shipbuilding, developed a successful silk industry in this period, by copying Byzantine secrets; and Florence tried to do the same now that the international market in fine woollens had contracted. The problem for Ferrante was that others had conquered the market first. Southern Italy's advantages would presumably lie in a combination of the ability to produce silkworms on a large scale and (it was hoped) a skilled labour force able to create the finished product. The conclusion must be that Ferrante's innovations were not entirely remarkable given the long history of government intervention in the south Italian economy; what may have been relatively new was a more sophisticated understanding of the operation of the economy, which was not simply seen as a fiscal tool.

Reality

The central question must be whether these intentions were translated into action. Ferrante's inheritance was not especially auspicious: Alfonso I had placed his political interests first, and saw the reformed government of the *Regno* as a source of supply for funds to be spent largely outside the region. He also left Ferrante the task of securing recognition for his royal title, potentially an expensive business if (as happened) the Angevins reappeared in southern Italy. On the other hand, Alfonso had scored a striking fiscal success with his pastoral reforms. In 1444/5 the income from the *mena delle pecore* was 38,516 ducats; in 1448/9 it was 92,973 ducats; but by 1449/50 it was 103,012 ducats, the proceeds of over a million

[59] E.M. Jamison, *Admiral Eugenius of Sicily: His Life and Work* (London, 1957), doc. IV, pp. 323-32.
[60] David Abulafia, *Frederick II: A Medieval Emperor* (London, 1988), pp. 335-36.
[61] R. Caggese, *Roberto I d'Angiò e i suoi tempi*, 2 vols. (Florence, 1922-30), i, 530-31.

sheep.[62] The monarchy was able to take advantage of the rural depopulation that followed the arrival of plague, while demand for wool (particularly the fine wools of the Abruzzi) remained healthy. The gains were short-lived since the wool of Castile captured the Italian market by the end of the fifteenth century. However, Ferrante clearly had a solid base on which to build. A second legacy was the favouritism that had always dominated Alfonso the Magnanimous' approach to government. According to John Marino, Ferrante made few substantial changes in the management of the Apulian pastures. Foggia grew in importance as the setting for a Spring fair specialising in pastoral products. Yet corrupt management of the flocks culminated in 1474 in the death of 700,000 sheep (41 per cent of the total) when inadequate grazing facilities were provided during a severe winter. Ferrante's approach remained that of his father; the *mena* was a valuable source of revenue, and if that meant taking sides with the great pastoralists against agricultural interests he was prepared to do so. There were frequent worries about whether the fisc was receiving all its dues from the *mena*. Even so the number of sheep had reached about 1,700,000 by 1496/7, and control of its revenues became a French ambition during the wars for control of Naples.[63]

Seen from Naples, the *mena* appeared to be a qualified success story. Revenues increased significantly over the years, and the main difficulty remained that of placating a wide variety of competing interests: owners of flocks and of land, powerful nobles with a stake in the pastoral economy, and petty pastoralists who had little clout at court. However, there was little success in creating an export-oriented woollen textile industry, and much of the best wool was sent outside the kingdom by foreign merchants; the very repetitiveness of attempts to stimulate the woollen industry into life suggests how far the king was from achieving his objectives.[64] The next question has therefore to be whether the monarch explored other ways to gain an important stake in the management of exports. The most ambitious attempt to do so was surely the creation of a trade route linking Naples to England. Once again the origins of this enterprise have to be sought in Alfonso's reign, when the first Neapolitan galleys ventured to Flanders and England (1451-52).[65]

[62] Marino, pp. 24-28, Ryder, pp. 361-62.

[63] Marino, p. 27.

[64] For relatively positive views, however, see G. Coniglio, 'L'arte della lana a Napoli', *Samnium*, xxi (1948), 62-79; and Silvestri, *Commercio*, p. 9n, mentioning an attempt in 1473 to clear an area of Naples so that industrial plants could be set up for wool production. In 1480 Ferrante invited Spanish, Genoese, Ragusan, Milanese, Bolognese, Florentine and other skilled workers to come and establish textile workshops in the *Regno*: Silvestri, *Commercio*, p. 10n; Bianchini, p. 166.

[65] C. Marinescu, 'Les affaires commerciales en Flandres d'Alphonse V d'Aragon, roi de Naples (1416-58)', *Revue historique*, ccxxi (1959), 35-36; M. Mallett, *The Florentine Galleys in the Fifteenth Century* (Oxford, 1967), p. 92n.

Under Ferrante there were further stimuli to this trade. In 1468 King Edward IV of England entered into a treaty with Ferrante; this seems to have had concrete results, since it is known that in 1473 or 1474 two of Ferrante's galleys, captained by Agnello Pirocco, were attacked on their way from England back to Italy by a notorious French pirate named Coulon, who also served as vice-admiral of Louis XI. Pirocco demanded compensation from the French king.[66] The same Neapolitan captain was in Southampton in 1478, and it is reasonable to assume that for much of the decade a couple of galleys, apparently owned by Ferrante himself, were travelling each year to the Atlantic.[67] Ruddock asks whether Ferrante was attempting to imitate the regular sailings of the Florentine and Venetian state galleys to England and Flanders.[68] This is likely enough: the state galleys regularly visited the ports of the *Regno*, and unloaded cloths, sugar, hides and other goods there, taking on board not merely food supplies but raw wool and the raw silk of Calabria.[69] The Neapolitan galleys continued to play a major role in the defence of the kingdom, which suggests that in times of peace several galley-based trade routes may have operated. One route that was probably not dependent so much on galleys as on round ships was the trading link to Tunis, along which the Neapolitans were promised freedom of navigation by a treaty with the Tunisian ruler in 1477. The Neapolitans were to receive privileges identical to those of the Genoese and the Venetians, and these rights were extended not merely to *regnicoli* but to others, in Ferrara, Urbino, Piombino and Faenza, who had political ties to King Ferrante.[70] It is possible that many of the galleys were rented out to foreigners: the galley *Ferrandina* is documented in the 1460s and 1470s, manned by Florentines and probably hired by the Medici from the king of Naples. It was active on the Florentine account not merely in Flanders but in the Levant – both Alexandria and Constantinople.[71] Such activities may have brought Ferrante some profit, but they did little to stimulate a renaissance of long-distance trade among the *regnicoli*.

The most extensive evidence for the role of Ferrante's subjects in international trade comes from the commercial contracts of the fair of Salerno in 1478, published by Silvestri. The role of the *meridionali* was in fact respectable: 211 merchants mentioned in Silvestri's collection were

---

[66] A. Ruddock, *Italian Merchants and Shipping at Southampton, 1270-1600* (Southampton, 1951), pp. 67-68.

[67] *Calendar of Patent Rolls, 1476-85* (London, 1901), p. 88.

[68] Ruddock, p. 68.

[69] Mallett, pp. 125-26.

[70] Pontieri, p. 179; J. Ribera, 'Tratado de paz ò tregua entre Fernando I el Bastardo, rey de Napoles, y Abuamer Otman, rey de Tunez', *Centenario della nascita di Michele Amari* (Palermo, 1910), ii, 373.

[71] Mallett, pp. 102-3.

southerners, as against forty-three north Italians, twenty-three Catalans, eight French and a single German.[72] These figures must themselves be modified in favour of the south Italians since several so-called foreigners had taken up permanent residence in the *Regno*. Removing the names of those who only appear as witnesses, we have twenty-three north Italians whose trading activities are recorded, seven Catalans, five Frenchmen and the single German, plus 104 south Italians. But the most important group of foreigners was not the Florentines, who were most numerous overall (ten *operatori* and fourteen witnesses); it was the slightly smaller group of the Genoese (thirteen *operatori* and five witnesses).[73] The Genoese bought goods to the tune of 6,704 ducats and sold goods for the slightly higher sum of 7,563. Florentine purchases totalled a mere 700 ducats, though sales totalled 4,525. The Catalans have a more modest profile: purchases at 1,128 and sales at 1,244. The French, primarily from Languedoc, come low down the scale, with 47 ducats in purchases, but 563 in sales.[74] Their real importance lay in the goods their home towns produced, rather than in their visible presence.

These figures must be qualified, since there is no guarantee that the source, the Neapolitan notary Petruccio Pisano, recorded a typical cross-section of the business of the Salerno fairs. It is not even clear what a notary from Naples was doing at Salerno. However, his records are strikingly consistent, whether he was working at home or in Salerno. In a group of his acts from Naples, dating to 1465-66, we find eight Florentines, seven Frenchmen, five Catalans, three Genoese, two Sienese and one Pisan.[75] We also find the same concentration among the foreign merchants on the sale of foreign cloths. Thus in July 1466 a merchant of Montpellier sold Languedoc cloth to a Neapolitan purchaser;[76] it was the revived strength of the cloths of Languedoc and Roussillon that brought southern French and some Catalan merchants to Naples and Salerno at this period.[77] In the Salerno acts of 1478 Languedoc has first place in the number and value of woollen cloths sold: 451 woollen cloths were traded, worth a little over 4,149 ducats; but the average price of these cloths was rather low: 9.1.0.[78] (In the Naples contracts of 1465-66 the cloths of Languedoc also hold first place, with 164 cloths worth a total of just over

[72] Sapori, p. 448.

[73] Sapori, pp. 452-53; Grohmann, pp. 229-31.

[74] Sapori, p. 448.

[75] Coniglio, 'Mercanti forestieri', p. 79.

[76] Ibid, p. 80.

[77] Ashtor, pp. 253-54.

[78] A good example of a sale of Languedoc cloth is Silvestri, *Commercio*, doc. xcix, p. 86, where Taddeo de Alborea, a Gaetan merchant resident in Naples, declares that he owes Geronimo de Scozio 267 ducats for the purchase price of 'pannorum viginti octo de Linguadoca de lana novorum diversorum colorum et racionum'. Scozio was a Neapolitan: Silvestri, ibid., pp. 132-33.

1,327 ducats, making an average of 8.3.0 per cloth.) By comparison, Florentine woollen cloths averaged a price of 45.4.3 a piece, and fifty-six of them were traded at a total of 2,566.[79] Florentine silks worth 318 ducats were also exchanged. English woollen cloths, apparently absent in the acts of 1465-66, were in 1478 worth only a little less on average than Florentine ones (43.0.18), and 78½ of them were exchanged, making a total of 3,390 ducats, that is to say much more than the value of Florentine cloths.[80]

It was Catalonia that made a rather poor showing, probably in the wake of the destructive civil wars of the 1460s. Ten Catalan and 33½ Barcelona cloths were traded, for 517 ducats; the cloths of Barcelona were of nearly twice the value per piece of the other Catalan cloths.[81] In addition there were cloths from the major Catalan industrial centres of Perpignan (a city now at issue between France and Aragon) and Majorca. Perpignan cloths were on average worth 31.4.17, and seventeen of them were sold, making a total of 543;[82] Majorcan cloths were on average worth 11.0.6 and a good 74 were sold, adding up to 819 ducats.[83] In 1465-66 one sale of a Majorcan cloth in Naples is recorded, worth 24 ducats.[84] Some cloth of Verona and Piedmont was sold at Salerno, but the major north Italian supplier other than Florence was Genoa, with 239 cloths at an average of 6.2.15 per piece and a total of 1,566 ducats.[85] These were evidently much more modest cloths than those of Florence, Perpignan or even Barcelona.[86] However, the contracts serve as a reminder that labels attached to cloths may indicate type rather than provenance: there is a reference to Genoese cloth in the style of Majorca, whose average price is closer to the Genoese than the Majorcan norm.[87] But the most modest

---

[79] See for example Silvestri, *Commercio*, doc. liii, pp. 72-73, an interesting contract for the purchase both of Florentine woollen cloth and of fine silks.

[80] Silvestri, *Commercio*, doc. xxix, p. 66, shows a Catalan merchant resident in Naples buying London cloth (as it is described) from some prominent Genoese traders, Manuele de Almano, Giuliano de Mari and Francesco Lomellino. See also Sapori, pp. 454-55; Ashtor, pp. 254-55.

[81] Silvestri, *Commercio*, doc. xxxi, p. 67, reveals a sale of various types of Barcelona cloth by the prominent Catalan merchant Bartolomeo Camporodone, on whom see also Silvestri, *Commercio*, pp. 99-100. He handled skins and grain as well, and made loans to the king.

[82] See e.g. Silvestri, *Commercio*, docs. xi-xii, p. 62, for sales of Perpignan cloth involving merchants of Roussillon, Catalonia and the south Italian towns.

[83] Thus Silvestri, *Commercio*, doc. lxv, p. 77, indicates a sale of one Majorcan cloth for twelve ducats.

[84] Coniglio, 'Mercanti forestieri', p. 79.

[85] Genoa was also a source of canvas, not surprisingly: Silvestri, *Commercio*, doc. xlii, p. 69.

[86] Sapori, p. 455; Ashtor, p. 255.

[87] 'Pannorum decem et novem de Janua legatorum a la maiorchina de lana novorum': Silvestri, *Commercio*, doc. lxxxiv, p. 82, and doc. lv, p. 73; also ibid., p. 54.

cloths were those known as *arbasio* or *orbace*, which sold for about 2.0.19 a piece, and of which 73 were traded; these would be relatively rough and heavy cloths, not all (as Sapori assumed) of Tuscan origin, but in most cases south Italian or Sicilian.[88] In fact, Ferrante had tried in 1465 to ban the import of cheap woollen cloths in the hope of eliminating competition for south Italian cloths in domestic markets. Not merely do the acts of 1478 suggest how unsuccessful he was; in 1477 the city of Barcelona requested the king of Aragon to intercede with his kinsman of Naples to lift the ban on cheap Catalan cloths.[89] It is therefore hard to say whether in the early 1460s cheap Catalan cloths would have been more visible in the market-places of the *Regno*. The acts of Petruccio Pisano drawn up at Naples in 1465-66 refer to twelve pieces of Catalan cloth, worth 156.0.5, so these appear not to be especially cheap textiles.[90]

The acts also reveal heavy imports of leather and of untreated skins, notably from North Africa and England.[91] The provenance of the 3,074 skins traded at Salerno in 1478 is not easy to judge; many were certainly south Italian and there is also a reference to 'coirorum centum quadraginta pilusorum de Sardinia' in a contract that links members of the Strozzi bank and south Italian businessmen.[92] Grain is not greatly in evidence among exports, but there are references to wine from Somma and Tropea;[93] there is a particularly important mention of unworked silk from Calabria, worth 769½ ducats, purchased on credit by a Genoese merchant;[94] and in particular there is a mention of silk to be worked at Taverna and Cosenza worth 716.1.10.[95] Thus southern Italy continued to supply silk, but not solely for domestic producers.

The *regnicoli* present at the Salerno fair were not by any means all from the immediate region. Giovanni Campani of Tropea in Calabria bought five pieces of French woollen cloth, already dyed, for 72 ducats; he promised to repay either in specie or in kind or in a combination of the two. The offer in kind consisted of red or white wine to be received either in Naples or in Tropea, according to his partner's choice.[96] It is thus clear

---

[88] Sapori, p. 456n; Ashtor, p. 255. See Silvestri, *Commercio*, doc. xl-xli, p. 69, for examples. For its presence in Sicilian internal trade, see S.R. Epstein, 'The Textile Industry and the Foreign Cloth Trade in Late Medieval Sicily (1300-1500): a "Colonial" Relationship?', *Journal of Medieval History*, xv (1989), 162-63.

[89] Silvestri, *Commercio*, p. 54n; Bianchini, p. 166.

[90] Coniglio, 'Mercanti forestieri', p. 79; Ashtor, p. 255.

[91] Coniglio, 'Mercanti forestieri', pp. 82-84.

[92] Silvestri, *Commercio*, doc. lxxxi, p. 82.

[93] Silvestri, *Commercio*, doc. i, p. 59; doc. xlix, p. 71. The one transaction involving grain is Silvestri, *Commercio*, doc. lvi, pp. 73-75, a deal between the Coppolas and Bartolomeo Donato of Genoa.

[94] Ibid., doc. xcvii, pp. 83-84.

[95] Ibid., doc. xcviii, p. 86; cf. doc. lii, p. 72.

[96] Ibid., doc. xlix, p. 71.

that he was active in trade from Tropea to Salerno and Naples, and was not simply a displaced Calabrian.[97] Among other towns whose merchants were present at the fair in 1478 were Amantea (with about twenty-nine merchants), Castellamare di Stabia (about fifteen), Aversa (about eight) and in pride of place Naples (at least 88).[98] The emphasis of the Salerno fair thus appears to have been on the supply of Campania and particularly Naples, but additional internal trade routes radiated outwards as far south as Calabria.

The five richest merchants or merchant partnerships of south Italian origin had a turnover that was over half of the entire turnover recorded for south Italian merchants; they were Raimondo and Fabiano Cassavergara of Naples, Luigi and Francesco Coppola of Naples, Giovanni di Paolo of Cosenza, Pietro Oliva of Naples and Geronimo Scozio of Naples. The total turnover for all south Italian merchants was 14,071 ducats in purchases and 8,827 in sales, as against 8,635 and 13,897 ducats for the foreign merchants.[99] In other words, the turnover of native merchants was 366 ducats higher, but the balance between purchases and sales was approximately reversed.

The impression therefore is that south Italian businessmen trading at Salerno could not in general command the resources of their north Italian, Catalan or southern French partners; there were only one or two exceptionally wealthy figures, such as the two Coppolas who possessed ties to the royal court.[100] In general the entry of foreign goods into the *Regno* was handled by foreign businessmen, and often (though not always) they handled goods originating in their home region. It is striking too that the Florentines, whose government had at just this point broken with Ferrante, still maintained a high profile in the trade of the Mezzogiorno. The strong Genoese presence may have been enhanced, however, by the friendly approaches of Ferrante to Genoa, and the greater importance of the Florentines in Petruccio's Neapolitan acts of a dozen years earlier may reflect the normal state of business in the major ports of the kingdom. Equally the Catalan presence was certainly stronger in the 1440s and 1450s, when Alfonso I was at war with Florence and gave massive encouragement to Catalan traders in southern Italy, so much so that they rapidly surpassed the Florentines in numbers and scale of investment. The stunning lead gained by Catalan cloths is visible in a register of the royal customs from Naples probably dating from 1457. In October and November of that year 665 Catalan cloths are said to have been sold in

---

[97] Three other Tropeans are recorded at the fair of 1478 according to Sapori, p. 450, echoed by Coniglio, 'Mercanti forestieri', p. 81; Grohmann, p. 227, identifies only the one Tropean, and is correct.

[98] Sapori, p. 450.

[99] Ibid., pp. 448, 451.

[100] Silvestri, *Commercio*, pp. 104-5.

Naples, rather more than half of the total cloth traded; French cloth came a strong second with 374 cloths (nearly a third), but Florentine sales at 68 pieces were down to about a tenth of Catalan sales.[101] This was not to last. The internal crisis of Catalonia, and the favours Ferrante found it necessary to heap on Florence, deprived the Catalans of a secure lead, even if their presence remained significant. As Manuel Peláez has pointed out, the Salerno acts of 1478 are certainly not evidence for a cataclysmic collapse in Catalan trade after the civil wars.[102] Equally they date from a period when Catalan trade had passed its fifteenth-century peak.

Conclusion

The debate over economic dualism in medieval Italy has suffered from a tendency for its participants to talk at cross purposes. Terms such as 'under-development', 'exploitation', 'colonialism' have been used with abandon.[103] The argument that penetration of south Italian, Sicilian and Sardinian markets helped to generate growth in the north Italian towns and in Catalonia is not necessarily the same as the argument that the northerners took over and ruthlessly manipulated the economy of those regions. Equally it would be wrong not to lay considerable stress on the failure of the south Italian maritime cities to maintain an active international trade in the face of north Italian and Catalan competition. Amalfi did decline. The question is when and why, not whether, it did so.[104] Yet there were important internal markets that Amalfitans, Neapolitans and others continued actively to supply; and the Salerno fair was one of the major regular opportunities they had to gain access to finished products that were simply not available from domestic suppliers. And attempts to stimulate internal production met with only a limited success. Ferrante's initiatives were frustrated by the growing complexity of international trade. The *Regno* was a valued source of raw materials, not least silk, but by the early fifteenth century concentrated investment in silk and other good-quality textiles had enabled several north Italian cities, and the towns of Languedoc-Roussillon, to gain or strengthen their grip on the international trade in textiles. This trade was itself dominated by famous names: Majorca, Florence, Barcelona, among many Mediterranean examples. Naples failed to add itself to the list, and

---

[101] Del Treppo, *Mercanti catalani*, p. 244; Ashtor, p. 254.

[102] M. Peláez, *Catalunya després de la guerra civil del segle XV* (Barcelona, 1981), especially 166-69, where he remarks of the 1470s that 'la vinculació entre el commerç de Nàpols i el de Barcelona fou, sens dubte, una realitat'.

[103] See the work of Bresc and Day for fairly extensive use of these terms; compare the stern strictures of Epstein in his forthcoming book: note 5 *supra*.

[104] See del Treppo and Leone, *Amalfi medioevale*, for the best discussion of the contraction of its trade to a mainly Tyrrhenian orbit by 1400.

investment in the production of raw silk or wool resulted in an increase in the sale abroad of unworked fibres, rather than creating a domestic industry on a large scale.

It has to be remembered that Ferrante and Carafa were not hostile to the foreign commercial presence. Ferrante did see the commercial and financial links to Florence, Genoa and Catalonia as a means to win wealth for the kingdom. Carafa's recommendations were imaginative and closely reasoned. He and his king observed precisely enough the desirability of providing a sound industrial and agrarian base in the *Regno*. What they were not actually able to do was to conjure the image into life.

X

Gli italiani fuori d'Italia

1. *Gli emigrati nella storia dell'Italia medievale.*

Durante il Medioevo, in un certo senso, il concetto degli italiani fuori d'Italia è irreale: i mercanti italiani si consideravano anzitutto fedeli alla città madre da cui essi, o i loro avi, provenivano; e in generale era soltanto agli occhi degli estranei che essi venivano talvolta assimilati in un unico gruppo di *Lombardi* o *Rûm*, sebbene fossero anche spesso descritti dai cronisti come «nazioni» separate (ad esempio) di pisani e genovesi[1]. Sotto molti aspetti, è comunque possibile parlare di una comunità di espatriati italiani nel Mediterraneo e oltre dal 1250. In primo luogo, i tre gruppi dominanti di mercanti occidentali che commerciavano con il Levante e con il Nord Africa erano composti da cittadini delle repubbliche rivali dell'Italia del Nord di Genova, Venezia e Pisa; questa rivalità sconvolgeva la pace dei mari attorno all'Italia in numerose occasioni; e fu precisamente la mancanza di cooperazione tra di esse, unita però alla somiglianza dei loro propositi, a far identificare agli estranei questi gruppi come mercanti italiani. Cosí gli imperatori bizantini cercarono di mettere Venezia contro Pisa e Genova nel XII secolo, e Genova contro Venezia nel XIII, consapevoli delle ambizioni comuni, ma tra loro contrastanti, delle repubbliche dell'Italia del Nord. Visto in questa luce, il termine «italiano», se applicato ai mercanti, era quasi una connotazione peggiorativa, che suggeriva un tipico stile di comportamento, litigioso e insensibile ai richiami di autorità superiori. In secondo luogo, esisteva una dimensione positiva dell'identità italiana fuori d'Italia: le attività delle tre principali città marinare avevano un effetto di stimolo sulla vita economica dell'entroterra italiano. I numerosi toscani che commerciavano sotto la bandiera di Pisa, anche se erano abitanti di Siena o di San Gimignano o di Firenze, traevano vantaggio dalla protezione offerta dai governanti stranieri ai cittadini delle tre grandi repubbliche e ai loro alleati[2]. L'espansione di Pisa, Genova e Venezia era lontana dal rappresentare un fenomeno esclusivo di quelle città; nella scia degli italiani delle città marinare seguivano gli abitanti di Verona, Piacenza, Arezzo, contribuendo a finanziare i legami commerciali che collegavano gli italiani dell'interno ai mercati di Spagna, del Levante e del Nord Africa.

Resta tuttavia impossibile tracciare confini precisi, che dividano gli «autentici» italiani dai loro vicini. I provenzali erano costretti all'occorrenza a commerciare attraverso Genova e Pisa, e potevano perciò talvolta reclamáte benefici fiscali oltremare, come se fossero stati di fatto degli italiani. E alcune aree dell'Italia moderna, specialmente la Sicilia e la Sardegna, furono culturalmente ed etnicamente distinte dal continente fino a che, nel XII e XIII secolo, vi ebbe inizio la massiccia immigrazione che trasformò almeno la Sicilia in un Nuovo Mondo di colonizzatori italiani, dominatori dei mercati che una volta erano stati la riserva di musulmani e greci. La trasformazione stessa della popolazione delle isole serve a ricordare che, nelle isole come sul continente, l'espansione demografica delle città era resa possibile soltanto da una costante corrente di immigrati, non tutti di origine peninsulare. In altre parole, il cittadino italiano aveva il viaggio nel sangue: le città erano principalmente abitate da immigrati e dai loro discendenti, alcuni dei quali provenienti dal vicino contado, altri da Francia, Germania, Dalmazia. E forse, in conseguenza a ciò, il senso di appartenere alla comunità non consisteva semplicemente in un sentimento per la città come luogo. Ciò che contava di più era il senso della città come comunità: in effetti, il cittadino poteva fare i bagagli e viaggiare ad Acri, a Palermo, a Maiorca o in qualunque altro luogo senza perdere uno stretto contatto con la propria comunità. I mercanti italiani disseminati per il Mediterraneo costituivano dunque una vera diaspora, tenuta insieme non solamente dai casi della stirpe, ma dal comune senso di una identità speciale [3]. E tale identità veniva espressa non tanto culturalmente, quanto dal punto di vista legale: in quei diritti di esenzione fiscale o nell'accettazione della giurisdizione di un console [4].

2. Tipi di emigrati italiani.

Alcune di queste osservazioni si applicano chiaramente in misura diversa a quegli emigrati italiani che non erano mercanti: gli ecclesiastici che viaggiavano quali emissari papali in Inghilterra, come il legato Pandolfo all'inizio del XIII secolo, o coloro ai quali si concedevano diocesi in terre di frontiera recentemente conquistate, come il formidabile Daimberto da Pisa, patriarca di Gerusalemme al tempo della prima Crociata. Le figure intellettuali dominanti dell'Europa del Nord alla fine dell'XI secolo, Lanfranco e Anselmo, entrambi abati di Bec in Normandia ed entrambi arcivescovi di Canterbury, venivano da territori che formano parte dell'Italia moderna; e il più influente teologo del XIII secolo, Tommaso d'Aquino, era naturalmente un «regnicolo» che lasciò l'Italia per lo stimolante ambiente

intellettuale di Parigi. Allo stesso modo, l'esistenza di grandi ordini internazionali come i benedettini e le loro ramificazioni, o come i francescani
e i domenicani, comportava il movimento di un grande numero di italiani
attraverso le Alpi al servizio del loro ordine. Infine, c'erano molti cavalieri
italiani che servivano Cristo partecipando alle Crociate: non semplicemente i crociati navigatori delle repubbliche marinare, ma i cospicui contingen-
ti lombardi della prima Crociata o i cavalieri di Bologna, che furono attivi
nella quinta Crociata (1218-21) e assunsero il controllo di parte della città
di Damietta, allora conquistata'.

I monaci e i frati viaggiatori possono apparire lontani dalla storia economica d'Italia, e piú occupati, in certi casi, a condannare i comportamenti
da usurai dei mercanti piuttosto che a promuovere l'attività finanziaria.
Ma la Chiesa Romana giocò un ruolo altamente significativo nello sviluppo
della diaspora italiana. La primissima penetrazione ben documentata dei
finanzieri italiani nell'Europa del Nord riguarda i *mercatores camere* che vi
si recarono per conto del papa allo scopo di raccogliere tasse per Roma; e
il rapido sviluppo nel XIII secolo della decima clericale, usata per finanziare
guerre contro i nemici della Chiesa (come Manfredi di Svevia), si risolse in
un impiego piú diffuso di agenti italiani per la raccolta delle entrate. È difficile accertare se gli italiani venivano impiegati perché possedevano già capacità speciali, o se essi acquisivano tale particolare destrezza a seguito della loro nomina ad esattori papali; quello che è chiaro è che le opportunità
offerte dal papato alimentarono la vasta espansione degli affari italiani a
nord delle Alpi nel XIII e nel XIV secolo. La presenza italiana in Irlanda, ad
esempio, fu determinata sia dalla ricerca di lana di buona qualità, sia dal
desiderio del papato di estorcere tasse dai suoi estremi territori annessi.

Il secondo gruppo principale di emigrati italiani era formato dagli artigiani. La presenza ad Avignone di un largo numero di orafi e di altri ope-
rai qualificati, durante il periodo della residenza papale, trasformò la città
da un centro provenzale in un centro di cultura internazionale; tra coloro
che provvedevano alle esigenze del papato ad Avignone c'era Simone Martini, uno dei grandi artisti del primo Trecento. Ma c'erano anche esperti
tessitori di origine italiana in centri tessili stranieri, come Montpellier nel
tardo XIII secolo.

3. *Coloni ed emigranti.*

In generale, è ragionevole distinguere due tipi di emigrati italiani: quelli che si stabilivano permanentemente oltremare – noti a Costantinopoli
intorno al 1150 sotto il nome di *bourgesioi* – e quelli che non desiderava-

no mettere radici. I mercenari del Nord Africa, che certamente includevano italiani, o i crociati, o alcuni degli artisti piú famosi, avevano solitamente intenzione di ritornare a casa; ma c'erano anche autentici coloni, alcuni dei quali li troviamo signori attorno a Tiro, nel regno di Gerusalemme, o proprietari terrieri nella Creta veneziana; e, oltre a loro, c'erano negozianti a Costantinopoli, a Durazzo o nella Francia meridionale. Gli esempi piú importanti di emigrazione su larga scala sono visibili, entro il territorio dell'Italia moderna, nella forma della colonizzazione latina di Sicilia e di Sardegna. Nella Corsica meridionale, Bonifacio divenne il punto focale di una fitta rete commerciale controllata, dal 1195 in avanti, dai genovesi, e interessata soprattutto allo sfruttamento della Sardegna settentrionale (piuttosto che della Corsica stessa). Furono gli emigrati italiani del continente a dominare questo commercio, a costruire e popolare le città della Corsica (con emigrati sardi come compagni a Bonifacio). E furono monaci italiani a cercare di sottomettere l'interno della Corsica. Nel tardo XIII secolo Bonifacio era divenuta una città autonoma, governata a tutti gli effetti dai suoi coloni, che curavano i suoi interessi non meno di quelli di Genova. Il caso corso presenta molte analogie con la penetrazione italiana in altre aree del Mediterraneo e oltre: Creta, Chio, il Mar Nero, l'Andalusia[6].

La presenza italiana fuori d'Italia fu cosí espressa anche nella costruzione di città, nella formazione di una classe mercantile residente di espatriati, e nella creazione di reti commerciali sussidiarie che spesso non erano legate alla città madre in Italia, ma guardavano in direzioni completamente opposte. I veneziani nella Costantinopoli del XII secolo erano particolarmente attivi nel commercio con l'Italia, ma erano anche coinvolti nell'esportazione di prodotti greci ad Alessandria, in Siria e sulle coste della Grecia e dell'Asia Minore. Esaminando diversi esempi dell'espansione italiana oltremare nel Medioevo, sarà possibile identificare l'importanza che i mercanti italiani insediati oltremare attribuivano al commercio con la città madre, e agli altri tipi di contatto con la propria terra natale, e sarà possibile individuare il loro grado di integrazione nella vita economica della società che ne ospitava l'attività[7].

4. Comunità organizzate d'oltremare.

Una delle caratteristiche piú significative delle comunità mercantili italiane nel Mediterraneo e oltre era la cristallizzazione della loro vita corporativa in una serie di istituzioni permanenti. Persino dove pochi italiani passavano la loro vita dalla nascita alla morte nelle basi oltremare, come in Tunisia o ad Alessandria, esistevano funzionari permanenti il cui dovere era di rappresentare i mercanti italiani (divisi, naturalmente, tra veneziani, pisani, genovesi, siciliani e altri sottogruppi) dinanzi al governo locale; gli stessi consoli (per citare il loro titolo piú frequente) giudicavano anche le dispute tra i mercanti, amministravano la proprietà ceduta alla città madre – il fondaco, o magazzino, la pesa pubblica, e, con l'aiuto ecclesiastico, la chiesa della comunità. Il paradosso è che, per facilitare il commercio dei visitatori temporanei, era essenziale creare istituzioni permanenti. I diritti dei consoli riguardo ai coloni fissi nei porti oltremare erano piú incerti; fin dalla metà del xii secolo l'imperatore bizantino Emanuele Comneno cercò di allontare i coloni permanenti veneziani di Costantinopoli dalla giurisdizione del balio nominato dalla repubblica. Evidentemente, quello che gli italiani cercavano (ma raramente, o quasi mai, ottenevano) era la giurisdizione consolare su tutti i loro concittadini negli insediamenti oltremare, e su tutti i procedimenti legali in cui erano coinvolti i loro compatrioti. Ma persino nel regno latino di Gerusalemme non furono in grado di ottenere una giurisdizione cosí ampia come quella che gli era stata promessa.

Alla metà del xiii secolo, i consoli pisani di Acri erano uomini relativamente giovani, di buona famiglia, non necessariamente ricchissimi: per loro, si trattava di una tappa sulla strada della nomina politica nella città madre[8]. Particolarmente importante per l'ascesa dei consoli appare la crescita di una vera e propria burocrazia locale nelle colonie italiane d'oltremare: i privilegi degli imperatori bizantini, che autorizzavano i veneziani a impiegare i loro pesi e misure, indicano che i veneziani potevano imporre le proprie tasse sui loro connazionali, come pure tariffe per pesare le merci, entro l'area degli insediamenti veneziani; persino dove i privilegi sembrano stabilire altrimenti, i mercanti non erano realmente esenti da tutte le imposte, ma le pagavano alla propria comunità piuttosto che al governo locale. Gli storici hanno allegramente dimenticato che, nella misura in cui le colonie crescevano, cresceva anche l'onere finanziario di amministrarle. Tutto ciò suggerisce che i consolati non erano diretti come liberi servizi pubblici; ci si aspettava che essi producessero entrate molto considerevoli, e non semplicemente per coprire i costi dell'amministrazione.

I consoli erano i rappresentanti di intere comunità, e si assumevano responsabilità non solo per i loro autentici connazionali, ma anche per coloro che provenivano da città italiane limitrofe e aderivano volontariamente. Il console pisano di Acri aveva un mandato papale di protezione sui mercanti di San Gimignano. Ciononostante, qualunque acquisizione finanziaria non andava agli alleati ma a Pisa stessa; le proprietà dei sangimignanesi che morivano in Siria vennero espropriate dal console pisano, come se essi fossero pisani, cogliendo cosí alla sprovvista il governo della piccola città toscana[9]. Ma dal tardo xiii secolo è visibile un nuovo sviluppo: il potere della capitale fiorentina, e le profonde divisioni politiche entro Firenze stessa, condussero alla concessione di privilegi da parte dei governanti stranieri a singole banche toscane, e non semplicemente a tutti i fiorentini; Carlo d'Angiò era pronto a difendere soltanto gli interessi di specifiche compagnie dei guelfi fiorentini, nel commercio della Provenza e dell'Italia del Sud, e una tendenza simile è visibile in Inghilterra, nel Delfinato e in qualsiasi altra parte dove i governanti erano meno interessati al vessillo guelfo dei loro creditori, ma cercavano di stabilire un rapporto diretto con coloro che effettivamente controllavano le maggiori quantità di capitale[10]. Questo tipo di relazione influenzava direttamente i mercanti delle repubbliche marinare, perché era spesso su navi genovesi, ad esempio, che i banchieri fiorentini trasportavano le loro merci in Spagna, in Tunisia e nel Levante. Vediamo cosí, dal 1300, due tipi di comunità di mercanti d'oltremare: i grandi fondachi, organizzati intorno ad un console, che parlava per la comunità in presenza dell'emiro, sultano o imperatore; e le filiali bancarie, strettamente controllate dai loro quartier generali in Toscana, spesso con diretto accesso al sovrano e con diritti molto speciali di esenzione dalle tasse, anche se tecnicamente parte della piú larga comunità degli espatriati italiani.

5. Gli Italiani nel Mediterraneo.

La storia delle colonie italiane deve essere esaminata caso per caso; ci fu scarsa uniformità nell'atteggiamento che i governanti adottavano nei confronti degli italiani, e anche nell'atteggiamento assunto dagli italiani quando acquistavano per se stessi il controllo delle città mediterranee e delle isole. Come regola generale, sembra che gli italiani del primo XII secolo desiderassero ottenere una totale esenzione dalle tasse, pieni diritti di giurisdizione interna, controllo sui propri magazzini, pese pubbliche, chiese, e altre facilitazioni essenziali, e, se possibile, l'esclusione degli altri gruppi che avrebbero potuto minacciare il loro primato commerciale. Tali aspirazioni erano realizzate molto raramente, se mai lo erano, nonostante fossero state fatte promesse in tal senso dagli imperatori bizantini e dai governanti franchi in Siria. Ma è chiaro che la Siria e Bisanzio forniscono due degli esempi piú significativi di acquisizione di uno status privilegiato da parte degli italiani, tanto piú in quanto essi sono ben documentati. Un terzo esempio, Tunisi, rivela le difficoltà a cui gli italiani dovettero far fronte in ambiente arabo, trovandosi confinati in uno specifico quartiere della città e dipendendo pesantemente dalla benevolenza del signore; fortunatamente, la colonia genovese a Tunisi ha lasciato una notevole documentazione delle proprie attività quotidiane alla fine del XIII secolo negli atti notarili di Pietro Battifoglio, conservati a Genova. Infine, la piú lenta penetrazione degli italiani in Spagna solleva il problema della capacità degli italiani di coesistere con i rivali latini della Catalogna e della Francia del Sud, nell'occupazione dei territori recentemente riconquistati. Verso la fine del XIII secolo, gli italiani erano attivi nella creazione di rotte marittime verso l'Inghilterra e le Fiandre, attraverso la Spagna meridionale, e qui vediamo il consolidamento dei legami esistenti tra l'Italia e le città tessili dell'Europa del Nord, in parte manifestati dallo sviluppo dei quartieri italiani a Bruges, Londra e altrove.

5.1. Bisanzio e il Mar Nero.

I legami commerciali tra l'Italia e Bisanzio non furono mai completamente interrotti nel primo Medioevo: la continua fioritura di Napoli come centro di commercio addirittura nel VI secolo fornisce la prova che, sebbene si fosse verificata, nel primo Medioevo, una netta contrazione del commercio tra Est e Ovest, non ci fu nessun periodo di lunga durata in cui la navigazione nel Mediterraneo fosse cessata interamente. Dai primi del X secolo le rimanenti aree di sovranità bizantina in Italia, intorno alle lagune veneziane e lungo la costa della Puglia, stavano conducendo un traffico abbastanza intenso che legava i Balcani occidentali all'Italia, al quale partecipavano i mercanti di Amalfi e di Gaeta, soggetti a Bisanzio soltanto nel senso piú simbolico del termine. Dagli anni ottanta dell'XI secolo, come afferma Anna Comnena, Durazzo nella moderna Albania era abitata per metà da veneziani e per metà da amalfitani e (anche se in ciò vi è una certa esagerazione) il coinvolgimento italiano con il fianco piú occidentale dei Balcani rimase una caratteristica molto importante del commercio a Bisanzio durante il Medioevo[11]. Tuttavia ciò che venne rapidamente a caratterizzare i rapporti tra Venezia (in particolare) e Costantinopoli fu il grado di reale indipendenza che i supposti *duli*, o 'sudditi', dell'imperatore possedevano[12]. I veneziani furono completamente esentati dalle imposte commerciali da pagare al governo bizantino a partire dal 1082 e, benché nessun altro gruppo di italiani ottenesse una tale posizione di privilegio, i veneziani, i genovesi e i pisani beneficiavano tutti di un livello di tassazione inferiore rispetto a quello gravante sui sudditi greci dell'imperatore. Questo non significa, come si ritiene comunemente, che gli italiani acquistassero dalla metà del XII secolo una posizione di comando nel commercio del mondo bizantino, né che la tesoreria imperiale fosse privata della maggior parte delle sue entrate in seguito alle presunte attività parassitarie degli italiani; i beneficiari erano tanto gli imperatori bizantini, che garantivano flotte per perlustrare i mari Egeo e Ionio, quanto gli stessi italiani. Ma i mercanti italiani acquistarono probabilmente un posto predominante nel commercio a lunga distanza del mondo bizantino, sia verso l'Italia sia nell'Egeo. Questa può essere stata, nondimeno, una sorpresa per gli imperatori greci, dato che si è sostenuto che il privilegio del 992, e probabilmente quello del 1082, riguardavano l'esenzione dalle tasse nel rispetto del commercio bilaterale soltanto tra Italia e Bisanzio, e che non ci si aspettava che le Bolle d'Oro si risolvessero in un pesante coinvolgimento veneziano nel commercio interno bizantino[13]. Di fatto, nel periodo successivo gli imperatori si preoccuparono di non fare concessioni cosí generose ad altri gruppi di italiani, cosicché i genovesi constatarono come il meglio che Emanuele I avrebbe offerto loro sarebbe stata una riduzione della principale imposta (il *kommerkion*) del 4 per cento, e ciò solo nel caso di commercio diretto tra Costantinopoli e Genova o viceversa.

Il privilegio del 1082 conteneva due affermazioni reciprocamente contraddittorie. Da un lato, i veneziani dovevano essere liberi di commerciare attraverso l'intero impero; dall'altro, dovevano essere provvisti di una lista di trentatre città, inclusa la capitale, dove potevano commerciare liberi da tasse; queste città erano di fatto tutte nell'Adriatico, nello Ionio e nell'Egeo, ed è chiaro che gli imperatori non volevano lasciar entrare i veneziani nel Mar Nero. Cipro e Creta, in un primo momento escluse, furono aggiunte alla lista dalle concessioni piú tarde del 1126 e del 1148. Quale che fosse l'intenzione del *basileus*, subito ci furono coloni veneziani in città mai menzionate da una qualunque crisobolla, come Halmyros, e non esistono visite documentate dei veneziani ad altre città che invece figurano nelle crisobolle, come Demetrias (in realtà, molto vicina ad Halmyros)[14]. Esiste persino la prova del possesso di terre veneziane intorno ad Halmyros nel XII secolo.

Sarebbe sbagliato, comunque, supporre che le colonie italiane a Bisanzio fossero un prodotto naturale generato dalle generose condizioni del privilegio del 1082. Non soltanto gli imperatori cercavano di recuperare tutto quanto, o molto di ciò che avevano concesso, ma essi concedevano assai meno di quello che generalmente si suppone. Sappiamo adesso che i veneziani nel 1082 non ricevettero un quartiere a Costantinopoli, ma proprietà isolate nel principale quartiere di affari della metropoli, con punti di attracco fisicamente staccati da alcuni dei loro altri possedimenti[15]. La creazione di un quartiere veneziano fu in parte opera di un imperatore ostile, Emanuele (1143-80), che vide nei conflitti dei veneziani e dei genovesi per le strade della città, come anche nell'ostilità veneziana verso gli interessi di politica estera di Bisanzio, una forza potenzialmente dirompente; egli creò un ghetto virtuale per i veneziani, dando loro in delega (per esempio) i quartieri francesi e tedeschi, in modo da consolidare i loro possessi in un unico quartiere.

Nel XII secolo queste colonie a Bisanzio non erano controllate direttamente dalla città madre in Italia. Dal 1107 il patriarca di Grado aveva a tutti gli effetti interesse ad esercitare controlli nella stessa Costantinopoli; da lui il comune di Venezia affittava la terra, sebbene egli pagasse anche un affitto di 160 lire all'anno al doge per il suo diritto di sfruttare i bagni pubblici, il panificio, il forno, le misure del vino e dell'olio e i negozi intorno alla chiesa veneziana nella città. Nel 1206 il veneziano Pascale Bollano pagava 72 hyperperi all'anno al patriarca di Grado per l'uso dei pesi e delle misure della comunità veneziana di Costantinopoli[16]. Era la Chiesa veneziana a dominare le colonie oltremare. Sull'isola di Lemno l'oratorio di San Biagio era un possedimento di San Giorgio Maggiore.

Ma com'era la comunità veneziana di Costantinopoli? Un censimento del 1206 rivela che Enrico Alemanno era un residente tedesco nei territori del patriarca di Grado a Costantinopoli, mentre lo stesso documento nomina anche i greci Alexios e Theodoros di Durazzo, essa stessa una delle maggiori stazioni commerciali veneziane dell'impero. Venezia si poneva come intermediaria tra luoghi come Costantinopoli, Acri, Alessandria e la Lombardia, la Germania e oltre; nel tardo XII secolo il celebre mercante tedesco Bernardus Teutonicus gettava le basi di quello che sarebbe divenuto il fondaco dei tedeschi a Venezia[17]. E alcune delle storie di maggior successo nella Venezia del XII secolo riguardavano mercanti che non erano di origine veneziana, come Dobromir Stagnario, uno schiavo schiavone che prese il nome di famiglia del suo padrone patrizio[18]. I veneziani d'oltremare erano dunque un gruppo sfuggente, certamente dominato dalle grandi e autentiche famiglie veneziane, gli Ziani, i Tiepolo, i Dandolo, che esercitavano la direzione delle comunità e investivano capitali nelle maggiori imprese commerciali; sotto di loro, beneficiando della loro presenza, c'erano veneziani, veronesi, lombardi, slavi, tedeschi che venivano integrati nella vita delle colonie, accettando la giurisdizione del balio nominato da Venezia. Indubbiamente, il governo veneziano trattava persino gli ebrei della sua colonia a Negroponte come veneziani quando questi commerciavano ad Acri, in un momento in cui gli ebrei erano scoraggiati dallo stabilirsi nella stessa Venezia[19].

Il problema più difficile di tutti è come giudicare l'effetto di queste attività sull'economia della penisola italiana. Nel X e nel primo XI secolo, il commercio italiano con Bisanzio era sotto molti aspetti un commercio al minuto e su piccola scala; i principali consumatori delle merci che gli amalfitani e i veneziani portavano in Italia erano le corti principesche di Milano, Pavia, Roma, Montecassino e, in misura sempre crescente, oltre le Alpi. Erano la seta di Costantinopoli e le pellicce della foresta provenienti dalle steppe, comprate nella capitale bizantina, ad attirare mercanti occidentali nei territori greci. Ma nel XII e nel XIII secolo le relazioni economiche tra l'Italia e Bisanzio assunsero un carattere diverso. I mercanti italiani risposero alla caduta della quantità e della qualità dell'argento occidentale, con il quale generalmente pagavano le merci orientali, esportando i tessuti lombardi o fiamminghi in Oriente. Una *ars dictandi* del 1140 circa contiene un modello di lettera mandata, presumibilmente, da Costantinopoli da un mercante italiano del Nord a un collega tornato a casa, nella quale è contenuta un'ordinazione per del tessuto di Piacenza[20]. È questo un primo accenno alla merce che doveva alimentare il commercio degli italiani a Bisanzio, nel Levante e in Sicilia. Le prove sono piú abbondanti per le esportazioni di prestigio di tessuti di alta qualità fuori d'Europa; ma è difficile determinare quale proporzione della forza lavoro tessile nelle città italiane fosse veramente impegnata nella produzione per i mercati esteri. Dal 1200, comunque, i mercanti italiani che commerciavano in Grecia erano ampiamente coinvolti anche nello smercio di vino greco, olio e frumento, una parte dei quali era importata nell'Adriatico per nutrire la crescente popolazione di Venezia e dell'Italia nord-orientale, e un'altra veniva traghettata nella direzione opposta, verso la capitale, un centro di consumo ancora piú ampio per i surplus agricoli. Indubbiamente, il commercio di Venezia o Ancona con Bisanzio era costituito da una significativa capacità di cabotaggio lungo le coste della Dalmazia e dell'Albania nello Ionio e nel Golfo di Corinto.

Tuttavia lo sfruttamento del commercio di Bisanzio allo scopo di alimentare le città italiane non doveva rimanere una peculiarità delle città adriatiche. Dopo il collasso dell'impero latino di Costantinopoli nel 1261, tenuto in piedi per breve tempo, i genovesi ricevettero favori da Michele VIII Paleologo paragonabili a quelli precedentemente concessi ai veneziani, e trassero pienamente vantaggio dalla loro posizione privilegiata penetrando nel Mar Nero e sviluppando un massiccio commercio internazionale di cereali, di frutta e di altri generi alimentari[21]. Dal 1300 Genova non soltanto riceveva queste merci: i generi alimentari sul mercato erano trasportati, attraverso la Sicilia e Gibilterra, nelle Fiandre e in Inghilterra. In un momento di crescita demografica, anche il frumento del Mar Nero, ottenuto a basso costo, era richiesto con urgenza in Europa occidentale, e, dato il livello elevato dei prezzi in Europa, il costo del suo trasporto non sembra averlo posto fuori dal mercato.

Un secondo fenomeno collegato al predominio genovese nel commercio italiano con Bisanzio fu la formazione di grandi colonie largamente autonome di residenti genovesi su suolo greco. Come risultato del rapido disin-canto di Michele VIII nei confronti dei genovesi dopo il 1261, essi furono obbligati a trasferire i loro affari a nord del Corno d'Oro, nei sobborghi di Costantinopoli. L'insediamento di Pera o Galata acquistò un grado di in-dipendenza che la comunità veneziana nella Costantinopoli del XII secolo non aveva mai posseduto, diventando, dal 1318, una Genova in miniatura governata dal proprio *podestà*, con una popolazione di una decina di mi-gliaia di persone, legata alla tradizionale politica ghibellina di Genova, che la differenziava dalla città madre in Italia, ora guelfa. Naturalmente, anche qui i residenti non erano solo genovesi: il rapido sviluppo del traffico degli schiavi tra la Crimea e l'Egitto portò a Pera numerosi schiavi circassi e tar-tari, parte dei quali riuscí a stabilirvisi. Cosí anche nella colonia piú lonta-na di Caffa esisteva dal 1280 una comunità mista di genovesi, altri 'lom-bardi', siciliani, catalani, greci, come anche schiavi e liberti di origine locale.

Quello che si deve porre in rilievo nel periodo del dominio genovese sull'economia bizantina è la riassunzione da parte dei genovesi del ruolo che i veneziani avevano svolto nei secoli precedenti, come tramite princi-pale tra Costantinopoli e il Mediterraneo occidentale. Sotto l'influenza ge-novese il raggio geografico del commercio venne enormemente allargato, e attraverso il Mar Nero si stabilí un contatto con i vasti mercati dell'im-pero mongolo. La *pax mongolica* del XIII secolo rese disponibili sete cinesi e altri oggetti esotici di lusso dell'Estremo Oriente, al punto d'arrivo di vie commerciali lunghe e ben sorvegliate; anche i veneziani giunsero a Tana, oltre Caffa, in cerca di merci del genere, e Tabriz in Persia divenne, verso il 1300, un'altra base per la ricezione da parte degli italiani di merci orien-tali, con una chiesa latina e altre agevolazioni speciali.

Dal 1350 circa, è ragionevole distinguere tipi diversi di imprese colo-niali a Bisanzio e nel Mar Nero: da un lato vi erano le isole poste sotto il dominio diretto di una città madre, i cui principali esempi erano Creta e il Negroponte veneziani; poi, le isole genovesi, come Chio (prima conqui-stata da Benedetto Zaccaria alla fine del XIII secolo, e riacquistata poi dai Giustiniani nel 1346), che erano amministrate da privati, su licenza del go-verno genovese; infine, c'erano anche molte navi di corsari – i Gattilusi a Lesbo, i Sanudo nell'arcipelago – che mantenevano una residua fedeltà verso Genova o Venezia. Le basi corsare fornivano protezione alle forze navali della città madre, ma non erano di per sé importanti centri di com-mercio. Sìa Creta sia Chio svolgevano la funzione di importanti fornitori dell'Italia, la prima in quanto fonte di frumento e di generi alimentari par-ticolari, la seconda inviando non solo mastice, frutta e vino, ma anche l'al-lume di Focea. Ci sono anche somiglianze sorprendenti con la Crimea genovese, o con gli insediamenti sulle coste bulgare e rumene, dove il controllo sulla campagna circostante veniva mantenuto con la costruzione di fortezze, e dove l'interesse principale era quello di garantire il libero movimento di frumento, diretto a Genova, e di schiavi, diretti all'Egitto mamelucco. Per contro, la colonia di Pera rientra in una seconda grande categoria, poiché i coloni non potevano ottenere il controllo sulla campagna ed erano essenzialmente impegnati ad alimentare il commercio fuori del Mar Nero, nel Mediterraneo. Verso il 1400 Pera era il principale quartiere commerciale di Costantinopoli. Qui la giurisdizione dell'imperatore bizantino era praticamente nulla; a Chio e a Lesbo essa veniva completamente ignorata.

Queste colonie erano solo in parte interessate ad acquisire agevolazioni per il commercio con la città madre in Italia. La loro grandezza e stabilità le trasformò anche in notevoli centri di consumo, e i loro abitanti svilupparono un senso di attaccamento locale che poteva, all'occasione, scavalcare le richieste di Venezia o Genova. Così la ribellione cretese del 1363 non fu solo una rivolta di greci oppressi; anche i proprietari veneziani locali vi svolsero una parte molto importante.

Accanto a queste basi c'erano naturalmente quartieri o magazzini genovesi o veneziani in territori in cui essi non avevano alcuna possibilità di stabilire un controllo politico. Gli italiani gareggiavano per ottenere favori alla corte degli imperatori Comneni di Trebisonda, e usavano Trebisonda sia come base per penetrare nella Persia del Nord (soprattutto a Tabriz), sia come fonte di metalli preziosi, nocciole e altri beni disponibili sul luogo[22]. Un caso simile si può riscontrare per i molti italiani (inclusi non solo genovesi e veneziani, ma anche fiorentini, anconetani, siciliani) che commerciavano attraverso l'Armenia cilicia a Laiazzo (Ayas); essi rifornivano i re rupenidi dell'Armenia con merci di lusso e viaggiavano oltre, nel territorio arabo e mongolo. In questa zona la loro base principale verso il 1300 era Famagosta a Cipro, un'isola su cui gli interessi finanziari dei genovesi prima e dei veneziani più tardi dovevano gettare a lungo un'ombra[23].

5.2. La Terra Santa.

La massiccia presenza degli italiani a Cipro fu essenzialmente il risultato della perdita di Acri nel 1291; il commercio del Levante si spostò dalle coste della Palestina e Famagosta divenne un punto centrale attorno al quale si incrociavano vie commerciali dirette in Armenia, a Beirut e in Egitto. È ora necessario esaminare la storia precedente del commercio nel Levante, e in particolare la formazione delle colonie italiane negli stati crociati.

Per lungo tempo c'è stato accordo sul fatto che le prime Crociate fecero la fortuna degli italiani del Nord nel commercio nel Levante, e che, a parte il coinvolgimento veneziano a Bisanzio, prima del 1100 circa si effettuavano pochi traffici tra l'Italia del Nord e il Mediterraneo orientale[24]. Senza dubbio, il più importante privilegio concesso da Bisanzio a Venezia precede l'appello per la prima Crociata nel 1095 di solo tredici anni, e si potrebbe sostenere che la prospettiva di una simile ricompensa dette ai sedicenti rivali di Venezia, Genova e Pisa, lo stimolo per un'espansione nel Mediterraneo orientale. Contro questa tesi, ci sono prove, riscontrabili in fonti come i testi della *Geniza* del Cairo, di visite occasionali da parte di navi genovesi o pisane in Egitto verso la metà dell'xi secolo. Di fatto, né l'xi secolo, né la prima Crociata segnano il reale inizio del commercio italiano con il Levante; non ci fu nessun big bang, nonostante i generosi privilegi concessi dai governanti franchi a Est attraessero gli italiani nei porti del Levante in numero crescente.

Nella prima fase, fino al 1200 circa, i diversi gruppi di italiani concentrarono le loro energie nello sviluppo di basi rivali in Terra Santa[25]. Ai veneziani fu assegnato un terzo di Tiro nel *Pactum Warmundi* del 1123, un trattato tra il patriarca di Gerusalemme e le grandi flotte veneziane che dovevano aiutarlo a conquistare la Tiro araba. Un patriarca precedente, Daimberto, aveva garantito diritti ai pisani nel suo dominio di Giaffa. Nel frattempo i genovesi poterono beneficiare della concessione di diritti non solo ad Acri ma anche a Gibelletto, nella contea di Tripoli, dove era stata concessa la signoria ai patrizi Embriachi. Fu però Acri a divenire gradualmente la base delle operazioni italiane in Terra Santa; il suo porto era manifestamente superiore a quello di Giaffa, ed era evidentemente un punto terminale per il commercio nell'interno, attraverso le colline di facile transito della Galilea e attraverso le alture del Golan verso Damasco e Aleppo. Tiro, nonostante possedesse un porto adeguato, era meno accessibile dall'interno, tagliata fuori da Damasco dal monte Hermon e dai picchi libanesi. Acri occupava anche una buona posizione per il commercio sotto la costa palestinese verso Damietta e Alessandria; era generalmente attraverso l'Anatolia, la Siria e la Terra Santa che le navi occidentali raggiungevano l'Egitto, dato che i venti e le correnti lungo quella rotta erano molto più facili da domare rispetto alla pericolosa rotta del Nord Africa[26].

Ciò trasformò Acri in un *entrepôt* per il commercio sia verso l'Egitto sia verso l'interno siriano; non era un importante centro industriale, né la Terra Santa produceva di per sé molto (reliquie a parte) di quello che i consumatori occidentali richiedevano[27]. Ma i crociati avevano conquistato il controllo dei crocevia commerciali del Medio Oriente, e dal xiii secolo le entrate commerciali erano la fonte principale del reddito regale – senza dubbio, i feudi monetari erano di frequente tratti dalle entrate commerciali di Acri".

I veneziani in particolare si trovarono in una straordinaria posizione, senza paragone con qualunque altra loro acquisizione a Costantinopoli. A Tiro, fu messo in atto il loro diritto a un terzo della città, con il risultato di assumere la giurisdizione veneziana sui non italiani che si erano stabiliti in quella parte della città; vi si trovavano residenti fissi veneziani, che stabilirono dinastie a Est, inclusi forse membri di casati illustri come i Falier e i Contarini. È ancora più importante il fatto che i veneziani potessero rivendicare i propri diritti su un terzo del territorio attorno a Tiro, grazie al trattato del 1123. Sembra che i cavalieri veneziani nella campagna intorno a Tiro fossero soggetti alla corona per il servizio militare, ma da tutti gli altri punti di vista la comunità veneziana a Tiro era un corpo autonomo, che forniva consiglio al re ma insisteva sui propri speciali diritti di esenzione".

Sul quartiere veneziano ad Acri esiste una buona documentazione, che fa risalire le sue origini fino al 1110, quando i veneziani furono ricompensati per il loro aiuto nell'assedio di Sidone. Esso fiancheggiava il porto di Acri, in una eccellente posizione, e dalla metà del XIII secolo era circondato da mura proprie, diventando di fatto una città nella città. Si può ancora rintracciare sul terreno il suo fondaco; conteneva negozi e magazzini, alcuni affittati a mercanti in visita (con un affitto più alto al secondo piano) e altri usati per i materiali della comunità da immagazzinare, come il legname e la pietra. Qui viveva anche il prete della chiesa di San Marco e l'usciere di corte. Nel quartiere veneziano il comune amministrava nel complesso direttamente quattordici case, inclusi trentun negozi e settantaquattro stanze o appartamenti. Una situazione simile nel quartiere genovese conferma che gli italiani ad Acri erano una miscela di mercanti emigranti e coloni da molto tempo; i residenti non genovesi e non pisani nei quartieri italiani erano considerati dagli italiani soggetti alla giurisdizione italiana, anche se i governanti del regno si opponevano a questa rivendicazione.

Non c'è alcun bisogno di esaminare in dettaglio i diritti arrogatisi da ciascuna comunità ad Acri. Ciò che è importante è che la città era governata da molte giurisdizioni autonome, persino in conflitto tra loro. Il re cercava di garantire che l'esenzione dalle tasse riconosciuta agli italiani fosse applicata soltanto quando essi commerciavano entro il regno; se si spingevano oltre, nella Siria araba, erano ufficialmente soggetti a essere considerati come mercanti senza privilegi". Questo provvedimento esprimeva perfettamente l'atteggiamento della corona verso i suoi ospiti italiani. Il loro status speciale, e soprattutto la loro libertà dalla maggior parte delle tasse, era tollerabile perché avevano trasformato Acri e Tiro in *entrepôt* at-

traverso i quali i siriani e altri mercanti orientali, che pagavano le tasse alla
corona, erano avidi di commerciare, facendo transitare le merci tramite
mani latine o in Occidente o in Egitto. In altre parole, la presenza di italiani esenti dalle imposte moltiplicava le entrate dei re latini, provenienti
da coloro con i quali gli italiani solitamente facevano affari. Se i mercanti
italiani fossero penetrati regolarmente nell'interno, e avessero reclamato
i diritti di esenzione tornando ad Acri, questo redditizio ma ancora blando
sistema di controllo sarebbe crollato.

Ci sono poche prove che gli italiani riuscissero a rompere queste restrizioni. Intorno al 1156 Ansaldo Baialardo si stava preparando a uscire da
Genova verso l'Est latino, con la possibilità di continuare il suo viaggio
verso Damasco, Alessandria o la Sicilia; il suo finanziatore era il facoltoso
patrizio Ingo della Volta[11]. All'inizio degli anni quaranta del XIII secolo,
ad Aleppo si trovavano dei sangimignanesi. Generalmente, comunque, la
penetrazione all'interno era più semplice dall'Armenia o persino da Trebisonda; la funzione di Acri era precisamente quella di agire come intermediaria tra l'Europa e l'interno siriano, o tra l'Europa e l'Egitto. I vantaggi ottenuti dai mercanti latini da una base in territorio cristiano non
possono essere esagerati. Essi non erano soggetti all'umiliazione del sistema poliziesco che, in molte città arabe, li confinava in un quartiere; erano
in grado di giocare un ruolo politico significativo nel regno di Gerusalemme; erano in buona posizione per controllare il movimento dei tessuti, delle verghe d'oro e d'argento e di altri articoli di lusso nelle tre zone commerciali che servivano, la Siria, l'Egitto e l'Italia.

5.3. Tunisi e il Maghreb.

Le condizioni per le quali i mercanti italiani poterono penetrare in territorio arabo sono vividamente illustrate dall'esempio di Tunisi. I legami
commerciali italiani con l'Ifriqiya, approssimativamente la moderna Tunisia, possono essere rintracciati sin dal X e dall'XI secolo; indubbiamente,
fu soltanto quando gli italiani ebbero stabilito i loro rapporti con i governanti della Tunisia che essi poterono sperare di spostarsi oltre il Mediterraneo centrale e di sfruttare i mercati del Levante. La pirateria musulmana
fuori di Mahdia e delle altre basi sulla costa tunisina rimaneva un serio
problema, che Ruggero II risolse con inventiva: egli ottenne il diretto controllo delle principali città di Ifriqiya e di Tripolitania, anche se la stessa
Tunisi, che avrebbe in breve tempo sostituito Mahdia come maggior centro commerciale della regione, non fu mai conquistata dai Normanni[12].
L'attrattiva di Mahdia e di Tunisi risiedeva nel loro accesso, non sempre
disponibile, alle provviste d'oro dell'Africa nera, e nei mercati affamati

che esse frequentemente rifornivano di grano siciliano. Già nel 1117 a Mahdia si trovavano agenti commerciali siciliani, che rappresentavano il conte Ruggero; in questo stadio essi sarebbero dovuti essere presumibilmente arabi, ma due secoli dopo erano mercanti latini di Messina coloro che amministravano un fondaco e una chiesa a Tunisi. L'approvvigionamento di frumento, vino e formaggio siciliani in Africa è ben documentato per tutto il Medioevo, e quello che colpisce è il ruolo che gli italiani del Nord acquistarono rapidamente nel commercio a breve distanza tra la Sicilia e la Tunisia. In parte ciò accadde perché molti italiani del Nord avevano posto la loro base a Palermo e a Messina, e potevano mobilitare capitale più velocemente delle loro controparti siciliane, con l'aiuto delle banche fiorentine (per esempio); ma la corona era ansiosa di trarre vantaggio dalla dipendenza africana verso i rifornimenti siciliani, irritandosi per l'interferenza degli italiani del Nord: cosí Federico II impose un embargo nel 1239-40, impedendo che le navi straniere portassero grano a Tunisi colpita dalla carestia, e vendendo il proprio grano sulle proprie navi a un prezzo molto elevato. Alla lunga, comunque, i tentativi di controllare la presenza degli italiani del Nord in questo commercio non riuscirono; la testimonianza del notaio siciliano Adamo de Citella nel periodo della guerra dei Vespri indica che il coinvolgimento dei fiorentini e dei genovesi nel traffico di grano per il Nord Africa e nel traffico d'oro da questa regione era molto intenso".

Ma l'immagine più chiara dell'interesse italiano in Ifriqiya deriva dagli atti notarili genovesi stilati a Tunisi nel 1289". La prima impressionante caratteristica di questi atti sono i problemi incontrati dai genovesi per assicurarsi, da parte del governo locale, il rispetto dei diritti loro garantiti. Un tipico esempio è fornito da un atto del 1° maggio 1289, nel quale il console di Genova a Tunisi dichiara al capo del servizio doganale che i patti tra il comune di Genova e il signore di Tunisi devono essere da questi rispettati, e che egli deve accordare udienza al console due volte al mese. Le garanzie fornite dalla corte reale includevano chiaramente una promessa di protezione per le merci dei genovesi, e di indennità qualora fossero state sottratte illecitamente: cosí la corte acconsentí nel rifondere l'enorme somma di 20 393 bisanti ai genovesi per danni perpetrati nel porto di Tunisi a La Goletta, dove gli aggressori pisani avevano oltraggiato i genovesi. Il valore attribuito a una nave era di oltre 14 000 bisanti; il suo carico conteneva perlomeno 2000 giare di olio. Ma il vino italiano era un altro prodotto che gli italiani commerciavano attraverso Tunisi. Fu precisamente un tentativo del signore hafsida di aumentare le tasse sul vino che portò a una lite tra questi e il console; il console prese il provvedimento un po' drastico di mettere sotto chiave il magazzino del vino e di dare la chiave al prete genovese residente, Tealdo. Una lite per l'imposta sull'olio, parte della quale doveva essere pagata dalla corte hafsida al console, secondo le clausole dei trattati esistenti, sfociò persino nella violenza; il senso di insicurezza avvertito dagli italiani a Tunisi era chiaramente molto piú grande che nel regno di Gerusalemme o in altri stati italiani. È chiaro che, come nella Costantinopoli del XII secolo, la comunità italiana a Tunisi comprendesse una maggioranza di mercanti, presenti solo per alcuni mesi, ma una significativa minoranza di residenti permanenti che provvedevano ai bisogni dei mercanti. Le chiese delle varie comunità potevano divenire oggetto di certe piccole restrizioni, per esempio una proibizione di suonare le campane e di costruire campanili, malgrado i tentativi veneziani di evitare la seconda di queste limitazioni". Gli emiri di Tunisi valutavano troppo il loro commercio per negare ai mercanti italiani ragionevoli facilitazioni, ma i mercanti vivevano, in effetti, in un ghetto e dovevano regolarmente rinegoziare i propri diritti. Non era, come in Terra Santa, un trattato permanente tra il governante e i mercanti italiani, ma soltanto un patto temporaneo, quale era consentito dalla legge islamica.

Gli atti notarili di Pietro Battifoglio, comunque, indicano che i mercanti italiani stabilitisi a Tunisi usavano la città come base per commerciare non soltanto con la Sicilia e l'Italia; la città stava a cavallo su vie commerciali che penetravano sia nel Mediterraneo occidentale sia in quello orientale, e ci sono segni di un commercio attivo, finanziato in parte da investimenti italiani, con Maiorca, Montpellier e i porti della Sardegna occidentale. Gli italiani erano soci dei catalani nel commercio tra Tunisi e le terre della corona d'Aragona, mentre le ambizioni politiche delle case di Aragona e di Angiò in Tunisia erano un fattore significativo nell'incoraggiare l'amicizia genovese verso Pietro d'Aragona piuttosto che verso il suo rivale Carlo I di Sicilia.

Le grandi colonie italiane a Tunisi, Bugia e altri centri africani di commercio divennero punti focali di reti commerciali autonome che ignoravano Genova o Pisa. Il mercante italiano era sempre stato fortemente coinvolto nel trasportare merci lontano dalla propria città natale; ma alla fine del XIII secolo questo commercio separato, diretto al di fuori della città natale, ricevette un fondamentale stimolo dall'apertura della rotta marittima attraverso lo Stretto di Gibilterra. È necessario adesso volgersi alla presenza italiana in Spagna, nell'Atlantico e nelle Fiandre; vale a dire, lungo la nuova via del Nord.

6. Gli italiani in Spagna e nell'Atlantico.

6.1. La Spagna e le isole Baleari.

Si può sostenere che nel XII secolo la costa della Spagna mediterranea attraesse il mercante italiano soprattutto come scalo sulla rotta verso destinazioni molto piú valutate; i porti dell'Africa del Nord-Ovest, dove è possibile individuare una presenza genovese dal 1160 circa[16]. Ceuta fu gradualmente scoperta come fonte di oro, cuoio e persino grano; il passaggio fu facilitato, almeno per i genovesi, da un trattato con ibn Mardanish o *rex Lupus*, signore di Valencia in quello stesso periodo. Persino la Catalogna fu solo superficialmente penetrata da genovesi e pisani nel XII secolo; la principale ragione dei trattati degli italiani del Nord con la casa d'Aragona in questo periodo fu, piuttosto, un tentativo di rendere libero il passaggio sui territori della Francia del Sud, dove gli aragonesi possedevano diritti di signoria. Ma i loro interessi in Spagna erano generalmente determinati dall'utilità delle basi spagnole riguardo alla penetrazione nelle rotte commerciali del Maghreb; un punto focale delle loro attività divenne perciò Maiorca, conquistata per breve tempo dai pisani all'inizio del XIII secolo, e costantemente bersaglio di incursioni da parte delle flotte latine fino alla sua definitiva conquista nel 1229. Gli italiani cercarono di stringere rapporti amichevoli con i governanti delle isole Baleari che, nel tardo XII secolo erano un gruppo isolato di emiri almoravidi, che mancavano di alleati sia nella Spagna almohade che in Africa o in Occidente. Cosí, immediatamente dopo la conquista catalana di Maiorca, i genovesi e i pisani cercarono sia di ottenere conferma dal nuovo governante cristiano dei loro diritti commerciali esistenti, sia di estendere ulteriormente questi diritti, sostenendo (nel caso di Pisa) che di fatto Pisa stessa poteva a buon diritto reclamare le Baleari come faceva la Catalogna, e (nel caso di Genova) che un antico conte catalano aveva fatto sostanziali promesse di privilegi qualora le isole fossero state occupate. Sospese tra le acque del circuito del Tirreno, dominate dai pisani e dai genovesi, e le acque recentemente divenute catalane piú a ovest, le Baleari vennero a giocare un ruolo speciale ed estremamente importante nel commercio italiano durante il XIII e il XIV secolo: come Tunisi, Maiorca fu un punto nodale in un sistema regionale di commercio che si irradiava in tutte le direzioni, verso Valencia, l'uscita di Gibilterra, il Nord Africa, la Sicilia, la Sardegna e, non ultima, la Francia del Sud (anche, di certo, verso la Catalogna, ma là i catalani stessi restavano assolutamente dominanti)[17]. Era un centro per la riparazione delle navi italiane sulla rotta del Nord Africa e verso le destinazioni atlantiche. Era anche un centro per l'affitto dei vascelli; il commercio dei genovesi e dei fiorentini con l'Inghilterra e con le Fiandre veniva occasionalmente effettuato su agili navi maiorcane. E le isole Baleari erano valutate mercati a pieno titolo, dapprima produttori di poche merci, a parte il sale di Ibiza, anche se più tardi doveva crescere un'industria tessile maiorcana: la totale assenza di terra da coltivare spinse gli italiani a giocare un'ampia parte nell'approvvigionamento di grano e di altri prodotti fondamentali. Il successo degli italiani fu tale che, nel 1269, quattro anni dopo che misure simili erano state prese a Barcellona, il re aragonese espulse da Maiorca tutte le compagnie di mercanti senesi, fiorentini, piacentini e lucchesi; simili decreti furono ripetuti frequentemente nei secoli seguenti, sebbene avessero poco effetto sulla presenza di genovesi e pisani. I genovesi avevano la propria *lonja* che era sia una corte di mercanti che una camera di commercio; fu là che il genovese Ingeto Contardo si impegnò in una sorprendente serie di discussioni con un ebreo di Maiorca sui rispettivi meriti del giudaismo e della cristianità[38]. La presenza pisana sopravvisse a lungo alla sconfitta di Pisa alla Meloria nel 1284; la testimonianza del *Lou dels Pisans* suggerisce un commercio molto vivo tra la Toscana e le Baleari ai primi del XIV secolo[39].

6.2. Fiandre e Inghilterra.

La conquista di Maiorca rese possibile l'apertura, quasi cinquant'anni più tardi, dello Stretto di Gibilterra e la creazione di una rotta marittima verso le Fiandre. Ma la presenza italiana nelle Fiandre è già documentata molto prima: c'erano italiani a Bruges nel 1127, l'anno calamitoso dell'assassinio del conte Carlo il Buono. Durante il XII secolo, i contatti tra le Fiandre e l'Italia divennero eccezionalmente intensi; l'esportazione a Genova di tessuti di lana fiamminga, e in una certa misura di lino, è registrata molto precisamente nelle minute dei notai della città, e la tendenza era chiaramente verso una sempre più vasta mole di esportazioni, in quanto i mercanti italiani svilupparono l'arte di vendere questi prodotti a Bisanzio e nel mondo islamico invece di compiere pagamenti in argento o in altro modo. Un esempio a caso dalle registrazioni notarili rivela il carattere essenziale di questo commercio: il 7 maggio 1205 Rubeo della Volta, un patrizio genovese, ricevette a Genova da Nicola Tinivelle, di Arras, tessuto del valore di 53 lire[40]. Quello che colpisce è l'alto numero di documenti che si riferiscono a vendite di tessuto a Genova da parte di commercianti del Nord; ma esistono anche prove di una lenta, meno chiaramente visibile, crescita di visitatori italiani a nord delle Alpi. Nel XII e ai primi del XIII secolo la maggior parte di questi viaggiatori italiani non andò più lontano dello Champagne, alle grandi fiere dove si trovava un'ampia varietà di tessuti provenienti dalle Fiandre, dal Brabante, dalla Francia del Nord-Est e dall'Inghilterra; molti, fino al 1250 circa, sembra fossero originari di Asti, sebbene Piacenza fosse sempre meglio rappresentata. Alla metà del XIII secolo il ricco mercante genovese Simone di Gualterio, nonostante fosse attivo nell'acquisto di tessuti attraverso lo Champagne, in realtà non viaggiava al Nord, ma indirizzava i tessuti tramite la propria città natale verso la Sicilia e il Levante[41]. Il declino delle fiere dello Champagne nel tardo XIII secolo fu in parte il risultato dell'estensione delle vie commerciali per terra (ed, eventualmente, marittime), cosicché i mercanti italiani cominciarono ad arrivare in gran numero a Bruges, Gand e in altri centri industriali o commerciali del Nord, per comprare alla fonte. Ma si dovrebbe sottolineare il fatto che, durante il XIII e il primo XIV secolo, la maggioranza dei mercanti genovesi di tessuti andavano ad acquistare ancora le loro merci fiamminghe o della Francia del Nord fino al Sud delle Fiandre, specialmente a Montpellier e nelle città della Provenza. Alle fiere dello Champagne i cittadini di Montpellier avevano il loro console, che rappresentava anche i provenzali; gli italiani, insolitamente, cercarono di formare un singolo gruppo, sotto i capitani della nazione lombarda, per poter trattare in termini piú egualitari con i conti dello Champagne.

Non si può sottolineare troppo enfaticamente che il commercio italiano nel Mediterraneo era e doveva essere nutrito dal commercio dell'Europa transalpina: il poco studiato legame tra Venezia e la Germania, o quello, meglio indagato, tra Genova e le Fiandre, rese possibile da solo una continua influenza italiana nel commercio mediterraneo. Ma c'erano altri fattori che portarono gli italiani verso nord. La classica tesi che gli italiani arrivarono per la prima volta in Inghilterra intorno all'anno 1218 come esattori delle tasse papali è stata giustamente criticata sulla base del fatto che le entrate dall'Inghilterra, ai primi del XIII secolo, erano scarse, e che gli esattori italiani in questo periodo sembrano aver intascato il denaro invece di mandarlo a Roma[42]. Fu solo alla fine del XIII secolo che il papato trovò agenti italiani veramente affidabili (nelle vesti dei Mozzi, degli Spini, e, nella giusta misura, dei Bardi e dei Peruzzi). Il papato, inoltre, accrebbe le sue richieste verso i regni europei usando le decime per pagare guerre ambiziose in Italia e altrove; ciò pose enfasi ancora maggiore sul ruolo degli italiani come esattori papali. Negli anni ottanta del XIII secolo, i Ricciardi di Lucca ricevettero e misero a profitto il ricavato della decima clericale del 1274, e ulteriori tributi nel regno di Edoardo I consolidarono la posizione dei lucchesi, dei senesi e infine dei fiorentini come banchieri reali e papali[43]. Ma ci furono anche altri fattori, di carattere piú locale, che accrebbero la prosperità degli italiani. I fiamminghi furono esclusi dal commercio inglese durante la contesa anglo-fiamminga del 1270-74, un conflitto le cui origini si trovano nelle lamentele espresse dai mercanti inglesi per il cattivo trattamento ricevuto nelle Fiandre; ciò lasciò agli italiani mano relativamente libera in Inghilterra. In secondo luogo, il declino dell'influenza finanziaria degli ebrei creò un vuoto che i creditori italiani furono in grado di riempire, su una scala quasi mai raggiunta dai loro predecessori ebrei. L'espulsione degli ebrei dall'Inghilterra sanzionò questi cambiamenti, per cui la corona, come il papato, dovette ammettere che la pratica del credito da un cristiano a un altro non possedeva in alcun senso carattere di usura. La clientela dei banchieri italiani includeva non solo l'alta nobiltà e i vescovi, ma anche la municipalità di Londra; e un singolo finanziere genovese, Antonio Pessagno, 'Sir Anthony Pessaigne', traeva fondi dalle grandi compagnie fiorentine, con le quali, alternativamente, teneva a galla le finanze dello sfortunato Edoardo II[44]. Ciò non si risolse interamente a beneficio di Edoardo, dato che mise in grado il re inglese di combattere una disastrosa guerra scozzese. E l'esistenza di una fonte alternativa, italiana, di entrate, venne vista dalla nobiltà del reame come una grave sfida alla propria influenza finanziaria sul re.

Implicita negli investimenti italiani era, naturalmente, la ricerca della lana. Coinvolti dapprincipio nel trasporto della lana nelle Fiandre, dove i loro compatrioti potevano acquistare tessuti finiti di lana, gli italiani diversificarono il raggio geografico dell'esportazione di lana, inviando lana grezza inglese sulla nuova linea navale che collegava l'Inghilterra e le Fiandre al Mediterraneo (e venne anche fatto un certo uso della via di terra per l'Italia). Firenze poté cosí ottenere direttamente lana inglese o irlandese, tramite gli intermediari italiani che spesso penetravano nelle aree di produzione dello Yorkshire, dove le eccellenti lane dei monaci cistercensi venivano largamente affidate sotto contratto agli italiani[45]. Sarebbe completamente sbagliato ritenere che gli italiani esportassero in Italia la maggior parte di ciò che essi acquistavano; per tutto il primo XIV secolo le Fiandre e la Francia del Nord rimasero importanti consumatori. Senza dubbio le colonie italiane a Londra non guardavano soltanto alle loro città madri nel Mediterraneo per commerciare; i mercanti italiani si integrarono bene nella vita commerciale delle zone connesse delle Fiandre, della Francia del Nord e dell'Inghilterra, specializzandosi nel movimento della lana, dei tessuti raffinati e delle merci di lusso mediterranee o orientali importate via Southampton o Bruges. Una importazione di particolare significato era l'allume usato come fissativo nell'industria tessile; dalla metà del XIV secolo i genovesi e i loro soci fiorentini in affari avevano creato una rete commerciale, che in alcune sue vie ignorava la Liguria e la Toscana, collegando le miniere di allume di Focea alle manifatture tessili dell'Europa del Nord, attraverso la Sicilia e l'Andalusia.

Ci furono ostacoli alla penetrazione italiana nell'Europa del Nord: la linea di divisione venne tracciata a Bruges, dove i luoghi ancora visibili dei magazzini dei genovesi e dei baltici rivelano il ruolo del porto come punto d'incontro tra italiani e anseatici. Comunque sia, l'opposizione dei mercanti dell'Ansa agli intrusi mediterranei nel Mare del Nord e nel Baltico non precluse completamente la Germania agli italiani. Ai primi del xiv secolo, principi tedeschi del Reno dalla mentalità finanziaria si servirono di banchieri lombardi o ebrei: di solito, o degli uni o degli altri, non di entrambi contemporaneamente. Dalla metà del xiv secolo esistevano colonie italiane, formate da maestri coniatori e da specialisti finanziari, nei regni in espansione dell'Europa dell'Est: a Kutna Hora (Kuttenberg) in Boemia, anche a Cracovia in Polonia, dove la rotta del Mar Nero incontrava le rotte via terra dall'Ovest in un grande circolo, e a Buda nell'Ungheria angioina, dove Buonaccorso Pitti doveva dilapidare la sua ricchezza nel gioco d'azzardo con compatrioti italiani⁴⁶.

7. Gli italiani oltremare: colonie ed economie sussidiarie.

Una rapida indagine degli italiani fuori d'Italia serve a sottolineare due caratteristiche della loro attività economica. Una è quella per cui, in larga misura, essi cercarono di far fronte alle esigenze della stessa economia italiana, e in tale processo crearono una rete integrata di vie commerciali e di servizi finanziari, ottenendo accesso alle corti reali, ai centri di produzione rurale, alle miniere; al suo apice questo sistema implicava il trasporto diretto di merci dal Mediterraneo orientale al Mare del Nord, ma l'obiettivo finale era evidentemente di creare una catena di rifornimenti culminante nel commercio dei tessuti nel Mediterraneo. In altre parole, il mercante italiano può essere caratterizzato come un brillante impresario tra l'Islam, il precedente impero bizantino, l'Italia, la Spagna e l'Europa del Nord. Ma in un altro senso ciò che colpisce del mercante italiano è precisamente lo sviluppo di circuiti commerciali secondari, in parte o anche interamente staccati dalle grandi reti; questo è particolarmente vero per le aree in cui si stabilirono grandi e privilegiate colonie di italiani: la colonia veneziana a Costantinopoli, la colonia genovese a Pera, i coloni italiani nella Spagna del Sud e persino a Tunisi. Pera non è molto differente, ai primi del xiv secolo, dal modello di un'antica colonia greca; era una ramificazione della città madre, dalla quale aveva acquisito un'effettiva indipendenza. A parte Creta, le isole egee sotto il controllo italiano erano generalmente controllate da signori locali di stirpe italiana, e solo Chio e Creta giocavano un ruolo molto significativo nell'economia della città madre.

La grande rete era piú importante del commercio locale? Chiaramente la risposta è che la grande rete, dominata dalle grandi case mercantili di Venezia, Genova, Firenze e cosí via, era sostenuta dal capitale dei patrizi urbani e dei loro alleati nelle arti maggiori. Questa grande rete doveva giocare una parte speciale nell'espansione economica della Toscana e della Lombardia medievali, fornendo ricchi consumatori alle corti reali in tutto il mondo conosciuto. Tuttavia le reti secondarie avevano anch'esse una considerevole importanza in un'epoca di carestie, di guerre navali, di valute preziose fluttuanti: il mercante medio di grano, nato nell'Italia del Nord, che lavorava tra Tunisi e Trapani, non solo riusciva a realizzare profitti decenti, ma contribuiva a legare insieme le economie di regioni divise dalla religione, dalla politica e dall'attività economica. Cosí anche in Andalusia e (sebbene secondo criteri diversi) nelle Fiandre o persino in Boemia.

Tutte queste attività rispondevano ai bisogni di un'Italia del Nord densamente popolata, piuttosto povera di risorse agricole, dipendente dai profitti commerciali per la sussistenza di un numero cospicuo dei suoi abitanti. Molti mercanti emigrati, forse la maggior parte, avevano intenzione, alla fine, di tornare in patria con le proprie ricchezze; molti non lo fecero, e l'iniezione di capitale italiano, permanentemente o temporaneamente, nelle industrie tessili dell'Europa del Nord, o quella del potere di acquisto italiano nei mercati di spezie del Levante, contribuí ad animare e a connettere tra loro le economie di regioni distanti come l'Egitto e l'Inghilterra.

---

[1] Per esempio, EUSTAZIO DI TESSALONICA, *La espugnazione di Tessalonica*, a cura di S. P. Kyriakidis e V. Rotolo, Palermo 1961, pp. 57-58. L'idea degli italiani come gruppo emerge nel primo XIII secolo, per esempio nei lavori di Jacques de Vitry.

[2] D. ABULAFIA, *The Levant trade of the minor cities in the thirteenth and fourtheenth centuries: strenghts and weaknesses*, in «Asian and African Studies», Haifa 1988 (numero speciale in memoria di Eliyahu Ashtor, a cura di B. Z. Kedar e A. Udovitch).

[3] Sul concetto di diaspora, si veda P. CURTIN, *Cross-cultural trade in world history*, Cambridge 1984.

[4] Indubbiamente, un'altra poderosa manifestazione di questo senso d'identità è rintracciabile tra i numerosi patrizi esuli che furono espulsi (o che fuggirono) dalle loro città natali durante i conflitti civili tra guelfi e ghibellini del XIII e XIV secolo; la maggior parte rimase in Italia, sebbene molte figure di primo piano apparissero in Catalogna alla vigilia dell'invasione aragonese della Sicilia nel 1282, o anche (come l'avventuriero Enrico di Castiglia) nella Tunisi musulmana dello stesso periodo. Molti conservarono a lungo memoria dei loro diritti ancestrali di generazione in generazione, e un potente sentimento per la città madre, che era determinato, in una certa misura, dalla loro estromissione. Su questo si veda R. STARN, *Contrary Commonwealth: the theme of exile in medieval and renaissance Italy*, Berkeley - Los Angeles

1982. Il fervore di Dante verso Firenze fu espresso, con minore eloquenza, da altri italiani contemporanei. Si potrebbe suggerire che l'idea di «italianità» crescesse anzitutto e piú rapidamente fuori d'Italia, che essa fosse un'importazione dalle colonie d'oltremare di mercanti, artigiani ed esuli?

⁵ Gli effetti economici delle Crociate sulle terre d'origine dei crociati sono oggi considerati piú sostanziali di quanto si sia a lungo supposto: per equipaggiarsi il crociato spesso ipotecava o addirittura vendeva le proprie terre, talvolta alla Chiesa, e almeno in Francia la partenza della prima Crociata ebbe un impatto significativo sulla ricchezza fondiaria della Chiesa e portò a un'immediata caduta dei prezzi della terra.

⁶ G. PETTI BALBI, Genova e Corsica nel Trecento, Istituto storico italiano per il Medioevo, Studi storici, Roma 1976; F. FERNANDEZ-ARMESTO, Before Columbus: exploration and colonization from the Mediterranean to the Atlantic, 1229-1492, London 1987, p. 99.

⁷ Ma occorre sottolineare che le possibilità di integrazione erano limitate dal carattere religioso delle terre che essi penetravano: nella Siria latina la casta dominante era cattolica, sebbene rappresentasse una piccola minoranza, mentre a Bisanzio gli italiani mantenevano generalmente le distanze dalla Chiesa Ortodossa e avevano il permesso di frequentare le proprie chiese latine; in Egitto, nel Maghreb e in certe parti della Spagna mediterranea, essi si trovarono isolati in una società musulmana. L'esperienza degli italiani nell'Europa del Nord, d'altra parte, era completamente diversa: essi si trovavano tra correligionari cattolici, e tuttavia erano spesso ansiosi di affermare la propria identità come veneziani, fiorentini o altro, ad esempio mantenendo le proprie cappelle laterali nelle chiese esistenti. Vale la pena di aggiungere che le città mercantili dell'Italia del Nord possedevano un'omogeneità religiosa che mancava in Catalogna, in Provenza o nell'Italia del Sud: esse permettevano a pochi ebrei di stabilirsi, e, malgrado il loro intenso traffico con il mondo arabo, avevano ben pochi residenti fissi musulmani. Il loro aggressivo carattere latino fu posto in rilievo dalla spedizione di flotte in aiuto alle prime Crociate, dalla loro devozione a santi patroni come San Marco e San Giorgio, il cui emblema in un luogo lontano come Bruges annunciava le case dei veneziani e dei genovesi.

⁸ D. ABULAFIA, Crocuses and crusaders: San Gimignano, Pisa and the Kingdom of Jerusalem, in Outremer: studies in the history of the crusading kingdom of Jerusalem presented to Joshua Prawer, Jerusalem 1982, pp. 233-34.

⁹ Ibid., pp. 235-39.

¹⁰ ID., Southern Italy and the Florentine economy, 1265-1370, in «Economic History Review», serie 2, XXXIII (1981), p. 379.

¹¹ ANNA COMNENA, Alexiad, libro V, 1.1.

¹² R. J. LILIE, Handel und Politik zwischen dem byzantinischen Reich und den italienischen Kommunen Venedig, Pisa und Genua (1081-1204), Amsterdam 1983.

¹³ È questa la posizione di David Jacoby in un importante saggio, non ancora pubblicato, presentato al Symposium di Studi Bizantini a Oxford nel 1984.

¹⁴ Su questo si veda LILIE, Handel cit., pp. 184, 187-90.

¹⁵ Questo è il punto di vista del professor Jacoby, espresso nel saggio citato alla nota 13.

¹⁶ S. BORSARI, Il commercio veneziano nell'Impero bizantino nel XII secolo, in «Rivista Storica Italiana», LXXVI (1964), pp. 982-1011, e Per la storia del commercio veneziano col mondo bizantino nel XII secolo, ivi, LXXXVIII (1976), pp. 104-26; cfr. C. M. BRAND, Byzantium confronts the West, 1180-1204, Cambridge (Mass.) 1968, pp. 205-6, per la colonia pisana.

¹⁷ W. VON STROMER, Bernardus Teutonicus e i rapporti commerciali tra la Germania meridionale prima dell'istituzione del Fondaco dei Tedeschi, in «Quaderni del Centro tedesco di studi veneziani», VIII (1978); K. E. LUPPRIAN, Il Fondaco dei Tedeschi e la sua funzione di controllo del commercio tedesco a Venezia, ivi, VI (1978).

¹⁸ Si veda BORSARI, Il commercio cit. e Per la storia cit.

[19] D. JACOBY, *L'expansion occidentale dans le Levant: les Vénitiens à Acre dans le second moitié du treizième siècle*, in «Journal of Medieval History», III (1977), pp. 225-67.

[20] D. ABULAFIA, *The Two Italies: economic relations between the Norman Kingdom of Sicily and the northern communities*, Cambridge 1977, pp. 74-75.

[21] M. BALARD, *La romanie génoise*, 2 voll., Atti della Società ligure di Storia patria, Ecole française de Rome, 1978.

[22] S. P. KARPOV, *L'impero di Trebisonda, Venezia, Genova e Roma, 1204-61. Rapporti politici, diplomatici e commerciali*, Roma 1986.

[23] D. JACOBY, *The rise of a new emporium in the eastern Mediterranean: Famagusta in the late thirteenth century*, Meletai kai Hypomnemata, Idryma Archiepiskopou Makariou III, Nicosia 1984, pp. 145-79.

[24] La principale affermazione della continuità, fatta propria in seguito da B. Z. Kedar, G. Airaldi e altri, è quella di C. CAHEN, *Orient latin et commerce du Levant*, in «Bulletin de la Faculté des lettres de Strasbourg», XXIX (1951), pp. 328-46.

[25] Sull'intera storia della presenza italiana nel regno di Gerusalemme del XII secolo si veda ora M. L. FAVREAU-LILIE, *Die Italiener und das Heilige Land*, Amsterdam 1988; cfr. anche gli Atti del convegno italo-israeliano tenuto a Gerusalemme e Haifa nel 1984, a cura di B. Z. Kedar e G. Airaldi, *I comuni italiani nel Regno crociato di Gerusalemme*, in «Collana storica di Fonti e Studi, Istituto di Medievistica, Università degli studi di Genova», XLVIII (1986).

[26] Sull'importanza di fattori come i venti e le correnti nel Mediterraneo, si veda J. H. PRYOR, *Geography, technology, and war* («Past and Present Series»), Cambridge 1988.

[27] Si confronti il punto di vista di CAHEN, *Orient* cit., secondo il quale Alessandria era sempre una base più importante di Acri per il commercio nel Levante; cfr. anche E. BACH, *La Cité de Gênes au XIIe siècle*, Copenhagen 1955, pp. 72-73, per la questione se le navi andassero ad Alessandria via Acri e poi tornassero direttamente a ovest. Sembra chiaro adesso che la maggior parte delle imbarcazioni per Alessandria ricorresse all'uno o all'altro porto nella Terra Santa sia all'andata che al ritorno.

[28] Tiro conseguí un'importanza paragonabile solo dopo il 1257, quando il conflitto tra i genovesi e i veneziani si risolse nell'espulsione dei primi da Acri e dei secondi da Tiro, dopo di che Tiro divenne la principale base genovese nell'Est latino.

[29] Per le colonie di Tiro e di Acri vedi J. PRAWER, *The Italians in the Latin Kingdom*, nella sua raccolta di studi *Crusading Institutions*, Oxford 1980, pp. 217-49, originariamente pubblicata in versione ridotta come *I veneziani e le colonie veneziane nel Regno latino di Gerusalemme*, in *Venezia e il Levante fino al secolo XV*, 2 voll., Firenze 1973, pp. 625-56. Vedi anche il prezioso studio di JACOBY, *L'expansion* cit.

[30] J. RILEY-SMITH, *Government in Latin Syria and the privileges of the foreign merchants*, in D. BAKER (a cura di), *Relations between East and West in the Middle Ages*, Edinburgh 1973, p. 120.

[31] G. ASTUTI, *Rendiconti mercantili inediti del Cartolare di Giovanni Scriba*, Torino 1973.

[32] D. ABULAFIA, *The Norman Kingdom of Africa*, in «Anglo-Norman Studies», VII (1985), pp. 25-49.

[33] ID., *A Tyrrhenian Triangle: Tuscany, Sicily, Tunis, 1276-1300*, in *Studi di Storia economica toscana nel Medioevo e nel Rinascimento in memoria di Federico Melis*, Biblioteca del Bollettino storico pisano, XXXIII, Pisa 1987, pp. 53-75; ID., *Sul commercio del grano siciliano nel tardo Duecento*, in *La società mediterranea all'epoca del Vespro*, XI Congresso di Storia della Corona d'Aragona, 4 voll., Palermo 1983, II, pp. 5-22.

[34] Gli atti di Pietro Battifoglio furono per la prima volta analizzati da G. JEHEL, *Catalogue analytique et cronologique des actes du notaire Petrus Batifolius*, in «Cahiers de Tunisie», XXV (1977), pp. 69-135, ormai sostituito dalla preziosa edizione di G. PISTARINO, *Notai genovesi in Oltremare, Atti rogati a Tunisi da Pietro Battifoglio (1288-1289)*, in «Collana storica di Fon-

ti e Studi, Istituto di Medievistica, Università degli studi di Genova», XLVII (1986). Si veda anche FERNANDEZ-ARMESTO, *Before Columbus* cit., pp. 109-11.

[35] R. BRUNSCHVIG, *La Berbérie orientale sous les Hafsides des origines à la fin du XVe siècle*, 2 voll., Paris 1940-47, pp. 453-54.

[36] G. PISTARINO, *Presenze ed influenze italiane nel Sud della Spagna (secc. XII-XV)*, in *Presencia italiana en Andalucia, siglos XIV-XVII, Actas del I Coloquio hispano-italiano*, Publicaciones de la Escuela de Estudios hispano-americanos de Sevilla, CCXI, Siviglia 1985, pp. 21-51; M. GONZÁLEZ JIMÉNEZ, *Genovesos en Sevilla (siglos XIII-XV)*, *ibid.*, pp. 115-30.

[37] Tra gli studi fondamentali sul commercio attraverso Maiorca si trovano i contributi di A. Santamaria Arández (*La reconquista de las vias maritimas*), M. T. Ferrer i Mallol e altri negli *Actas del Primero Congreso internacional de historia mediteranea* (Palma de Mallorca 1973), in «Anuario de Estudios medievales», X (1981); vedi anche F. SEVILLANO COLOM e J. POU MUNTANER, *Historia del Puerto de Palma de Mallorca*, Palma 1974.

[38] O. LIMOR, *The disputation of Majorca, 1286. A critical edition and introduction*, 2 voll., Hebrew University of Jerusalem, 1984.

[39] T. ANTONI, *I 'Partitari' maiorchini del «Lou dels Pisans» relativi al commercio dei Pisani nelle Baleari (1304-1322 e 1353-1355)*, Biblioteca del Bollettino storico pisano, XVIII, Pisa 1977.

[40] R. DOEHAERD, *Les relations commerciales entre Gênes, la Belgique et l'Outremont d'après les archives notariales génoises aux XIIIe et XIVe siècles*, Institut historique belge de Rome, Etudes d'histoire économique et sociale, vol. II (Textes), Brussels-Rome 1941, p. 96.

[41] R. D. FACE, *Symon de Gualterio: a brief portrait of a thirteenth-century man of affairs*, in *Economy, society and government in medieval Italy: essays in memory of Robert L. Reynolds*, a cura di D. Herlihy, R. S. Lopez e V. Slessarev, Kent (Ohio) 1969.

[42] T. LLOYD, *Alien merchants in England in the High Middle Ages*, Brighton 1982, p. 169.

[43] Si veda R. W. KAEUPER, *Bankers to the Crown: the Riccardi of Lucca and Edward I*, Princeton 1973; dello stesso autore, anche *The Frescobaldi of Florence and the English Crown*, in «Studies in Medieval and Renaissance History», I (1973).

[44] N. FRYDE, *Antonio Pessagno, king's merchant of Edward II of England*, in *Studi in memoria di Federigo Melis*, Napoli 1978, vol. II.

[45] LLOYD, *Alien merchants* cit., p. 200; M. PRESTWICH, *Italian merchants in late thirteenth and early fourteenth century England*, in *The Dawn of Modern Banking*, New Haven 1979, pp. 77-104.

[46] V. BRANCA, *Mercanti scrittori: ricordi nella Firenze tra Medioevo e Rinascimento*, Milano 1986, pp. 366-67.

THE LEVANT TRADE OF THE MINOR CITIES
IN THE THIRTEENTH AND FOURTEENTH CENTURIES:
STRENGTHS AND WEAKNESSES

Discussion of the Mediterranean economy during the Middle Ages has, understandably, been dominated by the rise of Genoa, Pisa and Venice, plus eventually Barcelona; the place of the other Western cities known to have been active in long-distance trade has received much less attention.[1] Since Venice obtained the lion's share of the spice trade with Egypt by 1400 and Genoa was master of the Black Sea grain trade in the same period, such emphases reflect the realities of medieval business. But what we know of the commercial history of Marseilles, despite a multitude of records, was largely summarized by Edouard Baratier in 1951;[2] Montpellier — despite its undoubted importance regionally and internationally — is only now receiving adequate attention from Kathryn

---

[1]   This article attempts to analyze and organize evidence about several trading communities which I have discussed individually and in detail elsewhere. Several of these articles were composed with the benefit of the advice of the late Professor Ashtor. See my 'Marseilles, Acre and the Mediterranean, 1200-1291,' in P.W. Edbury and D.M. Metcalf (eds.), *Coinage in the Latin East*, Oxford 1980, pp. 19-39; 'Crocuses and Crusaders: San Gimignano, Pisa and the Kingdom of Jerusalem,' in B.Z. Kedar, H.E. Mayer and R.C. Smail (eds.), *Outremer: Studies in the History of the Crusading Kingdom of Jerusalem presented to Joshua Prawer*, Jerusalem 1982, pp. 227-243; 'The Anconitan Privileges in the Kingdom of Jerusalem and the Levant Trade of Ancona,' in G. Airaldi and B.Z. Kedar (eds.), *I comuni italiani nel regno crociato di Gerusalemme*, Genoa 1986, pp. 525-570; 'The Merchants of Messina: Levant Trade and Domestic Economy,' *Papers of the British School at Rome* 54 (1986); 'Narbonne, the Lands of the Crown of Aragon and the Levant Trade, 1187-1400,' *Montpellier, La Couronne d'Aragon et les pays de Langue d'Oc (1204-1349). Actes du XIIe Congrès d'Histoire de la Couronne d'Aragon, Montpellier 26-29 septembre 1985*, in the *Mémoires de la Société Archéologique de Montpellier* 15 (1987): 189-207.

[2]   E. Baratier, *Histoire du commerce de Marseille publiée par la Chambre de Commerce de Marseille*, ed. G. Rambert, vol. 2, Paris 1951.

Reyerson;[3] Leonhard's recent study of Ancona in the Middle Ages says less than it should about commercial developments;[4] the Levant trade of Dubrovnik has fared better, but its principal historian does not claim an outstanding role for Ragusan merchants before the sixteenth century.[5] All this may reflect an accurate judgment on the relative significance of what Professor Ashtor called 'the minor trading nations;' and yet Ashtor's own monumental *Levant Trade in the later Middle Ages* presented a startling amount of evidence — fragmentary, of necessity — for the continuous presence of merchants from Narbonne, Messina, Ancona and elsewhere in the ports of Egypt, Cyprus, Syria and Lesser Armenia during the fourteenth and fifteenth centuries.[6] Many of these merchants traded under the cover of privileges permitting tax reductions, recognized warehouses and the appointment of consuls to oversee their affairs and their relations with the local rulers. And, particularly at times when the Venetians quarreled with the Mamlūk sultans, the presence of the merchants of the 'minor nations' in Alexandria and Beirut ensured a reasonably continuous flow of pepper, ginger and Eastern luxuries to Western consumers.

The question of the role of the 'minor nations' is not, however, simply one of weighing their much slighter investments alongside those of the Genoese, Venetians and Catalans, who generally came in large numbers to the trading stations of North Africa and the Levant: they had access to the ruler's ear and knew that the wishes or displeasure of their home government counted in the diplomatic and financial calculations of the Muslim rulers. Thus, even when the king of Aragon sent legates to Egypt to discuss access to the Holy Places for Christian pilgrims, the Mamlūk sultan steered negotiations toward the current difficulties in commerce between Egypt and Catalonia. In 1305 and in 1327 the sultan insisted that unrestricted trade between his domains and those of the Aragonese king was a pre-condition of his protection to Christian pilgrims and their shrines.[7] Venice, too, could alarm the money-conscious sultans with its threats to find common cause with their rivals to the north and east, and to sever

---

3   See especially Kathryn Reyerson, *Business, Banking and Finance in Medieval Montpellier*, Toronto 1985, and, for the present subject, idem, 'Montpellier and the Byzantine Empire. Commercial Interaction in the Mediterranean World before 1350,' *Byzantion* 48 (1978): 456-476.

4   J. F. Leonhard, *Die Stadt Ancona im Spätmittelalter: Politik und Handel*, Tübingen 1983 — notwithstanding the title!

5   B. Krekić, *Dubrovnik (Raguse) et le Levant au Moyen Age*, Paris–The Hague 1961.

6   E. Ashtor, *Levant Trade in the Later Middle Ages*, Princeton 1983.

7   Ashtor, pp. 33-34.

trading links with the Nile Delta.[8] Such tactics were hardly feasible for Ancona or Dubrovnik, still less for Messina, whose ruler in the mid-fourteenth century was a powerless child-king.

Unable to achieve striking results on their own, the merchants of the lesser trading cities understood the necessity of cooperation between their home towns, across inconvenient political boundaries; this brought not merely extra weight at foreign courts, but additional sources of capital and manpower. Thus the merchants of Narbonne (in the kingdom of France), of Montpellier (held by the kings of Majorca until 1349), of Marseilles (held by the two Angevin dynasties), of Perpignan (Majorcan and later Aragonese territory) worked together on the routes to the Levant throughout the fourteenth century.[9] These links also reflected a relative degree of economic specialization, for the inland towns such as Narbonne concentrated more on industrial activities, notably cloth production, while Marseilles emphasized the provision of shipping services; Montpellier offered highly-developed banking facilities as well as an elaborate distribution network. A lack of expertise in one or another economic speciality could thus be compensated by cooperation. Cooperation was reflected in the grant of trade privileges not to individual cities but to groups of towns; an early example is the privilege for trade in Tyre of 1187, in favor of Barcelona, Montpellier, Nîmes, Saint-Gilles and Marseilles.[10] One historian has expressed surprise that the Italian merchants trading to England in the late Middle Ages were not granted privileges as a group as were the Hansa traders; but the Venetians and Genoese, in the Mediterranean and beyond, unlike the smaller fry, were notoriously reluctant to share their rights with one another.[11] Nor were their needs and interests at all uniform.

The intention of this article is to examine the ways in which merchants of the 'lesser trading nations' intruded themselves into Levantine commerce during the thirteenth and fourteenth centuries. It will be apparent that there were three means of access: by going east as partners or agents of the greater, privileged, merchants and being counted, therefore, as members of a Pisan, Genoese or Venetian trading party; by adopting the nationality of a host group, usually their neighbors in the Western lands from which they came; and by requesting and obtaining privileges of their own, as Anconitans, Sicilians, southern French or

8   Ashtor, pp. 57-61.
9   Abulafia, 'Narbonne.'
10 Abulafia, 'Marseilles;' H.E. Mayer, *Marseilles Levantehandel und ein akkonensisches Fälscheratelier des XIII. Jahrhunderts*, Tübingen 1972.
11 T. H. Lloyd, *Alien Merchants in England in the High Middle Ages*, Brighton 1982, pp. 166-167.

whatever. At the risk of over-simplification, it can be suggested that some communities moved from the first through the second to the third process, as their own involvement in the Levant trade grew and their special needs, political as much as commercial, came to be more clearly defined. Occasionally it was the ruler rather than the merchants who propelled a community toward recognition of its special status, substituting a tax of, say, two percent for the total tax exemption merchants could claim by trading under the flag of Genoa or Venice. Privileges were not always generous favors. They imposed obligations and they even limited freedom. Historians tend to assume they were generally desirable. So they were for first comers; but those who arrived in their wake often saw reason to submerge their identity, and trade instead as members of the most favored and most powerful communities.

A further problem of definition arises from the fact that the minor trading cities absorbed large numbers of immigrants, themselves often natives of Venice, Genoa or Barcelona. Benjamin of Tudela remarked on the large number of foreign visitors to Montpellier in the mid-twelfth century;[12] but even in 1356 the French king received a report on Montpellier in similar terms: 'plus de deux parties [i.e. half] des habitants d'icelle sont d'estranges parties, les uns Cathalains, les autres Espaignols, Jeunevois, Lombars, Venessiens, Chiprois, Provensals, Allemains et d'autres plusieurs estranges nations.'[13] Around 1300 Benvenuto of Pistoia, an inhabitant of Agrigento, was trading from Sicily (probably from Messina and Palermo) to Cyprus and back.[14] In 1383 Pierre de Puysec, originally of Narbonne, now of Montpellier, organized a sailing to Alexandria out of Marseilles.[15] Such figures had chosen a base, away from the town of their birth, but traded from other cities too; and the permanent residents of several Latin trading centres included vast numbers of immigrants and their descendants, particularly in the over-populated years before the Black Death. Messina, Palermo, Ciutat de Mallorca (modern Palma) and, though far more slowly, Valencia were repopulated by Genoese, Tuscan, south Italian, Catalan, Provençal settlers. Pietro di Vitale *ianuensis* of Messina was a prominent member of the Messinese trading confraternity at the end of the thirteenth

12 M. N. Adler (ed.), *The Itinerary of Benjamin of Tudela*, London 1907, pp. 2-3 (English text), p. 3 (Hebrew text); cf. Mayer, pp. 60-65, where, however, Benjamin is not cited.

13 L.J. Thomas, *Montpellier, ville marchande. Histoire économique et sociale de Montpellier des origines à 1870*, Montpellier 1936.

14 R. Pavoni (ed.), *Notai genovesi in Oltremare. Atti rogati a Cipro da Lamberto di Sambuceto (6 luglio — 27 ottobre 1301)*, Collana storica di fonti e studi, vol. 32, Genoa 1982, no. 125.

15 Baratier, end table.

century; he moved among the Sicilians and the Genoese at Famagusta, in Cyprus.[16] Such men could claim the benefit of tax concessions conferred on the Genoese, or whichever community they claimed in membership. The far-flung diaspora of Italian and Catalan merchants was too large in numbers and too extensive in size to make it possible for merchants to be identified by personal knowledge of their origins and status. A Venetian of the Rialto and a Jew of Negropont were subject to the same jurisdiction in the Venetian colonies overseas;[17] Genoese of Pera and Caffa might never set foot in Italy. Thus the question 'who were the Genoese, or Catalans, or Venetians?' remains germane. There existed the notion of a commonwealth of merchants under the jurisdiction of the consuls of one or another city; but to be a Pisan in the eyes of the ruler of Tunis or the consul of the Pisans there did not mean citizenship of, or origin in, Pisa itself, in all or even the majority of cases.

The first way in which merchants from lesser towns found themselves counted as merchants of greater ones can be examined quickly. Business partnerships between merchants of unprivileged inland or maritime towns and merchants of the great maritime republics abound in the Genoese and Venetian notarial contracts.[18] The Florentines hardly constituted a 'minor trading nation' by 1300, but they had no shipping of their own, and partnerships with Catalans, Genoese and Anconitans were necessary if they were to manage effectively the grain trade between Sicily and Africa or the trade in textiles and raw materials through Cyprus to Little Armenia, Syria and Egypt.[19] From Piacenza came the bankers Scotti and Borrini, and they, like the moneymen of Siena, traded to the East by way of Marseilles as well as the Tuscan port of Pisa.[20] The Sienese only received a privilege for trade in the Holy Land in 1268, and then from the questionable

16   V. Polonio (ed.), *Notai genovesi in Oltremare. Atti rogati a Cipro da Lamberto di Sambuceto (3 luglio 1300 — 3 agosto 1301)*, Collana storica di fonti e studi, vol. 31, Genoa 1983, no. 65; Abulafia, 'Merchants of Messina,' pp. 206–207.

17   Ashtor, p. 45 (in general); cf. D. Jacoby, 'L'expansion occidentale dans le Levant: les Vénitiens à Acre dans la seconde moitié du treizième siècle,' *Journal of Medieval History* 3 (1977): 225–264, especially 237, 247, 249.

18   See, for instances, the acts of Lamberto di Sambuceto cited in notes 14 and 16: Pavoni, nos. 181, 185 (a merchant of Genoa, of Ancona and a ship-owner of Fermo), 203 (a Syrian Christian, a Cypriot, a Ragusan shipper and, apparently, a Venetian); Polonio, no. 71 (a Messinese and two Genoese).

19   Polonio, p. 550, s.v. *Florencia* gives some idea of the scale of penetration of Cyprus by representatives of the Peruzzi, Bardi, Mozzi and other houses.

20   Ashtor, p. 39.

hand of Conradin of Hohenstaufen;[21] they were evidently there earlier, with merchants of Volterra and the Tuscan hill-towns, as also of Marseilles, and it can be surmised that they injected capital into trading expeditions whose main protagonists were Tuscan and Provençal shipping entrepreneurs.[22] Equally, the inhabitants of lesser Catalan towns such as Perpignan, Tarragona and Ciutat de Mallorca followed in the wake of the merchants of Barcelona and Montpellier, the two prime centers of international trade in the Crown of Aragon before 1300. The fact that privileges in Byzantium or Armenia mentioned only Barcelona or only Montpellier did not act as a brake on the activities of fellow Catalans and Provençaux, who invested alongside them and were counted as Barcelonese or Montpelliérains.[23]

These practices shade imperceptibly into a more controversial issue, that of the flag of convenience. It was one thing to be counted as a Pisan or Venetian because the consul and his officials in an overseas port indicated that a merchant formed part of a company of merchants mainly from the home city. But the tax concessions conferred on the merchants of the greater cities were attractive bait to merchants from, say, San Gimignano or Volterra. By posing as Pisans in the port of Acre they could escape most of the customs dues normally levied on Latin merchants, under the terms of a royal privilege of 1187.[24] There is the famous story, recounted by Giovanni Villani, of the Tunisian ruler who assumed all his Tuscan visitors were Pisans until he saw a gold florin flashing in the hands of an Italian merchant; further enquiry revealed the existence of a commercial and industrial center far mightier than Pisa, where the florins were minted: Florence.[25] When in 1257 the *bailli* of the Kingdom of Jerusalem conferred a tax privilege on the merchants of Ancona, it was expressly stipulated that:

> Toutes manieres danconitens, qui se sont franchi jusques au jor duy per Jeneueis ou per pisans, ou per Venetiens, que il reuiegnent a la Seignorie, et seient en la Condition des autres anconitans.[26]

21 G. Müller, *Documenti sulle relazioni delle città toscane coll'Oriente cristiano e coi Turchi fino all'anno 1531*, Florence 1879, no. 70; cf. Abulafia, 'Marseilles,' n. 39 and 'Crocuses and Crusaders', p. 243.

22 For the links between Siena and Marseilles, see L. Blancard, *Documents inédits sur le commerce de Marseille au moyen âge*, 2 vols., Marseilles 1884, e.g., Cartulaire d'Almaric, no. 230.

23 Abulafia, 'Crocuses and Crusaders,' p. 238.

24 Ibid.

25 Giovanni Villani, *Cronica*, 6. 54; see also David Abulafia, 'A Tyrrhenian Triangle. Tuscany, Sicily, Tunis, 1276-1300,' in *Studi di storia economica toscana nel Medioevo e nel Rinascimento in memoria di Federigo Melis*, in the *Biblioteca del Bollettino storico pisano, Collana storica* 33 (1987): 53-75.

26 Edition of privilege in Abulafia, 'Ancona,' Appendix I, pp. 560–563.

There was to be no attempt to take advantage of even lower tax rates permitted to other groups; Anconitans had to identify themselves as what they really were. Since (at least by 1300) Anconitans were trading to the Levant often in partnership with Venetians and Genoese, this must have made the new rules hard to follow. Ownership of goods passing through the Chaine in Acre, or another customs house, could be hard to establish without close enquiry; business practices, involving advance purchase, sale under guarantee, and complicated transfer of title through third parties, were hardly conducive to a simple separation of Anconitan goods from those of their possible partners. Clearly, too, the Anconitans had not all suffered from the lack of special privileges before 1257; there were ways of evading customs duty that were widely known, even to the rulers of the Latin states.[27] Thus the Anconitans were also admonished not to admit to their group outsiders in search of tax exemption:

> Et se il y aueit aucun des anconitans qui ne fust Habitans a ancone, ou el destreit dancone, et il ne vousist estre en cest Condition, que ceaus dancone sont tenus de bannirles en cors et en aueir.[28]

This was actually a highly restrictive clause, defining Anconitans as residents of the city and its contado; an Anconitan resident in Apulia, for instance, would therefore be excluded. Ancona itself was continuing in this period to attract immigrants from central Italy and Dalmatia, so that the task of defining its 'habitans' cannot have been an easy one.

What is striking is that the Pisans, Genoese and Venetians do not seem to have minded the way outsiders placed themselves under their flag to claim trade privileges. There is no need here to repeat the story of how the authorities in San Gimignano became aware, during 1245, that the town's merchants were posing in the Holy Land as Pisans, and were benefiting from Pisa's privileged status in the customs régime of Acre.[29] It was argued in the courts of San Gimignano that many, though not all, Tuscan merchants accepted the authority of the Pisan consul in Acre, and that they were then allowed the rights of the Pisans, except

---

27   Cf. the attempts to ensure that Venetian merchants do not travel to Muslim territory and trade there with foreigners who would have had to pay full taxes on goods imported into the Kingdom of Jerusalem: J. Riley-Smith, 'Government in Latin Syria and the Commercial Privileges of Foreign Merchants,' in D. Baker (ed.), *Relations between East and West in the Middle Ages*, Edinburgh 1973, p. 120. Venetians who crossed the frontier were themselves held liable for the taxes the crown failed to receive from their Syrian business partners, even though normally Venetians were exempt from dues.

28   Abulafia, 'Ancona,' Appendix I, p. 561.

29   Abulafia, 'Crocuses and Crusaders,' pp. 235-239.

only that they did not participate in the election of new consuls. *Illi qui nolunt non subsunt et non coguntur nisi velint se conficeri Pisanos*: in return for recognition of the consul's authority — however such recognition was expressed — Tuscan merchants obtained the protection of a great trading city which was also a political force in the Kingdom of Jerusalem. But they were also liable to certain obligations, notably the surrender to the Pisan consul of one-third of the goods of a merchant who died in Syria. It is worth adding that in some regions of the Mediterranean the merchant had to do nothing in order to find himself placed under the authority of the consul: Pere de Grau, a Majorcan merchant in Sicily, was summonsed by the Catalan consul in Palermo, and failed to extricate himself from the consul's court by arguing that, as a Majorcan, he was not subject to the jurisdiction of the consul of the king of Aragon. It was assumed around 1299 that the king of Majorca's subjects were also the brief of the Catalan consul in Sicily.[30]

The real problem is not so much the advantage that these extraneous merchants gained from their submission to a foreign consul as it is the advantage the relationship gave the consul and his home city. For Pisa, a city already past its peak in the Levant trade, other Tuscan merchants provided additional capital for overseas voyages, in which Florentines, Sienese and Sangimignanesi, all shipless, were keen to invest; they paid rent for their lodgings in the Pisan quarter; they gave numerical strength to a community of merchants that had failed to sustain the challenge of Genoese and Venetian competition. Above all, there was the simpler question of jurisdiction. The more Pisans and pseudo-Pisans that fell under his authority, the more chance the consul had of cutting a *bella figura* in the Haute Cour.[31] At the other extreme, the proliferation of privileged smaller communities of merchants, not just of Ancona but of the inland Italian towns, would erode the financial and political power of the three great Italian communities in the Holy Land. So much for this case. In other instances the basis of such relations was often friendships formed between neighboring cities back in the West: Marseilles and Montpellier, for instance, on

---

30 David Abulafia, 'Catalan Merchants and the Western Mediterranean, 1236-1300: Studies in the Notarial Acts of Barcelona and Sicily,' *Viator* 16 (1985): 238-239. Cf. Antoni Riera Melis, *La Corona de Aragón y el Reino de Mallorca en el primer cuarto del siglo XIV*, vol. 1, *Las repercussiones arancelarias de la autonomía balear*, Madrid–Barcelona 1986, pp. 211, 213, 217, 278, where evidence is presented that in 1300 the kings of Majorca arranged to establish an independent consulate in Bougie, thus by-passing the authority of their overlords the kings of Aragon.

31 Exercise of criminal jurisdiction (with the help of his gendarmerie) is revealed in Abulafia, 'Crocuses and Crusaders,' pp. 240-242. It should be remembered that the three main merchant communities, along with the major Military Orders, possessed special political status in the Latin Kingdom, despite their apparent exemption from royal interference in their internal affairs.

the Cyprus run in the early thirteenth century;[32] or Barcelona and Majorca, its daughter-city and its partner along many Mediterranean trade routes. In yet further instances the basis lay in the domination of smaller cities by greater: the lordship of the Genoese over the commune of Savona brought the latter carefully controlled access to the markets of the East, through the port of Genoa; its merchants would be counted as Genoese except in the restricted sphere of the western Mediterranean where Savonese ships were allowed to trade unhindered. Venice extended membership of its communes in the East to merchants of Istria and of the coastlands between the lagoons and its rival Ancona: so, too, several Dalmatian cities, such as Dubrovnik, could send their merchants to selected destinations under Venetian protection.[33]

The disadvantages lay in the fact that rulers failed to distinguish between real and ersatz merchants of a particular Western town when they turned their wrath against them. The growing problem of reprisals meant that innocent traders of an inland Italian town might have their goods seized by the Mamlūk sultan in recompense for the faults of a vanished merchant of Venice or Genoa.[34] To guard against this a separate privilege, such as that held by Ancona in the Holy Land, was a useful asset. It was even possible to enlist Levantine rulers in aid of merchants of the 'lesser trading nations' and to encourage the use of reprisals on their behalf. In 1289 a merchant of Messina, Natalis, recorded the unusual circumstances that had led him to appeal against the Genoese consul in Caffa to the courts of Constantinople. The consul in Caffa had seized 172 cow-hides from Natalis, apparently quite arbitrarily; the judge in Constantinople provided restitution by seizing from a certain Benedetto Scotto of Genoa four bales of Smyrna silk. As a Genoese Benedetto was simply held liable for the offence caused to Natalis, even though he and Natalis had never had any dealings before these events. Benedetto was able to redeem the silk by paying Natalis for the cow-hides, though they were far away in Caffa and were not at all what he wanted to buy.[35] He was to all intents still out of pocket. But on balance governments were more likely to hold pseudo-Genoese or pseudo-Venetians to blame for the errors of their supposed mother-city than they were to leap to their aid in this way.

The final means of privileged access to Eastern markets for merchants of the

32   Abulafia, 'Marseilles,' p.29.
33   Ashtor, p. 31; Krekić, p. 115 and nos. 74, 206.
34   For reprisals in an inland Tuscan town, see W.M. Bowsky, *A Medieval Italian Commune: Siena under the Nine, 1287-1355*, Berkeley–Los Angeles 1981, pp. 232-46.
35   M. Balard (ed.), *Gênes et l'Outremer, I: Les Actes de Caffa du notaire Lamberto di Sambuceto 1289-1290*, Paris–The Hague 1973, no. 55.

192

minor trading centers was the acquisition of specific privileges. The case of Ancona has been examined already. Particularly after the fall of Acre, the beleaguered ruler of Cilician Armenia showered privileges on Western merchants, hoping thereby to encourage the crusading plans of French, Aragonese and other kings. The Catalans received a grant in 1293; Montpellier, in the kingdom of Majorca, was given favors in 1314 and 1321; the Venetians, too, were potential allies against the Mamlūks, and they were suitably showered with 'privileges in 1307, 1321 and after.[36] Even the merchants of Sicily were permitted a reduction in imposts so that from 1331 they had only to pay two percent on goods brought into or out of Armenia; they were allowed to operate their own courts in Armenia, subject to the oversight of the royal judiciary.[37] Trasselli is probably right to see Messina as the main beneficiary of the Sicilian privilege, and encouragement to the Aragonese kings of Sicily to help defend Armenia as the main motive. So, too, privileges for trade in Cyprus had their origins in a mixture of diplomatic endeavor and desire to attract foreign merchants to an island that had rapidly and successfully replaced Acre as a well-placed entrepôt for trade, licit and illicit, with the Muslim world. The notarial registers of the Genoese Lamberto di Sambuceto, of around 1300, indicate the presence of several Messinese, Narbonnais, Montpelliérain and Catalan merchants, not to mention Anconitans and Ragusans.[38] The Venetians and Genoese remained dominant, and by the time Pegolotti was in Cyprus they traded free of *commercium*, while the merchants of Provence, Catalonia, Ancona and Narbonne paid only two percent.[39] Visitors from Messina no doubt passed themselves off as Catalans, that is to say subjects of one of several Aragonese kings then ruling, or as members of whichever north Italian community they could claim links to by descent — Pietro Vitale *ianuensis* of Messina was presumably careful to pay no taxes at all, as a Genoese visitor to Cyprus.

36   V. Langlois (ed.), *Le Trésor des Chartes d'Arménie ou Cartulaire de la Chancellerie royale des Roupéniens*, Venice 1863, nos. 28, 33 bis, 34, 37, 38, etc.
37   Langlois, no. 38; C. Trasselli,'Sugli europei in Armenia: a proposito di un privilegio trecentesco e di una novella di Boccaccio,' *Archivio Storico Italiano* 122 (1964): 471-491.
38   A good introduction to Lamberto's evidence is M. Balard, 'L'activité commerciale en Chypre en l'an 1300,' in P.W. Edbury (ed.), *Crusade and Settlement: Papers read at the First Conference of the Society for the Study of the Crusades and the Latin East and presented to R.C. Smail*, Cardiff 1985, pp.251-263; see also D. Jacoby, 'The Rise of a New Emporium in the Eastern Mediterranean: Famagusta in the Late Thirteenth Century,' *Méletai kai Ipomnimata* 1 (1984): 145-179.
39   Francesco Balducci Pegolotti, *La Pratica della Mercatura*, ed. A. Evans, Cambridge, Mass. 1936, p. 84.

The case of Narbonne serves as a reminder that single cities of secondary importance could also find themselves blessed with royal favors and an autonomous consulate in Cyprus;[40] by 1400 the merchants of Narbonne also possessed a *funduq* in Alexandria, known as the '*funduq* of the pilgrims.'[41] It is possible that Narbonne was favored, in Cyprus at any rate, because its merchants were subjects of the French crown; the Lusignans of Cyprus could hope for French gratitude and further enthusiasm for that elusive and long-planned crusade. A privilege to the 'Provençaux' would, of course, benefit Angevin subjects in Marseilles and possibly Majorcan ones in Montpellier; Narbonne owed its successes to its specifically French political identity, and to judge from Lamberto di Sambuceto it capitalized fairly handsomely on these offers. Clearly, it should not be assumed that privileges involved a de facto recognition of the past commercial successes of the beneficiary city or cities; not merely the Christian rulers of Armenia and Cyprus saw diplomatic advantage in the conferral of tax exemptions, for the Mamlūks were as anxious to discourage would-be crusaders as the Armenians were to attract them.[42] Mention must also be made of a more tortuous combination of crusading diplomacy and commercial favor: Pope Innocent IV, with the encouragement of the Marseillais and of their allies in the Kingdom of Jerusalem, confirmed a heap of twelfth-century trade privileges which Mayer has shown to be forgeries of a mid-thirteenth century workshop at Acre.[43] But the basic issue was the same for the inhabitants of the Latin East: to encourage Western goodwill and to pay for it with commercial rights. Whether or not Marseilles secured the exemptions it claimed, the decades after the publication of the forgeries mark the highpoint of the city's trade with the Holy Land.[44]

Marseilles, Messina, Narbonne, the Catalan cities: these were not autonomous maritime republics, like Genoa and Venice, exempt though their citizens often were from close interference by the crown. They could not mobilize their fleets for war on their own: the fleets were generally small and the kings of France, Aragon and Sicily or Naples allowed them little freedom in foreign policy. Thus these cities were not being rewarded solely for themselves,

40   For the consulate, Abulafia, 'Narbonne', pp. 192–194.

41   C. Port, *Essai sur l'histoire du commerce maritime de Narbonne*, Paris 1854, p. 132.

42   Trasselli, 'Europei in Armenia,' stresses the intended advantage to Armenia of treaties with Aragonese rulers in the West.

43   Mayer, pp. 196-207 and passim. Ancona also received favor from Innocent IV, though not in the form of confirmations of bogus privileges: Abulafia, 'Ancona,' pp. 530–534.

44   Abulafia, 'Marseilles,' pp. 34-35.

and for what they could offer the Cypriots or the Armenians. The privileges were in part a lever intended to activate sympathy at the court in Paris, Barcelona or Palermo. The subdued history of fourteenth-century crusading indicates that such successes were limited.[45] What succeeded instead was the penetration by the 'minor merchants' of Eastern markets, and to that it is now necessary to turn.

The first characteristic of the Levant trade of the 'minor nations' is, not surprisingly, the export of industrial goods produced in or near the Western city from which the Levant traders originated. The account books of Jacme Olivier, merchant of Narbonne, reveal that in the 1380s there were quantities of local cloth — blanquettes of Narbonne, as well as Perpignan cloth — reaching Alexandria and Beirut in the hands of southern French merchants.[46] Pegolotti also talks of these commodities in his *Pratica della mercatura.* [47] In fact, Jacme Olivier not merely exported the textiles of his home city, he even helped supply it with raw wool from Aragon, which passed via the customs house of Perpignan into French territory.[48] Blanquettes (originally: heavy white cloths — a word from which the modern 'blanket' derives) were sent overseas with vermilion, blue and green cloths. Of all southern French towns, Montpellier had the liveliest textile industry, and the foundations of its international trade, as of that of Florence, lay in the ability of its citizens to provide financial services, finished and semi-finished cloths, and an elaborate distribution network for imported Eastern luxuries.[49] There is an obvious contrast with Venice and Genoa, cities whose industrial activity, before the fifteenth century, consisted primarily in ship construction and whose primary economic function was that of commercial entrepôts. Indeed, the failure of an industrial proletariat to challenge the power of the ancient aristocratic élite, in Venice and to a lesser extent in Genoa, reflects the distinctive and restricted economic function of these two cities. Not so Barcelona, Florence or indeed Pisa; not so Ciutat de Mallorca or Montpellier: the two major Mediterranean trading cities lacked the large textile-producing proletariat of their lesser rivals.

A second characteristic of the 'minor nations' is the use of the Levant trade to supply raw materials for local industries. Here the competition between Ancona

45   See N. Housley, *The Avignon Papacy and the Crusades*, Oxford 1986.
46   A. Blanc, *Le livre de comptes de Jacme Olivier, marchand narbonnais du XIVe siècle*, Supplément au Bulletin de la Commission archéologique de Narbonne, 2 vols., 1895-1902; Ashtor, pp. 543-544.
47   Pegolotti, pp. 37, 55, 58, 79, 84, 109, 111, 113, 167, 180, 204.
48   Blanc, p. 284, no. 18.
49   Thomas, *passim*.

and Venice in the cotton trade from Syria and Egypt is especially instructive. Venice was middleman, purveyor of raw cotton to the looms of Lombardy and, later, of southern Germany. Ancona sold its cotton to the workshops of the central Italian hill-towns, such as Jesi, Osimo or Fermo. It was a restricted market, because the Venetians forced treaties on Ancona, notably in 1264, which denied Anconitan merchants free access to the upper Adriatic.[50] Indeed, the intention of the Venetians was to deny Ancona the right to carry anything but pilgrims and local merchants between East and West. The Anconitans managed to infringe these terms with impunity, but even so they could never compete effectively with Venice in the trade in Eastern luxuries. Imports of sugar, pepper, incense and Eastern cloths seem mainly to have been directed to consumers in central Italy, such as the papal court, whose summer retreats in Umbria and the hills of Lazio were easily accessible to the Anconitans, themselves subjects of the popes. Attempts to make Ancona into an out-port for the Tuscan towns in their trade with the Balkans and the eastern Mediterranean, though well documented, appear not to have achieved significant success; as early as 1169 Pisa attempted to construct a network of land and sea routes linking Tuscany to Ancona, Split, Dubrovnik and, very probably, the Byzantine Empire; but then, as later, Venetian hostility remained implacable.[51]

A third feature of the Levant trade of the 'minor nations' was their involvement in passenger traffic rather than in freight. The truth behind the thirteenth-century Marseilles forgeries, pretending to an ancient, privileged status in the Holy Land, is that the Pisans had long tried to coerce Marseilles, Montpellier and the southern French towns into the carriage eastward solely of pilgrims.[52] Even in the mid-thirteenth century this was probably a major feature of Provençal traffic to the East.[53] The richer Italian republics may have perceived that cargo paid its way more handsomely than did pilgrims, and (given the limited shipping capacity of the thirteenth century) the release of space on board Italian ships for commercial uses was urgently required. But the pilgrim traffic entailed minor trade at least; on the return journey, when empty spaces were more likely to be found, there was a temptation to load goods; and even on the outward journey the captain and crew could not really be prevented from ferrying articles to the East for sale.

50   A. Cessi, *Venezia e il problema adriatico*, Padua 1943, pp. 75-82, Ashtor, p. 30.
51   David Abulafia, 'Ancona, Byzantium and the Adriatic, 1155-1173,' *Papers of the British School at Rome* 52 (1984).
52   Mayer, pp. 84-88.
53   Abulafia, 'Marseilles,' p. 34.

A fourth feature is the trade in local agricultural products — Western goods in short supply in the East or only available in poor quality. In the thirteenth century the Sicilians were involved in the carriage of grain to the ailing Latin states in the East, either on their own or with the help of Florentine capital. In 1283, for instance, Bonaggiunta de Scarlata of Messina was permitted by the Aragonese king to export 300 *salme* of wheat to Acre, on the ship of Conetto di Conetto of Pisa; here, Peter of Aragon was imitating the practice of his predecessor and rival Charles of Anjou, who had licensed exports of grain to the Holy Land by Amalfitans, Sicilians and north Italian visitors to his *Regno*.[54] The same year another Messinese merchant was allowed to add cheese to his cargo bound for Acre, if he wished to do so; cheese from Sicily was often exported on the grain ships, for it could be stored between decks above the hold, in spaces too confined for the carriage of grain.[55] The Cairo Geniza documents also record exports of cheese from Messina and Syracuse to Alexandria in 1241 and 1243; this was a trade in which Jewish merchants had a special interest, for some at least of the cheese was kosher and was intended for consumption by Egyptian Jews.[56] While cheese was probably a regular export to the East, grain depended more on fluctuations in the political climate or the real climate: poor harvests in Armenia (as at the end of the thirteenth century), or the general destitution of the Latin-controlled countryside in Syria before the fall of Acre.[57] When grain was exported to the Mamlūk territories, however, additional problems arose: could wheat, especially biscuit, be classified as a war material? If so, it was subject to papal embargo. But there are signs the trade continued nonetheless.

More specialized agricultural produce was also carried east by the minor merchants. Honey was in demand in Egypt, and according to Ashtor the agricultural decline of the Near East increased dependence on Western suppliers.[58] Although many Levant traders carried honey, the Languedoc merchants stood in an especially advantageous position. Languedoc produced

54 G. Silvestri (ed.), *De rebus regni Siciliae (9 settembre 1282 — 26 agosto 1283)*, Palermo 1882, p. 269; Ashtor, p. 16; E. Pispisa, *Messina nel Trecento: Politica, Economia, Società*, Messina 1980, pp. 8, 13; N. Nicolini, *Codice diplomatico sui rapporti veneto-napoletani durante il regno di Carlo I di Angiò*, Regesta Chartarum Italiae, Rome 1965, pp. 143, 155, seq.

55 *De rebus*, pp. 481-482.

56 S. D. Goitein, 'Sicily and Southern Italy in the Cairo Geniza Documents,' *Archivio storico per la Sicilia orientale*, 67 (1971): 15.

57 Y. Renouard, 'Une expédition de céréales de Pouille en Arménie par les Bardi pour le compte de Benoît XII,' *Études d'histoire médiévale*, Paris, 1968, vol. 2, pp. 793-824; Nicolini, pp. 143, 155; Ashtor, pp. 16-17, 30-31.

58 Ashtor, pp. 23-25, 50.

excellent export grade honey; Jacme Olivier of Narbonne even maintained a special series of Honey Accounts, and in 1387 we find him sending 42 jars of the commodity to Rhodes, Alexandria and Beirut, in partnership with Jacme Baron of Narbonne and Jacme Carquasona of Montpellier. Their ship was to travel east from Leucate, an out-port of Narbonne, but Jacme Olivier also had honey on board 'la nau de Monpeylier' which was due to depart, apparently, from Aigues-Mortes.[59] On another occasion his honey was loaded on a ship that set out from Collioure, the out-port of Perpignan. His career seems to prove the point made in a contemporary rhyme: 'Nule part n'ot remes mel meillour fors à Noirbonne.'[60] Marino Sanuto the Elder, author of plans for an economic war against the Mamlūks, saw honey as well as nuts and olive oil as significant Western imports into the Levant at the start of the fourteenth century.[61] The southern French merchants, natives of a région that produced some of the best honey, were able to capitalize very successfully on this demand. In return they could import an alternative sweetening agent — sugar — as well as pepper, ginger and cinnamon.

But the spice trade was not one-way. The minor merchants dominated the export of the major Western spice in demand in the Levant — high-grade saffron. The best saffron came from the hills of Tuscany, from the contado of San Gimignano. The product itself was of excellent quality, but no less importantly, the Sangimignanesi were known to control production carefully in order to prevent adulteration. In this respect the rival product of Volterra or Siena was less reliable. In the mid-thirteenth century a pound of San Gimignano saffron fetched over a pound of Pisan silver in the markets of the Levant. Moreover, this was an exceptionally versatile product, used as a dye for cloth, as a component of drugs and as a flavoring in its own right.[62] From Acre the merchants of San Gimignano carried saffron to Aleppo, Alexandria and 'Turchia,' and there are signs that they were involved in the saffron trade generally, not merely in the sale of saffron from their home city. Among competitors, the Sienese neighbors of San Gimignano not surprisingly have a

59 Blanc, pp. 128-131, 139-142, and, for his 'Lybre de la mel,' pp. xxxvi and 242.
60 Port, p. 72.
61 Ashtor, p. 23; C.J. Tyerman, 'Marino Sanudo Torsello and the Lost Crusade: Lobbying in the Fourteenth Century,' *Transactions of the Royal Historical Society* 5. 32 (1982): 60.
62 Abulafia, 'Crocuses and Crusaders,' p. 227; E. Fiumi, *Storia economica di San Gimignano*, Biblioteca storica toscana, Florence 1961, pp. 33-40; the ability of the contado to support an extraordinarily large population, not matched till the twentieth century, must surely be explained in the light of intense specialization — in the production and processing of crocuses (for saffron extraction) and in the cultivation of highly respectable vines.

special importance; in 1248 Dioteviva Alberto of Siena sent 171 1b. of saffron from Marseilles to Acre, using a Provençal factor.[63] In the same period other Tuscans trading in the Levant (generally under the Pisan flag) display different specialities: the Florentines, not surprisingly, were most interested in the sale of cloth.[64]

A further example of the exploitation of local resources to fund the Levant trade of a minor nation is provided by Messina, a city whose grain merchants have already been encountered. But Messina was isolated from the granaries of Sicily by the land-mass of Etna; its grain merchants were thus mainly involved in feeding the city, rather than in exporting local grain.[65] To pay for their imports of foodstuffs they could, however, export the local agricultural asset, which consisted of wine. Petronio de Puteo, a Messina merchant who died in the East in or before 1279, traded regularly between Messina and Acre, and sent Sicilian wine to the Holy Land, taking back in return pepper, sugar and luxury textiles.[66] Indeed, Alibrandi has insisted that one of the principal articles imported into the Levant by the Messinesi was wine.[67] It is therefore all the more striking that members of Petronio de Puteo's family should have possessed a vineyard in the vicinity of Messina.[68] It seems likely that they produced the same article as they exported. Typical or not (and the evidence from Messina is very fragmentary), the Puteo family expresses the fact that the city's Levant trade was based in part on specialization in a local commodity, produced to a high level of quality in the region of Sicily least able to feed itself directly from the soil. There was also an active wine trade between Sicily and North Africa in this period, though the western Sicilian towns are better documented in this respect.[69] The analogy with Narbonne and San Gimignano needs to be stressed: local honey, local saffron or local wine, handled in significant measure — though not exclusively — by local merchants enabled these towns to conduct an active Levant trade. This is a very different picture from that presented by Genoa and Venice, net importers of foodstuffs for their own bloated populations — cities whose function in the

63   Blancard, Cartulaire d'Almaric, no. 230.

64   Abulafia, 'Crocuses and Crusaders,' p. 239.

65   Pispisa, pp. 12, 14.

66   M. Alibrandi Intersimone, 'Pergamene dell'Archivio di Stato di Messina provenienti dal Museo Nazionale (1225-1770),' Rassegna degli Archivi di Stato 32 (1972): 501, no. 124.

67   M. Alibrandi, 'Messinesi in Levante nel Medioevo,' Archivio storico siciliano 3. 21-22 (1971/2): 102-103; Abulafia, 'Merchants of Messina,' 200-202.

68   Alibrandi, 'Pergamene,' p. 501, no. 128.

69   Abulafia, 'Tyrrhenian Triangle,' is mainly a study of Tuscan intermediaries in the wine trade from western Sicily to (of all places) Tunis.

Levant trade was in essence entrepreneurial.[70]To these instances of specialization others can be added, too. At the end of the fourteenth century the *Ste Catherine* of Narbonne, whose owners included Jacme Olivier, carried, predictably enough, southern French and northern textiles, probably honey too; but there was also coral on board, and here it was the merchants of Marseilles who dominated business.[71] Their fishing grounds lay off Alghero in northwestern Sardinia, but they supplied a large international market. So, too, the occasional Valencian merchant might trade across the Mediterranean, and even to England, in the rice and luxury fruits as well as the elaborate pottery that his region produced.[72] The Majorcans, though less involved than the Barcelonese in the Levant trade, undoubtedly drew much wealth from the exploitation of the salt-pans of Ibiza.[73] The southern French merchants also had easy access to salt along their marshy coasts. In this commodity, however, Venice dominated the Levant trade, and Catalans or Provençaux concentrated more on the valuable salt trade to northwest Africa. Yet here again local resources provided the means, or part of the means, for commercial take-off. Finally, it would be hard to deny that the trading successes of Dubrovnik had their origin in the town's hard-won access to the silver and base metals of the mountains of Bosnia. Slaves, too, were a local resource of some notoriety, though if they were Bogomils or Orthodox the issue was less controversial.[74]

Neither the dependence of the 'minor nations' on the Genoese, Venetians and Catalans, nor their independence of such greater interests, should be exaggerated. Several towns in Tuscany were able to gain access to Levantine markets under the Pisan flag of convenience; indeed, by the end of the thirteenth century the Florentines, if not the Sienese and Sangimignanesi, may well have

---

70 Narbonne in fact was sometimes involved with the export of Languedoc grain, though in the late thirteenth century its citizens begrudged Acre any share; see T. N. Bisson, *Assemblies and Representation in Languedoc in the Thirteenth Century*, Princeton 1964, pp. 200-211 and doc. no. 5, pp. 316-318.

71 Baratier, and table; this material is extended on the basis of the Datini archive in Prato by Ashtor, pp. 194-195 and 527-529 (Table A4). For the coral of Marseilles see also G. Lavergne, 'La pêche et le commerce de corail à Marseille aux XIVe et XVe siècles,' *Annales du Midi* 64 (1952): 199-211.

72 Ashtor; A. Ruddock, *Italian Merchants and Shipping in Southampton, 1200-1600*, Southampton 1950, p. 77.

73 J.C. Hocquet, 'Ibiza, carrefour du commerce maritime et témoin d'une conjoncture méditéranéenne,' *Studi in memoria di Federigo Melis*, Naples 1978, vol. 1, pp. 491-526, and especially pp. 496-499.

74 Krekić, pp. 79, 109-111.

dominated the Levant trade officially attributed to Pisa. Others were able to seize different coattails: Ancona could trade under a Genoese or Venetian shadow, at least until 1257; the southern French could take advantage of the privileges showered on the subjects of the House of Anjou in Marseilles, or of the Crown of Aragon in Montpellier until they, too, received grants of their own; the Sicilians were sometimes masked as Catalans after 1282.[75] Indeed, it may be wondered who actually paid the full *commercium* in Acre, Ayas, Famagusta or the Mamlūk domains. It is a situation reminiscent of that on the Ferrovie dello Stato in modern Italy, where no self-respecting citizen can fail to show that he is entitled to one or another *tariffa ridotto*. It has been seen that the rulers of the kingdoms of Jerusalem and Armenia sought to limit their privileges to bona fide Anconitans or Sicilians, but it has been seen also that such identity was hard to establish in cities with a highly mobile population, among which the most mobile elements of all were the merchants. What is to be made of Pierre Raymond de Montpellier, five times consul of Narbonne in the mid-thirteenth century?[76] The origin of his family is not in doubt, nor his citizenship, but as a businessman he would certainly exploit all opportunities open to him, as Narbonnais and Montpelliérain. So, too, Pietro Vitale, the *ianuensis* of Messina.

In the thirteenth and fourteenth centuries specialized interests enabled the merchants of Messina, Narbonne and elsewhere to maintain, in low profile, an active Levant trade of their own. Messina had its wine surplus available for export to the Christian East (at least), while Narbonne directed the honey of Languedoc toward consumers in Alexandria and Beirut. Moreover, *nerbonesi, pirpignani* and other southern French cloths were in high demand throughout the Mediterranean — so much so that the terms became generic ones, and by this period they may not even indicate origin in Narbonne or Perpignan.[77] Equally, there were limits to what such cities could achieve on their own, even with the patronage of French or Aragonese rulers; the merchants of Messina suffered the disadvantage of living under a cadet Aragonese house, weakened by internecine strife in Sicily during the fourteenth century. Despite occasional achievements,

---

75   But they had a separate consulate in Tunis (at least) to that of the Catalans, reflecting a long
      history of Sicilian-African trade before the Aragonese conquest. G. La Mantia, *Codice
      diplomatico dei re aragonesi di Sicilia Pietro I, Giacomo, Federico II, Pietro II e Ludovico, dalla
      rivoluzione siciliana del 1282 al 1355*, vol. 1: *1282-1290*, Palermo 1917, pp. 168-169, 204-207; the
      Sicilian consul was to be a Messinese.

76   R.W. Emery, *Heresy and Inquisition in Narbonne*, New York 1941, p. 28.

77   Pegolotti, p. 425, s.v. *Nerbonesi* and s.v. *Pirpignani*. Nonetheless many Nerbonesi and
      Pirpignani did come from the towns that gave them their name, as Jacme Olivier's accounts
      seem to indicate; and they fetched good prices overseas.

such as the Armenian privilege to the Sicilian merchants, or special rights and a consulate at Famagusta, in the case of Narbonne, these merchants had less powerful backing than did the Catalans of the Spanish mainland, not to mention the Genoese and Venetians. Ancona, too, drew strong encouragement from its overlord the Pope, but the Curia was able to achieve few concrete results on Ancona's behalf: Innocent IV's privilege to the Anconitans in Acre was surely a dead letter.[78] What mattered were the fighting fleets that Genoa, Venice and, at its peak, the Crown of Aragon possessed, enabling them to hold open access to the markets of the Levant and the Maghrib: the one truly effective lever in Mediterranean ports and courts. The lesser trading nations were rarely, if ever, able to gain first access to new markets in the region; they followed in the wake of the Genoese, Pisans, Venetians and Catalans. In Cyprus around 1300 they were even making extensive use of a Genoese notary resident at Famagusta to conduct their business; Narbonne had a consul, but apparently no scribe.[79] Occasionally, too, the 'minor nations' received in grant more than they could manage. The use of the Narbonnais *funduq* at Alexandria for pilgrims may reflect the heavy involvement of Narbonne in passenger traffic to the East, but it is more likely that it indicates the limited capacity of the Narbonnais to fill their warehouse with goods and merchants, so that they became obliged to act as innkeepers to pilgrims who came on any or all ships. But taken as a group, the merchants of what is now southern France did have capital resources and were able to send ships regularly to the East, combining in one vessel the investments of businessmen of Marseilles, Montpellier, Narbonne, Perpignan and inland towns such as Nîmes.[80] All this may still make the 'minor nations' sound unimportant. Certainly it is hard to estimate the cumulative value of their investments: taking all non-Venetians, non-Genoese and non-Catalans together, the annual investment in the Levant of the minor merchants is unlikely to have reached even ten percent of total East-West trade. What is important, however, is the link between the Levant trade of the 'minor nations' and the domestic economy of the cities or regions from which their merchants

78 Abulafia, 'Ancona,' p. 532; A. Theiner, *Codex diplomaticus dominii temporalis S. Sedis*, Rome 1861, vol. 1, p. 119, no. 210.
79 Further details of the consulate in Abulafia, 'Narbonne,' pp. 192–194; the Narbonne merchants used a French church in Famagusta, having none of their own. By 1344 the consul of the 'French' in Beirut appears — conceivably a Narbonnais or even Montpelliérain, possessing, or claiming, a wider brief: Ashtor, p. 49, cf. Baratier, p. 222.
80 For Nîmes, see still L. Ménard, *Histoire civile, écclésiastique, et littéraire de la ville de Nismes*, 6 vols., Paris 1750-5. The city was a beneficiary of the 1187 privilege to Barcelona and the southern French towns (Mayer, pp. 181-183), though with what effect it is hard to say.

originated. Produce of eastern Sicily and Languedoc was directed toward Eastern markets: raw materials from the East arrived in central Italy via Ancona, breathing life into the cotton industry of central Italy. Messina or equally Narbonne and Ancona were not simply command centers of a vast international trade network, contributing rather few commodities of their own — as might, without exaggeration, be said of Genoa and Venice during this period. The Levant trade of the lesser nations acted upon the surrounding countryside and on satellite towns close by — thus Aigues Mortes survived St. Louis' crusades to become a flourishing out-port for the Languedoc towns.[81] The minor cities were not just intermediaries distributing goods produced far afield, but processing centers for wine and cheese, or honey, or coral, and often for textiles too.

In other words, their long-distance trade was not an exceptional feature of their economic activity, divorced from the major local interests of each city; it was intimately linked to the domestic economy, by which it was stimulated and on which, in turn, it acted as a stimulus.

---

81 It now seems that the crusade was only one motive for the town's foundation and extension: B. Jehel, *Aigues-Mortes: les Capétiens et la Méditerranée*, Roanne 1985.

XII

THE MERCHANTS OF MESSINA:
LEVANT TRADE AND DOMESTIC ECONOMY

I

essina is often seen as the exception to a rule: whereas the towns of southern Italy
d Sicily performed a passive role as suppliers of raw materials to the merchants of
rthern Italy and Catalonia from the twelfth century onwards, Messina possessed
active community of entrepreneurs, and was the only southern town to compare
any way with the great merchant republics further north. In explanation, it has
en suggested either that the origins of Messinese vitality lay in an Amalfitan
odus to Sicily, consequent upon the decline of Amalfi under Norman rule; or,
ternatively, that Messina, more than any other Sicilian town, was isolated from the
od-producing interior of the island, so that its survival depended on trade along
e coasts, to Milazzo, Calabria and Catania. The need to pay for the grain the city
ported generated investment in oriental silks and spices, African skins and gold,
d stimulated the emergence of a group of merchants whose range eventually
tended as far as Egypt, Armenia and the Black Sea. To some degree this
planation involves the imposition of a model derived from eleventh- and twelfth-
ntury Genoa.[1] It is probably a more satisfactory explanation than the argument
r Amalfitan influence; for, although there was an Amalfitan quarter in Messina in
e thirteenth and fourteenth centuries, there were also Amalfitan merchants
attered through the west Mediterranean, active in the food trade as well as luxury
mmerce, well after the Norman takeover of Amalfi. Moreover, Messina, just like
malfi, was under Norman rule from the late eleventh century.[2]

A radically different approach denies the very existence of a large Messinese
ading community. A few of the city's inhabitants may have enriched themselves in
e wake of Genoese and Pisan expansion, by way of Messina, into the east
lediterranean; but it was others who led the way. Messina's notorious collection of
rged trade privileges, from the fifteenth century, discredit the idea of an active
erchant group in more ways than one.[3] There were plenty of merchants at Messina,

[1]For the debate about Messina see E. Pispisa, *Messina nel Trecento: Politica, Economia, Società*
Messina, 1980), which provides an excellent survey of the city's history; some useful additional
mments (focussed on the fifteenth century) in S. Tramontana, *Antonello e la sua città* (Palermo, 1981).
. Ashtor, *Levant Trade in the later Middle Ages* (Princeton, 1983), contains many references to Messina
nd its merchants. On the wider Sicilian setting, see especially A. Petino, *La politica commerciale di Pietro
II d'Aragona in Sicila* (Italiae Historia Oeconomica, xi, Messina, 1944), especially 18–22; A. Petino,
Aspetti del commercio marittimo della Sicilia nell'età aragonese', *Bollettino storico catanese, già Archivio
torico per la Sicilia orientale*, xi/xii (1946/7), 5–16, where (much more emphatically than Pispisa) 'aetate
eltibera Siciliae portus non solum transitus fuisse, ut legimus apud Doren, sed eosdem cum maximis
Mediterranei maris emporiis commercia explicavisse, auctor fontium notarum et ignotarum auxilio
emonstrat' (p.16). C. Trasselli, *Note per la storia dei banchi in Sicilia nel XIV secolo* (Banco di Sicilia,
ondazione per l'Incremento economico culturale e turistico della Sicilia 'Ignazio Mormino',
Quaderno i, Palermo, 1958) concentrates more on western than eastern Sicily.

[2]M. del Treppo, A. Leone, *Amalfi medioevale* (Naples, 1977).

[3]On which, C. Giardina, *Capitoli e Privilegi de Messina* (Palermo, 1937); C. Trasselli, *I Privilegi di
Messina e di Trapani, 1160–1355* (Palermo, 1949); Petino, *Politica commerciale*, 18–22.

but according to this view they were very largely foreigners. Here already problems arise. To argue that the Messina trading community was of non-Sicilian ancestry is not necessarily to argue that Messina lacked merchants born, bred and firmly attached to the city, little aware of their ancestry in Genoa, Tuscany or Languedoc. Indeed, it is clear that Messina experienced heavy immigration from the eleventh century onwards. Even under Muslim rule many of its inhabitants were Christian; but it was not a particularly large or important city until the conquest of the Holy Land made it a regular stop on the way east.[4] 'Here most of the pilgrims assemble to cross over to Jerusalem, as this is the best crossing': Benjamin of Tudela, writing before 1170, bears witness to the city's new-found importance. A little later, another Spaniard, the Moor Ibn Jubayr, described the excellence of Messina's port—an excellence compromised by the dangers of the rapids between Calabria and Sicily, strong currents that sank the ship in which he was sailing.[5]

Benjamin of Tudela talks of a sizeable Jewish community in Messina, though documents a century older, from the Cairo Geniza, do not seem to agree. Neither Jews nor Muslims could compare in influence with the Christians, who formed the bulk of the city's population even before the Norman conquest. Many of the Christians were Greeks (*Grifones*), presumably descended from the Greek Christians who had continued to inhabit the Val Demona and eastern Sicily under Muslim rule; the area had a reputation as a source of silks and heavy cloths, the silks probably manufactured in part from Calabrian raw silk.[6] Although the Greeks remained prominent throughout the Middle Ages, there are signs of tension between Latin and Greek, notably during Richard Coeur-de-Lion's visit to Messina on his way to the Holy Land. The castle of Matagrifon ('kill the Greeks') continued to stand after his departure.[7] However, the Greeks could exert influence at the royal court since the Basilian monastery of San Salvatore was one of the best-endowed landlords in Sicily. Its monks had trade privileges as early as the twelfth century, permitting them to sell wheat in north Africa, in exchange for which they obtained wax.[8] Further evidence for a Greek landed interest is provided by the surviving charters of the monastery of Santa Maria.[9]

But it was the Latins who gained more and more influence; virtually all of them must have been immigrants from southern Italy, Liguria, Tuscany and the shores of

[4]David Abulafia, *The Two Italies: economic relations between the Norman Kingdom of Sicily and the northern communes* (Cambridge, 1977), 42–5, remarking that 'Messina was a Norman phenomenon and a phenomenon of the crusades'.

[5]*The Itinerary of Benjamin of Tudela*, ed. M. N. Adler (London, 1907), 2, 76; cf. *The Travels of Ibn Jubayr*, ed. and transl. R. J. C. Broadhurst (London, 1952), 338, 348; Messina is described by Ibn Jubayr as 'the main mart of the merchant infidels', in 1184/5.

[6]S. D. Goitein, 'Sicily and southern Italy in the Cairo Geniza documents', *Archivio storico per la Sicilia orientale*, lxvii (1971), 12, 13; Abulafia, *Two Italies*, 44.

[7]*The Chronicle of Richard of Devizes of the time of the King Richard I*, ed. J. T. Appleby (London, 1963), 16–25.

[8]E. Caspar, *Roger II. (1101–1154) und die Gründung der normannisch-sicilischen Monarchie* (Innsbruck, 1904), Regesten, no. 95; David Abulafia, 'The crown and the economy under Roger II and his successors', *Dumbarton Oaks Papers*, xxxvii (1983), 5.

[9]A. Guillou, ed., *Les actes grecs de S. Maria di Messina* (Testi e monumenti dell'Istituto siciliano di studi bizantini e neoellenici, vol. viii, Palermo, 1963).

le western Mediterranean. From the early twelfth century onwards, attempts were
eing made to encourage Latin settlers from Apulia and Campania, and in
articular from the hinterland of Savona, to colonise eastern Sicily, a thinly
opulated area even before the Norman victories.[10] It was the towns—not merely
andazzo and Paternò, but Messina—that drew many of these settlers. Alongside
1em came short-term visitors from Genoa and elsewhere; the first privilege received
y Genoa in Sicily consists of a grant of land next to the sea at Messina, in 1116.[11]
urther privileges to Genoa, Venice and Pisa, especially the generous grant to Genoa
1 1156, enabled the north Italians to claim major tax reductions in the Sicilian
orts.[12] It is therefore hardly surprising that the inhabitants of Messina, not all of
/hom could benefit from these privileges, grew restive. In May 1160 Messina
eceived a major commercial privilege from King William I, whose authenticity is
.ot (for once) in doubt. 'All the Christians' of Messina were granted a reduction in
he main tax, the *commercium*, from ten per cent to three per cent, and this was
ssentially the same reduction as the Genoese had received in 1156 in Messina. But
ood coming into or going out of Messina was not to be taxed at all. This reflects the
pecial problems of Messina, a city without an extensive grain-growing hinterland.[13]
t was the export of local wine and fruit that enabled the Messinesi to pay for the
grain they needed.[14] One speciality of the region seems to have been bacon. In 1200
ome merchants of Marseilles drew up a contract for the export of ham or bacon to
Provence from Messina. Their cargo also included liquorice from Syria, the presence
of which emphasizes Messina's role as storehouse for imported luxuries from the
ast.[15]

The question here is who managed the storehouse: the Messinesi or the foreign
merchants who were so deeply entrenched in the city by 1200? If, as has been
suggested, imported eastern luxuries provided the citizens of Messina with a means
to pay for the grain and other staple goods the city required, then the question arises
who was importing those luxuries and how their sale and exchange was organised in
Messina. It is clear that some Messinese merchants concentrated heavily on the local
grain or wine trade, and ranged no further than Calabria or the northern and eastern
coasts of the island.[16] An Arabic trade contract of the mid-twelfth century,
concerning a certain Sir William and his Muslim business partners, may bear early

[10]Abulafia, 'Crown and the economy', 11–13.
[11]Abulafia, *Two Italies*, 62–4; I no longer believe there must have been a Latin original; it seems more likely the Greek text was the original, for production of Latin documents at the early Norman court was slight.
[12]Abulafia, *Two Italies*, 92.
[13]Giardina, *Capitoli e Privilegi*, 15–16; Trasselli, *Privilegi*, 13, 16; Abulafia, *Two Italies*, 117–21, and also 134–6 for Paganus of Messina, a Messinese merchant of this period who is documented both at Venice and at Genoa.
[14]Pispisa, *Messina*, 11–22, 108–112, 137–9, 141–6.
[15]A. Blancard, ed., *Documents inédits sur le commerce de Marseille au moyen âge*, 2 vols. (Marseilles, 1880–1), i, 3–5, doc. 1; cf. J. M. Tatlock, 'Un privilegio di dogana conceduto da Federico II di Svevia ai Provenzali nel 1200', *Archivio storico siciliano*, n.s., li (1931), 354–9.
[16]Pispisa, 22.

witness to this process.[17] But on the international trade routes, the Genoese (in particular) seem to have been the dominant group. Although occasionally deprived of privileges in Messina or all Sicily, they sought to consolidate their hold on eastern Sicily, laying claim even to the whole city of Syracuse.[18] Among the non-Genoese denizens of Messina, prominent place goes to the Pisans and their neighbours in Tuscany. A document of April 1239, preserved among the acts of Santa Maria di Messina, describes how Giovanni Chipulla and Donna Rosa, daughter of the late Roberto of Lucca, possess in common a warehouse (*fundicum*) in the new part of the city of Messina; this property is surrounded by the possessions of an Amalfitan and of a citizen of Ravello (now deceased). The eastern façade of the *fundicum* looks towards the sea, but the western side borders on the *rugam Pisanorum*, the street (or quarter) of the Pisans. Arrangements are made for the division of ownership of the warehouse between the joint owners.[19] A similar picture of the mixing of foreigners in Messina is presented in Boccaccio's famous story of the pot of basil; three brothers live in Messina, left rich after the death of their father, who had come from San Gimignano. Their principal factor was a Pisan called Lorenzo, who made the fatal error of falling in love with their sister, Lisabetta. Obviously the details of the story can be discounted, but as on other occasions Boccaccio's evidence for the conduct of trade in Sicily is entirely credible.[20]

Yet the Messinesi themselves were engaged in long-distance trade by the late thirteenth century. It will be necessary to return to the question how a Messinese merchant is to be defined, given the foreign ancestry of all the Latins. For the moment, a working definition is those merchants who, while from Messina, are not described in documents as 'habitator' or 'civis' of a second town, nor as Ianuensis, Pisanus and so on. Into this category of 'pure' Messinesi falls a group mentioned in an act drawn up in Acre on 16 October 1279.[21] Matteo Calciamira, Bulgarino de Castello and Brancaccio de Astingo, executors of the estate of Petronio de Puteo, dispose of his property in Acre in favour of Petronio's widow, Goffredina. Petronio had died in Acre, and possessed at the time of his death a quarter share in the ship *Sanctus Iohannes*; he had possessed such a share during the course of three voyages—

[17]S. Cusa, ed., *I diplomi greci e arabi di Sicilia*, 2 vols. (Palermo, 1860–82), ii. 502–4; 719; G. Trovato, *Sopravvivenze arabe in Sicilia: documenti arabo-siculi del periodo normanno* (Monreale, 1949), 73–6, for a defective translation. Dr J. Johns proposes to re-edit the document and he and I propose to supply a commentary to it.

[18]Their problems with Frederick II are outlined in H. Chone, *Die Handelsbeziehungen Kaiser Friedrichs II. zu den Seestädten Venedig, Pisa, Genua* (Berlin, 1902) and C. Imperiale di Sant'Angelo, *Genova e le sue relazioni con Federico II* (Venice, 1923); for Syracuse, David Abulafia, 'Henry Count of Malta and his Mediterranean activities: 1203–1230', *Medieval Malta: studies on Malta before the Knights*, ed. A. T. Luttrell (London, 1975), 110–4, 118–9.

[19]L-R. Ménager, ed., *Les actes latins de S. Maria di Messina (1103–1250)*, (Testi e monumenti dell'Istituto siciliano di studi bizantini e neoellenici, vol. ix, Palermo, 1963), 150–8.

[20]Boccaccio, *Decameron*, Day 4, novella 5; cf. David Abulafia, 'The reputation of a Norman king in Angevin Naples', *Journal of Medieval History*, v (1979), 135–47, and the discussion *infra* of the Armenian embassy.

[21]Maria Alibrandi Intersimone, 'Pergamene dell'Archivio di. Stato di Messina provenienti dal Museo Nazionale (1225–1770)', *Rassegna degli Archivi di Stato*, xxxii (1972), 501, no. 124; Maria Alibrandi, 'Messinesi in Levante nel Medioevo', *Archivio storico siciliano*, ser.3, xxi/xxii (1971/2), 97–110, especially 100–103.

o from Messina to Acre, one from Acre to Messina—and presumably intended to ain his share during the forthcoming return passage from Acre to Messina. tronio had not simply rented out his share in the ship to merchants looking for ace where they could store their goods; he had carried Sicilian wine and other erchandise to the east, apparently buying pepper, sugar and oriental textiles in change.[22] Pepper worth 247 besants 11 carats was to be consigned to Goffredina as e outstanding balance on Petronio's account, after the costs of his funeral and ductions for minor legacies had been dealt with. Petronio had also invested in a rtnership with his Messinese executor Bulgarino de Castello (whose name, cidentally, suggests Genoese antecedents); Petronio possessed a one-eighth share in small ship (*bucius*) called the *Santa Croce*. The document does not suggest enormous ealth: Petronio's partnership with Bulgarino was worth a mere 12 and a quarter nces of Sicilian gold; the 247 besants in residue, though perhaps only a fraction of tronio's assets in Acre, compare with the investments of second-rank merchants in e Levant at this period, of which more shortly. On the other hand, Petronio's ares in two ships would have necessitated a considerable capital investment. Back Messina, Petronio's widow owned land in the *Ruga sactarorum*, where she, in onjunction with the *tutrix* of Petronio's children, built three houses in 1283.[23] Other embers of the family had similar interests: Iacopo de Putheo received a vineyard in 288 from an aunt, herself a member of the Astingo family.[24] It has been seen that rancato de Astingo was one of Petronio de Puteo's executors in 1279. Probably, erefore, we are looking at examples of the commercial and landed interests of a losely-knit clan or kin-group of fairly wealthy Messinesi. They trade in the Levant, wn ships, invest in city property, but also retain an interest in the local prize roduct, wine. They are patricians with a broad portfolio of business interests, omparable in the range of those interests (but not in the scale of their wealth) to the atricates of Genoa or Pisa in the same period. If Alibrandi is right in assuming that he chief article imported into the Levant by the Messinesi was wine, then the nvolvement of the Puteo family in wine production in Sicily makes even more sense. The foundation of their commercial wealth becomes their agricultural assets on the dge of Messina. But clearly speculation must not be stretched too far here.

Examples of Messinesi in the east Mediterranean do not abound; but documents in the archives of the Crown of Aragon reveal similar characteristics to those identified in the case of Petronio de Puteo. On 24 November 1282 King Peter of Aragon, newly victorious in Sicily, notified Pere de Solavella, representing his authority in Syracuse, that a Pisan and a Messinese ship held by Pere at Syracuse should be released; the ships had arrived from Acre, but there were no enemies of the Aragonese king on board, nor were the goods the two vessels carried the property of enemies of the crown.[25] King Peter was writing from Catania, and was evidently anxious to curry favour with the merchants of Messina and Syracuse. In January

---

[22]Alibrandi, 'Messinesi in Levante', 102–3, insists on the importance of Sicilian agricultural goods in the trade from Messina to Acre; cf. Pispisa, 12, 14.

[23]Alibrandi, 'Pergamene', 501, no.125.

[24]Alibrandi, 'Pergamene', 501, no.128.

[25]G. Silvestri, ed., *De rebus regni Siciliae (9 settembre 1282–26 agosto 1283)* (Palermo, 1881), 190.

1283 King Peter is seen assuming the role of his arch-rival Charles of Anjou, who had encouraged the sale of Sicilian grain in the Holy Land (over which Charles, though not Peter, claimed a royal title). Peter ordered the Secrezia and the Master Portulans in eastern Sicily to permit Bonaggiunta de Scarlata of Messina to export 300 *salme* of wheat to Acre, on the ship of Conetto di Conetto of Pisa. This ship, the *San Nicolò*, was not to unload the grain anywhere else—above all in enemy territory!—and the arrival of the wheat in Acre was to be certified by the Master of the Knights of St John of Jerusalem and by the Pisan consul in Acre.[26] A similar document, of February 1283, permits Giuseppe di Viagio of Messina to act in a similar way, carrying grain and possibly cheese from Augusta to Acre, subject to the attestation of the Knights Hospitaller.[27] Conceivably, therefore, the grain was intended for the use of the Knights Hospitaller. It is certainly interesting that the Pisan consul was to attest the arrival of the cargo; this requirement confirms the strong suspicion that Messina, or Sicily, had no consul in Acre, and it is likely that Messinese merchants voluntarily placed themselves under the authority of the Pisans or other north Italians while in Acre. This would bring them tax advantages, and help guarantee their security. Other groups, such as the merchants of San Gimignano, certainly behaved this way.[28]

But there were Sicilian enemies of the crown engaged in the trade to Acre, also. On 15 January 1283 Niccoloso Mataraffo, loyal to the new dynasty, notified the royal court that he had entered into a commenda contract with the traitor Matteo di Riso, a member of a prominent Messinese family. Matteo had entrusted his partner with 30 ounces of gold, invested in wine and cheese, for carriage to Acre; 106 salme of red wine, and more than 51 cantaria of cheese were to be taken to the Holy Land; the cost of transporting these goods was five ounces three tari. Niccoloso delivered to the royal treasury the outstanding sums still owing to his partner after deduction of expenses, namely 28 ounces 1 tari 7 grani.[29] This document confirms the impression left by Petronio de Puteo's affairs: exports of wine and medium-grade foodstuffs had an important role in Sicilian trade with the Levant. Indeed, there are many references in the Cairo Geniza documents to exports of Sicilian cheese to Egypt from Syracuse and eastern Sicily, throughout the Middle Ages.[30] Tommaso da Sciacca, another Messinese (though apparently of western Sicilian origin) was allowed in February 1283 to export wool, cheese and other unnamed goods to Acre, providing that vegetables and other prohibited foodstuffs did not form part of his cargo.[31] Clearly some food supplies were being held back for the army and other domestic use. Tommaso da Sciacca was to sail from Syracuse on his ship the *San Nicola*: once again it is clear that the Messinese merchants used a variety of Sicilian

[26]*De rebus*, 260.

[27]*De rebus*, 481–2.

[28]David Abulafia, 'Crocuses and Crusaders: San Gimignano, Pisa and the Kingdom of Jerusalem', *Outremer: studies in the history of the Crusading Kingdom of Jerusalem presented to Joshua Prawer*, ed. B. Z. Kedar, H. E. Mayer, R. C. Smail (Jerusalem, 1982), 227–43.

[29]*De rebus*, 267–71.

[30]Goitein, 'Sicily and southern Italy', 15 (cheese from Messina and Syracuse to Alexandria, 1241 and 1243).

[31]*De rebus*, 482–3.

rts, Syracuse no less than Messina. Syracusans were themselves based at Messina: one da Siracusa, described as a merchant of Messina, was given permission in bruary 1283 to export 300 salme of wheat plus cheese to Syria, from the port of gusta near Syracuse. He was in partnership with Aldoina di Solano and Orlando Benedetto, both Messinesi; the ship *San Domenico* which was to carry the cargo was ned by two Messinesi, Perrono di Romano and Bulgarino de Castello.[32] The last me comes as no surprise: he was one of the executors of the estate of Petronio de teo more than three years earlier.[33] His presence in the Holy Land in 1279 and ain in 1283 confirms his status as a prominent Levant trader of Messina.

Clearly, then, the Messinesi possessed the ships and the expertise in the handling grain, wine and cheese that made their Levant trade both practicable and ofitable. It is a picture similar in many ways to that of the merchants of Amalfi in e same period. But, whereas the port of Amalfi had ceased being a major stopping- ace in the western Mediterranean, Messina could not but continue as a favoured rt: its position en route to the Levant led to the presence of very many foreign erchants, superior in the power of their capital, and quite probably in numbers, to e native Sicilians.

II

ome indication of the vitality of the foreign merchants at Messina in the late irteenth century is provided by fragments of a Genoese notarial register drawn up Messina by a Ligurian notary. This notary also worked in Naples, but his register in extremely poor condition and it is not intended to analyse it here.[34] Nicolas de amulio, presumably a native of Camogli near Genoa, was one of several Genoese otaries whose acts drawn up in overseas ports still survive in the Genoese archives. imilar material originally compiled in Bonifacio (Corsica), Tunis, the Black Sea nd Cyprus has also been identified.[35] It is the material from Cyprus, and to a lesser xtent from Caffa in the Crimea, that will be used here to illuminate the commercial ctivities of the merchants of Messina and other Sicilian towns, in the dozen years up o 1301. For the notarial registers of Lamberto di Sambuceto, who worked in Caffa uring 1289 and 1290, and in Famagusta from 1296 to 1301, shed light on the trade f Venice, Ancona, Barcelona, Languedoc and Sicily no less than on that of Genoa. amberto seems to have been employed by the Venetian community in the absence,

---

[32]*De rebus*, 453–4.

[33]Alibrandi, 'Pergamene', 501, no.124.

[34]Archivio di Stato, Genoa, Cart. Not. 122, c.137r–143v (January to March, 1298, Messina); ibid., c.166r–172v (April–May, 1298, Messina); the notary worked at the loggia of the Genoese in Messina. He was in Naples from September to November 1297: Cart. Not. 69, c.159r–169v. For further details of Nicolas de Camulio, see *Archivio di Stato di Genova: Cartolari notarili genovesi* (Pubblicazioni degli Archivi di Stato, vols. xxii and xli, Rome 1956–61).

[35]For Bonifacio see now Rosalind Brown, 'Social development and economic dependence: northern Sardinia, c.1100–1300', Cambridge University Ph.D. thesis (1985).

no doubt temporary, of their own notary, and he was popular with Latin, Syrian Christian and occasionally Jewish merchants also.[36]

Seven acts from Caffa speak of Messina or the Messinesi.[37] Since Messina lay on the most direct sea-route from Caffa via Pera to Genoa, it is not surprising that Genoese businessmen drew up among themselves contracts for trade in Messina. A clear indication of Messina's value as mid-way station, where Black Sea products could be sold for profit, is given by an act of 17 May 1289, in which Guglielmo de Predono receives G£3 in commenda from Andriolo de Sigestro, for trade in Messina. However, account is to be rendered, and the profits are to be divided, in Genoa itself.[38] On 11 August 1289 Bernardo Porcadello received goods from Bernardo Molietus, promising to pay him 2 oz. of Sicilian money within eight days of Molietus' arrival in Messina.[39] It is possible here that Messina is only the collection-point, not the intended place of disposal of goods. Deals were also drawn up among Genoese in Messina, with a view to settlement in Caffa. Piccamiglio Marocello admitted receipt of G£230 from Conrado Piccamiglio, on 18 June 1290; this sum was owed to Piccamiglio Marocello by a third party, Benedetto Marocello, 'ut constat publico instrumento, scripto manu publici notarii in Messana'; but in Pera Benedetto had commissioned Conrado Piccamiglio to settle the debt on his behalf.[40] The close co-operation of kin, all of distinguished Genoese birth, is typical of many acts. Non-Genoese trading from Caffa to Messina included the Catalan Bartomeu de Lovel, a shipowner who on 17 August 1289 engaged the Sicilian sailor Giacomo de Trapana (from Trapani) to serve on his ship the *Sanctus Julianus* as far as Messina.[41]

The Sicilians in Caffa included also Messinesi. But their activities are hard to disentangle from those of the north Italians with whom they did business. On 8 May 1289 Natalis de Messana appeared before Lamberto di Sambuceto to state that he had received from the Genoese Benedetto Scotto 140 hyperpers, in Constantinople, and to record the unusual circumstances behind this payment.[42] In Constantinople, the Messinese merchant had brought an appeal against a sentence or act of seizure against him in Caffa, where the Genoese consul Alberto Spinola had arbitrarily taken from him 172 cow-hides. A judge in Constantinople, acting in the name of the

---

[36]An introduction to this notary's picture of the Mediterranean is given in M. Balard, 'L'activité commerciale en Chypre en l'an 1300', in *Crusade and Settlement: papers read at the first conference of the Society for the study of the crusades and the Latin east and presented to R. C. Smail*, ed. P. W. Edbury (Cardiff, 1985), 251–63; see also the excellent article of D. Jacoby, 'The rise of a new emporium in the eastern Mediterranean: Famagusta in the late thirteenth century', Μέλεται καὶ Ὑπομνήματα (Ἵδρυμα Ἀρχιεπισκόπου Μακαρίου Γ', Nicosia, 1984), i.145–79.i.145–79.

[37]M. Balard, ed., *Gênes et l'Outremer, i. Les Actes de Caffa du notaire Lamberto di Sambuceto 1289–1290* (Documents et Recherches sur l'économie des pays byzantins, islamiques et slaves et leurs relations commerciales au Moyen Age, xii, Paris—The Hague, 1973); G. I. Bratianu, *Actes des notaires génois de Péra et de Caffa de la fin du XIIIe siècle (1281–1290)* (Académie roumaine, Etudes et Recherches, ii, Bucharest, 1927). Cf. Pispisa, 13.

[38]Balard, *Actes de Caffa*, no. 82.

[39]Balard, *Actes de Caffa*, no. 321.

[40]Balard, *Actes de Caffa*, no. 670.

[41]Balard, *Actes de Caffa*, no. 333.

[42]Balard, *Actes de Caffa*, no. 55.

reek emperor, had declared the seizure illegal and in reprisal confiscated from
enedetto Scotto four bales of Smyrna silk, on the grounds that he was a Genoese
tizen and was thus liable for the offence caused to Natalis. There is no evidence
hat Scotto had ever had any direct dealings with Natalis before this event. But the
mperor's representative made it clear that Scotto must recompense Natalis for the
ss of his hides, or suffer permanent loss of his own silk. Benedetto Scotto therefore
aid Natalis a sum in settlement of the Sicilian merchant's claim, and presumably
ecovered the silk. Natalis seems also to have engaged to record these proceedings
efore a notary in Caffa, so that Scotto could present his own claim in due course to
he Genoese consul there. However, it is clear from the document that Alberto
pinola had already ceased being Genoese consul at Caffa. Whether Scotto ever
ecovered his 140 hyperpers is uncertain. What is clear is that, as elsewhere in the
Mediterranean, Genoese merchants trading in Byzantine waters stood in danger of
cts of reprisal by the Greek authorities for offences committed by other Genoese
rading, perhaps, in entirely different places. The issue of reprisals was a constant
eadache in the Italian mercantile republics during the late thirteenth century.[43] It is
certainly striking that a Byzantine official regarded an illicit seizure apparently
carried out in the Crimea as the concern of the imperial government; a testimony, no
doubt, to the official view in Constantinople that the Italian settlements in the
Crimea were privileged communities on the territory of the Roman Empire.
Effective Byzantine rule had faded in Cherson long before.[44] It is likely, too, that the
seizure of the Sicilian merchant's goods was regarded as illegal because the
jurisdiction of the Genoese consul was confined to cases between Genoese and
Genoese. To interfere in the affairs of a Sicilian merchant was to go beyond the terms
of the chrysobulls conferred on the Genoese by Michael VIII Palaiologos.[45] More
than that: Michael VIII and his successors were aware that they had rewarded the
Genoese exceptionally handsomely for their help in restoring Greek rule at Constantinople in 1261. During the late thirteenth century they tried to claw back some of
the rights conferred on Genoa. By 1289 a further political issue helped determine the
Byzantine attitude: the invasion of Sicily by Michael VIII's distant ally, Peter of
Aragon, led the Byzantines to look with favour on Sicilian and, even more, Catalan
merchants. Natalis de Messina, as a subject of the king of Aragon, might expect some
favour from Byzantine officials when in dispute with the Genoese at Caffa.

In Caffa itself, Natalis' appearance before the notary was witnessed by
Raynerius Gallus de Messana, a member of a family whose members appear several
times in the documents from Cyprus (Pisanus Gallus filius quondam Raynerii Galli,
who appears in an act of 13 September 1301, may well be his son; conceivably his

[43]W. M. Bowsky, *A medieval Italian commune: Siena under the Nine, 1287-1355* (Berkeley-Los Angeles, 1981), 232-46.
[44]On the status of these colonies, see M. Balard, 'Les Génois en Crimée aux XIIIe-XIVe siècles', Ἀρχείον Πόντου, xxv, Ἀνακοινώσεις Συμποσίου Birmingham Μ. Βρεταννίας μὲ θέμα Ἡ Μαύρη Θάλασσα, (Athens, 1979), 205-6, making the important point that the Tatars, not the Byzantines, decided whether the Genoese could settle at Caffa. But Byzantium had an impressively long memory of past glories.
[45]On which see D. Geanakoplos, *Emperor Michael Palaeologus and the West, 1258-1282* (Cambridge, Mass., 1959), 81-91.

name points to Pisan ancestry in the family).[46] On 2 December 1289 Thomas de Cantulo of Messina, acting also on behalf of Oberto di Santo Stefano, received a sum of silver from Oddino Bancheta de Ceva, a Genoese; he promised to repay him in kind with sixty pounds of wax (according to the heavy pound of Caffa), at a rate of $34\frac{1}{2}$ aspers for each pound.[47] The wax was to be of best quality: 'cere pulcre, nictide et mercantilis, projecte in panibus'; such wax was one of the prize exports of the Crimean ports, though its place of origin could lie much further to the north in the east European forests. But it is clear that Thomas de Cantulo was engaged in a usurious transaction. No sum of money is indicated to have been received on 2 December; the document merely states that the wax when delivered, before the end of April 1290, is to be worth 2070 aspers. Oddino Bancheta would have handed over a smaller sum than this, in effect receiving as profit the difference between what he paid and 2070 aspers. Oddino is, moreover, a Genoese—his name reveals this— and Oberto di Santo Stefano sounds Genoese too. Thus a Messinese businessman involved in the wax trade takes partners from the dominant merchant community in Caffa. Broad, too, are the links of Oberto di Messina, who sent Federico Panzano to Caffa to settle a debt arising from a commenda between the Sicilian and two merchants of Treviso in north-eastern Italy (26 May 1290).[48]

The Messinesi in Caffa are not numerous, compared to the vast numbers of Genoese. But it was in the character of Genoese trade at Caffa that non-Genoese merchants should be discouraged from intensive competition. Only the Venetians, competitors too powerful to displease, were able to trade extensively in the Black Sea, but even so under a strong Genoese shadow. It is thus no surprise to find the Genoese consul attempting to confiscate the goods of a Sicilian merchant at Caffa. The Genoese regarded Caffa as entirely theirs. Interesting, however, is the involvement of the Messinesi in the trade in cow-hides and in wax, entirely typical products of the Black Sea. It is even possible that Black Sea grain was imported into Messina, simply because the city had such difficulty feeding itself from north-eastern Sicilian stocks. Crete, too, may have been a source of grain. A certain Marcus de Missina, apparently a Sicilian resident in Crete, bought wheat from a Cretan Jew in 1280, though there is no proof he exported the grain to Sicily.[49] Nor should one dreadful accidental import of 1347 be ignored: the trade links between Caffa and Messina brought the plague bacillus to Europe on a Genoese ship. Michele di Piazza is eloquent witness to the effect of pestilence in Messina.[50]

[46]Pavoni, no. 108 (for the full reference to this collection, see n. 50 *infra*).

[47]Balard, *Actes de Caffa*, no. 392.

[48]Balard, *Actes de Caffa*, no. 559.

[49]M. Chiaudano, A. Lombardo, eds., *Leonardo Marcello, notaio in Candia 1278–1281* (Fonti per la storia di Venezia, sez. iii, Archivi notarili, Venice, 1960), nos. 12, 303. This Marcus is described as 'habitator in Castro Temallo'. Another Marcus de Missina 'habitator Castri Themeni' appears in a document from Crete of 1352: A. Lombardo, ed., *Zaccaria de Fredo, notaio in Candia 1352–1357* (Fonti per la storia di Venezia, sez. iii, Venice, 1968), no. 62. Many of the acts of the Venetian notary Pietro Pizolo, in Crete, were witnessed by Nicolaus de Misina in 1300: S. Carbone, ed., *Pietro Pizolo, notaio in Candia*, vol. i, (1300) (Fonti per la storia di Venezia, sez. iii, Venice, 1978), docs.1, 2, 4, 7, 11, 12, etc.

[50]Michele da Piazza, *Cronaca, 1336–1361*, ed. A. Giuffrida (Fonti per la storia di Sicilia, ed. F. Giunta, Palermo-São Paulo, 1980), cap. xxvii, 82–3; also S. Tramontana, *Michele da Piazza e il potere baroniale in Sicilia* (Messina-Florence, 1963).

III

ver fifty Messinesi appear in the acts of Lamberto di Sambuceto from Cyprus,
blished by Balard, Polonio and Pavoni, and varying in date from 1296 to 1301.[51]
here are other Sicilians too, from Trapani, Marsala, Agrigento, Palermo, Malta
d, nearer to Messina, Syracuse and Lipari, whose islands were closely bound to
rth-eastern Sicily by maritime trade. But Messina is the clear leader; the great
ajority of Sicilian merchants mentioned in the acts are from there, and this picture
confirmed by the frequency of reference to its merchants in other late medieval
urces, compared to those from other towns. What needs to be established,
wever, is the meaning of the term 'Messinese'. Lamberto di Sambuceto describes
me Messinesi as *civis*, some as *habitator*, and many as *de Messana* only. Most are
early Latins, some may be Greek or Jews. Occasionally merchants from Messina or
her Sicilian towns are evidently of north Italian origin or ancestry. Benvenuto of
stoia, an inhabitant of Agrigento, owned a ship which was sailing in 1297 from
yprus to Messina or Palermo.[52] Oberto Manayra of Savona, near Genoa, is
scribed as an inhabitant of Marsala in Sicily.[53] Pietro del fu Pietro Vitale (Vidalis)
Messina is actually said to be a *Ianuensis*, a Genoese.[54] His career and associates
eserve further attention.

Pietro Vitale conducted business with merchants from a wide area. He first
ppears on 27 October 1300, selling the Anconitan merchant Giovanni de Paternanis
sixth part of the ship *Sanctus Johannes Baptista* for 175 Saracen besants;[55] Pietro
romises to abide by and defend the sale come what may, except in the face of King
harles II of Naples (*excepto a rege Karulo*), a comment reflecting the continued
ruggle between Angevins and Aragonese in the central Mediterranean, which was
ot settled until the Peace of Caltabellotta two years later. Among his other business
artners were exiles, or the descendants of exiles, from the destroyed Latin states in
yria: Giovanni di Castello from Acre, perhaps a Genoese;[56] Giacomo Leo from
ripoli, now an inhabitant of Famagusta, who received in commenda from Pietro
he equivalent of 984 white besants, invested in a furnace or oven and in fuel with
vhich to operate the plant.[57] Pietro may well have invested, therefore, in small-scale
ndustry in Cyprus. He also took commissions from other merchants anxious to
ecover sums owing to them; the Genoese Lanfranco de Bulgaro, member of an
mportant family, appointed Pietro his procurator (7 March 1301) and was handed
he sum of 500 Armenian dirhems within a month, recovered by Pietro from

---

[51]M. Balard, *Notai genovesi in Oltremare. Atti rogati a Cipro da Lamberto di Sambuceto (11 Ottobre 1296–23 Giugno 1299)*, (Collana storica di fonti e studi, xxxix, Genoa, 1983); V. Polonio, *Notai genovesi in Oltremare. Atti rogati a Cipro da Lamberto di Sambuceto (3 Luglio 1300–3 Agosto 1301)*, (Collana storica di fonti e studi, xxi, Genoa, 1982); R. Pavoni, *Notai genovesi in Oltremare. Atti rogati a Cipro da Lamberto di Sambuceto (6 Luglio–27 Ottobre 1301)*, (Collana storica di fonti e studi xxxii, Genoa, 1982).

[52]Balard, *Cipro*, no. 36.

[53]Pavoni, no. 125.

[54]Pavoni, no. 125.

[55]Polonio, no. 65.

[56]Polonio, no. 197. But there were de Castellos at Messina too: Alibrandi, 'Pergamene', 501, no. 124.

[57]Polonio, no. 128.

Giuliano de Bulgaro.[58] This agreement with Lanfranco de Bulgaro was witnessed by 'Petrus, faber, de Messana, qui moratur iuxta stacionem notarii', a further reference, perhaps, to Sicilian involvement in local industry.

But Pietro Vitale appears most frequently as executor (with Giovanni di Castello of Acre), winding up the estate of the late Zaccaria Roberti, merchant of Messina. His task here was to settle debts owed to or from Zaccaria Roberti, many of whose business colleagues had also come from Messina. Assets collected in Cyprus needed also to be transmitted back to Zaccaria's legatees in Sicily. On 31 October 1300 159 white besants (money of Cyprus) were returned to the estate of Zaccaria Roberti by Ianino Bonavita of Messina, himself acting on behalf of his deceased brother Bartolomeo di Bonavita.[59] Equally, there were items in Zaccaria's hands, at the time of his death, that the executors had to return to their proper owners. On 1 December 1300 Pietro Vitale and Giovanni di Castello received a quittance from Giacomo Zanterio of Messina, himself acting on behalf of Giacomo, nicknamed Puccio, son of Giovanni Dati of Messina, for goods returned in this way. They included finely-wrought silver, such as a small silver shield, candle-sticks, inlaid gilded covers, and also silk purses, some embroidered with gold wire; there was a silken scabbard, a Tatar knife adorned with gold and silver decorations; there were also, more modestly, a quire of paper, a mattress and other domestic goods.[60] It is thus clear that Zaccaria Roberti was closely involved in the sale of gold and silver objets d'art; whether he was more involved in their import to the west from Cyprus than vice-versa it is hard to say, for silk, gold and silver were available in Sicily no less than the Levant; but the presence of a Tatar knife suggests that he imported finely-wrought weapons via the ports of Armenia, of which more shortly.

Zaccaria Roberti raised money in Cyprus by taking loans from native bankers. Giovanni di Castello and Pietro Vitale paid Giacomo de Signago 70 white besants on 20 January 1301; this was in settlement of a loan made 'pro usuris' by Giacomo to Zaccaria Roberti, in the form of 450 gros tournois.[61] Repayment in a different currency was a handy way to avoid accusations of charging excessive interest, since the interest payment could be concealed behind a weighted exchange rate. Even so, quite large sums of money accrued to the estate of Zaccaria Roberti. Guglielmo di Benedetto came out to Cyprus in late 1300 or early 1301, acting on behalf of Zaccaria's widow Rosa, and Zaccaria's sisters Anna and Dulcis; a third sister, Flora (Flos) was represented by her husband Ardizzone Gallo of Messina. The widow and sisters received no less than 2,771 white besants, to be distributed one half to the widow and one sixth each to the sisters.[62] It seems that Zaccaria Roberti's assets in Cyprus compare well with those of the Genoese, Venetian and Anconitan merchants who are documented in Lamberto di Sambuceto's cartulary. His business associates included several of the Messinesi who appear most often in Lamberto's acts: Puzio

---

[58]Polonio, nos. 268, 321. For the Bulgaro family, see S. Origone, 'La famiglia "de Bulgaro" a Genova (secc. XII–XV)', in *Genova e la Bulgaria nel Medioevo* (Collana storica di fonti e studi, xlii, Genoa, 1984), 125–47, especially 140.

[59]Polonio, no. 72.

[60]Polonio, no. 135. 'Chianterius' and 'Zanterius' are variant spellings of one name.

[61]Polonio, no. 197.

[62]Polonio, nos. 231, 317, 346.

.to of Messina issued a quittance in favour of his own procurator, Giacomo di nterio, for goods recovered from the estate of Zaccaria Roberti (27 April 1301).[63] fact, there were marriage ties linking Zaccaria Roberti to other trading families, t least the Gallo family. Ardizzone Gallo, procurator and brother-in-law of ccaria Roberti, in conjunction with Guglielmo di Benedetto, raised a loan of 200 ite besants on 9 January 1301 from Giovanni di Castello;[64] the quittance, dated April 1301, was witnessed by Petrus faber de Messana and by Iacobus 'qui oratur iuxta palacium domini regis in Messana'.[65]

It is likely Zaccaria Roberti had died in Cyprus or nearby. For he actually opears alive in the record. On 17 June 1299, at Famagusta, he received a quittance om the Pisan Zolus de Campo for the sum of 1,100 hyperpers of gold. Zolus' ship ad been seized off Rhodes by another Messinese, Giovanni de Dondo, who bsequently appointed Zaccaria Roberti as his agent to make restitution.[66] Other essinesi approached the problem of acquiring a ship in a more respectable manner. n 14 March 1299 Matteo Beacqua and Giacomo Dato (member of a Messinese mily that is often mentioned in the Cypriot acts) bought the ship *Santa Caterina* *ancta Cathalina*) from a shipowner of Marseilles named Gherardo de Andrio, for 50 Saracen besants.[67] As well as Sicilian shipowners, there were Sicilian carpenters . Cyprus: on 27 January 1301 Giovanni 'magister axie' of Messina promised that he ould 'servire et operari de meo magisterio et de arte marinarie' on the ship *Sanctus nthonius*, now in port at Famagusta. He was paid 80 white besants for three months' ork. The shipowner was a Genoese.[68]

Once at sea, ships owned or operated by Messinesi did not always head for Messina. Viviano de Milleo of Messina was part-owner of the ship *Sancta Maria de cara*; his partner in ownership of the vessel was no less a person than Roger de auria, admiral of the king of Sicily. The ship was leased out to two merchants of nstated origin, in order to carry cotton, alum and skins to Venice, in spring 1297.[69] n November of that year Viviano de Milleo, acting under the guarantee of another Messina merchant, paid 1,550 Saracen besants to a business colleague, probably of Genoese origin; Viviano was, therefore, not an insignificant figure. Indeed, his family ad been active in the grain trade to north Africa since the 1270s.[70] Gherardo Nam vas another Messinese with interests that stretched further than the Cyprus-Sicily rade route. He advanced a sum in Cypriot money to two members of the Spinola amily of Genoa on 9 September 1300; in return he was to receive G£383.6.8 in Messina, but if access there proved impossible the money was to be repaid in Genoa

---

[63]Polonio, no. 359.
[64]Polonio, no. 175.
[65]Polonio, no. 339—and compare the note at the end of no. 175.
[66]Balard, *Cipro*, no. 155.
[67]Balard, *Cipro*, no. 108.
[68]Polonio, no. 204.
[69]Balard, *Cipro*, no. 34.
[70]Balard, *Cipro*, no. 17. Antonio de Milio of Messana is mentioned in the grain export permits of Charles of Anjou, in 1276: N. Nicolini, *Codice diplomatico sui rapporti veneto-napoletani durante il regno di Carlo I di Angiò* (Regesta Chartarum Italiae, Rome, 1965 [original print date 1942]), 143, 155; a number of other Messinesi also appear.

itself. No doubt the 'impedimentum' mentioned in the document was the vicious war at sea off the coasts of Sicily and southern Italy, between Angevins and Aragonese of Sicily.[71]

The Sicilian merchants were linked also to the ports of Asia Minor; Cyprus, after all, functioned in large measure as entrepôt for goods from Armenia, 'Turchia', Syria and Egypt. One important target in Asia Minor was Makri in Lycia. On 30 October 1300 Bartolomeo de Astexano, from Syracuse, declared to Giovanni de Pando of Messina that he had received 280 white besants from Giovanni; these were to be used to make ready Bartolomeo's ship *Sanctus Nicolaus*, before a voyage to Makri.[72] But Giovanni de Pando had much bigger investments in this sailing. He had already placed 2,500 besants on board the same ship in September 1300; no destination is indicated in the earlier contract.[73] Interestingly, the September contract describes him as 'Iohanes de Pando de Marffi', of Amalfi; the October contract describes him as a merchant of Messina. It is thus clear that he is one of the Amalfitan settlers in Messina, where, as has been seen, there was a 'ruga Amalfitanorum' of some antiquity.[74] The same merchant appears in October 1300 selling to a Pisan a black male slave from Spain, bought originally from a Messina banker named Ugolino, (a witness, moreover, is Petrus de Lipari).[75]

Probably Armenia was an even greater attraction than Makri, for from Laiazzo (Ayas) roads ran north into Turkish territory, across to the Black Sea and to Tabriz and the Caspian. The Genoese did not neglect their opportunities here, at least before the fourteenth century; and merchants of Ancona, Narbonne and Messina followed in their wake. It has been seen that Pietro Vitale handled Armenian dirhems; but it can also be shown that Messinesi reached Armenia itself. Giacomo de Rocha, a Genoese from Voltri, declared in February 1301 that he had received Cypriot money from Giacomo de Zanterio of Messina, and promised to repay him to the tune of $1,295\frac{1}{2}$ new dirhems of Armenia within twelve days of the arrival in Armenia of the ship of Guido Butegarius, a Pisan. Guido Butegarius also carried some of Giacomo de Zanterio's money without the use of an intermediary. He agreed to take 250 white besants belonging to the Sicilian merchant to Laiazzo, to trade there; the contract was drawn up on 13 February and a quittance issued already on 1 April 1301, so business was conducted quickly and smoothly.[76] There were in fact plenty of Italian ships based in Cyprus that specialised in the commercial shuttle service between Laiazzo and Famagusta, unloading their Asian goods in Cyprus for trans-shipment to the west.

The activities of the Messinesi in Cyprus are in all respects similar to those of other groups of Italian merchants: they own and lease ships, they trade to Armenia and Makri, they sell slaves and carry cotton, alum and chased metalwork to the west, both to their home city and to the major commercial centres in Europe. They conduct their business to a considerable extent among themselves, but also have

[71] Polonio, no. 9.
[72] Polonio, no. 71.
[73] Polonio, no. 28; for him as an Amalfitan, see also no. 24; for him as a Messinese, nos. 62, 63, 71.
[74] Pispisa, 6, 9, 311.
[75] Polonio, nos. 62, 63; cf. no. 66.
[76] Polonio, nos. 220, 224, 224a; cf. also nos. 222, 222a.

artners from Genoa, Ancona, Pisa and elsewhere. Colleagues appear from Syra-
use, Lipari and other parts of Sicily. Moreover, the trade of the Messinesi seems to
e dominated by a small group of related families—'seems to be', because there is no
nowing how many Messinesi made use of other notaries. The names Gallo, Dato,
e Zanterio recur, and the Genoese denizen of Messina, Pietro Vitale, has very close
nks with them, acting as partner or at least witness in several of the documents. A
econd circle of Sicilian businessmen can also be identified. Viviano de Milleo,
learly a man of some standing, in view of his link to Roger de Lauria, appears as a
ebtor in a will drawn up by Pilastro of Messina in January 1299.[77] Pilastro's
xecutor was to be Bartolomeo de Cossa or Corsa, member of a Messinese trading
amily that appears repeatedly in the Cypriot acts, though mainly in the witness
ists.[78] Pilastro's colleagues included Puzio de Dato of Messina, and the 'societas de
Morrinis', a group of merchants or bankers who may have originated from
Syracuse—a Guglielmo Morena of Syracuse received a loan of $2\frac{1}{2}$ oz. of gold from a
merchant of Messina in October 1296, the sum to be repaid in Sicily itself.[79] It is,
hen, important to stress that the group of Messinesi analysed here by no means
constituted the whole of the Sicilian merchant community in Famagusta.

IV

The merchants of Messina, though beneficiaries of royal privileges in Sicily itself, do
not seem to have possessed special rights of tax exemption in Cyprus. By the 1320s
Genoese, Venetians, Pisans, Narbonnais, Provençaux, Catalans and Anconitans were
all privileged in some way; the Genoese and Venetians paid no *commercium* at all, the
other merchants only two per cent.[80] Possibly the Sicilian merchants passed
themselves off as Catalans or as subjects of another town; this was common practice;
and occasionally the privileges conferred on merchants of Barcelona by Mediterranean rulers were assumed to apply to all merchants from lands ruled by Aragonese
dynasties, even when those lands were at war with one another. In north Africa,
Sicilians and Catalans probably had separate warehouses at this period, but the
Sicilians had very old privileges of their own at Tunis and elsewhere, antedating the

[77]Balard, *Cipro*, no. 96.

[78]E.g. Polonio, nos. 79, 185, 328, 412; Pavoni, nos. 113, 127.

[79]Balard, *Cipro*, no. 14; one witness is Nicoleta nepos Nicolai de Malta—Nicolaus de Malta
indulged in pawn-broking, to judge from Polonio, no. 165, had houses in Famagusta (Pavoni, nos. 84,
115) but was also a *Ianuensis* (Pavoni, no. 115). He appears also in Pavoni, no. 126, as neighbour of a
Genoese who makes his will, and as a witness in Balard, *Cipro*, no. 13. Possibly he was not from Malta,
but a descendant of the Genoese pirate, Henry of Malta, whose son, active in the 1230s, was also called
Nicholas: Abulafia, 'Henry Count of Malta', 124.

[80]Francesco Balducci Pegolotti, *La Pratica della Mercatura*, ed. A. Evans (Cambridge, Mass., 1936),
84. For Messina itself, see 107–111; for a comparison of Messinese or Sicilian weights and measures with
Armenian ones, 60, 63. For Ancona, see D. S. H. Abulafia, 'The Anconitan privileges in the Kingdom of
Jerusalem and the Levant trade of Ancona', in B. Z. Kedar and G. Airaldi, eds., *I comuni italiani nel regno
crociato di Gerusalemme* (Genoa, 1986); for Narbonne, D. S. H. Abulafia, 'Narbonne, les pays de la
couronne d'Aragon et le commerce du Levant, 1187–1400', *Actes du XIIe Congrès de la Couronne d'Aragon,
Montpellier, 1985* (forthcoming).

Aragonese conquest of Sicily.[81] An important exception to the lack of Sicilian privileges in the Levant is provided by the privilege of King Leo of Armenia to the Sicilians of 1331, published by the Armenian monks of Venice on the basis of a manuscript in Messina, and later complemented by the publication of a Latin text in their own possession.[82] The privilege states that Sicilian ambassadors came to the king of Armenia, who, out of regard for King Frederick of Sicily, granted the Sicilians a tax reduction so that in future they would have to pay only two per cent on exports and imports. The Sicilians were warned not to pass off as fellow-Sicilians merchants from other countries; this would lead to cancellation of tax exemption for any Sicilian engaged in such tax evasion, even on behalf of another person. Disputes between Sicilian and Sicilian or Sicilian and Armenian would be referred to the royal court if they resulted in the drawing of blood. Other complaints made by Armenian subjects to the crown against Sicilians would be referred to the Sicilian community in Armenia who themselves had to report to the courts or royal court in Sicily. In other words, the jurisdiction of the Sicilian community is carefully circumscribed, without being entirely suppressed. At the same time, the Sicilian community in Armenia is held responsible for serious offences against Armenians; the principle of reprisal, seen at work already in the Byzantine world, reigns here too. Carmelo Trasselli has related this treaty to a long history of diplomatic links between Sicily, Aragon and Armenia, whose origins lay in the eastern policy and crusading plans of James the Conqueror of Aragon, as early as the 1260s, before Aragon conquered Sicily at all. Trasselli has also suggested that the account of a twelfth-century Armenian embassy to Sicily under King William the Good, proferred by Boccaccio in his *Decameron* (Day V, novella 7), has a stronger historical basis than has usually been supposed. Armenians had come west to Aragon (rather than Sicily) to discuss plans for a crusade. The long history of attempts by Armenians and Aragonese to unite forces against the Mamluks culminated in the marriage of Princess Constance of Sicily to Leo V of Armenia in 1331; in other words the privilege to the Sicilian merchants (by whom Trasselli understands in first place the Messinesi) is a direct reward to King Frederick of Sicily for his willingness to make real those tentative promises of alliance, already 70 or more years old.[83]

The argument can be extended further. A Siculo-Armenian alliance against the Mamluks would threaten the interests of Sicilian merchants trading in Egypt itself. Compensation must be offered for the loss of access to Alexandria and Damietta, and to the newly-important harbour at Beirut, all of which would be cut off in the

---

[81]G. La Mantia, *Codice diplomatico dei re aragonesi di Sicilia Pietro I, Giacomo, Federico II, Pietro II e Ludovico, dalla rivoluzione siciliana del 1282 sino al 1355*, i (1282–1290) (Palermo, 1917), 168–9, 204–7, indicating separate warehouses for Sicilians and Catalans; 299–306, indicating that the Sicilian consul in Tunis was to be a separate individual to the Catalan consul, and to be a Messinese.

[82]V. Langlois, ed., *Le Trésor des Chartes d'Arménie ou Cartulaire de la Chancellerie Royale des Roupéniens* (Venice, 1863), 186–90, doc. xxxviii (Armenian text with French translation); C. Trasselli, 'Sugli europei in Armenia. A proposito di un privilegio trecentesco e di una novella del Boccaccio', *Archivio storico Italiano*, cxxii (1964), 471–91, for the Latin text, which is on display in the Museum of the Armenian monastery (Padri Mechitaristi) on the island of San Lazzaro, Venice.

[83]Trasselli, 'Europei in Armenia', 481–91; Princess Constance had links with Cyprus too—she was wife of King Henry II from 1317 to 1324. Cf. R-O. Bertrand, 'Jean XXII et le mariage de Constance de Chypre avec l'infant Pierre d'Aragon', *Annales du Midi*, lxiii (1951), 5–31, especially 29.

ent of Sicilian campaigns against the Mamluk sultans. Nor, indeed, can the Sicilian
ivilege be isolated from a series of grants by the Armenian kings to Catalans,
:netians, Pisans and southern French. Montpellier, a city under the overlordship of
e King of Majorca, received privileges in 1314 and 1321.[84] It is likely, as has been
:n, that Sicilians would shelter under privileges conferred on their allies, such as
e Genoese, Catalans and Montpelliérains, until granted rights of their own. The
31 privilege to the Sicilians, by outlawing such 'sheltering', only demonstrates that
was a common problem, here as elsewhere.

Documents from Messina suggest that, in the long term, access to the Mamluk
>mains was not hindered. The hopes raised in 1331 came to little. In 1346 a
.essinese and a Syracusan made a deal for trade between their cities and Beirut,
yprus, Beirut again, whence the journey was to head back to Trapani, Syracuse or
Iessina.[85] A document drawn up in Famagusta in 1352, in the loggia of the
atalans, reveals the continuing presence of Messinesi;[86] the location is suggestive of
e close economic links between the lands of the Crown of Aragon, even when under
fferent rulers. The acts of the Venetian notary Nicola de Boateriis, working in
amagusta around 1360, reveal that Messinese merchants were still active on the
nes linking Cyprus to Venice and Cyprus to Crete.[87] It is clear that the merchants of
Iessina retained considerable vitality in the years around 1300; the predominance
f Genoa and other cities in the trade through Messina did not entirely suffocate
Iessina's own merchant community. Indeed, links with Genoa—migrants, capital,
iipping services—helped Messina to grow. Here at least the presence of the
ortherners might be argued to have stimulated local merchant enterprise.[88]

[84]Langlois, 163, doc. xxxviii (Catalans, 1293); 166-9; doc. xxxi (Venetians, 1307); 176-7,
Ioc. xxxiii bis (Venetians, 1307); 178, doc. xxxiv (Montpellier, 1314); 182-4 (Venetians, 1321); 185-6,
doc. xxxvii (Montpellier, 1321), etc.; Trasselli, 'Europei in Armenia', 489.
[85]Alibrandi, 'Pergamene', 503, no. 140; Alibrandi, 'Messinesi in Levante', 103-4.
[86]Alibrandi, 'Pergamene', 504, no. 143; Alibrandi, 'Messinesi in Levante', 105-6.
[87]A. Lombardo, ed., *Nicola de Boateriis, notaio in Famagosta e Venezia 1355-1365* (Fonti per la storia di
Venezia, sez. iii, Venice, 1973), nos. 21, 22, 23 (Cyprus to Venice); no. 84 (Cyprus to Crete).
[88]My warm thanks are due to Dr Enrico Pispisa (Messina) and to Dr Pietro Corrao (Palermo and
Oxford) for their help.

THE ANCONITAN PRIVILEGES IN THE KINGDOM OF JERUSALEM AND THE LEVANT TRADE OF ANCONA

I

Before the fourteenth century, the Levant trade of Ancona is hard to document: the medieval archives of Ancona have mostly been destroyed, and citizens of Ancona make only fitful appearances in the records of the kingdom of Jerusalem. This has not prevented attempts to elevate Ancona to the rank of a "Repubblica marinara italiana," alongside Genoa, Pisa and Venice, as early as the late twelfth century[1]. Those documents which concern Anconitan rights in the kingdom of Jerusalem — some papal letters, and a privilege issued in the kingdom in 1257 — outwardly suggest that the Latin east was an important target of Anconitan shipping, and that there existed an Anconitan colony in Acre; but closer examination of the circumstances in which these rights were granted is long overdue[2]. The lack of commercial contracts from Ancona is particularly frustrating; and, in compensation, it is necessary to turn to notarial registers from other Italian or Adriatic ports which mention Anconitan traders. The archives of Dubrovnik offer references to Anconitan merchants, but have little to say on the Levant trade of Ancona (or indeed Dubrovnik itself) before the fourteenth century[3]. More promising are the Genoese cartularies

---

[1] *Ancona Repubblica Marinara. Federico Barbarossa e le Marche. Atti del Convegno di Studi storici, Ancona, 19-20 aprile 1969* (Città di Castello, 1972) is largely committed to this view; but compare G. Franceschini's contribution, "Ancona e le repubbliche marinare", ibid., pp. 56-9.

[2] W. Heyd, *Histoire du commerce du Levant*, trans. F. Raynaud, 2 vols. (Leipzig, 1885-6), 1 : 318, seems the only contribution to the subject.

[3] B. Krekić, *Dubrovnik (Raguse) et le Levant au Moyen Age* (Paris, The Hague, 1961).

compiled in Cyprus by the notary Lamberto di Sambuceto[4]. These provide clear evidence for Anconitan involvement in the Levant trade ten years after the fall of Acre. It would obviously be dangerous to assume that everything the Anconitans did in Cyprus had also been done earlier in the kingdom of Jerusalem, where their legal status may have been entirely different; but it is certainly striking that they enjoyed close relations in Cyprus with a group of Greek merchants of Syrian origin, and that they were heavily involved in the transport of cotton from the Levant to Italy. Lamberto di Sambuceto has preserved not merely contracts drawn up in Cyprus but summaries of contracts or instructions drawn up in Ancona itself, very rare material at this period[5]. And, in a more general sense, the Cyprus documents give some clues to the intensity of Ancona's ties to the Latin east at the end of the thirteenth century, and to the nature of its ties to Genoa, long a firm friend in view of Ancona's own difficulties with Venice.

The rivalry between Ancona and Venice, far from hindering Ancona's eastward trade, may actually have helped foster it[6]. The evidence here concerns Ancona's contact with Constantinople, not Acre or Tyre, but it provides important information on the range of Anconitan commerce at the end of the twelfth century. Shortly after 1201 the north Italian rhetorician Buoncompagno da Segni wrote an eloquent glorification of Ancona's unbending resistance to the army of Christian of Mainz and

---

⁴ C. Desimoni, "Actes passés à Famaguste de 1299 à 1301 par devant le notaire génois Lamberto di Sambuceto," *Archives de l'Orient latin* 2 (1884), 3-126; *Revue de l'Orient latin* 1 (1893, 58-139, 275-312, 321-353; V. Polonio, *Notai genovesi in oltremare: atti rogati a Cipro da Lamberto di Sambuceto (3 luglio 1300 - 3 agosto 1301)*, Collana storica di Fonti e Studi, 31 (Genoa, 1982); R. Pavoni, *Notai genovesi in oltremare: atti rogati a Cipro da Lamberto di Sambuceto (6 luglio - 27 ottobre 1301)*, Collana storica di Fonti e Studi, 32 (Genoa, 1982), and the further volume of Cypriot acts edited by M. Balard.

⁵ Pavoni, §§ 221-3.

⁶ For a general account, see F. Lane, *Venice: a maritime republic* (Baltimore, 1973).

the navy of Venice in 1173, the *Liber de obsidione Ancone*[7]. Buoncompagno, writing thirty years later, may occasionally have intruded information about the size and commerce of Ancona which fitted the circumstances of his day better than those of 1173, but he makes clear the close political and economic ties between Ancona and the Byzantine empire during the 1170s[8]. As early as 1155 the commune of Ancona had entered into an alliance with Manuel Comnenus, and was rewarded with gold and, very possibly, trading privileges[9]; in 1173, at the time of the Venetian blockade, Buoncompagno states that "multi Anchonitani aberant, qui causa negotiandi erant in Alexandria, in urbe Constantinopolitana et Romania;" and it is almost certain that after the siege Manuel conferred further gifts or grants on Ancona[10]. Two years before, the Venetians had been expelled from the Byzantine empire, and Manuel was well-disposed to the Anconitans not merely for their resistance to Barbarossa's army but not their success in defying and damaging the Venetian fleet. It remains to be asked whether competition in the Levant trade was an important factor in Venetian hostility to Ancona. The events of 1171 certainly encouraged the Doge to

---

[7] *Buoncompagni Liber de Obsidione Ancone* [a. 1173], ed. G. C. Zimolo, in RIS. NS 6, 3.

[8] See my article "Ancona, Byzantium and the Adriatic, 1155-1173," *Papers of the British School at Rome* 52 (1984), 196-216; among other literature see also P. Schreiner, "Der Dux von Dalmatien und die Belagerung Anconas im Jahre 1173. Zur Italien- und Balkanpolitik Manuels I.," *Byzantion* 41 (1971); A. Carile, "L'assedio di Ancona del 1173. Contributo alla storia politica e sociale della città nel secolo XII," *Atti e Memorie della Deputazione di Storia Patria per le Marche* 7 (1971-3), 23-57, and a later version of the same article in *Studi Veneziani* 16 (1974), 3-31; S. Borsari, "Ancona e Bisanzio nei secoli XII - XIII," in *Ancona Repubblica Marinara*, pp. 67-76; J. - F. Leonhard, *Die Stadt Ancona im Spätmittelalter: Politik und Handel* (Tübingen, 1983), discusses these events too.

[9] Io. Kinnamos, *Epitome rerum ab Ioanne et Alexio Comneno gestarum*, Corpus scriptorum historiae byzantinae (Bonn, 1836), p. 170.

[10] Buoncompagno, p. 17; cf. Zimolo, in Buoncompagno, p. 12; also Buoncompagno, p. 37.

turn on Byzantium and its allies: before Ancona was attacked, Dubrovnik also was besieged and the coasts of Greece were ravaged[11]. But rivalry with Ancona was undoubtedly concerned with other issues too: command of the Adriatic shipping routes; access to the ports of Dalmatia, especially those, such as Split, which were under Byzantine suzerainty; competition for trade in grain, metals and other raw materials. This was in no sense an equal competition: Ancona was by no means the size of Venice; Buoncompagno offers a figure of over ten thousand inhabitants in 1173, which can be taken as a very rough estimate, intended to convey the impression of a good-sized maritime city[12]. The physical area of medieval Ancona was certainly smaller than that of the three major maritime republics; nor did Ancona possess a small empire of subsidiary coastal towns, as did Genoa and Venice. Its neighbours, such as Fano and Senigallia on the coast, and Jesi and Osimo inland, competed for control of the March of Ancona, and many neighbours participated in the siege of 1173, on the German and Venetian side. Ancona possessed only a small contado and, as Buoncompagno says, it was an example of a city which could not survive on local resources, and therefore turned to trade as a means to exist[13].

Buoncompagno mentions Anconitan trade with Byzantium and Egypt, but not with the Latin east. It is generally assumed that the Anconitan colony in Costantinople, based at the church of Santo Stefano, antedates the Fourth Crusade[14]; but even

---

[11] D. Abulafia, "Dalmatian Ragusa and the Norman Kingdom of Sicily," *Slavonic and East European Review* 54 (1976), 412-28.

[12] Buoncompagno, p. 23, referring, admittedly, to siege conditions.

[13] Buoncompagno, p. 17; cf. p. 9.

[14] C. Ciavarini, ed., *Statuti Anconitani del mare, del terzenale e della dogana e patti con diverse nazioni*, 1 (Ancona, 1896), 61, rubrica 80. Cf. A. Pertusi, "The Anconitan Colony in Constantinople and the report of its Consul, Benvenuto, on the fall of the city," *Charanis Studies: Essays in honour of Peter Charanis*, ed. A. Laiou - Thomadakis (New Brunswick, 1980), pp. 199-200.

if the colony survived, the intimate political tie between Ancona and Constantinople did not. Ancona had to turn to other patrons for aid in the acquisition of rights in foreign ports. Between 1228 and 1232 the commune of Ancona took advantage of attempts by Pope Gregory IX to build a strong bloc in the Marches, capable of resisting the imperial army of Rainald von Urslingen[15]. In 1231 the first signs emerge that Anconitan loyalty to the pope, as overlord of the Marches, was being rewarded with benign interest at the papal curia in the overseas trade of Ancona. The Gregory IX sent a stern letter to the Sultan al-Kāmil, complaining that Anconitan merchants, the pope's "fideles," had been despoiled and arrested in Alexandria.

> Rem novam et insolitam, rem detestabilem et horrendam rumore audivimus obstupendo, quod videlicet mercatores Anconitanos fideles nostros apud Alexandriam sub tue securitatis solita fiducia commorantes faci fecisti, detinesque captivos bonis omnibus spoliatos, quod est utique contra fidem et pacem, quarum predicabaris hactenus inviolabiliter custoditor[16].

The exact circumstances of these arrests cannot be identified, but once again it is clear that the Anconitans were engaged in trade with Egypt, and that they believed themselves to possess certain guarantees of immunity from al-Kāmil. Gregory IX's letter suggests that the Anconitans were already a defined community, not sheltering under the privileges of friendly merchants (such as the Genoese or the Greeks), but claiming privileges of their own. It will be seen shortly that their position in the kingdom of Jerusalem was different in several respects, at least before 1257.

---

[15] D. Waley, *The Papal State in the thirteenth century* (London, 1961), pp. 124-9.

[16] *Annales Ecclesiastici ad anno MCXCVIII ubi desinit Cardinalis Baronius, auctore Oderico Raynaldo*, ed. J. D. Mansi, 2 (Lucca, 1747), 52, no. 56; RRH no. 1025.

II

A letter of Frederick II, of 1224, indicates that there were already some Anconitans at Acre, and that the commune of Ancona was thought capable of controlling their actions far away in the east [17]. The emperor informs the government of Ancona that fighting has broken out between the Genoese and the Pisans in Acre; Frederick has already written to the Genoese asking them to allow passage to Anconitan merchants. Whatever their actions on this occasion, the Anconitans apparently did not favour the emperor two decades later, when they received their first known privileges for trade in the kingdom of Jerusalem. Pope Innocent IV informed the Podestà, Council and Popolo of Ancona that henceforth

> mercatores Civitatis Anconitane libere possint emere ac vendere per Civitatem Acconensem et Regnum Jerosolimitanum, ac inde merces extrahere sine cuiuslibet solutione Doane [18].

Two further letters forbade interference with these rights in the March of Ancona ("provincia tua") and instructed the bishop of Acre of the terms of the privilege [19]. A fourth letter informed the city of Ancona that the right of free passage applied in the same terms to "totam Apuliam et Regnum

---

[17] E. Winkelmann, *Acta Imperii inedita seculi XIII*, (Innsbruck, 1880), 1 : 241, § 263; RRH no. 1025; cfr. Heyd, 1 : 157, 318, 346.

[18] Archivio Segreto Vaticano, Registro Vaticano 21, ep. 43, fol. 219 v.; the best edition is that of A. Theiner, *Codex diplomaticus dominii temporalis S. Sedis*, 1 (Rome, 1861), 119, § 210; also ed. by C. Rodenberg, *Epistolae a regestis Pontificum Romanorum*, MGH Epistolae Selectae, 1 : 94, no. 125; and registered by E. Berger, *Les Registres d'Innocent IV*, 1 (Paris, 1884), 214, § 1404; RRH no. 1025.

[19] Registro 21, ep. 44-5, fol. 219 v; Theiner, *loc. cit.*; Berger, § 1405-6.

Sicilie, nec non per omnes terras et aquas ecclesie Romane." [20]. Altogether this series of papal privileges is very different in character from the grants received by Italian communities from rulers in the Latin east. The papal letters speak broadly of exemption from all taxes — "solutione Doane" should probably be understood to refer to the whole gamut of imposts, and the same vague phrase is used for the kingdom of Sicily as for that of Jerusalem. The letters are not a series of privileges to an exempt group, which claimed special territorial or judicial rights, but favours towards a subject city in the papal state, anxious at the activities of Frederick II and reasonably loyal to the curia; but the curia was based, in 1245, not in Italy but at Lyons. The privileges of 1245 were no more than an attempt to win the firm support of Ancona in the early phases of the struggle between Innocent IV and the Hohenstaufen. They include Sicily and Apulia because Innocent during the same weeks deposed Frederick from the kingdom of Sicily, "quod est speciale patrimonium beati Petri" (as he continually insisted); as overlord of a kingdom lacking a ruler, Innocent regarded himself as perfectly free to issue trade privileges concerning that kingdom, to grant lands to his followers, or to make other dispositions intended to enhance his party's interests — whether they could be put into effect was another matter [21]. The issue of a privilege for trade in Jerusalem may also be based on the principle that this was a kingdom without a king, since Conrad of Hohenstaufen had not arrived to claim

---

[20] Registro 21, ep. 46, fol. 219 v; Theiner, *loc. cit.*; Rodenberg, *loc. cit.*; Berger, § 1407. Another example of privileges linking the kingdom of Jerusalem with that of Sicily is provided by the grant to Siena, made by Conradin in 1268: G. Müller, *Documenti sulle relazioni delle città toscane coll'Oriente cristiano e coi Turchi* (Florence, 1879), 100-1.

[21] A phrase repeated again and again in Innocent IV's letters: Registro 21, fol. 209 v (denunciation of Frederick II); compare the insistence that "Regnum Sicilie Rege ad presens careat," e.g. in Registro 21, ep. 895, fol. 411 r, enabling Innocent to grant fiefs in southern Italy to supporters in his struggle against Frederick II.

his right; if so, the papacy was extending its rights of intervention past the normal limits, but in that case Ancona was not the sole beneficiary. Later on, Marseilles also received privileges for trade in the east from Innocent IV, at the instigation of that city and of its allies in the kingdom of Jerusalem. These grants contained confirmation of older privileges, attributed to past rulers of the kingdom; it is therefore possible that the Anconitans also argued at the papal curia that they possessed ancient privileges, which they requested the pope to confirm. However, there is no visible reference to such privileges in the grants made to them by Innocent IV [22]. So soon after his act of "deposition" of Frederick, Innocent may not yet have developed to the full his policy of later years. More probably, the pope was simply exploiting his lordship over Ancona, in the vague and no doubt vain hope that papal vassals armed with papal letters might be able to claim rights of exemption. It is thus possible that — as in the case of Apulia — the papacy did not expect activation of the rights of exemption so handsomely conferred on Ancona in the Holy Land; this was a bid to gain support from Ancona by promises that in the future the papacy would guard the city's interests in the east and in southern Italy. Such manoeuvres were entirely typical of papal policy in the central and eastern papal state during the 1240s; as Daniel Waley has shown, other privileges to the towns took the form of exemptions from provincial taxation or of a reduction in military obligations [23]. Nor was Ancona alone in receiving a trade privilege: Spoleto was another beneficiary, though not of course for the Levant trade; a privilege for an unnamed town in central Italy conferred rights in Apulia and Sicily (but not beyond) identical to those besto-

---

[22] J. Riley-Smith, *The Feudal Nobility and the Kingdom of Jerusalem, 1174-1277* (London, 1973), pp. 213, 305; cf. H. E. Mayer, *Marseilles Levantehandel und ein akkonensisches Fälscheratelier des XIII. Jahrhunderts* (Tübingen, 1972), especially pp. 207-12, nos. 23-26.

[23] Waley, *Papal State*, pp. 150-1.

wed upon Ancona[24]. These privileges were also, perhaps, an embarrassment; Ancona seems to have lost access to the wheat supplies of Apulia after 1245, in view of its adherence to the papal cause. A privilege of Innocent IV, of 1246, allowed the Anconitans free passage to Durazzo in Albania (then in Epirote hands)[25]. The pope explains that Ancona was ringed by enemies who interfered with its food supplies, and that access to Durazzo was essential for Ancona's survival. From 1244 to 1247 Ancona was the only town on the east coast to adhere to Innocent IV, a "long period of isolation," as Waley remarks, but clearly commercial as well as political isolation[26]. The privilege for Durazzo was surely of greater immediate value to Ancona than that for Acre or Apulia[27].

Nevertheless, the letters of 1245 reveal that the Levant trade was a matter in which the Anconitans were interested, either on the basis of past results or on that of future prospects. A papal letter of 1243 indicates that inhabitants of the March of Ancona were selling forbidden items to the Muslims and to the schismatic Greeks: participants in this trade were given an opportunity to support Christian enterprises against Muslims and Greeks instead[28]. Anconitan Franciscans may have been

---

[24] Archivio Segreto Vaticano, Registro 21 A, ep. 551, fol. 261 r (Spoleto); BN, MS lat. 11867, fol. 34 v, ed. K. Hampe, "Aus verlorenen Registerbänden der Päpste Innocenz III. und Innocenz IV.," *Mitteilungen des Instituts für österreichische Geschichtsforschung* 24 (1903), 231, no. 68 (unnamed city).

[25] Registro 21, ep. 863, fol. 408 r; Theiner, 1 : 124-5, § 227.

[26] Waley, *Papal State*, p. 149.

[27] For links between Ancona and Durazzo, see A. Ducellier, *La façade maritime de l'Albanie: Durazzo et Valona du XIe au XVe siècle*, (Thessalonika, 1981), pp. 284, 419, 564, 566.

[28] Registro 21, ep. 73-4, fol. 12 v - 13 r; edited by Th. T. Haluščynskyj and M. M. Wojnar, *Acta Innocentii PP IV (1243-1254), e Registris Vaticanis aliisque fontibus*, Pontificia Commissio ad redigendum Codicem Iuris Canonici Orientalis. Fontes, 3.4.1 (Rome 1962), p. 7. § 5 (ep. 73 only); Berger, § 73-4.

involved in missions to the Bulgars, Vlachs, Slavs, Nubians, Nestorians, Georgians and other eastern Christians in 1245 [29]; Ancona was certainly a good point of access to the Bulgarian empire and to Serbia, by way of Durazzo and the Dalmatian ports. And there was an Armenian convent in Ancona by 1248, when it was taken under the protection of Innocent IV [30]. On balance, then, it is likely that there did exist regular contact with east Mediterranean ports at the time of Innocent's privileges to Ancona.

III

Venetian rivalry with Ancona helped reinforce links between Ancona and Genoa. Not surprisingly, the Anconitans are listed among the supporters of Genoa and Philip de Montfort in the War of Saint Sabas, just as the Provençaux, rivals of Genoa, appear among the supporters of Venice [31]. Another group within the Genoese faction was the Hospital of Saint John, and it is in the Hospitaller archive in Malta that a trade privilege in favour of Ancona, dating from the height of the War of Saint Sabas, is preserved [32]. It will be suggested later

---

[29] Haluščynskyj and Wojnar, pp. 48-9, § 21, a document preserved in the Franciscan archive of Ancona. Cf. RRH no. 1209 b of 1260.

[30] Registro 21 A, ep. 197, fol. 49; Haluščynskyj and Wojnar, pp. 119, § 66; Berger, § 4189.

[31] *Annali Genovesi di Caffaro e de' suoi continuatori*, ed. C. Imperiale di Sant'Angelo, 4 (Rome, 1926), 36: "all were against the Genoese except the Hospital of St. John and except the Anconitans and the Catalans."

[32] National Library of Malta, Arch. 5 (originally 6), no. 55, records of the order of St. John; cf. Z. Gabaretta, J. Mizzi, *Catalogue of the*

how the document might have ended in the hands of the Knights of Saint John. The privilege of 1257 (which is in French) is issued in the name of John of Ibelin, lord of Arsur, constable and bailli of the kingdom of Jerusalem, and of his followers, including the lord of Tyre, Philip de Montfort, whose conflict with the Venetians played an important part in the civil war [33]. The document is thus a product of the conflict, an attempt by one faction to win over, or more likely reward and encourage, a group of Italian merchants who did not yet enjoy the special legal status of the Genoese or the Venetians. Indeed, it can be deduced from the privilege that the complete tax exemption envisaged by Pope Innocent IV was not recognised by the bailli and the Frankish Seigneurie; the taxes Anconitan merchants were to pay were much lower than those paid by unprivileged merchants, but they were not granted tax exemption on the

---

records of the order of St. John of Jerusalem in the Royal Malta Library, 1, *Archives 1-72* (Malta, 1964), 36, where it is catalogued as follows: "Jean d'Ibelin, seigneur d'Arsur, Connestable et Lieutenant General de Royaume de Jerusalem. (Text in French), 10, VIII.1257. (No seal extant)." I am grateful to Dr. A. T. Luttrell, formerly of the University of Malta and to Mr J. B. Sultana of the National Library of Malta for their help. There exists an edition with an accompanying translation into more modern French: G. Paoli, *Codice diplomatico del sacro ordine gerosoli-mitano oggi di Malta*, 1 (Lucca, 1733), pp. 157-61, no. 132. For further details of Arch. 5, see Gabaretta and Mizzi, *Catalogue* 2-3, 32. RRH no. 1259 for a summary of the privilege. The orthographical oddities of Paoli's edition have induced me to offer a new edition at the end of this article.

[33] For the War of St. Sabas see J. Prawer, *Histoire du royaume latin de Jérusalem*, 2 (Paris, 1970), 359-371; G. Caro, *Genova e la sua supremazia nel Mediterraneo*, in *Atti della Società ligure di storia patria*, 88 (Genoa, 1974), 1 : 36-49, 72-79; H. E. Mayer, "Ibelin vs. Ibelin: the Struggle for the Regency of Jerusalem, 1253-1258," *Proceedings of the American Philosophical Society*, 122 (1978), 25-57, and especially 48-9, making the identity of the Ibelin factions clearer; cf. P. W. Edbury, "John of Ibelin's title to the county of Jaffa and Ascalon," *English Historical Review* 98 (1983), 115-133, especially 132-3. Also, Riley-Smith, *Feudal Nobility*, p. 216.

scale of that practised by the Venetians[34]. Before 1257, the privilege indicates, Anconitans traded in the Latin kingdom under several possible categories. Those who came in their own right, as Anconitans, paid the full taxes, it appears; but many, perhaps most, declared themselves to be Genoese, Pisan or Venetian merchants, especially when they had entered a business partnership with a privileged merchant. A later example of this may be "Nicolaus de Parte de Ancone" who was in Cyprus in 1300, but is described as Genoese[35]. However, the 1257 privilege insist that all Anconitans must henceforth be counted as members of the Ancona community, irrespective of whether they were "franchi jusques au jor duy per Jeneueis ou per pisans ou per Venetiens." Thus in 1257 the pro-Genoese party constituted the Anconitans into an autonomous body, separate from the Genoese; but far from being a neutral body, the community of Ancona was expected to provide armed help to the de Montfort faction, and it was promised land adjacent to that possessed in Acre by the Genoese — a repetition of the border dispute between Genoese and Venetians over the convent of Saint Sabas was clearly not expected between Genoese and Anconitans. Indeed, a number of leading Genoese witnessed the privilege: Ansaldo Ceba, Giovanni di Castagna, Guglielmo Guercio, Guglielmo Spinola, Lanfranco di Carmadino, Antonio Grimaldi[36]. The witness list of the Ancona privilege has received attention recently from H. E. Mayer and Peter Edbury. Mayer emphasizes the Genoese presence and argues that all the members of the Haute Cour mentioned in the privilege were, by 1257, adherents of John of Arsur. One, Stephen of Savigny, must,

---

[34] For an exposition of these rights, see in particular J. Riley-Smith, "Government in Latin Syria and the commercial privileges of the foreign merchants," in *Relations between East and West in the Middle Ages*, ed. D. Baker (Edinburgh, 1973), pp. 109-32.

[35] Polonio, p. 173, § 150.

[36] For some of these figures see e.g. Caro, *Genova*, 1 : 36, 166, 167 and 82 or 127.

according to Mayer, have switched sides from John of Jaffa's faction to John of Arsur's in late 1256 or 1257. Other witnesses were, according to Mayer, also adherents of the Arsur faction, even though their earlier allegiance is hard to prove. Edbury, on the other hand, argues that the witnesses were residents in Acre, regular participants in the Haute Cour who regarded it as their duty to attend since John of Arsur was legitimately entitled to convene the Haute Cour, as regent of the kingdom. Edbury states that "to regard them as members of John's « party » may be reading too much into the evidence". On the other hand, Edbury's caution does not really modify the signs that the privilege to Ancona was issued with Genoese encouragement, and in order to further the interests of John of Arsur's faction. The presence of neutral or even hostile witnesses seems to have had no effect, however hard it may be supposed they argued against the proposed favours to Ancona. In other words, the 1257 privilege still represents a victory for the Genoese and for the bailli. Nor was this simply an agreement between the Anconitans of Acre and the Genoese faction. The commune of Ancona sent its own representatives to the east, to negotiate the terms:

> Ce est a sauer que mesire Johan de Guide, et mesire Bienuenu de Vidal, Syndiques procureors, et actors, et speciaus messages dou Comun dancone, receueors et stipuleors de par leur Comun, et de par les Homes Singuliers de la Cite et dou destreit dancone.

The Podestà of Ancona itself and the Anconitan consul in Acre were to swear each year to observe the terms of the agreement, and within two years (that is, by August 1259) a copy of the text, bearing the seal of the commune of Ancona, was to be returned to the bailli of the kingdom of Jerusalem. This again reveals the reluctance of the Frankish barons to be drawn into a treaty with a few resident merchants who claimed to represent an Italian town but lacked any influence over its policies. It should be stressed that what survives in Malta is a copy which seems originally to have carried the seals of some or all of the Frankish barons who agreed the terms — John of Arsur, Philip de Montfort, and others. According to the manuscript, two copies were made on a single sheet of parchment, which was then divided (in the form of a chirograph); one text was given to the Anconitans and one to somebody whose name cannot be read, probably the bailli. The phrasing used at this point, "cestui a les Anconitans et lautre a le [...]," suggests that the copy which now survives is the text which was consigned to the Anconitans themselves. If that is right, additional problems arise. According to the terms of the agreement, as has been seen, one copy was to be sent to Ancona and confirmed there, before being sent back to the bailli. But this version would carry the seals of the government of Ancona, not of the Frankish barons. Possibly, therefore, the bailli's copy was the one actually sent to Ancona, unsealed or only partly sealed, and this surviving copy was held by the Anconitan community in the kingdom of Jerusalem. But it is also possible that among the lost seals were not merely seals of the barons but Anconitan ones also, affixed in Ancona before the document was sent back.

The privilege has close analogies to those granted earlier to other Italian communities in the Holy Land [37]. Thus the Anconitans are permitted a tax reduction at the *cour de la Chaine* in Acre, both on goods brought into Acre by sea from Christian lands and on goods taken out. They are to pay 1 % of the value of the goods carried ("un besans dentree per Centenal; un besans dissue per Centenal"). In future the "seur plus," a tax about which no further details are offered, would be set aside; this was probably a tax on the difference between the value of exports and that of imports, where the value of the exports stood higher than that of the imports. Riley-Smith has noted certain parallels in the commercial tax system of

---

[37] Riley-Smith, "Government in Latin Syria," 118-20; a handlist is provided by J. La Monte, *Feudal Monarchy in the Latin Kingdom of Jerusalem, 1100-1291* (Cambridge, Mass., 1932), pp. 261-75.

contemporary Egypt[38]. Goods brought by Anconitans themselves from "les terres de paienisme," however, or goods bought there and carried by sea into Acre, are not tax-exempt:

> les baillis de la chaene receuront deaus dreiture dentree enterinement ensi coment sont a Costume a paier gens remdables.

If these items were left unsold after importation, the tax paid on them would still not be remitted. Indeed, when these articles were re-exported, tax would have to be paid on them yet again, just as if the Anconitans were unprivileged merchants. This reluctance to allow concessions for goods imported directly from Muslim countries in Italian hands is also reflected in government policy towards the Venetians — a subject, indeed, which aroused the indignation of Marsilio Zorzi, the Venetian *bailo* in the 1240s[39]. As in the case of the Venetians, Anconitans who sought to combine trade with Aleppo, or even Alexandria, with trade in Acre were seriously penalised; and it is clear from what has been said already that Ancona did indeed possess sufficient business interest in "les terres de paienisme" to arouse papal concern.

Anconitan merchants were forbidden to indulge in the common practice of permitting foreign merchants to take their name and pass through customs as if they were exempt from tax. If an Anconitan extended his protection to "gens remdables" in this way, he would lose his own rights of exemption. But it does seem that the whole community was also liable to search out and remove from their midst all pseudo-Anconitans:

> se il y aueit aucun des anconitans qui ne fust Habitans a ancone, ou el destreit dancone, et il ne vousist estre en cest Condition, que ceaus dancone sont tenus de bannirles en cors et en aueir.

---

[38] Riley - Smith, *Feudal Nobility*, p. 93.

[39] RRH nos. 1114, 1116; Riley - Smith, "Government in Latin Syria."

This probably reflects a growing irritation at the presence of would-be Pisans and others in the Italian communities of Acre; the San Gimignano merchants, for instance, regularly passed themselves off as Pisans in Acre, a fact of which their own home government for long remained quite ignorant [40]. As has been seen, the privilege also insisted that Anconitans no longer enjoy that status themselves, as protected members of the Genoese, Pisan or Venetian jurisdiction, and those under Venetian patronage in consequence found themselves paying more taxes than before [41]. On the other hand there may have been few Anconitans working in close partnership with Venetians during the War of Saint Sabas. Thus the privilege leaves a narrow definition of Anconitans as men of Ancona and its surrounding area, and it is by no means clear that traders from Fermo, Fano or other central Adriatic ports were allowed to participate in Anconitan rights [42]. On the other hand, at least one of the Ancona merchants named in a Cyprus contract of 1301 has what is probably a Slav name, and throughout the thirteenth century Ancona clearly acquired many settlers from Dalmatia, Istria and the Italian interior [43]. In the last analysis, it was very difficult for any commune to exclude non-native merchants, because the Italian maritime towns were great foci of immigration.

As in the privileges of other Italian communities, arrangements were made for the exercise of Anconitan jurisdiction

---

[40] D. Abulafia, "Crocuses and Crusaders: San Gimignano, Pisa and the Kingdom of Jerusalem," in *Outremer: Studies in the History of the Crusading Kingdom of Jerusalem presented to Joshua Prawer*, ed. B. Z. Kedar, H. E. Mayer and R. C. Smail (Jerusalem, 1982), pp. 227-43.

[41] Venetians paid almost nothing: Riley - Smith, "Government in Latin Syria."

[42] For a ship owned by a citizen of Fermo, bound for Ancona, see Pavoni, pp. 225-6, § 185.

[43] Pavoni, p. 1, § 1.

over commercial cases in the kingdom of Jerusalem. The Anconitans were permitted a consul or consuls, who would judge "per l'usage de la terre," by which seems to be meant the Latin kingdom itself [44]. Among their responsibilities was the question who was entitled to be counted as an Anconitan and to enjoy tax rights. But criminal jurisdiction did not belong to the consuls. The Anconitans had territory as well as jurisdiction, under the terms of the privilege. Two overlapping sites are named for their colony. The first site was to be a piece of land alongside the « garden of the Genoese, » running down to the sea-walls; here they could build a church and a communal palace, as well as a hostel ("une place ausi por eaus herbergier"). There would be an open space near the sea, just inside the walls, where they could bring, and presumably store or sell, their merchandise. But there was some uncertainty, the document says, whether all this land could be made available by the Frankish Seigneurie: it seems likely that some of the land was simply in other hands, and the uncertain conditions within Acre during 1257 must have made the assignment of city land hard to enforce. In the event of difficulties, the Anconitans were to buy the house of Sire Iohan Grip, Sire Iop and Sire Iorge; the Seigneurie would then give them the land between those houses and the sea, for lodging and also for loading and unloading. Since these lands gave less good access to the port, the Anconitans would be allowed free use of the nearest city gate to transfer their merchandise into their quarter. In addition to the problem of civil war, the bailli and his allies had to face the sheer dificulty of assigning a compact area of land to a group of foreign merchants in a crowded city, where building space was in short supply. Thus the Seigneurie would have to alienate some of its own property in favour of the Anconitans, and this property seems not to have been entirely contiguous. For that reason, property in the hands

---

[44] Riley-Smith, *Feudal Nobility*, p. 269; Mayer, *Marseilles*, p. 186 (no. 5), indicating a similar limitation on the merchants of Marseilles.

of certain knights might have to be assigned instead, so that the Anconitan quarter was not split into parts. The main aim, then, was to create a coherent patch of territory, with a church, palace, warehouse and other facilities, similar to those possessed to a greater or lesser degree by the other privileged communities of merchants[45]. But, interestingly enough, the only block of territory assigned to the Anconitans was in Acre; the document mentions no other lands, although subsequent events make it possible that the Anconitans acquired some rights and territory in Tyre.

The knights whose houses were to be bought, if necessary, by the Anconitans deserve closer attention. One, Sire Johan Grip, had other property interests. A document of 1260, formerly in the Malta archive, records that "Iohannes Grifus miles Acconensis" and his wife Agatha willed land in the bakers' district of Montmusard, as well as a money-fief worth sixteen besants a year to the Knights of Saint John, from whom, indeed, part of the estate was already held[46]. Johan Grip or Grifus is thus a reasonably wealthy Acre landowner, who possesses fairly valuable and extensive property in Montmusard and — to judge from the privilege of 1257 — in another part of Acre too. The connection with Grip probably explains the survival of the charter among the documents of the Knights of Saint John. The Ancona privilege has nothing itself to say about the Hospitallers, though as has been seen the Hospitallers were allies of the Genoese in the War of Saint Sabas, and thus also of the Anconitans. It is possible that the Hospital, as legatee of Johan Grip, received documents previously in his hands, which he had because they concerned his own property rights. Even so,

---

[45] On the physical geography of Acre, see B. Dichter, *The maps of Acre* (Acre, 1973); D. Jacoby, "Crusader Acre in the Thirteenth Century: Urban Layout and Topography," *Studi medievali* 2.20 (1979), 1-45.

[46] RRH no. 1291 (and *Additamentum* no. 1291); Paoli, *Codice diplomatico*, 1 : 297-8, § 19. For Montmusard, see D. Jacoby, "Montmusard, Suburb of Crusader Acre," in *Outremer* (cited in n. 40 *supra*), pp. 205-17.

it is not clear why Grip should have possessed an original rather than a notary's transumpt.

The Anconitans were not to constitute an entirely exempt community, free from military service [47]. They were expected to give something valuable in return for their privilege: not money, so much as men, both on land and at sea. Fifty soldiers, "armes de fer au meins," were to be made available to help in the defence of the city and port of Acre, and elsewhere; those who served at sea would receive food rations from the Frankish Seigneurie but would not receive equipment or other necessities. They were to be ready two years hence (1259) on the feast of All Saints, and if the consul of the Anconitans did not have them ready by then, a forced levy would be imposed, to raise fifty men at the expense of the Anconitan community. Moreover, all Anconitans actually in Acre would be bound to aid the Frankish barons to the best of their ability in time of need. Two questions arise here. The prescription "two years hence" need not imply that no aid was provided during 1257 or 1258; it must be assumed that the Anconitans won their privilege partly through their willingness to support Genoese interests against Venetian, even by the sword. Moreover, the insistence that the Anconitans in Acre must always "ayder la Seigno-rie ... de tout luer poeir" can be taken to mean that, during an emergency, the Anconitans would not fail to provide military help, and 1257 saw just such an emergency. Second, fifty men was quite a sizeable force, assuming the men were drawn from the Anconitan community. This number might represent one heavily-armed ship, carrying marines. If a land force were raised, it is likely that many of the men would be paid soldiers of non-Anconitan origin. Outside an emergency, Anconitans would only be made to serve if the consul failed to provide

---

[47] Some Venetian settlers around Tyre were liable for military service, but it is still not clear what obligations bound the Venetian and other communities as a whole; see in due course the study of the Italians in the kingdom of Jerusalem by Marie - Luise Favreau - Lilie.

the promised squadron. It should be stressed that the defense arrangement was not a one-way arrangement; the Seigneurie promised to protect the Anconitans and to indemnify them against loss in time of war; and if the Seigneurie made peace with its enemies, it was to ensure that the Anconitans were included within that peace. Here, certainly, is a further echo of the War of Saint Sabas, a time of obvious danger to merchants trying to operate from Acre.

The need for indemnification was particularly apparent when the Genoese attempt to control part of Acre collapsed, and the merchants of Genoa sailed north to Tyre, to occupy the Venetian quarter and to take advantage of Philip de Montfort's protection (1259) [48]. There is reason to suppose that Venetians in Acre did not respect the terms of Ancona's privilege, for in 1264 the Venetians imposed an agreement on Ancona, limiting its trading activities to the Adriatic and nearby regions; the Levant trade of Ancona was to be suppressed. Venice seems, therefore, to have carried the War of Saint Sabas into the Adriatic, in the form of a limited conflict or challenge to Ancona, which Ancona proved quite unable to resist, for the moment at least. It is thus highly unlikely that the provisions of the agreement of 1257 were put into effect, at least in Acre, in the form described in the privilege. This is not to exclude the possibility of a later return to Acre or of a transfer to Tyre, nor that certain rights, such as the use of a church, were enjoyed [49]. There is simply no substantial evidence. The privilege of 1257 thus has several characteristics which set it apart from those received by rival Italian communes. It was conferred by a faction in the kingdom of Jerusalem, to strengthen their hand in a war with the Venetians and other internal foes; the

---

[48] Prawer, *Histoire*, 2 : 370-3; Caro, *Genova*, 1 : 72-9.

[49] B. Dichter lists an Anconitan church in Acre among the city's Latin churches in his compendium, *The Orders and Churches of Crusader Acre* (Acre, 1979, p. 31, but same of his statements about the Anconitans seem difficult to prove.

wars to which the document refers are not — as in twelfth-century privileges to the Italians — wars with the Muslims, but wars between Latin and Latin.

From 1257 onwards rare references to Anconitans in the Latin kingdom do occur. In 1257 the lord of Sidon had among his men Peter of Ancona, John the Old of Pisa and John of Genoa (or Geneva), a combination which fits very well into the known pattern of association of Anconitans [50]. In 1267 the list of witnesses to an act concerning the lands of Sancta Maria Latina reveals the presence of Iohannes of Ancona, Nicolaus of San Gimignano and Bonannus canonicus of Pisa [51]. The former document, if not the latter, suggests that Anconitans, like other citizens of the Italian maritime towns, occasionally settled in the east and took a lord there. But there are very many more appearances in witness lists of Genoese, Pisans and Venetians, and it can be said with confidence that the Anconitan settlement in the kingdom of Jerusalem was very modest in scale.

IV

1264, even more than 1259, marks a serious crisis in Ancona's Levant trade. That year, the Venetians managed severely to restrict Ancona's freedom of navigation, not merely in the Adriatic but also in the eastern Mediterranean. Cessi, and more recently Ashtor, have discussed the treaty of 1264 between Venice and Ancona in which the Anconitans were forced to

---

[50] RRH no. 1253.

[51] RRH no. 1356. Occasionally the words "Ancona" and "Accone" may be confused, and it is not always clear whether one or the other is intended: see RRH no. 1388 of 1273.

agree not to carry the merchandise of foreigners to places beyond the Adriatic, nor to import such goods *intra culfum*. Items taken directly to Venice, against the terms of the agreement, would be treated as contraband [52]. Yet the limitations were resisted. The Anconitans tried to persuade Pope Gregory X to cancel the provisions, in 1274, to no effect. They were aware that the unequal treaty with Venice destroyed at a stroke Ancona's function as middleman in the trade between Lombardy, Tuscany or the Romagna and the east, though they remained free to carry east clerics, crusaders and other pilgrims. So too were local merchants of the March of Ancona free to trade in Anconitan vessels bound for the east — vessels that carried, officially at any rate, pilgrims in the main. The treaty of 1264 thus marks a significant victory for Venice in its rivalry with Ancona. The restrictions placed on Ancona are analogous to those placed on such cities as Savona or Montpellier by the Genoese a century earlier: an attempt to make the more powerful city into the staple through which eastern goods had first to pass.

It is especially interesting to find, in the 1264 agreement, that the Venetians sought to stifle the Anconitan cotton trade: Apulian cotton could not be carried to Venice, to the coast north of Rimini, nor to Dalmatia. For it becomes clear, from an analysis of documents drawn up ten or so years after the fall of Acre, that the international cotton trade was a major target of Anconitan investment; nor were the Venetians able, in the long term, to exclude Anconitan competitors. This is not to claim that the Anconitans were as successful in the penetration of Lombard, let alone German, markets as were the Venetians.

There is plentiful evidence that Anconitan merchants were active in the Cyprus trade around 1300. The notarial acts of Lamberto di Sambuceto from Famagusta, now preserved in

---

[52] R. Cessi, *Venezia e il problema adriatico* (Padua, 1943), pp. 75-82; E. Ashtor, *Levant trade in the Later Middle Ages* (Princeton, 1983), p. 30.

Genoa and edited by Desimoni, Polonio and Pavoni, refer frequently to Anconitan ships and traders, and they include a number of commercial contracts between Anconitans and Greek, Pisan, south Italian and of course Genoese investors or partners. Obviously great care must be taken before it can be concluded that the activities of the Anconitans in Cyprus mirror those of the Anconitans in Acre, a decade and more earlier; there is no clear indication whether any of the merchants named in the Genoese cartularies had previously been involved in direct trade with the kingdom of Jerusalem, although the Anconitans in Cyprus did enjoy close relations with Greek merchants of Syrian origin; and occasionally Latin merchants of Syrian ancestry or origin too. Cyprus functioned as a distribution port for goods brought from, and bound to, Egypt and Cilician Armenia, while contact with the once-favoured markets of Syria became more restricted after the fall of Acre [53]. Some of the commodities acquired by Anconitans in Cyprus were also exported in quantity from the erstwhile kingdom of Jerusalem, particularly sugar and cotton, though Indian cotton could also be had in Egypt [54]. However, the heavy involvement of the Syrian Greeks alongside the Anconitans in the cotton trade may indicate that the cotton, like the Greeks, came from Syria.

A good example of a partnership between an Anconitan and a Greek, using a ship from Ancona, is provided by a contract of 14 October 1300, recorded by Lamberto di Sambuceto. Tomaso de Rogerio of Ancona declared to Cosmas de "Lezia", which may mean Laodicea, that he had received from him, in commenda, cotton worth 1444 white (or Cypriot) besants; this cotton was to be carried to Ancona, and sold there, aboard the ship of Barone Pellegrini de Galante, also of Ancona [55]. With

---

[53] For a valuable discussion of the rôle of Cyprus, see David Jacoby.

[54] For the cotton trade in general, see M. F. Mazzaoui, *The Italian Cotton Industry in the Later Middle Ages, 1100-1600* (Cambridge, 1981).

[55] Polonio, pp. 56-7, § 48.

the proceeds of the sale Tomaso de Rogerio was to purchase goods "per totam marcham Ancone et totam Ampuliam", and to export them to Cyprus. A regular flow of goods between Ancona and southern Italy on the one hand and Cyprus on the other is indicated by the terms of the contract; and indeed all the individuals mentioned so far reappear again and again in Lamberto di Sambuceto's cartulary, both in 1300 and in 1301. Tomaso was only one of several merchants who were employed by Cosmas of Laodicea ("Lezia") for an identical purpose, the carriage of cotton to central Italy, an enterprise in which Cosmas had exceptionally large business interests. But Cosmas himself was only the leading member (as far as can be seen) of a large group of Laodicean merchants [56]. He and his brother Damian arranged to send wheat worth 3800 white besants from Cyprus to Armenia in May, 1301 [57]; and it is possible that this wheat was one of the items imported from the March of Ancona and Apulia by Cosmas' Anconitan agents: evidence published by Renouard indicates that Cyprus and Armenia drew grain from Apulia in the early fourteenth century, and the close links between Ancona's interests in Apulia and its interests in the east seem indicated by the papal letters of 1245 [58]. Cosmas and his family also traded with Ancona using Greek Syrian *socii negociantes*: in October 1301 Cosmas and his brother Nicholas (Nicolinus) entrusted a cargo of cotton worth 5215 white besants to Simon, son of Joseph of "Lezia," "burgensis Famagoste," to be carried by Joseph to Ancona aboard the ship of Barone de Galante, now back in Cyprus from his winter venture of 1300-1. [59]. Damian of

---

[56] See, e.g., Polonio, §§ 31, 48, 50, 54, 368, 368 a (Cosmas); §§ 30, 31, 32, 33, 34, 54, 368, 368 a, 390 (Damian).

[57] Polonio, pp. 442-3, § 368.

[58] Y. Renouard, "Une expédition des céréales des Pouilles en Arménie par les Bardi pour le compte de Benoît XII," *Mélanges d'archéologie et d'histoire de l'Ecole française de Rome* 53 (1936), 287-329.

[59] Pavoni, pp. 234-5, § 193.

"Lezia" invested a further 4650 white besants in the same enterprise [60]. Cosmas also acted as intermediary for other merchants: he sent 2004 white besants' worth of cotton to Ancona with Simon of Laodicea, on behalf of Thomas Megibel of "Lezia", "burgensis Famagoste" (October 1301) [61], and he made use of another Simon, described as "de magistro Nicolao de Ancona", to recover the sum of 100 Saracen besants from a second Anconitan merchant, probably in Ancona itself [62]. However, it was not just Anconitans who benefited from Greek investment: Cosmas and Damian also made use of the ships of Nicola Sten and Marino de Aragusia, that is, of Ragusa or Dubrovnik; these ships were bound for Venice, and in one contract Damian placed on board cotton worth 2662 Saracen besants (or 9317 white besants) while in another Cosmas placed cotton worth 3568¼ white besants [63]. The Laodicean merchants in Cyprus thus had wider interests than the cotton trade with Ancona, but trade with the Adriatic remained their prime recorded interest.

Anconitan investment in trade with Italy received other backers than the Laodiceans. A large bundle of 36 contracts survives in Lamberto di Sambuceto's cartulary, listing invest-

---

[60] Pavoni, pp. 243, pp. § 202.

[61] Pavoni, 249-50, § 208.

[62] Pavoni, pp. 239, § 197.

[63] Pavoni, pp. 243-4, § 203; 245, § 204. But other investments were also made by Cosmas and Damian: Pavoni, p. 247, § 206; pp. 249-50, § 208; pp. 252-3, § 211-12; pp. 253-4, § 212, not to mention documents concerning other Laodicean merchants: Pavoni, pp. 251-2, § 210 ("Michelinuș, filius quondam Theodori de Lezia," agent of "Georgio, filio Michaelis de Lezia," who appears as agent of Cosmas and Damian in § 211-2); pp. 254-5, § 213 (Michelinus for Costas of Antioch); pp. 255-6, § 214 (Michelinus for "Manueli, filio Bechie de Antiochia"); pp. 256-7, § 215 (Michelinus for "Symoni Iosepe de Lezia"); pp. 257-8, § 216 ("Symon de Iosepe de Lezia" for "Saono, filio Manssor, burgensi Famagoste"). Pavoni § 203-7, mentioning the ships of Nicola Sten (probably a Venetian) and Marinus of Dubrovnik, but § 210-216, § 218-219 mention only the ship of the latter.

ments made from 2 to 9 October, 1301 [64]. Apart from Cosmas and his group, there were Genoese investments: Ansaldo de Sexto of Genoa sent five sacks of cotton, worth 250 Saracen besants, with Lipo di Pietro of Ancona, to Pula (Pola) "et deinde per totum Gurffum Venecianum," thence back to Cyprus [65]; and he sent six sacks of cotton, worth 265½ Saracen besants to Ancona itself, with Baldovino Benevenuti of Ancona, aboard the ship of Barone de Galante [66]. George Tiratira of Famagusta, probably a Greek, sent 863 white besants with Lipo di Pietro of Ancona on board a ship owned or operated by a trader from Fermo, an Adriatic port near Ancona [67]. A Greek Syrian of some importance was Costas of Antioch; he despatched cotton worth 1500 white besants to Ancona, aboard Barone de Galante's ship, and commissioned Simon Dimitri of Laodicea to act on his behalf [68]; he sent a further 2000 besants worth with Simon, son of Joseph of "Lezia." [69] This Simon was to take 1700 besants' worth of cotton to Ancona on behalf of another Antiochene, Manuel "filio Bechie." [70]

The Anconitans always appear either as ship-owners or as travelling partners; they do not operate as *socii stantes* based in Cyprus. There appears to be a regular traffic between Ancona and Cyprus, managed, to a considerable extent, by Anconitan shipping entrepreneurs, but the investors at the Cypriot end of the route are commonly Greeks from Syria, resident in Cyprus. Of course, the Anconitan travelling partners

---

[64] Pavoni, pp. 220-66, § 181-222; but §§ 184, 189, 190, 191, 209, 217 are clearly extraneous to the series, § 201 is a fragment begun in error, § 184 should probably be redated 2 October from 2 September, in which case it can be re-admitted to the group. Seé appendix II *infra*.

[65] Pavoni, pp. 226-7, § 186; cf. 220-1, § 181, clearly for the same sailing.

[66] Pavoni, pp. 229-30, § 188.

[67] Pavoni, pp. 225-6, § 185.

[68] Pavoni, p. 237, § 195.

[69] Pavoni, p. 238, § 196.

[70] Pavoni, pp. 239-40, § 198; cf. 255-6, § 214 (for Venice).

of the Greeks can expect a quarter share of the profit from commenda enterprises[71]; but — as will emerge shortly — investment in Anconitan - owned capital takes place at the Ancona end, not in Famagusta. A regular cycle exists: investment by Anconitans in Italy, making possible voyages to Cyprus, where Greeks help finance a further round trip to Italy and back. In other words, ships such as that of Barone de Galante are moving seasonally between capital investors at both ends of the trade route, year-in, year-out.

The picture provided by the documents of October 1301 holds true, with some minor modifications, for the contracts of autumn 1300 also. Cosmas of Lezia appears, of course[72]; but Anconitans received investments from Florentine investors, one of whom required Venetian silver[73]; and on one occasion two Anconitans arranged for the transport of 2200 moggia of salt to Ancona or Venice, also on behalf of the Peruzzi bank[74]. Lacking a flett of its own, Florence had to make use of Anconitans, Catalans, Genoese and others for transport. Tuscans also operated as factors along the trade route between Cyprus and Ancona; the Anconitans and their Greek partners did not hold a monopoly of access to Ancona. On 11 April 1301 Belluco de Belluchis "de Accon," a Pisan previously of Acre, arranged to carry cotton and sugar valued at the heady sum of 2540 Saracen besants and 7 carats, to "Veneciam, Anconam et totum Gurffum et Apuliam et exinde redire Ciprum."[75] This suggests

---

[71] This was normal in commenda-type contracts; see e.g. Pavoni, pp. 220-1, § 181, where Flancolinus quondam Thome de Ancona agrees to take three bales of cotton, worth 450 white besants, to Pula on behalf of a Savonese member of the Genoese community, "ad quartum proficui michi inde habendum." This is entirely typical. He is to bring canvas goods back to Cyprus (2 October 1301).

[72] Polonio, pp. 56-7, § 48, 58-9, § 50; pp. 62-3, § 54.

[73] Polonio, p. 67, § 58; see note 89 *infra*.

[74] Polonio, pp. 72-4, § 64.

[75] Polonio, pp. 387-8, § 323.

that Ancona was seen as one among several useful distribution points for Levantine cotton — most probably, as a centre from which looms in central Italy and above all Tuscany were supplied.

In addition to the Tuscan partners and rivals, there were Anconitans in Cyprus whose origins may have lain outside the Marches. "Ivanus de Galvano, mercator," who appears as a witness and as a debtor, owing an unnamed sum to Guirardo, "draperius de Accon," has a Slav first name and may be Dalmatian [76]. Among the witnesses to an act of November 1300 appears a certain "Nicolaus de Parte de Ancone", but he and the other two witnesses are labelled "omnes Ianuenses." [77] He may have passed as a Genoese at the customs - house, or have been a Genoese resident originally in Ancona. But what is rare is evidence that Anconitans were permanent residents in Cyprus. Giacomo of Ancona, "tabernario, qui habitas in Famagusta in contrata Tortosa" evidently qualifies; he appears in Lamberto di Sambuceto's cartulary paying bail-money after another Italian escaped or avoided galley service [78]. In the winter of 1300-1 few Anconitans are mentioned at all in the cartulary, even as witnesses, and it is evident that many Anconitans had left the island at the time of the October sailings to Italy. Some, like Tomaso de Rogerio and Barone de Galante, did return in 1301 [79]. Fanellus Iacobi de Ancona, who appears in a witness list with the Venetian consul Nicola Zugno, probably spent the winter in Cyprus, for the document is dated 3 November [80]. The principal Anconitan to whom the document refer during this winter recess is Ciriaco de Ancona, bearer of the name of Ancona's patron saint. Unlike the other Anconitans encountered so far, Ciriaco seems to have specialis-

---

[76] Pavoni, pp. 1-2, § 2.
[77] Polonio, p. 173, § 150; cf. 240, § 204.
[78] Polonio, pp. 375-6, § 313.
[79] Pavoni, pp. 229-30, § 188; 240-2, § 199-200.
[80] Polonio, pp. 95-6, § 82; cf. p. 81, § 70.

ed in moneylending, though never on a massive scale. Thus on 8 November 1300 he lent Domenzio of Cervia the lowly sum of 5½ white besants[81]; a day later he lent Symonicius of Manfredonia 8½ white besants[82]. On 15 February 1301 Ciriaco lent 100 white besants to a Pisan merchant bound for Armenia, and arranged for payment of interest; the debt was settled in three weeks, as the cartulary reveals[83]. Ciriaco's work also included the recovery of bail money, owed by or on behalf of those who fled from galley service, and here again his clients included Pisans[84]. Finally, Ciriaco was involved in the slave trade; on 8 March 1301 he sold a Turkish male slave, aged about twelve, to Bellotus of Barletta, one of a group of Apulian merchants then (to judge from the witness list) visiting Cyprus[85]. It might be added that evidence for Anconitan involvement in the slave trade is rather slight, compared to involvement in the cotton or sugar trade. Anconitan merchants could, of course, acquire slaves across the water from their home-city, in Dalmatia or the Slav hinterland; but there is little evidence that Anconitans took an interest in a local slave trade in the waters around Cyprus. Nicola son of Stefano de Margato, of Ancona, sold a slave from Romania, named Maria, to Manssor or al-Mansūr of Tripoli in Syria ("de Castro Pellegrini"). A literally redeeming feature of this dubious contract to sell a Christian to a Muslim (or so it appears) is that Manssor was obliged to release Maria unharmed after

---

[81] Polonio, pp. 113-4, § 98.

[82] Polonio, p. 119, § 103.

[83] Polonio, pp. 264-5, § 225, with quittance attached — see also p. 323, § 271.

[84] Polonio, pp. 406-7, § 342; pp. 431-2, § 360.

[85] Polonio, pp. 321-2, § 270. The witnesses are "Paschalinus de Barleto, Nicola de Barleto et Iacobus de Manfredonia"; cf. also "Iacobus Rubeus de Barleto", a witness to § 225, and "Symonitius de Manfredonea" in § 103.

four years [86]. To return, however, to Ciriaco de Ancona: he was still in Famagusta on 24 July 1301, when he appears as witness to an act concerning a Genoese merchant bound for Armenia, as "Cliachus de Ancona," and it must be assumed that Ciriaco was a long-term resident in Cyprus, but not one of a great community of resident Anconitans [87].

Among the acts of Lamberto di Sambuceto there can be found a remarkable group of documents, recording that goods have been loaded on the ship of Barone Pellegrini de Galante bound for Ancona, in accordance with the instructions of the *socii stantes* in Ancona itself. These three contracts, of 9 October 1301, illustrate the dimension normally missing from the Cyprus documents: the terms of the contracts under which Anconitan merchants came to Cyprus to purchase goods on behalf of investors in Italy. And, given the lack of commercial contracts from this period in the archives of Ancona, these are the only documents that survive on the basis of which the lost commercial contracts can be reconstructed. In the first document Leonarduccio de Dominico of Ancona says that he has loaded on the ship of Barone de Galante items bought with the money provided to him, in Ancona, by a number of merchants [88]. Sixteen commenda contracts are listed, worth 1988 Saracen besants according to Lamberto di Sambuceto; though by adding up the figures given for each contract, we reach a slightly higher sum — 1991 besants. Leonarduccio invested a further 488 Saracen besants of his own. Only one merchant is described as "de Ancona," but no other origin is attributed to fourteen other investors; the sixteenth, Guglielmo de Griffolino, comes from San Severino, in southern Italy. One of the investors,

---

[86] Pavoni, pp. 284-6, § 239.

[87] Pavoni, pp. 18-19, § 16. Other Anconitans probably wintering in the east were Amador Iacobi de Ancona (Polonio, pp. 113-4, § 98); Gracia de Ancona (Polonio, p. 182, § 158); Nicola de Parte (Polonio, p. 173, § 150; p. 240, § 204).

[88] Pavoni, pp. 262-4, § 220.

"Puzius," or Puccio "qui travasa oleum," was apparently involved in the oil trade. Some merchants instructed Leonarduccio to buy cotton only, but for most he purchased cotton, sugar, pepper, incense and gold, as well as 47 buckram cloths; the actual amount of cotton he loaded was not large — nine sacks only. A useful clue to the nature of the commercial ties between Ancona and the east is provided by the reference to purchase of gold. Now, the value of the items purchased by Leonarduccio is stated, merchant by merchant, in Saracen besants, that is to say gold; it is possible, but not inherently likely, that he bought gold in some form with Saracen besants, but it is much more likely that the sums in Saracen besants indicate the value of items as agreed or estimated in Cyprus, and do not indicate that the money brought to Cyprus in payment for the cotton, gold and so on consisted of Saracen besants [89]. In other words, the Anconitans must have brought, in the main, western commodities such as grain and western bullion, in the form of silver, when they came to Cyprus. Indeed, the third document in their series cites a value in pounds of Ancona, not in money of the east, and this fits well with a picture of the Adriatic ports — especially Venice — as major exporters of silver mined in Germany, southern Italy and elsewhere, and despatched as far as Egypt and the emirate of Aydin [90].

Leonarduccio's document was witnessed by the notary of the ship on which the goods were to be conveyed, "Iacobus

---

[89] A point surely confirmed by Polonio, p. 67, § 58, with its reference to the acquisition of Venetian grossi in Venice by Giovanni de Paternanis of Ancona, though it cannot be stated for certain that the grossi were exported back to Cyprus.

[90] Pavoni, pp. 265-6, § 222; cf. D. Abulafia, « Maometto e Carlomagno: le due aree monetarie italiane dell'oro e dell'argento,» *Storia d'Italia. Annali, 6: Economia naturale, economia monetaria*, ed. R. Romano, U. Tucci, (Turin, 1983), pp. 224-70, especially pp. 267-8; Ph. Grierson, « Le gillat ou carlin de Naples-Provence: le rayonnement de son type monétaire,» *Catalogue de l'Exposition centenaire de la société frànçaise de numismatique (1865-1965)*, (Paris, 1965), pp. 43-56.

de Philipo, scriba dicte navis," as well as by merchants of Frankish Syrian ancestry or origins — Thomas of Sidon, John of Acre, described later as "habitatores Famagoste."[91] The second charter, of the same date, and concerning the same ship, lists the goods loaded by Lipo de Egidio of Ancona[92]. Five investors are named, in addition to Lipo himself; and the total amount mentioned is 1871 Saracen besants, to which Lipo has added 325 besants of his own. The commodities for export are the same as those purchased by Leonarduccio, but all except one investor placed fairly small sums in the expedition, less than Lipo himself. The overwhelming amount of money came from Vidalis de Rogerio, who was to receive eight sacks of cotton, sugar, pepper, incense, buckram and gold, altogether worth 1400 Saracen besants. The third document, representing eight commenda contracts and nine investors from Ancona, lists goods worth £ 3,500 in money of Ancona, and as has been seen it was in that money that the original investments were most probably made. In this document Leonardo Salembene of Ancona declares that he is loading no less than 45 sacks of cotton, as well as 22 cases of sugar, 125 pieces of buckram, packed in boxes, "vegete due de colloquinte" and a large quantity of gold wire[93].

These three documents help explain the nature of Ancona's trade with the Levant, in about 1300. In Ancona itself, there were clearly numerous willing investors, anxious to acquire cotton in the first place, gold and luxury items in second place. They were probably sending silver bullion, grain and raw materials to Cyprus, and some of the grain was forwarded from there to Cilician Armenia. In Cyprus, on the other hand, there was no large settled community of Anconitan merchants, at least to compare with the Genoese or Venetian presence in Cyprus and on the shores of the Black Sea. Those who

---

[91]   Pavoni, p. 266, § 222.

[92]   Pavoni, pp. 264-5, § 221.

[93]   Pavoni, pp. 265-6, § 222.

invest, at the Famagusta end, in trade with Ancona or aboard Anconitan ships are either other Italians, not of Ancona, or, very frequently, Greeks of Syrian ancestry, perhaps refugees from the lost principality of Antioch. It is possible, of course, that the picture is distorted by the obvious preference of Cosmas of "Lezia" for the services of Lamberto di Sambuceto, whom he used even though his own business was with Ancona, Venice and the Adriatic rather than with Genoa or the Black Sea. Actually, Lamberto was popular with the Venetians too, and clearly did possess a wide clientele for a Genoese notary[94]. Even without claiming that this notary is fully "representative," we can see some consistent strains in the evidence he provides. The role of the Ancona merchants as carriers between the Adriatic — not just Ancona — and the Levant is amply revealed, but it is certainly a modest role compared to that of the Genoese, Pisans and Venetians. The Anconitans can probably be ranked with the merchants and shippers of Marseilles, Messina or, a little more grandly, Barcelona, in the Levant trade of the late thirteenth century.

Ancona drew its real fortune from Adriatic trade in the thirteenth century, not from long-distance voyages to Syria, Cyprus or Egypt. Its success lay in its ability to hold the

---

[94] It has been seen that "Nicolaus Zugno, consul Venetorum in Famagosta," was a client: Polonio, p. 70, § 81; pp. 95-6, § 82; so too does "Bernardus Faxit, consul Nerbonensium in Famagosta" appear with some frequency — see e.g. Polonio, pp. 58-9, § 50. Polonio, in her introductory remarks, believes that the Venetians may have made extra use of Lamberto di Sambuceto because they temporarily lacked enough notaries of their own; but in any case merchants of Catalonia, Provence, Sicily and elsewhere made considerable use of his services. Lamberto di Sambuceto worked earlier in the Genoese Black Sea colonies; some of his contracts survive, and there too occasional references to Anconitan merchants can be found. M. Balard, *Gênes et l'Outre-Mer*, 1. *Les Actes de Caffa du notaire Lamberto di Sambuceto, 1289-1290*, Documents et recherches sur l'économie des pays byzantins, islamiques et slaves 12 (Paris-The Hague, 1973), §§ 13, 38, 85, 258, 293, 320, 481, 514, 578, 583, 686.

XIII

Venetians at bay in the middle Adriatic, where it competed, often violently, for access to stocks of grain and other primary products. In the late thirteenth century the Anconitans probably began to divert surplus grain supplies from central and southern Italy to markets in the east, taking advantage of shortages in Cyprus, Armenia and — perhaps — in Syria before the Frankish collapse. The Anconitans certainly had interests in Apulia and its grain stocks. Surplus silver too — the profits from Adriatic trade, and particularly from penetration of Bosnia and the silver-bearing mountains of the Slav interior — must have provided capital for eastern ventures. These were clearly quite regular by 1300, for Barone de Galante and some of the Anconitan merchants were sailing back and forth between central Italy and Cyprus. No doubt the acquisition of substantial quantities of raw cotton enhanced Ancona's standing as a source of supply for those Levantine goods which were in demand in the industrial towns of north-eastern Italy and of Tuscany: the port could take good advantage of its geographical position. But Ancona did not possess or acquire the leverage, political and commercial, that the Venetians and Genoese enjoyed in the markets of the Levant, at least before the end of the fifteenth century [95].

Yet the limitations imposed by Venice were partially ignored or circumvented by 1300. In the period immediately

[95] J. Earle, « The commercial development of Ancona, 1479-1551, » *Economic History Review*, 2.22 (1969), 28-44; for a detailed bibliography see also Leonhard, *Die Seestadt Ancona*, who, however, has rather little to say about the Acre privilege or about the Cyprus trade of Ancona, (Leonhard, pp. 300-1, 328). It is a pleasure to thank David Jacoby of the Hebrew University of Jerusalem for his generosity in providing information about Cyprus and Lamberto di Sambuceto, and also for his hospitality during my stay in Jerusalem in 1983. This research was also made possible by the help of the Archivio Segreto Vaticano, the Biblioteca Vaticana, The British School at Rome and the National Library of Malta. The British Academy provided generous support. I am grateful to Jonathan Riley-Smith for valuable advice on the Latin Kingdom of Jerusalem.

after the grant of rights in the Holy Land by John of Arsur, the activation of Ancona's special status must have been almost impossible. The Genoese withdrawal from Acre and the Venetian treaty of 1264 together make it unlikely that Ancona ever managed to create a functioning quarter in Acre, or to trade intensively with the Latin Kingdom of Jerusalem. Equally, the trade of the Anconitans in Cyprus, though identifiable only after the fall of Acre, reveals their range of commercial interests and connections. The history of Ancona's rights in the east, before 1300, is, it seems, a story of aspirations, not achievements.

APPENDIX I

Privilege of 10 August 1257, issued at Acre in favour of the Commune of Ancona. Parchment. Original (chirograph).

National Library of Malta, Valletta. Records of the Order of Saint John, Arch. 5 (formerly 6), no. 55.

Previous edition: G. Paoli, *Codice diplomatico del sacro militare ordine gerosolimitano oggi di Malta*, 1 (Lucca, 1733), 157-61, no. 132. (= P).

Johan dybelin seignor darsur Conestable et bail dou Reaume de Jerusalem, par lassent et la volonte des homes lige de la Seignorie Cest a sauer Mesire Phelippe de Mont fort Seignor de Sur, et mesire Johan Laleman Seignor de Cesaire, et mesire Johan de Valencenes Sire de Cayphas, et mesire Jaque de la Mandelee, et mesire Tybaut de Bessan, et mesire Symon de Malembec, et mesire Balian Anteaume, et mesire Johan de Flori, et de plusors autres Homes de la dite Seignorie, et mesire Estiene de Sauvegni, Syndiques et procureor des chevaliers Homes de la Seignorie dou Reaume de Jerusalem, qui espe-cielment est ordene a ce, por eaus et por leur Successors, ou nom dou deuant dit Reaume ont veu et regarde la greignor utilite et le manifest profit dou dit Reaume, vindrent a tel Composition et Convention, et transaction, seur la franchise que les Anconitens demandoient. Ce est a sauer que mesire Johan de Guide, et mesire Bienuenu de Vidal, Syndiques pro-cureors, et actors, et speciaus messages dou Comun dancone, receueors et stipuleors de par leur Comun, et de par les Homes Singuliers de la Cite et dou destreit dancone. Ce est a sauer, que de toutes celles chose qui dreiture [a] deuront a la Chaene

que les anconitens ou Home dou destreit dancone auront achat-
tees en terre de Crestiens, dou leur propre, que il mettront a
Acre per mer, les baillis de[b] la chaene dacre requerront et
receuront deaus un besans dentree per Centenal et non plus.
Et de toutes les choses qui dreitures deuront a la chaene que
il trarront dacre per mer, receuront et prendront dyaus les
deuant dit baillis, un besans dissue per Centenal et non plus.
Et tout le seur plus que il solent paier ala chaene seit quite
et absolu perpetuelment. Et de toutes les choses remdables que
il apporteront de les terres de paienisme, ou achatteront en
les terres de paienisme, et les mettront per mer en acre ou
vendront ou alieneront en acre, les baillis de la chaene recouront
deaus dreiture dentree enterinement ensi coment sont a Costume a paier gens remdables. Et se il ne les vendissent ou
alienassent, et les trahissent dehors dacre, si perseront enterinement la dreiture au bailli de la chaene alissue itel Coment
sont a Costume de paier gens remdables. Se est a sauer que
seur zo que il auront paie dentree si compliront enterinement
la dreiture delissue. Et celui Home des Anconitens qui fran-
chira auec de gens remdables, il perdra sa franchise a tout
jors et son auer. Et que de toutes manieres les[c] querelles,
que len demande a les Anconitens en quei iustises nasierent
quelles se puissent et doient juger et determiner par leur
consele. Et se aucun valeur que les Consels les menast per
lusage de la terre, que il soient tenu dou faire. Et que toutes
manieres danconitens, qui se sont franchi jusques au jor duy
per Jeneueis ou per pisans, ou per Venetiens, que il reuiegnent
a la Seignorie, et seient en la Condition des autres anconitans.
Et se il y aueit aucun des anconitans qui ne fust Habitans a
ancone, ou el destreit dancone, et il ne vousist estre en cest
Condition, que ceaus dancone sont tenus de bannirles en cors
et en aueir. Et que il puissent auer Consels, et placier, et
baston. Et la Seignorie leur baillera et donra ades ou Jardin
des Jeneueis une piece de Terre juste le murs de la ville pres
a la mer, a edifier une Iglise por eaus, et un palais por leur
Comun, et une place ausi por eaus herbergier en tel maniere
que desus la mer ne puissent edifier Maisons mais mettre et
tenir la les leur choses. Et se la Seignorie ne leur poet ce doner
les Anconitens achatteront les Hosteaus de Sire Johan Grip, et
de Sire Jop et de Sire Jorge, et la Seignorie leur donra a des
la place, et la terre qui est entre ces hosteaus et la mer por
eaus Herbergier. Et tout les raisons que la Seignorie a en
deuant dit hosteaus, Et que les anconitens puissent charger et
descharger leur choses pres de ceaus hosteaus et metre et
traire per la porte dou Seignor la plus prochaine. Et se les

anconitens achatteient autres Hosteaus, ou terre por eaus herbergier, la Seignorie leur donra la raison que elle a, en celle
terre, et que il puissent pres dicele terre charger et descharger
les leur choses si com il est dit de sus que il poeient faire en
lautre place. Et les anconitens aideront la Seignorie dou Reaume
de Jerusalem Contre toutes gens de Cinquante Homes armes
de fer au meins, au beisoing de la dite Seignorie quant elle
aura guerre et Contens contre aucune maniere de Gens por
le fait de la dite Seignorie en acre et au port [d] dacre, per
entel mainiere que cil qui iront per mer aient la viande de la
Seignorie et non autre chose. Et ces Cinquante Homes sont
tenus les Anconitens dauer de ceste premiere feste de tous
sains qui vient en dous ans en auant, au besoing de la dite
Seignorie, si com il est de sus dit. Et se celui qui sereit par
les anconitens a acre ne baillast les dit Cinquante homes au
besoing de la Seignorie que celui qui sera seur le fait de la
Seignorie puisse retenir les dit Cinquante Homes a leur sous
seur les biens des anconitans. Et par de sus ce, tout les autres
anconitans qui seront en acre, tant com il seront en acre, sont
tenus dayder la Seignorie en la maniere, quil est de sus dite
de tous luer [e] poeir. Et la Seignorie est tenue dayder et garder
les Homes dancone Contre toutes gens a son poeir si com les
autres Homes de la dite Seignorie. Et se les anconitens rece-
veient damage des enemis de la Seignorie por achaison dou
fait dela Seignorie, la Seignorie est tenue deaus faire amender
le damage, si come le sien propre dicele gent qui le damage
aureit fait, seur les biens que les dits enemis auroient au jor
en acre sans deslay et sans fraude. Et se la Seignorie faseit
pais ou trieue ou fin a ses enemis elle est tenue de metre en
la fin et en la pais, et en la trieue les Anconitens si come se
meismes. Et toutes ces choses sont promises a tenir de lune
partie a lautre, fermes et estables et saint per leur Sagrement
et seur peine de lune partie a lautre de dis Milia besans. la
quele peine paiee, ou non, toutes les deuant dites choses seient
tenues fermes et estables perpetuelment. Ancores ont promis
et sont tenus les deuant dit procureors dou Comun dancone
que il feront et cureront en tel maniere que la poeste et les
Conseilliers dou Comun dancone, prometteront et jureront de
garder et mantenir la deuant dite Composition tout en la maniere de sus deuisee. Et de zo feront il faire publique instrument seelle dou Seel dou Comun dancone et Conferme de sos-
cription de plusors Notaire publique. Et cet instrument man-
deront et feront doner au bail dou Reaume de Jerusalem de
dens la tous sains prochaine qui est a venir en dous ans. Et
ancores feront il chasqun an jurer leur poeste et leur Conseille

dancone de garder et mantenir ceste Composition. Et feront mettre en leur statut senz remuer que ensi deient jurer. Et ensement deuent jurer les Consels et les Conseilliers se il les auront, qui seront par temporals en acre par le Comun dancone. Et les Syndiques dou bail et des cheualiers de la Seignorie jurera ensement chasqun an que bail se remuera, de garder et mantenir ceste Composition.

Haec acta sunt in Accon. Coram dominis Ansaldo Zeba, Johanne Castanea, Guillelmo Guercio, Guillelmo Lamfranci [f] Spinole, Lamfranco [f] de Carmadino, et Antonio de Grimaldi Januensibus; domino Egidio milite de Cayphas, et domino Filippo de Coxi milite, Johanne Boiamontis [g], Dago dauid, Nicola antonis Maurj, Petro Saluatici, et Nicola Comitis Anconitanis testibus rogatis. Dominice Incarnationis anno Millesimo Ducentesimo Quinquagesimo Septimo. Indictione Quintadecima, Die decima Mensis Augusti. Et nous dessus nomez [h] Bail dou Reaume de Jerusalem Seignor de Sur Seignor de Cesaire, Johan de Valencenes, Jaque de la Mandelea, Tyebaut de bessan, Symon de Malembec, Balian Antiaume, et Estiene de Sauuegnj, a greignor se et fermete, y auom mis nos seels de cire pendant. Et en sont feit.ij. enstrument parti per a. b. c. cestui a les Anconitans et lautre a le [...]

Ego Aliottus Uguiccionis Imperiali auctoritate Judex et Notarius publicus Interfui et predicta omnia rogatus fideliter seu bene in publicam formam redegi.

[a] P: dretture
[b] P: &
[c] P: de
[d] P: por
[e] Sic in MS. P: leur
[f] P: Lan-
[g] P: Roiamontis.
[h] P: nomnes

Other minor errors in P have not been listed; they are many, though not significant.

APPENDIX II:

COMMENDA CONTRACTS FROM FAMAGUSTA, 2 OCTOBER - 9 OCTOBER, 1301.

[Source: Pavoni, *Lamberto di Sambuceto*, § 181 - 222; see note 64 *supra*].

PAVONI No.	DATE	SOCIUS STANS	SOCIUS NEGOCIANS	VALUE	GOODS	SHIP-OWNER	ROUTE
181	2 Oct.	Georgius, Savonese (Genoa)	Flancolinus qd. Thome (Ancona)	450 b.a.	cotton (3 bales)	[Raynaldus de Salvaigo (Fermo)]	Pula
182	»	Falagius de Beleen, b.F.	Linardus Salembene (Ancona) Dominicus Symonis (Ancona)	1701 b.a.	cotton (10 bales)	[Barone Pellegrini de Galante]	[Ancona]
183	»	»	Symon Rubeus (Genoa)	2868 b.a.	cotton (20 bales)	[? »]	[— »]
184	"2 Sept." [probably error for 2 Oct.]	Michael de Robino	Octobonus Nizola (Genoa?)	300 b.a. in societate	Mongol slaves	?	?

— 565 —

PAVONI No.	DATE	SOCIUS STANS	SOCIUS NEGOCIANS	VALUE	GOODS	SHIP-OWNER	ROUTE
185	3 Oct.	Georgius Tiratira, h.F.	Lipus de Petro (Ancona)	863 b.a. 9 car.	cotton (6 bales)	Raynaldus de Salvaigo (Fermo)	Pula
186	»	Ansaldus de Sexto (Genoa)	»	250 b.s.	cotton (5 bales)	[»]	[»]
187	2 Oct.	Iacobus de Solario	Guillelmus de Bisacia, Savonese (Genoa)	832½ b.a.	scarlet cloth	?	Armenia
188	5 Oct.	Ansaldus de Sexto (Genoa)	Baldoynus Benevenuti (Ancona)	265½ b.s.	cotton (6 bales)	Barone de Galante (Ancona)	Ancona
192	7 Oct.	Cosma de Lezia	Symon Dimitri de Lezia, h.F.	5600 b.a.	cotton	»	»
193	7 Oct.	Cosma de Lezia and brother Nicolinus	Symon filius Iosepe de Lezia, b.F.	5215 b.a.	cotton	»	»
194	»	Georgius de Lezia	Symon Dimitri de Lezia, h.F.	2225 b.a.	cotton	»	»
195	»	Costa de Antiochia	»	1500 b.a.	cotton	»	»

PAVONI No.	DATE	SOCIUS STANS	SOCIUS NEGOCIANS	VALUE	GOODS	SHIP-OWNER	ROUTE
196	»	»	Symon filius Iosepe de Lezia	2000 b.a.	cotton	»	»
197	»	Cosma de Lezia	Symon de magistro Nicolao (Ancona)	100 b.a.	[appointment of procurator]	»	»
198	»	Manuel, filius Bechie de Antiochia	Symon filius Iosepe de Lezia	1700 b.a.	cotton	»	»
199	»	Cosma de Lezia	Thomas de Rogerio (Ancona)	2100 b.a.	cotton	»	»
200	»	Damianus de Lezia	»	1050 b.a.	cotton	»	»
202	»	»	Symon filius Iosepe de Lezia	4650 b.a.	cotton	»	»
203	»	»	Iacobus speciarius b.F.	2662 b.s.	cotton	Marinus de Aragusia (Dubrovnik) & Nicolas Sten (Venice?)	Venice
204	»	Cosma de Lezia	»	3568¼ b.a.	cotton	»	»
205	»	Georgius de Lezia	»	117 b.s.	cotton	»	»

PAVONI No.	DATE	SOCIUS STANS	SOCIUS NEGOCIANS	VALUE	GOODS	SHIP-OWNER	ROUTE
206	»	Symon Mosturii, scribe Templi (via Costa de Lezia)	»	506 b.s. 10 car.	cotton	»	»
207	»	Bee Aiupo de Tripoli	»	295 b.s.	cotton	»	»
208	»	Thomas Megibel de Lezia, b.F. (via Costa de Lezia)	Symon filius Iosepe de Lezia	2004 b.a.	cotton	Barone de Galante (Ancona)	Ancona
210	»	Georgius filius Michaelis de Lezia	Michelinus filius qd. Theodori de Lezia	1500 b.a.	cotton	Marinus de Aragusia (Dubrovnik)	Venice
211	»	Damianus de Lezia	»	700 b.a.	cotton	»	»
212	»	Cosma de Lezia	»	800 b.a.	cotton	»	»
213	»	Costa de Antiochia	»	2500 b.a.	cotton	»	»
214	»	Manuel, filius Bechie de Antiochia	»	2000 b.a.	cotton	»	»
215	»	Symon Iosepe de Lezia	»	1100 b.a.	cotton	»	»

PAVONI No.	DATE	SOCIUS STANS	SOCIUS NEGOCIANS	VALUE	GOODS	SHIP-OWNER	ROUTE
216	»	Saonus filius Manssor b.F.	Symon de Iosepe de Lezia [error for Michelinus de Lezia? Cf. § 193, 196, 215]	1336 b.a.	cotton	»	»
218	8 Oct.	Guido de Bando	Obertus de Rizardus (Pisa)	4676 b.a. 9 car.	cotton (28 bales)	»	»
219	»	Guzius de Campo (via Guide de Bando)	»	1084 b.a. 6 car.	(7 bales and one mattress)	»	»
220	9 Oct.	16 investors in Ancona	Leonarduzius de Dominico (Ancona)	1988 or 1991 b.s.	cotton, sugar, pepper, incense, buckram, gold	Barone de Galante (Ancona)	Ancona
221	»	6 investors in Ancona	Lipus de Egidia (Ancona)	1871 b.s.	cotton, sugar, pepper, incense, buckram, gold	»	»
222	»	8 investors in Ancona	Leonardus Salembene (Ancona)	£ 3500 of Ancona	cotton, sugar, buckram, coloquinta, gold-wire	»	»

XIII

Key:

b.a.	white besants
b.F.	burgensis Famagoste
b.s.	Saracen gold besants
car.	carats
h.F.	habitator Famagoste
qd	quondam

Place of origin of western merchants is indicated in brackets after name. [ ] indicates that the route and/or ship can be identified from later contracts mentioning the same *socius negocians*; [?] indicates that a route can be suggested, but not certainly identified.

XIV

NARBONNE, THE LANDS OF THE CROWN OF ARAGON, AND THE LEVANT TRADE 1187-1400

I

Though never part of the Crown of Aragon, Narbonne depended to an important degree on the maintenance of close economic ties with neighbours that did knowledge as lord the king of Aragon or king of Majorca. Montpellier to the east offered additional port facilities at Lattes, further sources of capital of investment, and even well-born settlers who became consuls of Narbonne : Pierre Raymond de Montpellier was five times consul of the *cité* of Narbonne ; his brother Guillaume Raymond twice consul, between 1242 and 1267.[1] Closer still, Perpignan to the west offered the port of Collioure, while the produce of Roussillon, Cerdagne and the hinterland of Languedoc was channelled through Narbonne (as also its neighbours), on its way into the Mediterranean.[2] Narbonnais merchants made use of shippers still further afield, too : there were close partnerships with shipping magnates of Marseilles in the fourteenth century, as also with Catalans of Barcelona and elsewhere.[3] Merchants from this wide area of the Mediterranean showed keen interest in the dyed cloths of Narbonne ; indeed, when Francesco Balducci Pegolotti speaks of Narbonne in the *Pratica della Mercatura*, it is generally of the city's cloths rather than its merchants.[4]

It will be argued here that the striking characteristic of Narbonne's relationship with the trading cities of Catalonia, Languedoc and Provence is its collaborative nature : no single southern French city was able to establish clear predominance in the trade between this region and the central or eastern Mediterranean, though of course within the western Mediterranean the balance was more and more weighted in favour of the Catalans. Montpellier certainly thrust itself forward as natural leader, claiming, for instance, a special status in the organisation of the trade to the north, to Champagne.[5] Such claims were resisted by the city's partners in southern France, and were not matched in the long-distance maritime trade of Montpellier. But it will also be argued that Narbonne's successes in Mediterranean trade owed much to the tutelage of Montpellier, Marseilles and other trading centres. It has been said that Montpellier was « tutor » to Barcelona ; arguably the same can be said for Montpellier's relations with Narbonne too.[6]

There is good evidence for the activities of Narbonnais merchants in the Levant trade to Cyprus, Armenia, Syria and Egypt, that speaks also for other merchants from the region Provence-Languedoc-Catalonia : the Genoese notarial registers of Lamberto di Sambuceto, recently edited by Balard, Polonio and Pavoni, provide ample data for the years around 1300[7]; from the late fourteenth century survive the accounts of Jacme Olivier, merchant of Narbonne, and much barely tapped information about his trading colleagues.[8] It is the period that encompasses the rise to commercial prominence of Narbonne and also its economic dilapidation ; a period in which the Levant trade, not simply in Narbonnais cloths, seems to play an especially important role in the city's maritime commerce. Much less plentiful is evidence for a Levant trade out of Narbonne in the twelfth and thirteenth centuries. A few Narbonnais merchants appear in Blancard's collection of commercial documents from Marseilles ; but references to other southern French merchants are much more common. Montpellier is wellrepresented.[9] Nor is this merely an *argumentum e silentio.* At the end of the twelfth century Narbonne was not counted as one of the southern French towns with commercial ties to the Levant. For the privilege of 1187, issued at Tyre by Conrad of Montferrat in favour of Provençal merchants, mentions Saint-Gilles, Montpellier, Nîmes and also Barcelona, as well as *'omnibus, qui predictorum comunium nomine censentur';* there is no specific mention of Narbonne.[10] Benjamin of Tudela, writing perhaps twenty years earlier, speaks with approval of the special status of the Jews of Narbonne, but says nothing about the city's trade ; however, when he comes to Montpellier, he does lay stress on commerce, but indicates – rightly, as Mayer's researches have shown – that Montpellier was still under Genoese and Pisan tutelage.[11] In the early thirteenth century it was Marseilles and Montpellier that continued to be taken as exemplars of Provençal trading centres, in privileges issued by Latin rulers in the east. King Henry I of Cyprus responded in 1236 to the pleas of 'Geraut Oliuer consele des Marseilles en Accre e Reymund de Conches'. The latter subsequently became Aragonese ambassador to the Mamluk sultan, in 1264 (one of his briefs was to look after the property of a Catalan merchant who had arrived in Alexandria on a ship of Narbonne, and had then died).[13] The Marseillais forged a large number of privileges for trade in the east, as Mayer has revealed; but the Narbonnais cannot be shown to have enjoyed privileges of their own, real or otherwise, before the fall of Acre in 1291. They must generally have traded under the umbrella of other patrons from Languedoc, Provence, Catalonia and also northern Italy. In the years around 1270 the consuls of Narbonne expressed an interest (not entirely positive) in the maintenance of the grain trade between southern France and the Kingdom of Jerusalem, at a time when local supplies in the Midi were dangerously short.[14] This was a traffic in which other southern French towns, not least Aigues-Mortes, were also much involved.

By contrast, in the early fourteenth century we do find the Narbonnais merchants recognised as a distinct group, still bound closely by ties of trade to their Provençal brethren, but possessing special rights of their own in what remained of the Latin east – the island of Cyprus. They had a consul and specific tax reductions. Pegolotti, who spent the years between 1324 and 1329 (if not longer) in Cyprus, states that, while the Genoese and Venetians were totally exempt from trade taxes at Famagusta, 'Pisani, nerbonesi, provenzali, catelani, anconetani' paid a 2% *commercium* on entering or leaving the port.[15] These years may well represent the high-water mark of Narbonne's Levant trade.

II

Each of the groups of merchants specified by Pegolotti is welldocumented in the cartularies of Lamberto di Sambuceto. Extensive use was made of this notary's services by merchants from Narbonne, Messina, Ancona and elsewhere, not merely for business with Genoese partners.[16] It is possible that the absence of their own notaries forced them to have recourse to a Genoese scribe instead. Indeed, even the Narbonnais consul in Famagusta made use of Lamberto: in March 1299 'Bernardus Faidir de Nerbona consul Nerbonensium' issued a quittance in favour of some Genoese galley-owners, members of the powerful Spinula clan. Bernardus Faidir was in partnership with Laurencius Deusaiuda and Bernardus Aimiel of Narbonne, as well as with a group of colleagues who had recently arrived in Cyprus on a ship from Marseilles.[17] Thus the close collaboration of merchants and shippers from the Provençal-speaking world is already made plain. The owner of the ship, Jofredus de Corvieria, was carrying a consignment of goods destined for the same Genoese galley-owners; very probably the goods were being transferred from the Marseillais vessel to the Genoese ones before they were run across to Armenia or another Levantine destination, for Cyprus had come to serve as interchange point for the trade-routes of the Latins in the eastern Mediterranean.[18] But Jofredus' ship not surprisingly carried many Marseillais merchants too, and on their behalf the consul of Marseillais merchants, Ugo Raymondus, issued a quittance of his own.[19] The separation of the Narbonne merchants from those of Marseilles, signified by the appearance of a separate consul for the Narbonne section of the Provençal trading community, is thus clear by 1299. The merchants of Montpellier also had their own consul: Petrus de Podio is seen acting on their behalf as consul for Cyprus and Armenia; in two documents of 23 June 1299 he receives the goods of a Montpellier merchant who had died in Turkish territory.[20]

The name of the Narbonne consul gives rise to difficulties. In 1300 « Bernardus Faidir » seems to be replaced by « Bernardus Faxit, *consul Nerbonensium in Famagosta* » ;[21] there is a record of a 'Bernardus Saxit', almost certainly a scribal error ;[22] the name Fayditus also surfaces, in the form of Raymondus Fayditus.[23] There is a Raymondus Faxit whose partners in December 1300 were partially the same as those of Raymondus Fayditus a little later.[24] This leads to the conclusion that 'Faidir', 'Faxit' and 'Fayditus' are versions of the same family name. But there was more than one Bernardus Faxit, too : a document of 5 December 1300 reveals that Bernardus Faxit de Nerbana, *mercator nerbonensis'*, had died on a trading visit to the east ; he was the son of a Bernardus Faxit, resident in Narbonne, and the father of a little Bernardus Faxit, also in Narbonne.[25] It is not clear where he died : possibly in Armenia, for a notarised version of his will could not be drawn up before his death, and had to be compiled in the presence of his trading colleagues, several of whom certainly spent time in Armenia. They then brought the existing text to Lamberto di Sambuceto, in order publicly to affirm its validity and to have it entered in his register. When he died he was expecting the arrival of goods from the west, with the merchant Bernardus Inardus, also of Narbonne, a close colleague who later became a procurator of his estate. Certainly, Faxit's links with Cyprus were close : he asked to be buried in the Dominican church at Famagusta, a request that may indicate there was no Narbonnais church in the town, even though possession of a community church was a desirable objective of foreign merchants. He left fairly small sums for the chanting of masses on behalf of his soul ; he gave donations to the churches of the Franks *(de Flancis masculis et Flancis feminabus)* in Cyprus. The legacies leave the impression of a merchant who was fairly but not outstandingly wealthy. He may have ceased being consul by the time of his death, since a document of 23 May 1299 is witnessed by Bernardus de Capodolao, *consul Nerbonensium.*[26] It should be added that the apparent youth of Bernardus Faxit is no impediment to the identification of the deceased merchant with the consul. He had very young children and a father still living, but consuls were by no means always men of very high political standing or wealth, as the experience of the Pisans in Acre reveals. Nor did they eschew oppotunities to trade in their own right.[27]

Nevertheless, there are signs he was able to gain access to royal courts; within the Narbonnais community in the Levant, he was quite possibly an eminent merchant, though that does not mean he could compete with Genoese and Venetian visitors to the island. On 30 May 1301 Faxit's procurator and executor *Bernardus Inardus* appointed two other Narbonne merchants, *Guillelmus Rebollus* and *Iohannes Gibertus,* to recover 2,797 Armenian dirhems *(daremi)* originally owed to Faxit by none other than the king of Armenia. This money had been made over to a third party, Laurencius Deusaiuda, another prominent merchant of this community.[28] By 2 October 1301 the money had been successfully recovered, and a quittance was issued; in fact it had been paid in the form of 754 white besants of Cyprus, the proceeds, in whole or in part, of a quantity of silver despatched by the Armenian ruler.[29] It seems that the king had provided the silver as a guarantee of his debt – the document speaks of *pignora argenti,* though what form the pawn took, bullion or coin or objets d'art, is not specified. A second document of the same date makes plain the complexity of the credit arrangements between King Hetoum of Armenia and the merchants of Narbonne. *Bernardus Inardus,* acting in conjunction with other merchants of Narbonne, takes note of a statement by *Laurentius Deusaiuda* that a sum of 600 dirhems remains owing to the king of Armenia from the estate of the late *Raymondus Fayditus.* The document may well be garbled here: it may make better sense to substitute the name Bernardus for Raymondus and to assume a scribal error.[30] The 600 dirhems formed, according to Laurentius, a *caparra,* or deposit, given by the king to *Raymondus* (i.e. *Bernardus Faxit)* or to *Bernardus Trencherius,* himself in the past a close colleague of *Bernardus Faxit.* When *Trencherius* next came before a notary, in Famagusta or elsewhere, he was to be invited to swear that the sum was still owing. On 1 December 1301 such an oath, or satisfaction in some other way, was obtained, for Lamberto di Sambuceto adds a note to his text that *dictus Laurencius iussit michi Lanberto de Sambuxeto, notario, dictum instrumentum debere cassari.*[31]

King Hetoum II of Armenia, a vassal of the Mongols, was a relative by marriage of the king of Cyprus ; and his obligations to his overlord included military service in Syria. He had troublesome brothers, and his political career thus constituted a delicate juggling act. His need for funds to prosecute his varied political interests is easy to perceive. But whether he saw the Narbonnais as a source of loans or as a source of desirable western goods it is impossible to say.[32]

Bernardus Faxit had interests in other parts of the Mediterranean, too. Cyprus had been intensively penetrated by Venetians, and it is not surprising that a Venetian merchant, Marino Segnolo, pressed claims against Faxit's estate. The executor, *Bernardus Inardus*, on 7 August 1301 declared himself ready to stay in Famagusta until the demands of the Venetian were settled by arbitration.[33] It appears Segnolo had already brought the case before the Castellan's court in Famagusta ; there is no mention of any attempt to involve or consult the consuls of the foreign communities, but disputes between merchants of different origins would normally have to be settled in a neutral court. In any case, *Bernardus Inardus* was too preoccupied with the affairs of *Bernardus Faxit* to be able to pursue his own commercial objectives outside Cyprus. On 7 June 1301 he had already appointed *Petrus Faber, Iohanes Gibertus* and *Iohanes de Salicata*, all of Narbonne, as agents for the recovery of sums owing from *Elia de Ferrandia de Martello* and *Guillelmus de Nulas de Caerci*, the latter probably a native of Cahors or of the surrounding region, Quercy.[34] These sums were to be sought for *specialiter in Candea, in Veneciis et in insula de Cretis*, or indeed anywhere else where his debtors may be. It is interesting to find that one of his witnesses was a Catalan, Borras Taliada de Barcellona. Although *Bernardus Inardus'* tranding activities (as opposed to his procuratorial activities) are poorly documented, it is possible he had relatives in Cyprus who were able to give their time to trade. *Bernardus Inardus* and the prominent Narbonne trader Iacobus Andrea witnessed an act on 6 July 1301, in which Raymundus de Cuzac of Narbonne acknowledged receipt of £50 worth of blanquettes of Narbonne, white woollen Narbonne cloths, as well as canvas and unprocessed cloth, all of which had been delivered to Iohanes Inardus of Narbonne on behalf of a businessman based back home in southern France.[35] This Iohanes also witnessed acts concerning *Bernardus Inardus*.[36] He appears as *Iohanes Isarnus* de Nerbona in an act of 27 September, 1301, making a loan, *gratis et amore* (a phrase of variable meaning !), worth £40 of Tours, to Peire *Gibertus* de Beerci, probably a native of Bercy.[37]

There are several Narbonnais who reappear again and again in Lamberto di Sambuceto's acts, mainly associates of *Bernardus Faxit* and of *Bernardus Inardus*. The are plenty more who only appear once as witnesses, so it is clear that the Narbonnais group was by no means confined to the circle of Faxit and *Inardus*.[38] *Bernardus Trencherius* and Peyre Amarre of Narbonne belonged to that circle, however. On 24 September 1300 they appointed procurators for the recovery of some cotton brought from Laiazzo (Ayas) in Armenia to Cyprus, but carried off by the Genoese Francesco Squarzaficio.[39] One of these procurators, Raymundus Deusaiuda, bears a familiar surname. Bernardus Trencherius possessed a large number of business partners, and worked closely with fellow-Narbonnais. On 7 December 1300 he issued a quittance in favour of Bernardus Bonushomo of Narbonne, who also appears elsewhere as a witness.[40] A similar picture emerges of *Bernardus de Quilano*.[41] More wide-ranging, perhaps, were the contacts of *Guillelmus Rebollus*; he has already appeared among the procurators of *Bernardus Inardus*, with links to Armenia.[42] He acted too as procurator for *Gerardus Aymaroni* of Narbonne for the recovery of sums in the hands of Guillelmus de Tiro, of Tyre, a draper now resident in Famagusta, and of *Belfaragius*, that is, Abulfaraj, de Jerusalem, another draper settled in Cyprus, as well as two other residents of Nicosia.[43] The arrival in Cyprus of refugees from the Latin states in Syria has been commented upon by historians.[44] *Guillelmus Rebollus* was also appointed procurator by a non-Narbonnais merchant: on 25 September 1301 *Poncius de Soiulis* of Montpellier turned to him as agent for the recovery of all sums owing.[45]

Other Narbonne merchants had close contact with Catalan business colleagues. On 14 February 1301 Iacobus Andreas of Narbonne acknowledged receipt of goods worth £800 of Barcelona, sent on the ship of *Guillelmus de Orto*. This sum was owed by Iacobus' relative *Bernardus Rassus* of Narbonne to a merchant of Barcelona, *Iacobus Carbonus*, who had provided *Rassus* with a sea-loan of 1966 2/3 besants of Acre, the old money of the Kingdom of Jerusalem, on 5 July 1300. Among the goods on board ship were seven bales of Châlons cloth, a favourite Catalan export, vermilion cloths of different types (possibly Narbonne products, given the importance of Narbonne in this industry), and forty-five *cantaria* of salted meat.[46] In other words, the Catalan had employed *Rassus* as his agent for the delivery of cloth and salted meat to Cyprus, sending him back to Languedoc or Catalonia the summer before; thence he despatched the required goods to his own agent in Famagusta. The close reliance on agents and procurators is by now in no way unusual; to travel in person with the promised goods was not necessary, given the business methods in general use by 1300.

The social standing of the Narbonne merchants in Cyprus was, in some cases at least, high. On 8 June 1301 *Petrus Capaneria* of Narbonne issued a quittance to a group of fellow-Narbonnais, including *Bernardus de Quilano*;[47] Petrus was acting on behalf of Guillelmus Vitalis and *Bartholomeus Taulerius*, the latter perhaps being a member of a prominent Narbonne family, some of whom had been sentenced for heresy and other crimes in the mid-thirteenth century.[48] The sum involved, 160 white besants, was not very large, but it was only part of a bigger partnership worth 600 besants. By comparison with the partnerships involving Anconitan, Venetian and Genoese merchants this and other Narbonnais investments in Cypriot trade cannot be described as particularly substantial. Even the debt of the king of Armenia was valued at only 754 besants.[49] The contrast between the Narbonne merchants and their richer rivals has wider implications, too. In 1301 we can see groups of Venetians and Anconitans filling round ships with vast amounts of raw cotton and other goods.[50] The Narbonnais were not in this league ; even Ancona, a city of second rank, had far heavier investments in the trade of Cyprus than did Narbonne. Partly, of course, this reflects industrial realities of the early fourteenth century : northern and central Italy drew cotton from the east for the textile industries, but southern France specialised in the production of woollen cloths ; thus there was no real need to buy vast quantities of unprocessed cotton in the east. This takes us again to Pegolotti's observations, stressing the market for Narbonne cloth in the east, at Constantinople, Satalia (alongside *pirpignani),* Famagusta and, presumably, in Laiazzo too.[51] Although it has been suggested that by the early fourtheenth century the terms *nerbonesi* and *pirpignani* were increasingly generic terms, applied to cloths of diverse origins, generally heavy woollens, it seems likely, to judge from the Cyprus documents, that merchants of Narbonne continued to play a major role in the export of such goods to the east.[52] The use by the Catalan *Iacobus Carbonus* of a Narbonnais merchant for the export both of linen of Châlons and of bright red cloth typical of southern France, is suggestive here.[53] But it is also plain that the Narbonnais relied at least in part on the shipping capacity of their neighbours, such as Marseilles, in the transport of luxury goods to the Levant. Within Cyprus they formed a distinct cricle, with consuls, intense intra-group relations and, perhaps, specialised functions as purveyors of cloth ; but their presence there was partly possible through the agency of more powerful neighbours, including Montpellier and Barcelona, with whose merchants they maintained regular business contacts.

III

The years around 1300 may mark the high point of Narbonne's Levant trade, even though it has been suggested here that the scale of that trade should not in any case be exaggerated. Whatever one's view of overall developments in the late medieval economy, it is difficult not to be impressed by the chorus of historians who, in ewamining the southern

French ports, have seen the period from the mid-fourteenth century as one of decline.[54] Baratier's studies of Marseilles indicat a weakening of the city's trading position during the fourteenth century, briefly relieved by a recovery in the years before 1400 ; during that period we also see Narbonnais merchants partnering the Marseillais on the routes to the east.[55] Speaking of Montpellier, Germain observed : « *Ce serait donc vers la limite chronologiquement indiquée par la fin du second tiers du XIVe siècle et le commencement du XVe qu'il conviendrait de placer la crise à l'issue de laquelle, sous la délétère influence des malheurs publics, s'est arrêtée la période ascendante de la vie commerciale de Montpellier.* »[56]

The ravages of the Great Companies, the policies of the Duke of Anjou in Languedoc, not to mention the interruption of important maritime trade routes, may all have had considerable impact on Montpellier's ability to sell its goods overseas.[57] Célestin Port, in what remains the only overview of Narbonne's commercial development, believed rather than Montpellier flourished in the mid-fourteenth century at the expense of Narbonne – « *c'était en effet, la vraie, la seule rivale de Narbonne* » ; he saw in the late fourteenth century a period of marked decadence in Narbonne's trade, identifying the expulsion of the Jews and the decay of the bed of the River Aude as vital factors also.[58]

What is clear is that Narbonne's « decadence » was not absolute ; the attempts to found a proper port at Leucate, though without firm outcome, indicate continuing vitality around 1400, as do references to Narbonnais consuls and merchants in Egypt, Syria and elsewhere. The consul of the Narbonnais in Alexandria was known as the 'official consule de Nerbonne et des pélerins', according to Simon of Saarbrucken, who was there in 1395 ; pilgrims were obliged to reside there and in no other Latin fondouk.[59] This in itself may imply that the Narbonnais did not have sufficient manpower to make full use of a warehouse and inn granted to them by the Mamluk sultan. Yet it is also plain that there were western products, brought from Narbonne to Egypt and Syria, which were in healthy demand out east ; and that the Narbonnais, as before, were closely partnered in this trade by colleagues from Marseilles, Montpellier and Perpignan. Their presence in Rhodes around 1350 is well-documented, sharing the provision of banking services to the Knights of St John with colleagues from Montpellier.[60] The book of accounts of Jacme Olivier, a Narbonnais merchant of the late fourteenth century, provides precious information on this score, and also overlaps substantially with a series of charters analysed by Baratier, concerning the Levant trade of Marseilles in the same years.

In May 1381 Jacme Olivier sent goods to Alexandria on a ship of Narbonne. He loaded on this vessel twenty-four cloths, bound in three bales, and valued at 240 Francs ; he then added further bales of cloth in later months.[61] The ship was to sail from Cap Leucate under the command of G. Bertran. He received in return for his overseas trips ginger from Alexandria and, from a voyage to the Byzantine empire, raw cotton.[62] In 1382 he sent a variety of cloths, bound in twelve bales, *en lo vyage de Barut e d'Alysandry, am la nau dels senhos de Narbona et de Monppelyer;* but the ship was to leave from the shore of neither city : *partyt del port de Masela,* that is, Marseilles.[63] The account book specifies the colour of each cloth in each bale, and states that the value per piece was 11 3/4 florins, making a total of 928 1/4, or £928. 5. 0.[64] But because of the distance to Marseilles, sums had to be counted for portage from Narbonne to Aigues-Mortes and thence to Marseilles ; three bales were to come from Perpignan, and their despatch alone would cost 9 Francs 5 grossi 3 denarii, or £11. 13. 4.[65] The next year Jacme Olivier turned his interest towards Damascus, too, whence he imported pepper,[66] as also to Romania *am la nau dels senhos de Montpey-lier.*[67] But the prime concern remained Alexandria, and here again it was a ship of Narbonne, setting out from Leucate under Bertomieu Teuleyra and Jacme Vydal de Crastas, that he utilised ;[68] the name Teuleyra has already been encountered in the Cypriot documents of around 13000, and this figure seems to have been a regular associate of Jacme Olivier. Part of his own accounts survive, indicating that he hired out ship space to Olivier for the transport of cloth and honey :

Moss s. Jac. Holyvyer deu per rolyt de 88 draps, a 11 g° per drap, monta : 60 li. 10 s.
It. pus deu per rolyt de 45 q. mel :22 li. 10 s.[69]

On this enterprise Berthomieu Teuleyra was partnered by the prominent Narbonnais Jacme Baron, an association that indicates too the high standing of Jacme Olivier among the merchants of Narbonne.[70] Teuleyra acted again on Jacme Olivier's behalf in 1384, when he carried nineteen 'draps de Narbona' at 9 florins 7 grossi the piece, and 79 quintals 50 li. of honey to Alexandria. Here too Jacme Baron was a partner of Jacme Olivier.[71] In 1385 it was honey – fifteen jars, or sixteen quintals – and cash that were sent by Olivier to Alexandria, on the ship of P. Jaufren, which *partic del port d'Aygas Mortas.*[72] The reference to cash is a reminder that the west was in deficit in its Levant trade, and had to balance its payments by the export of coin and bullion : indeed, this may have been a particularly dfficult period in this respect, marked by bullion shortages.[73] Thus the ability of the Narbonnais merchants to substitute their own textiles and the honey of Languedoc for cash payments, at least on occasion, is impressive tribute to their home region's economic strength even at this period.

The same year twelve bales of cloth, containing seventy-six cloths, were sent to Damascus, on the ship *Sant Johan e Ssanta Magdallena,* bound (presumably) for Beirut, and to be loaded in Aigues-Mortes. The cargo was valuable indeed : the total, including cost of packing and sending to Aigues-Mortes, taxes at the French port and loading on board, came to £678. 14.2.[74] In 1386 Jacme Olivier settled bills with Bertomieu Teuleyra for imported ginger and other costs.[75] He then despatched to Alexandria 36 jars (41 1/2 quintals) of honey, cloths and a bill of exchange worth £106 ; these were to be carried on a vessel that would set out from Collioure, the port of Perpignan, but put in at Leucate also.[76] A long section of accounts gives the proceeds of sales of spices brought from Damascus and Alexandria – pepper, ginger, cinnamon – some of which were transported to Montpellier by Jacme Baron, apparently for sale there ;[77] we also find recorded in 1387 the sale of coarse cloths at Montpellier *(baracans),* apparently imported from the east, but individually of rather low value compared to the cloths of Narbonne sent out to the east – £2 or so a piece.[78]

In 1387 Bertomieu Teulyer or Teuleyra and Jacme Baron themselves arranged to travel east from Leucate to a combination of destinations : Rhodes, Alexandria and Beirut. Twelve bales, containing 88 1/2 cloths were to be sent out, at 8 Francs a piece, but there was also a consignment of linen cloth of Châlons, used to wrap the bales *(per anvoya),* but worth 3 florins a piece. Then there were 42 jars of honey (47 quintals 5 1/2 li). The value of this consignment was considerable : £925. 4. 3., in which Jacme Carquasona (by origin not from Carcasonne but Montpellier) placed over £400 and Jacme Baron £200.[79] But in addition Jacme Olivier sent goods east on a second ship, *la nau de Monpeylier,* carrying honey (some in partnership with Simonet Bardocho, of Montpellier) ; the document was based on a notarial record of 'P. Rostan, notary d'Ayguas Mortas', so that it seems this ship was to depart from that port.[80]

1388 saw no relaxation of involvement in the east. Rhodes and Beirut were to be visited by the ship of En P. Terrassa of Collieure, *lacal es a Coplieure... e partit del port de Coplieure,* carrying eight bales of Jacme Olivier's cloth, plus miscellaneous textiles, together worth £400.[81] As for Alexandria, that was to be served not by a ship of Perpignan but by one of Montpellier : once again Jacme Baron was to be aboard, and Beirut was also to be visited.[82] There seems then to be a gap in the record until 1391, when £224 worth of cloths, plus four blanquettes at £10 each, were sent to Alexandria and Beirut, but the ship's point of departure is not indicated.

What can be deduced from Jacme Olivier's accounts ? There are some very striking features : the fact that his trading interests overseas are heavily concentrated on Egypt and Syria ; his close links to shippers and merchants from Perpignan, Montpellier and Marseilles ;[84] but also his heavy involvement in local trade – in the carriage of wheat, barley and wool from the Languedoc countryside (where he had agents of his own) to Narbonne.[85] He possessed a *lybre de la mel,* a separate account book for his honey stocks ;[86] and, as has been seen, honey, almost certainly local in origin, was a major commodity in his trade to the east. The honey of Languedoc had indeed a good reputation ; Célestin Port quotes a medieval poem :

> *Nule part n'ot remes mel meillour*
> *Fors à Noirbonne.*[87]

But Jacme Olivier was also involved in the supply of raw wool to the looms of Narbonne ; and they were the great money-spinners in the Levant trade – blanquettes, vermilion, blue and green cloths. A laisser-passer from the customs-house of Perpignan, published by Blanc, indicates Jacme Olivers's interest in the raw wool trade : *Leysatz pasar per la mar que dels iij dr. per li. an Jac. Olivier de Narbona que as pagat asi a Perpenya, una saqua en que a vint et seys pugesals de lana d'Arago migana, costa seys li. deta s. ; a pagat lo dret.*[88] Thus wool was being imported from the Aragonese highlands, via the Aragonese possession of Perpignan, to Narbonne in order to help sustain the city's cloth industry in the difficult economic climate of the late fourteenth century. An account of Jacme Carquasona, who originated from Montpellier, also refers to sales of sacks of wool to Jacme Olivier.[89]

How typical was Jacme Olivier ? Ashtor, seeking to identify southern French merchants in Alexandria around 1400, found two Narbonnais there in that year, one in 1401, three in 1402 ; for Montpellier his figures are 1, 3, 3 and for Marseilles 4, 7, 2.[90] But clearly this is to rely on very fragmentary references. He points to the presence of Narbonne cloth not merely in Olivier's consignments, but in those of Bartolomeo Bera, who brought these textiles, plus honey, on a Genoese ship in 1398-9.[91] Taken together with evidence for the activities of merchants from Perpignan, Montpellier, Marseilles and Nîmes, the signs become clear that the towns of what is now southern France were still quite active in Alexandrian trade in the 1380s and 1390s. But the most important evidence for the wider context of Jacme Olivier's trading activities comes from Marseilles ; there is no need to repeat the arguments of E. Baratier in this respect.[92] He points out how Marseilles took advantage of the strife between Genoa and Venice to revew its Alexandria traffic in 1379 ; although soon subject to disruption, as a result of the Neapolitan ambitions of the dukes of Anjou, which diverted the city's ships to other uses, a Levant trade involving Marseilles continued under the aegis of shippers from Narbonne and Montpellier. Baratier cites notarial acts of

Marseilles that record the passage of Narbonnais ships ; often on their return from the Levant they would call at Marseilles even before Leucate. Bertomieu Teuleyra and his ship *St Jean-Baptiste et Ste Marie Madeleine* appear in the Marseillais record in 1380, 1382, and (under other patrons, it seems) 1383 and 1385, when it appears also in Jacme Olivier's accounts. The 1383 passage was accomplished under the direction of Pierre de Puysec, by origin Narbonnais, but now a resident of Montpellier. Another shipper, Guillaume Pons of Barcelona, may have originated in Narbonne ; he travelled from Aigues-Mortes to Rhodes and Alexandria in September, 1388. But according to Baratier the last passage of a ship of Narbonne to the Levant in the fourteenth century is that of the *Ste Catherine,* one of the owners being Jacme Olivier himself ; Rhodes and Alexandria were to be the destinations. It carried coral (the produce of Marseillais fishing off Sardinia) and cloths. Indeed, the Marseilles merchants often loaded coral on these boats, whether they came from Narbonne, Montpellier or Catalonia ; it was their specialised export, rather as honey was Narbonne's. The personnel on board also reflects the mixed character of these sailings : Bérenguer Gniolon of Nîmes, factor of Arnaud Raynaud of Montpellier, was to be found on Bertomieu Teuleyra's ship *St. Jean-Baptiste et Ste Marie Madeleine,* bound for Beirut in 1380 ; on board was coral, as well, no doubt, as honey and cloths sent by Jacme Olivier and his peers (Olivier's accounts only begin in 1381, so this is mere guesswork). The same year the *Ste Marie* of Narbonne carried to Alexandria the Valencian factor of merchants from Avignon and Barcelona, as well as merchants of Narbonne ; in 1403 merchants of Montpellier and Narbonne travelled to Rhodes and Alexandria on the nef *St. Jacques* of Marseilles. The cargo included French and Languedocien cloths, as well as honey. The *St. Esprit* of Narbonne, of 1386, had as patron a shipper from Collioure near Perpignan ; it set out from Leucate but was robbed by the pirate fleet of Guillem Ramon de Moncada, Sicilian nobleman, near the coast of Crete ; restitution was eventually obtained at the Aragonese court.[93]

The intention of presenting these examples is simply to reiterate Baratier's point : « *Ainsi s'affirme la collaboration toujours plus étroite qui unit en cette fin du XIVe siècle les commerçants de Marseille, de Montpellier et de Narbonne* »[94] He points to the way merchants would divide their cargoes between ships departing from (say) Leucate, Aigues-Mortes and Marseilles to guard against loss at sea. This argument can be pressed further : the situation visible in the 1380s and 1390s was not entirely new. The long-distance trade of the Provençal and Languedocien merchants was characterised by similar interdependence far earlier. The blanket privileges granted to Marseilles, Montpellier and all other *provinciales* in the Latin east ; the mixing of commercial interests in Cyprus around 1300, where Catalans and

Montpellierains, as well as Marseillais, acted as shippers and trading partners for the merchants of Narbonne; the links between Jacme Olivier and colleagues in Perpignan, Montpellier and elsewhere, all serve to show that this interdependence was a continuous feature of Languedoc's Levant trade. It would be wrong, then, to be misled by the occasional reference to Narbonne's separate consuls and fondouks in the east. Sometimes, as Pegolotti seems to say, the consuls may have negotiated tax reductions specifically for the Narbonnais, but in fact such reductions, at least in Cyprus, were no greater than those gained by the Anconitans, Catalans or indeed Provençaux as a whole. Indeed, it cannot always have been plain who was a Narbonnais, given the immigration of other southerners into Narbonne, and the use by merchants of Narbonne of partnerships with other traders from the same region.

The Levant trade of Narbonne thus seems to cross the political boundaries dividing Perpignan and (until 1349) Montpellier from Narbonne, or (after 1349) Montpellier and Narbonne from Perpignan. Nor is this picture confined to the east Mediterranean trade of Narbonne. On 29 May 1309 Bernard Tankredi of Narbonne exported 200 salme of wheat from Palermo (or rather Agrigento); but his partner was Raymond Riccardi of Montpellier. The wheat was to be loaded on a Majorcan ship bound for Cagliari in Sardinia and Aigues-Mortes.[95] Henri Bresc's brief study of Narbonne merchants in Sicily refers again and again to such partnerships: relations between Narbonnais and merchants of Perpignan, Montpellier and elsewhere.[96] He is no doubt right to link the presence of Languedoc merchants in Sicily to the existence of an active southern French Levant trade, too, which passed the island; and his observation of a lessening of the Occitan presence around 1350 fits well enough with the argument that the southern French merchants had passed their peak by then.[97]

To place the argument in an Aragonese context: the overseas trade of Montpellier cannot be disentangled from that of Narbonne and other towns in the region without doing violence to the evidence. The same goes for Perpignan. Germain's *Histoire du commerce de Montpellier* and Port's *Essai sur l'histoire du commerce maritime de Narbonne* in a sense concern a single subject, to a much greater degree than could be said of a comparable history of the Italian maritime republics. Collaboration surpassed competition.

NOTES

1) R.W. Emery, *Heresy and Inquisition in Narbonne* (New York, 1941), 28.

2) Célestin Port, *Essai sur l'histoire du commerce maritime de Narbonne* (Paris, 1854), 72-9. There are even reports that Narbonne functioned for a time as commercial intermediary between England and Egypt : W. Heyd, *Histoire du Commerce du Levant*, transl. F. Raynaud, 2 vol. (Leipzig, 1885-6), I. 422n2, citing information from thirteenth-century Arabic sources. Goods are said to have been sent via Bordeaux and Aquitaine (then under English overlordship) across Languedoc to the sea via Narbonne.

3) E. Baratier, *Histoire du commerce de Marseille*, publiée par la Chambre de Commerce de Marseille sous la direction de Gaston Rambert, vol. II (Paris, 1951), 220-4, 229-35 ; E. Baratier, 'Marseille et Narbonne au XIVᵉ siècle d'après les sources marseillaises', *Narbonne : archéologie et Histoire*. Narbonne au moyen-âge (XIVᵉ Congrès organisé par la Fédération historique du Languedoc méditerranéen et du Roussillon, Montpellier, 1973), 85-92. For general accounts see C.-E. Dufourcq, *La vie quotidienne dans les ports méditerranéens au moyen âge* (Paris, 1975), 14, 21-2 and passim ; and (more briefly) M. and M. Lacave, *Bourgeois et marchands en Provence et Languedoc* (Avignon, 1977).

4) Francesco Balducci Pegolotti, *La Practica della Mercatura*, ed. A. Evans (Cambridge, Mass., 1936), 37, 55, 58, 79, 84, 109, 111, 113, 167, 180, 204.

5) A. Germain, *Histoire du commerce de Montpellier, antérieurement à l'ouverture du port de Cette*, 2 vol. (Montpellier, 1861), I. 201-4 (documents of 1246).

6) J.L. Shneidman, *The rise of the Aragonese-Catalan empire, 1200-1350*, 2 vol. (New York), II 381 – a worthwhile point in what is otherwise a very disappointing work.

7) M. Balard, Notai genovesi in Oltremare. Atti rogati a Cipro da Lamberto di Sambuceto *(11 Octobre 1296-23 Giugno 1299)*, (Collana storica di fonti e studi, XXXIX, Genoa, 1983) ; V. Polonio, Notai genovesi in Oltremare. *Atti rogati a Cipro da Lamberto di Sambuceto (3 Luglio 1300 – 3 Agosto 1301)*, (Collana storica di fonti e studi, XXXI, Genoa, 1982) ; R. Pavoni, Notai genovesi in Oltremare. *Atti rogati a Cipro da Lamberto di Sambuceto (6 Luglio – 27 Ottobre 1301)*, (Collana storica di fonti e studi, XXXII, Genoa, 1982).

8) A. Blanc, *Le livre de comptes de Jacme Olivier, marchand narbonnais du XIVᵉ siècle* (Supplément au Bulletin de la Commission archéologique de Narbonne, 2 vol., 1895-1902) ; Baratier, *Commerce de Marseille*, 229-35 and « Marseille et Narbonne », 90-2.

9) L. Blancard, *Documents inédits sur le commerce de Marseille au Moyen Âge*, 2 vol. (Marseilles, 1880-1, repr. in one vol., Geneva, 1978), II 128, no. 635, for an act of the *campsor* W. de Narbona, who is, however, a *civis Massilie*. Cf. « Table alphabétique des noms des ports, places et pays de commerce », II 517, s.v. Montpellier, Narbonne. An act of 1233 records the export of 300 sestiers of wheat flour from Narbonne to Majorca by merchants of Marseilles : I. 55-6, n° 41.

10) H. E. Mayer, Marseilles Levantehandel und ein akkonensiches Fälscheratelier des 13. Jahrhunderts *(Bibliothek des Deutschen Historischen Instituts in Rom,* XXXVIII (Tübingen, 1972), 181-3, nº. 4 ; David Abulafia, « Marseilles, Acre and the Mediterranean, 1200-1291 », *Coinage in the Latin East: the fourth Oxford Symposium on Coinage and Monetary History,* ed. P. W. Edbury and D. M. Metcalf (Oxford, 1980), 19-39, esp. 20.

11) M.N. Adler, ed., *The Itinerary of Benjamin of Tudela* (London, 1907), 2-3 (English translation), 3 (Hebrew text). The reference to Montpellier's trade being « al yedey beney Yeynuvin u-Pisanin », in the hands of Genoese and Pisans, fits well with Mayer's observations : Marseilles Levantehandel, 60-5, where, however, Benjamin is not cited. Narbonne also found itself under a Genoese shadow from 1166, or even 1132, with its annual pilgrim ship to the east being forbidden to pick up pilgrims from Montpellier, Saint-Gilles and Provence proper : Mayer, 61-2 ; cf. the documents in C. Imperiale di Sant'Angelo, *Codice diplomatico della Republica di Genova,* 3 vol. (Rome, 1936-42), I 73-5, II 49-52. For Benjamin of Tudela, see also Y. Levanon, *The Jewish travellers in the twelfth century* (Lanham, 1980), 86-8, 324-5. The views of A. J. Zuckerman, *A Jewish princedom in feudal France,* 768-900 (News York, 1972), are unacceptable : A. Grabois, « La dynastie des « Rois Juifs » de Narbonne (IXᵉ-XIIIᵉ siècles) », *Narbonne : archéologie et histoire.* Narbonne au moyen âge, 49-54.

11) Mayer, 193-5, doc. 10 ; also 90-1.

12) E. Ashtor, *Levant trade in the later Middle Ages* (Princeton, 1973), 13 ; Mayer, 90, Anm. 172 ; Germain, I 201-4, 253 ; W. Heyd, I 364, n.3.

14) T.N. Bisson, *Assemblies and Representation in Languedoc in the Thirteenth Century* (Princeton, 1964), 200-211 and doc. 5, 316-8. I hope to return to the grain traffic on a subsequent occasion.

15) Pegolotti, 84 ; for Pegolotti's career inCyprus, XX-XXI.

16) For Ancona, see David Abulafia, 'The Anconitan privileges in the kingdom of Jerusalem and the Levant trade of Ancona', The Italian communes in the crusading kingdom of Jerusalem : *Acts of a conference at the Van Leer Institute,* Jerusalem, 1984 (Genoa, forthcoming) ; I am preparing a study of the Messinese merchants in Cyprus. A valuable survey is provided by M. Balard, « L'activité commerciale en Chypre en l'an 1300 », *Crusade and Settlement : papers read at the first conference of the Society for the study of the crusades and the Latin east* and presented to R. C. Smail, ed. P. W. Edbury (Cardiff, 1985), 251-63, especially 254, mentioning *Bernardus Faxit* and *Bernardus Benedictus.*

17) Balard, Notai, nº. 103.

18) Balard, nº. 104.

19) Balard, nº. 105.

20) Balard, nᵒˢ. 159, 160.

21) Polonio, nº. 50 : *Bernadus Faxit* witnesses a quittance issued by a merchant of Ancona to Cosma de Lezia (of Laodicea in Syria), on whom see Abulafia, 'Anconitan privileges'.

22) Polonio, nº. 121.

23) Pavoni, nᵒˢ 178, 179.

24) Polonio, n⁰. 145 : *Raymondum Faxit, Petrum Pastorem et Raymondum Deusaiuda. Raymondus* is described as *fidecommissario* to Bernardus.

25) Polonio, n⁰. 145. There was also *Bartholomeus, bastardus meus.*

26) Balard, n⁰. 146 : *Poncius de Trignaco* of Narbonne appoints *Guilliemus* de Vadel, also of Narbonne, but resident in Armenia, as his procurator.

27) Abulafia, « Crocuses and crusaders : San Gimignano, Pisa and the Latin Kingdom of Jerusalem, » *Outremer : studies in the history of the Crusading Kingdom of Jerusalem* presented to Joshua Prawer, ed. B. Z. Kedar, H.E. Mayer, R. C. Smail (Jerusalem, 1982), 233.

28) Polonio, n⁰. 389, reding *Deusaiuda* for the scribal error *Visavida* – cf. Pavoni, n⁰. 178-9, making the identification certain.

29) Pavoni, n⁰. 179.

30) Pavoni, n⁰. 178. But the separate identity of Bernardus and Raymondus is clear : Polonio, no. 145.

31) Pavoni, n⁰. 178ᵃ.

32) T. S. R. Boase, « The history of the kingdom », in T. S. R. Boase, ed., *The Cilician Kingdom of Armenia* (Edinburgh, 1978), 28-9.

33) Pavoni, n⁰. 33.

34) Polonio, n⁰. 408.

35) Pavoni, n⁰ˢ 1, 3.

36) Pavoni, n⁰ˢ 33, 162, 178, 178ᵃ, 179. Since he does not appear in acts of 1300, it is possible that, like Bernardus Inardus, he only came to Cyprus in early 1301.

37) Pavoni, n⁰. 162. Pavoni, n⁰. 24, lists a Raymondus de Beerci amid a group of witnesses from Montpellier ; Pavoni, p. 332, s.v. Raymondus de Beerci de Montepessulano, clearly counts him as a resident of Montpellier, though the way the witness list is composed may indicate the opposite.

38) Ashtor, Levant trade, 39, remarks that 'the number of merchants of Narbonne must have been substantial, since the will of one of them drawn up in Famagusta in 1300 bears the names of thirteen witnesses who were natives of his town' – he refers to the will of Bernardus Faxit.

39) Polonio, n⁰ 5.

40) Polonio, n⁰. 144 ; other references : Polonio, n⁰ˢ. 99, 117 ; Pavoni, n⁰. 178.

41) Polonio, n⁰. 145, 257, 340, 409 ; Pavoni, n⁰. 156.

42) Polonio, n⁰. 389.

43) Polonio, n⁰ 99.

44) D. Jacoby, « L'expansion occidentale dans le Levant : les Vénitiens à Acre dans la seconde moitié du XIIIᵉ siècle », *Journal of Medieval History*, III (1977), 243-4.

45) Pavoni, n⁰. 160.

46) Polonio, n⁰ˢ. 226-7.

47) Polonio, n⁰. 409.

48) Emery, 95n, 104, 107 (Raymond Teulier) ; also 87n, 88, 156 (Guillaume Teuleria).

49) Pavoni, n⁰ 179.

50) Pavoni, n⁰. 181-229 contains much evidence here – see Abulafia, « Anconitan privileges ».

51) Pegolotti, 37 (Bianche di Nerbona, at Constantinople) ; 58 *(panni nerbonesi e pirpignani,* at Satalia) ; 79 *(Tolosani e nerbonesi, carcascioni, Bindersi e Pirpignano ;* also *Bianchi di Nerbona,* at Famagusta).

52) Evans, in Pegolotti, 425, s.v. *Nerbonesi* and s.v. *Pirpignani.*

53) Port, 57, for the dyes that made Narbonne cloth well-known.

54) No need here to reopen the debate between R. S. Lopez and H.A. Miskimin (« The economic depression of the Renaissance », *Economic History Review,* ser. 2, XIV (1961/2), 408-26) and Carlo Cipolla (ibid. XVI (1963/4) 519-24).

55) Baratier, *Commerce de Marseille,* 304-16. For the 'remonte' between 1380 and 1409, ibid. 308.

56) Germain, II. 51.

57) On the economic problems of Languedoc in this period, see especially E.R. Labande's studies : « Louis Iᵉʳ d'Anjou, la Provence et Marseille », *Moyen Age,* LIV (1948), 297-325 ; « L'administration du duc d'Anjou en Languedoc aux prises avec le problème du blé », *Annales du Midi,* LXII (1950), 5-14, both repr. in E.R. Labande, *Histoire de l'Europe occidentale,* XIᵉ-XIVᵉ siècles (London, 1973).

58) Port, 161-205, especially (for Montpellier) 167.

59) Cited in Port, 132.

60) For Rhodes, and the Seraller family of Narbonne, see L. de Mas-Latrie, « Documents sur le commerce maritime du Midi de la France, extraits de quelques Archives d'Italie », *Bibliothèque de l'Ecole des Chartes,* ser. 2, III, (1846), 203-13. Raymond Seraller is described as « de Narbonne, marchand habitant à Montpellier et bourgeois du roi de Chypre » (1357) – a classic example of the combination of interests found among Narbonne's Levant traders.

61) Blanc, 4-7.

62) Blanc, 12-13.

63) Blanc, 15-16.

64) Blanc, 17-18. Asthor, 543-4, makes errors in his computations of Jacme Olivier's accounts.

65) Blanc, 18. For the porterage system, see P. Carbonel, *Histoire de Narbonne,* Narbonne, 1954, 223.

66) Blanc, 30.

67) Blanc, 32.

68) Blanc, 36.

69) Blanc, 277, nº XI.

70) Blanc, p. XVIII-XIX.

71) Blanc, 66-7.

72) Blanc, 82.

73) John Day, « The great bullion famine of the fifteenth century », *Past and Present,* 79 (1980) 3-54 ; see now the comments by J.H. Munro, «Bullion flows and monetary contraction in late-medieval England and the Low Countries », in J.F. Richards, ed., *Precious metals in the later medieval and early modern worlds* (Durham, N.C., 1983), 97-158.

74) Blanc, 86-8.

75) Blanc, 89-90.

76) Blanc, 102.

77) Blanc, 104.

78) Blanc, 123.

79) Blanc, 128-31.

80) Blanc, 139-42.

81) Blanc, 168-70.

82) Blanc, 208.

83) Blanc, 255-6.

84) On links to Perpignan, etc., see also Blanc, 3, 123, 131, and many other references.

85) Blanc, 280-3, n° XV.

86) Blanc, p. XXXVI and 242.

87) Port, 72.

88) Blanc, 284, n°. XVIII.

89) Blanc, 285, n°. XIX.

90) Ashtor, 145.

91) Ashtor, 146.

92) Baratier, *Commerce de Marseille*, 230-41, and end table ; Baratier, « Marseille et Narbonne », 90-2.

93) Most of these data are drawn from the end table of Baratier, *Commerce de Marseille*, Etat des départs à destination du Levant des bâtiments marseillais et langue-dociens. This material has been extended by Ashtor, *Levant trade*, 194-5, and 527-9 (table A4), using the Datini archives in Prato.

94) Baratier, *Commerce de Marseille*, 234 ; cf. also 229.

95) H. Bresc, « Marchands de Narbonne et du Midi en Sicile (1300-1460) », *Narbonne :archéologie et histoire. Narbonne au moyen âge*, 93 ; more briefly, Lacave, 84-5.

96) Bresc, appendix I (1346), 96-7.

97) Bresc, 95, stressing the continuing role of Perpignan and (possibly) of Nice.

XV

GENOA AND THE SECURITY OF THE SEAS: THE MISSION OF BABILANO LOMELLINO IN 1350

For Genoa the 'crisis of the fourteenth century' had political as well as economic reality; the strife within the city and its colonies of Guelfs and Ghibellines was mirrored in its diplomatic affairs, as Genoa searched for friends in Guelf Naples or Ghibelline Sicily. The appearance of Catalan naval power presented a direct threat to Genoese shipping, however peaceful the intent of the latter might be; and attempts at co-operation between Genoa and Venice foundered on the banks of suspicion and envy. Commercial recession brought serious worry to what was still a trading, rather than industrial, centre, and there was a reluctance to waste valuable naval resources in attempts to eliminate Venetian or Catalan rivals.[1] This attitude was not confined to Genoa, and perhaps explains why the western trading cities were more anxious to settle their differences by negotiation and compromise than they had been in the thirteenth century. Severest problem of all was that of the 'pestifferam mortalitatem mundo totali occursam'; in the years immediately following the arrival of the Black Death (1347) the maritime cities found themselves suddenly deprived of invaluable manpower, and yet, paradoxically, they were not without the means to pay for the services of sailors and ship-builders if only these men could be found. Money, the money of dead men, there was in plenty; but neither the Genoese nor the Venetians knew how to adapt to the rapid change in the structure of demand that the pestilence engendered.[2]

These preoccupations affected the whole resident community in Genoa, Venice or their colonies. The bloated population of the first half of the fourteenth century needed food, and the Genoese played a subtle diplomatic game in order to keep available both the wheat of Naples and the wheat of Sicily. The Genoese colonies in the Black Sea, particularly at Caffa, supplied much needed grain to the mother-city and its allies.[3] Despite the depredations of Catalan pirates, the Genoese seemed by the 1340s to have established a stable relationship with grain-productive regions that did indeed enable their citizens to eat bread as they needed it. In the years before the Black Death two difficulties arose in the Black Sea that threatened this stability. Local wars with the Tartars interfered with the trade of Caffa and Tana; indeed, it was when the Tartars hurled the bodies of dead plague victims into Caffa that the disease spread to the Latin world.[4] Secondly, relations between Genoese and Venetians in the Black Sea were soured when the Genoese suspected their rivals of favouring the Tartars, trading with them in the hope of winning privileges, and possibly of winning help against Genoa. The Venetians had themselves been trading from Caffa and Tana, alongside and with the assent of the Genoese; when the Tartars besieged and took Tana the Genoese tried to blockade the town, and the

---

[1] Interesting from this angle is B. Z. Kedar's attempt to gauge the mood of Genoese merchants of the period: *Merchants in Crisis: Genoese and Venetian men of affairs and the fourteenth century depression* (New Haven, 1976).

[2] F. C. Lane, *Venice, a maritime republic* (New Haven, 1974), 173–9.

[3] G. Bratianu, *Recherches sur le commerce génois dans la mer noire du XIIIe siècle* (Paris, 1929).

[4] See e.g. P. Ziegler, *The Black Death* (London, 1969).

:netians, for their part, tried to break through and trade normally. The Genoese
:ued that the Venetians traded in Caffa on Genoese sufferance; the Venetians
:ued that the Tartar war was a Genoese and not a Venetian war.[5]

In the summer of 1350 the Venetian Senate deliberated with growing alarm on
: pretention of the Genoese. Reports were coming of Genoese seizure of the
:public's ships and goods in the Black Sea: satisfaction must clearly be demanded.
:t the Venetians trod carefully, still uncertain what war with Genoa might involve
the changed circumstances of the post-plague years; the Senate chose as ambassa-
:r Marin Falier and despatched him to Genoa with instructions to present his bill
:d obtain an apology. At the same time news was arriving of Genoese naval activity
: Greece—the signs of approaching war were now very clear. Possibly to pre-empt
:enoese attempts in this direction, the Senate tried to gain the goodwill of the
:zantine emperor, whose authority, though much attenuated, did extend over the
:rrows leading to the Black Sea, and over the Genoese trading colony of Pera, right
: the Golden Horn.[6] To tie the hands of the Genoese in Romania was, then, the
:ar aim of the Venetian Senate, but the Senate remained very pessimistic. Orders
:ere given to strengthen defences in Crete and to expedite negotiations with the
:ueen of Naples that promised to bring Corfu and the Ionian Islands under Venetian
:thority.[7] The Queen was short of money and anxious to sell, while the Venetians
:ew only too well that a hostile presence in the Adriatic entrance could strangle
:eir own trade and hamper their capacity to fight. Of course, the implication was
:at the Queen of Naples, the luckless Joanna I, would lean towards the Venetians
: the coming conflict, and here the Venetians felt they had hopes of success: Joanna's
:ntinuing fear that the Hungarian branch of the Angevin dynasty would return to
:uthern Italy to unseat her, induced the queen to make friends with others who
:oked askance at an extension of Hungarian royal power into, let alone across, the
:driatic.[8]

Genoa too could hope for positive gestures from Queen Joanna. The 1340s had
:itnessed a vigorous attempt by the Doges of Genoa to take advantage of the female
:uccession in Naples by asserting the rights of Genoa over the border between the
:epublic and the county of Provence.[9] Joanna, as countess of Provence as well as
:ueen of Naples, thus found herself pressed in both her realms by new and growing
:ifficulties. In 1345 Giovanni de Murta, Doge of Genoa, denied to the pope that his

---

[5]The main account is M. Brunetti, *Contributo alla storia delle relazioni veneto-genovesi dal 1348 al 1350*
Miscellanea di storia veneta, ser. 3, vol. ix, Venice, 1916), but it is based on the Venetian sources
:nly.

[6]F. Thiriet, *Régestes des délibérations du Sénat de Venise concernant la Romanie*, i (1329–1399) (Paris—
[r]he Hague, 1958), nos. 244, 245, 246, 248; F. Thiriet, *Délibérations des assemblées vénitiennes concernant
:a Romanie*, i (1160–1363) (Paris—The Hague, 1966), no. 579.

[7]Corfu and Cephalonia: *Délibérations du Sénat*, no. 249 (cf. no. 251); *Délibérations des assemblées*,
:o. 584; Crete: *Assemblées*, nos. 581, 582, 585.

[8]Following the mysterious death of Joanna's Hungarian consort Andrew, the king of Hungary
:nvaded Naples but was forced to retreat in 1348. For this queen see É. G. Léonard, *Histoire de Jeanne
:er reine de Naples, comtesse de Provence*, 3 vols. published (Monaco—Paris, 1932–1937). See also Brunetti,
139–42.

[9]Short comment by Léonard, *Jeanne Ier*, ii, 229.

citizens actually intended to invade Ventimiglia, but strongly affirmed that the lord-ship of Ventimiglia did indeed rest with Genoa, not the court of Provence; he argued that Joanna's father Robert the Wise (d. 1343) had seized Ventimiglia, taking full advantage of the civil strife that tore apart Genoa and the Genoese coast during the early fourteenth century.[10] The claim was not perhaps unjustified, for Genoa had acknowledged Robert as suzerain in 1318, and had presumably been obliged to accept his disposition of lands. So certain were the Genoese of the justice of their claims that the Doge refused all offers of papal intervention: simply look at our documents, he said, for it is all there.[11] Joanna remained obdurate and realised that the outcome might well be Genoese attacks on her coasts; she asked the pope to remind the Genoese that all who invaded her kingdom faced anathema.[12] Although the Genoese did not actually send a fleet against Joanna, they made contact with her Hungarian enemies, and seem to have regretted that the Hungarian pretender was forced to evacuate the Neapolitan kingdom in 1348. How extensive their contacts were is not easy to say; the Hungarian king had a Genoese admiral, but so did many rival monarchs, Sicilian, Neapolitan and French; he addressed a letter to the Genoese Doge in 1348 which spoke hopefully of future invasion plans, but which is not reflected by other evidence for Genoese–Hungarian co-operation.[13]

Genoa and Hungary: two mighty states with reason to contest the power of Venice, although for different reasons. In the long term an alliance did not emerge; Venice managed temporarily to settle its differences with Hungary, without losing the good regard of Queen Joanna or the golden opportunity to purchase Corfu (with Butrint) and to establish naval bases there. The eclipse of Hungarian pretensions affected Genoese interests also, of course, and in 1350 the Doge co-operated with the Neapolitan jurist Andrea di Isernia in a draft plan to end disagreement between Genoa and Joanna. Not merely was Genoa to have Ventimiglia, not merely were Genoese rights there to be recognised as ancient and legitimate, but Genoa was to supply three galleys until the end of September of that year, to help the Queen search out and destroy Hungarian adventurers who had remained in southern Italy after the retreat of their king—against his own orders, in fact.[14] Such an agreement could not, in consequence, fatally compromise Genoese relations with the Hungarian ruler in the long term. Most significant, perhaps, for the Genoese was a generous privilege permitting the republic to carry the white salt of Provence back home, and beyond to Pisa, Lucca, Florence, Siena, Perugia and all 'Tuscia'. In June formal promises were made by each side and in June or July Ventimiglia was handed to the Genoese; though the Doge had to be reprimanded for his failure to fulfil all conditions of the agreement by the pope himself, Joanna and the republic had at

---

[10]Léonard, *Jeanne Ier*, doc. nos. xvii, xviii, xix, 419, 421–2. Cf. xvi, 418.

[11]Ibid., no. xxxii, 432–5.

[12]Ibid., no. xxxiv, 436.

[13]P. Lisciandrelli, 'Trattati e negoziazioni politiche della Repubblica di Genova (958–1797), Regesti', *Atti della Società Ligure di Storia Patria*, n.s. i (1960), nos. 539–40; Léonard, *Jeanne Ier*, nos. xlv, xlvi, 449–50. Archivio di Stato, Genoa, Archivio segreto, materie politiche, no. 2727, docs. 32 and 33.

[14]Lisciandrelli, no. 546; Léonard, no. lv, 464–6 (1350 April 22). Archive no. 2727 (38).

ast established if not a friendly, at least a neutral relationship.[15] (When war be-
ween Genoa and Venice was under way, the Doge, true to form, established cordial
elations with Hungary after all: the Dalmatian interests of the Hungarians had
een reawakened, and the Genoese thought the opportunity for a stab in Venice's
ack too good to miss.[16])

Advances were also made in attempts to gain the co-operation of the king of
he island of Sicily, so that the Genoese could move freely in the disputed waters
round Messina and Milazzo: partisans neither of Sicilians nor of Neapolitans, the
Genoese could turn from the strife between Angevins and Aragonese to the conflict
immediately in prospect, between themselves and Venice. Since Aragon and Sardinia
ormed a separate realm to the kingdom of Sicily, ruled by a different branch of the
Aragonese royal line, Genoese difficulties with Catalan pirates did not compromise
attempts to secure the friendship of the King of Sicily. A treaty with Peter II had
been drawn up in 1342, but in 1350 efforts were made to renew contacts and to
ensure that relations remained unchanged after his death.[17]

A document survives in the Genoese archives that gives precious information
about Genoese activities in and off Sicily, Calabria, Apulia and Corfu in 1350.[18] It
must be seen in the context of Genoese successes in diplomacy vis-à-vis Angevins of
Naples and Aragonese of Sicily, as well as in the context of the Venetian war-threat;
it reflects the fear, indeed the near-certainty of war, as well as the reluctance of
Genoese, as of Venetians, to launch an immediate offensive. As has been seen, there
were good reasons in 1350 for doubts about the feasibility and desirability of war
between city-states already sapped by events beyond their control. This document
is the first set of instructions issued to a captain of the fleet in the war of 1350-3;
Babilano Lomellino is commanded to go and watch for Venetian galleys, to find
news rather than to engage in direct conflict. He is ordered also to give protection
to, or to supply from Sicilian stocks, grain-carrying ships bound for Genoa, and this
command probably reflects anxiety over Venetian interference with the shipping
route from the Black Sea, and equally over Catalan interference with trade contacts
with Sicily and southern Italy. Brunetti, who examined the Venetian–Genoese war
in a valuable study, looked solely at the Venetian material, and laid much the
greatest emphasis on the needs and problems faced by Venice in this war; but this
document can be taken to suggest that the outbreak of hostilities was viewed in
Genoa, as in Venice, with caution rather than enthusiasm.

It is clear from the instructions given to Babilano Lomellino that Genoa now
relied on the relative security it had obtained in Neapolitan and Sicilian waters, so
that it could freely send its ships there to watch for Venetian vessels, or engage in hot
pursuit into those waters. Noticeable too is the insistence of the Genoese authorities

[15]Lisciandrelli, no. 548 (Archive no. 2727 (40)); also nos. 549 and 550 (2727) (41–2)). Cf. M.
Villani, *Cronica* (Trieste, 1858 and other eds.), Lib. I, cap. xc.
[16]Lisciandrelli, nos. 579 and 582 (Archive nos. 2727 (54, 55)); Brunetti, 141–2.
[17]Lisciandrelli, no. 531 (2727 (28), two good copies, one of 1601 and one sixteenth century).
Cf. the document printed *infra*.
[18]Printed *infra* from Archivio di Stato, Genoa, Archivio segreto, materie politiche, 2737A, no. 69.
Cf. Lisciandrelli no. 551 for brief note; G. Meloni, *Genova e Aragona all'epoca di Pietro il Ceremonioso*,
i (1336–54), Padua, 1971, 60.

on the need to maintain grain supplies. Galleys are to be detailed to protect grain ships, and the Genoese fleet is also to endeavour to obtain grain in Sicily. Even the reduced post-plague population had every desire to ensure that good stocks existed in Genoa: the prospect of war was, equally, a prospect of reduced trade and diminished access to sources of food supply, of piracy and closure of markets. The line of operations recommended by the Doge's instructions was that bearing south to Messina and east to Romania—an essential trade route, particularly for grain; but of course the idea of moving north into the Adriatic, as far as Ragusa (Dubrovnik) was motivated primarily by the need to see how the Venetians were strengthening themselves in Italian waters. Even so the Genoese galleys were not to trespass in those areas where Venetian control, and the danger of direct attack, was strongest— the middle and upper Adriatic. That the Genoese Doge's plans were well advised is plain enough from the active attempts of the Venetians to gain control of Corfu, Butrint and the Ionian Isles. In 1351, on the outbreak of fighting between the two Doges, the Genoese did indeed send their admiral Pagano Doria to Messina and Dalmatia, to try to penetrate to the native sea of the Venetians.[19]

Babilano Lomellino, leader of the expedition of 1350, was a member of a noble family whose links with southern Italy in this period are well documented. A Leonello Lomellino had been chamberlain of King Robert, one of the many north Italians who found favour at the court of Naples during Robert's reign. In 1329 Franceschino Lomellino and Giorgio Spinola were given a licence to trade freely in Robert's realms, by which must be understood both Provence and Naples. And in 1345-6 Queen Joanna also showed her favour, when 'Angelus, Babilanus et Joannes Lomellini de Janua assecuratj a regina, et sub regia protectione recipiuntur'.[20] Thus Babilano already had reason to know the south Italian kingdom and its coasts.

The outcome of the Lomellino expedition is not recorded. That it was violent is certainly a possibility. In September, a month before Babilano received his instructions, the Genoese had already been attacked by the Venetians off Chios. The Genoese riposted with a vigorous attack on Venetian possessions in the Aegean —on Negropont and off the Morea: 'galee quoque Ianuensium tres armate per dominium Chiense virili actu ceperunt insulam et castrum de Cia, [Zea], cuius Veneti dominium obtinebant'. The war had already begun, a pan-Mediterranean war that extended far beyond the Lomellino brief.[21]

---

[19]Corfu, Butrint (Albania), etc.: see note 7 *supra*. Pagano Doria: Lisciandrelli 556-8 (2737A (73-75)); M. Balard, 'A propos de la bataille du Bosphore. L'expédition génoise de Paganino Doria à Constantinople (1351-52)', *Travaux et mémoires*, iv (1970), 431-69.

[20]A list of documents concerning the Lomellini in the Naples archives (originals now destroyed) was provided in 1610 by Petrus Vincentius, archivist of the Sicilian kingdom, to a Genoese client, and now constitutes Archivio Segreto 2727 no. 18 in the Archivio di Stato, Genoa. Fuller copies of two fourteenth-century documents cited by Vincentius were also provided (2727 (17), of 1326/7 and 2727 (19), of 1327/8), plus a stray text (2727 (20)) not listed in no. 18. Nine privileges, all of the fourteenth century are listed, which with 2727 (20) makes a total of ten documents.

[21]*Annales Genuenses di Giorgio Stella*, ed. G. Balbi (*Rerum Italicarum Scriptores*, ser. 2, vol. xvii, part 2), 150-1. For later developments, see A. Sorbelli, *La lotta tra Genova e Venezia per il predominio del Mediterraneo, 1350-5* (Bologna, 1921) (= *Memorie della R. Accademia delle Scienze dell'Istituto di Bologna, classe di scienze morali*, ser. 1, vol. v, sezione di scienze storico–fililogiche, 1911, p. 87-157 (parte prima)). This, like Brunetti, is based on the Venetian documentation only.

APPENDIX

chivio di Stato, Genoa, Materie politiche 2737A (busta 18A), no. 69.

In xpi nomine amen. MCCCL die xxvi ottobre.

Tractatus datus per magnificum dominum dominum ducem Januensem etc. nobili ro Babilano Lomelino Capitaneo duodecim Gallearum Comunis Janue et eius consilio.

Primo cum Galee ipse navigando secundum ordinem sibi datum deo duce pervenerint applicuerint in Messanam, studeant facere solicite et prudenter ut infra.

Viz. quod quam primum fuerint in ipso loco Messane procurent studiose et celeriter expedit per omnem modum per quem melius poterunt habere linguam et novam de enetis, et tam de Galeis duodecim que per eos nuper armate sunt in Venetijs, quam de aleis alijs que iverunt in Romaniam, et etiam de quibuscumque alijs condicionibus sorum.

Quibus quidem notitia et novis habitis de Inimicis ut supra, tunc Capitanei Consilium illi ad quos spectat diligenter avisent et revideant omnes undecim Galeas nostras, si bene rmate et parate sunt, et sufficientes ad facienda et complenda viriliter que infra dicentur.

Et si non ita sufficienter armate et parate essent, ut expedit ad faciendum que facere abebunt ut infra, tunc reducant dictas Galeas undecim ad decem, adhoc ut melius sint rmate et parate dicte x ad faciendum et exequendum, quod facere habebunt, ut dictum st.

Galea vero quam sic ut supra desarmaverint, pro rearmandis predictis decem ut upra, arment cum aliquibus paucis gentibus ad naverescam, et ipsam onerent Grano, et c onustam mutant Januam quam citius potuerint.

[f.1v) Si vero pro dicta Galea granum habere non possent in Insula, tunc illam imittant in dicto loco Messane cum quatuor vel vj custodibus prout eis videbitur, usque d eorum regressum.

Quibus omnibus ut supra soliciti et celeriter completis in dicto loco Messane et novis t notitia habitis de Inimicis prout melius poterunt, tunc in nomine domini recedant de licto loco Messane, et vadant ad Cotronam, et studiose et celeriter faciant ut infra.

Viz. cum fuerint in dicto loco Cotroni quia dominus dux nova habet per litteras quod redicte Galee xij.cim Venetorum de Venetia recesserunt die xij mensis presentis ottobris, t nescitur si dicte Galee xij iverint in Romaniam vel remanserint ad custodiam Gulfi, tudeant idcirco dicte Galee nostre cum fuerint ibi omni via et modo prout melius et elerius poterunt habere linguam et nova de dictis Galeis xij et de alijs Galeis que fuerint n Romaniam, ac etiam de omnibus alijs condicionibus Venetorum.

Et habitis et investigatis novis predictis in dicto loco Cotroni, tunc decem Galee incontinenti de ipso loca recedant, et demum festinanter et celeriter vadant ad Otrantum.

Cum autem fuerint in ipso loco Otranti, tunc ibi similiter studeant caute et celeriter omni via et modo per quem melius poterunt habere linguam et noticiam de supradictis Galeis Inimicorum, et tam de xij que de alijs que iverunt in Romaniam, et ut supra de omnibus condicionibus Venetorum, ad hoc ut semper vadant cum lingua et noticia de Inimicis in quantum poterunt.

Postquam vero predicte Galee fuerint in dicto loco Otranti et investigaverint diligenter de Galeis et condicionibus Inimicorum ut supra, [f.2r] tunc etiam ad melius habendum linguam de Inimicis, et tam de Galeis xij quam de alijs et eorum condicionibus ut supra, ut melius sciant quomodo facere et procedere habebunt, mutant unam de Galeis de dicto loco Otranti usque ad Caput Lingue, et deinceps usque Curfo, que Galea vadens ad dicta loca per omnem modum et viam ut melius et citius poterit investiget et procuret caute et solicite habere linguam et nova de predictis Galeis xij, et de alijs et omnibus ut supra, et postmodum confestim redeat ad galeas.

Que vero predicta Galea que ut supra iverit usque Curfo redierit in Otrantum, ubi dimiserit Galeas nostras, tunc Galee nostre secundum linguam et nova que reportaverit de Inimicis viriliter procedant et faciant ut infra.

Viz. quod si per ipsam Galeam nova haberent quod predicte Galee xij Venetorum remanserint ad custodiam Gulfi ut dictum est supra, tunc Galee nostre in nomine domini viriliter intrent Gulfum et celeriter et vigorose vadant ad dictas duodecim Inimicorum inveniendum et ad eas cum dei auxilio victoriose et viriliter capiendum.

Semper eundo caute et prudenter in Gulfo et faciendo viam suam per Sclavoniam et descendendo per eam usque ad Ragusiam et cum ibi fuerint non intrent Gulfum ulterius, secundum dictum teneant et veniant per Insulas versus montem sancti Angeli, et cum ibi fuerint, faciant viam per Apuliam versus Januam, dampnificando semper in eundo et redendo Inimicos in rebus et avere quantum poterunt, et de personis eorum capiendo quot poterunt habere, non tamen ipsos interficiendo, nec aliquam crudelitatem faciendo nisi quam minus poterunt, et in quantum poterunt evitare.

Item semper que dicte Galee fuerint in Messana et alijs locis ubi recupare poterunt de pilotis, sibi de ipsis provideant et se fulciant prout cognoverint expedire.

[f.2v] In omnibus supradictis et alijs que facere habebunt predicte Galee procedant dei auxilio invocato, prudenter, celeriter et viriliter secundum nova que habuerint et dispositionem quam invenerint, et prout Capitaneus eius Consilio et alijs ad quos spectat qui presentes erunt negotiis melius et salubrius videbitur procedendum, etiam et plus et minus quam dictum est in presenti tractatu.

Post supradictum Tractatum elusum et secretum [et quod non debet apriri citra Messanam, *above the line*] datum est alius tractatus seu commissio publica tenoris infrascripti.

In xpi nomine amen. MCCCL die. [*followed by space*].

Brevis commissio quam confititur vobis Capitaneo Galearum etc. de hijs que facere habebitis usque Messanam, de alijs autem que facere habebitis ab Messana ulterius, qui apriri non debet nisi cum fueritis ibi.

Primo separando de districtu Janue in nomine domini recte et celeriter quam tam potestis tendatis et faciatis viam vestram versus Gaietam Neapolim et alia loca prout fuerit oportunum. Et in eundo ut supra, si invenietis ligna aliqua vel navigia Venetorum illa secure et viriliter cum dei auxilio offendatis et capiatis et de ipsis faciatis per omnia prout vobis pro meliori videbitur faciendum.

Item memoratur et committitur vobis Capiti supradicto quod omnibus lignis et navigijs Januensium quorumcumque, onustis grano vel alijs victualibus quas invenietis precipiatis expresse pro parte Magistri domini Ducis sub penis illis de quibus vobis videbitur, quod omnino secundum aliqua excusaret declinent et veniant recto viagio cum dictis eorum oneribus ad portum Janue. Que quedem precepta per vos fienda ut supra faciatis diligenter notari [f.3r] ad hoc ut puniantur omnino que venerint continetur ipsa.

Cum autem fueritis in Messana, procuretis cum domino Regi cui in personam vestram facte sunt littere credentie et cum alijs quibusdam Baronibus ut videbitis habere tractam de salmis iiijc frumenti prout vobis locutum extitit per Jachinum de Castellano viz. pro denariis nostris.

Item recomendetis dicto domino Regi et alijs prout vobis videbitur Mercatores nostros Januenses qui apportaverunt Granum ad dictum locum Messane et qui sunt ibi cum navigijs suis, quatenus sibi placeat mandare et facere quod illis qui vendiderunt granum ibi satisfiat de pretio et illi qui non vendiderunt possint recedere cum eorum navigijs et onere et ire ad faciendum facta sua.

In omnibus autem alijs que facere habebitis in Messana et a Messana ulterius proceda-

et faciatis secundum ordinem vobis datum in tractatu alio supradicto, etiam et plus et
nus prout discretioni vestre et Consilij vestri, de que spes magna capitur, videbitur
cedendum et faciendum secundum ea que invenietis, et nova que habebitis.

[f.3v, f.4 are blank.]

XVI

Invented Italians in the Courtois Charters

IN PREPARING his *Studien zur Geschichte des Fünften Kreuzzuges* the historian Reinhold Röhricht had to face arduous difficulties. A larger version of his book was in the press in 1888 – the third in a trilogy of documents and studies on the Fifth Crusade; but its patron, the Comte Riant, died that year, and its publisher, the Société pour la publication de textes relatifs à l'histoire et à la géographie de l'Orient latin, also expired; part of Röhricht's manuscript went astray, and the *Studien* which appeared in 1891 are thus only a fragment of much fuller researches.[1] Even so, they contain references to, and summaries of, some very remarkable documents: records of loans by moneylenders, preponderantly Genoese, to participants in the Fifth Crusade – loans made mostly during the siege of Damietta.[2] Of particular interest is the way leading French crusaders guaranteed repayment of the loans, in a manner very similar to documented practice at the time of St Louis's later expedition to Damietta.[3] Thus, during September 1219, 'in castris juxta Damyetam', the seneschal of Champagne appears, sponsoring a loan of £90 of Tours to three of his followers; if they were unable to repay the Genoese bankers from whom the money was obtained, he himself would settle the debt.[4] Röhricht was not entirely happy with this document: 'scriptura cartae ornata est neque plane respondet scripturae ineuntis tertii decimi'; but he showed less reserve in handling other documents of this genre, such as the promise of the constable of Normandy to pay £1,000 of Tours to two Genoese merchants, in order to secure the release of nine of his followers.[5]

Röhricht's main source for this material was a manuscript in the Bibliothèque Nationale – MS Lat. 17803 – and he also employed printed texts from the works of the aristocrat Delley de Blancmesnil, the romantic historian Sub-Prefect Roger, the reputable numismatist Lavoix.[6] Röhricht agreed with Lavoix that MS 17803 contained documents of doubtful authenticity, but that most of the texts it provided could still be used as a major source for the financial history of the crusades:

> Wir wissen wohl, dass die Ächtheit einzelner Stücke bestritten worden ist, doch haben sich Stimmen genug erhoben, welche diese reiche Sammlung als im grossen und ganzen für authentisch erklären, wenn auch hier und da durch Nachcorrecturen manches Falsche hineingetragen worden sein mag.[7]

MS 17803, with its supplements 17803A and 17803B, contains well over four hundred texts, mostly copies – including repetitions of the same document, occasionally several times over.[8] The earliest charters carry the date 1190, the latest are attributed to the 1270s. Most of the copies are in nineteenth-century hands, but there are also photographs, lithographs and 'originals' on parchment or, less often, on paper.[9] Röhricht was struck by the fine seals some documents carry, apparently belonging to the French knights who guaranteed the loans made to their followers by the Genoese and their business rivals.[10] Individually, the documents do not massively alter the understanding of the crusades which can be obtained from other sources, such as the Trésor des Chartes or the remarks of Joinville and other chroniclers. They are repetitious, formulaic – differing mainly in the names of the Genoese or other bankers and of the French *armigeri*, *fideles* and other participants in the armies. Several of the more eminent figures mentioned appear also in the chronicles: Hugh comte de Nevers for instance.[11]

Nevertheless, the doubts which these documents generated in the minds of several critics were well-founded. Convincing though the 'originals' appeared, even to the best-trained eyes in France and elsewhere, they were all forgeries.[12] There is no need here to repeat the infamous history of M. Courtois and M. Le Tellier who sold these documents to French noblemen, full of assurances of their authenticity. About 200 forged charters were sold in the 1840s and 1850s; a further 350, the unsold residue, eventually reached the Archives Nationales and the École des Chartes; and MS 17803 contains copies of many sold and unsold charters, plus the few dozen 'originals' already mentioned.[13] Demand for these charters was fuelled by the decision of King Louis-Philippe to open the Salles des Croisades in a new wing of the Palace at Versailles; the king permitted those families whose ancestors had brought glory to France on crusade to display their coat of arms in the Salles.[14] Not surprisingly, the French court was flooded with requests for inclusion in the display by many noble, or would-be noble, families which had been left out of the original exhibition; additional Salles were quickly opened to satisfy demand. And while some families established their right to inclusion through the use of chronicle sources or the Trésor des Chartes, others were able to justify their claims only with charters purchased from M. Courtois.[15] Thus the Comtesse de Chastenay paid 500 francs; and in return she received an impressive piece of parchment, stating that Lazarino de Niela and Angelo Cavaccia of Genoa had provided a loan of 60 silver marks to three knights of a certain Johannes de Chastenaio.[16] The act was dated at Messina in February, 1190 – that is, during the passage eastwards of the Third Crusade. The document, now in the Bibliothèque Nationale, carries a particularly fine seal, showing a mounted knight; unfortunately, the comtesse had to be content with a damaged and illegible inscription.[17] Attached to the document is a much smaller piece of parchment, carrying a highly abbreviated text which states that reimbursement of the debt was duly made at Acre in June, 1191.[18] These miniature documents will attract attention again in a moment; they are very plentiful.

The exceptional facility with which Courtois and Le Tellier furnished charters to those in search of a crusader ancestry already aroused concern in the 1840s. The Prince de Joinville, on behalf of the king, corresponded with the leading French palaeographer, Léon Lacabane, and asked his opinion; Lacabane was prepared to accept the authenticity of the Courtois documents, and his major objection to the charters was of a different nature – the appearance of a name such as Chastenay was not necessarily proof that modern bearers of the same name were descendants of the person named on the original charter.[19] This attempt to dampen enthusiasm for the Courtois texts had, in a curious way, the opposite effect: Lacabane's comments created the illusion that he was satisfied with the documents as such, and merely dissatisfied with the use to which they were being put. Actually, Lacabane maintained close contact with Courtois and did not greatly disapprove of the way Courtois made money out of his collection. His dealings with Courtois did gradually arouse his suspicions – the way charters were slowly made available to him for inspection, a handful at a time, certainly disturbed Lacabane.[20] But Lacabane was not prepared to unleash a scandal by denouncing the Courtois collection in his own lifetime; in manuscripts he left to the Bibliothèque Nationale in his will Lacabane confessed his change of opinion, but even so access to these manuscripts (Add. Lat. 1667 and 1668) was strictly controlled after the library acquired them.[21] Thus it was perfectly possible for Reinhold Röhricht to accept the validity of the documents while working in the very library which contained, elsewhere on its shelves, Lacabane's denunciation of Courtois. Those who did gain access to Lacabane's notes either misunderstood or misrepresented them. Robert de Courson de la Villeneuve tried to settle the doubts of his contemporaries in 1898; he reported that he had seen Lacabane's comments, and that Lacabane's faith in Courtois had never wavered.[22] In fact, a reading of Lacabane's material creates a totally opposite impression. Lacabane states that the Courtois documents are 'le produit d'une fabrication moderne'; 'la non-authenticité me semble désormais démontrée'.[23] The miniature documents on paper or parchment were finally seen to be the product of sheer audacity and pure fantasy.[24] Courson de la Villeneuve interpreted Lacabane's view differently. Courson believed that Lacabane knew a great and sensitive secret about the Cabinet Courtois: the documents had been stolen from a Genoese archive – Courson postulated the archive of the Banco di San Giorgio – by French soldiers some time between 1793 and 1796, when Genoa was in the hands of revolutionary armies.[25] In view of their questionable origin, M. Courtois had not surprisingly provided only hints about the way he had obtained the collection – another example, by the way, of Courtois's chilling ability to create the impression that his charters were genuine. How so many Pisan, Sienese, Provençal and even north French charters reached M. Courtois was not explained by Courson.

There was, nonetheless, a strong and steady assault on the claims of the Cabinet Courtois throughout the mid-nineteenth century, culminating in Cartellieri's denunciation in 1906. Lainé objected that too high a proportion of the Courtois collection carried the names of possible ancestors of modern French noblemen; in the Trésor des Chartes one would find a much greater number of extinct families.[26] In effect, Lainé was saying that the documents were forged to appeal to the desire for ancestors of the new aristocracy of le Roi Bourgeois and of Napoleon III: which was true. But A. Borel d'Hauterive tried to rebut this objection by showing, with scant regard for statistical evidence, that the names of extinct families also appeared in the charters.[27] Actually, the forgers realised that it was generally enough to put only one or two supposed ancestors in each charter; space was filled with additional names, culled from genuine documents or invented out of thin air. A particularly powerful objection to the charters was the absence of reference to families with an established claim to descent from French crusaders: Montmorency, Rohan and so on. As soon as these objections were made public, the Cabinet Courtois released charters to show that, all along, the Montmorencys and their peers were of course also mentioned in charters from the collection.[28] Generally, however, the lure of profits from the sale of charters triumphed: the Courtois atelier began to produce 'blanks', filling in the names of supposed ancestors when news arrived that a particular family was wondering whether the Cabinet Courtois might by any chance contain reference to its forebears.[29] Léon Lacabane was apparently the unwitting collaborator of Courtois and Le Tellier in this process; he forwarded names to the Prince de Joinville and the authorities of the Salles des Croisades, for inclusion in the display there.[30] In 1843 Le Tellier wrote to Lacabane to claim a charter lent to the scholar, but now sold to a would-be descendant of crusaders:

> Monsieur, M. Constant de Ribecque me fait la demande immédiate d'un titre daté de Saint Jean d'Acre qui serait originaire de Normandie ou de Picardie et qui concernerait
> Jordanus de Burgo
> R. de Lambecurt
> J. de Constancia
> N. Perinus
> A. Babo
> Ces noms se trouvent effectivement sur une carte que vous avez eu la bonté de me dicter et je remarque que la pièce serait restée chez vous; je vous serais bien obligé si vous aviez la bonté de la remettre au porteur de ce mot.[31]

Professor Bautier has demonstrated with clarity what Courtois' critics believed: not a single document from the Courtois collection stands examination. Unfortunately, M. Bautier's work was not greeted with the acclaim it deserves. Some members of the Académie des Inscriptions observed that the relatives of those involved in the forgeries were still alive (this was in 1956), and that scandal should therefore not be unleashed.[32] But it is also a matter for concern that Courtois documents were still being utilised by scholars. Thus the comprehensive bibliography on French geneaology in 1968 lists Bautier's article underneath exceptionally untrustworthy defences of the Courtois material, such as that by Courson de la Villeneuve; the impression can be gained that the question of authenticity is not finally resolved.[33] But M. Bautier's discussion, based primarily on palaeographical criteria, is entirely convincing. Among features he has noted are the unusually neat edges of the charters, uncharacteristic of twelfth and thirteenth-century material – these resulted from the forgers' practice of using cut-away edges of genuine documents in order to provide blank parchment of about the right age. Occasionally, too, the parchment used is simply too fine for the period of Philip Augustus or the Fifth Crusade: the forgers used the blank edges of much later charters, written on much better parchment. Under ultra-violet light M. Bautier has seen fourteenth-century writing which lay beneath a supposedly thirteenth-century text. The paper documents show signs of artificial ageing, by the use of candle-smoke.[34] It was probably problems in the availability of raw materials which led the atelier to produce smaller and smaller documents of the highly-abbreviated type which has already been mentioned: some are no larger than postage-stamps. On the other hand, the seals of the documents, where attached, are genuine; we would probably be right in imagining a team of forgers at work in the Archives Nationales, snipping away the seals and borders of perfectly genuine charters. Generally, the seals were attached to the forged charters by a simple, effective method, involving the use of a heated strip to melt the inside of the seal. However, it is occasionally possible that the document carries the seal originally attached to the piece of trimmed parchment on which the forgers set to work – this may be true of some documents where a loan is guaranteed by a figure of eminence, such as Alfonso of Poitiers or Charles of Anjou, whose charters could be found ready-sealed in the Trésor des Chartes.[35]

Apart from the very small slips on parchment or paper, many of the forgeries are magnificent documents of their type, showing considerable skill. Many Courtois charters are securely behind bars, in the Bibliothèque Nationale or the École des Chartes; but there are certainly also large numbers of Courtois manuscripts in the hands of private owners, themselves descendants of those French nobles in search of ancestors who so plagued Louis-Philippe and so enriched M. Courtois. The Courtois documents still therefore deserve attention: individual charters will continue to surface and need to be identified. In certain cases it will not be possible to subject new crusader charters to close investigation, and it is perhaps worth suggesting some additional criteria for the investigation and identification of Courtois forgeries. This is particularly important where only copies in a modern hand come to light, in collections of transcriptions for example. M. Bautier remarks that 'le texte ... ne suffisait pas pour autoriser un jugement irrécusable', except perhaps in the case of the miniature documents; he points out that the forgers clearly had very extensive knowledge of the history of the crusades and of medieval diplomatic – here, perhaps, Le Tellier played an especially important role.[36] Thus many of the figures mentioned in the documents were genuine participants in the crusades, identifiable in contemporary chronicles. Hugh, duke of Burgundy plays a rôle in the Courtois charters commensurate with his real significance as intermediary between Philip Augustus and the Italians.[37] Thus the names that appear in the texts are of three types: genuine, fantastic and 'neutral' names, mostly invented but not intended to provide a pedigree for possible clients of the atelier.

However, there are several textual 'checks' which are possible. The forgers knew much about the crusades, but rather less about Italian merchants. The very tiny documents seem to have been offered, sometimes at least, as fragments cut from the notebooks or notarial registers of the Italian companies. Lacabane later reflected: 'ce qui m'étonne le plus, c'est qu'on ait pu arriver a imiter des *carnets* de marchands italiens sur *papier de coton'*.[38] Actual notebooks belonging to companies of Italian merchants do not exist from the time of the Third Crusade, nor indeed from early thirteenth-century Genoa, Pisa and Siena; but the Courtois forgeries bear not the slightest resemblance to what does survive – a few accounts of a Florentine firm, from 1211, or any of the very varied material in the notarial registers of Genoa, Siena and Marseilles.[39] The forgers seem to have imagined that the Italian bankers would work in fairly stable *societates*; both the large and the small documents contain references to merchant companies that have an anachronistic ring – 'Luchino Corsali et toti ejus Societati', an enterprise which, it is maintained, survived the thirty years from the Fifth Crusade to St Louis's Crusade, where it reappears.[40] Much more serious is the objection that nearly all the names of Genoese, Pisan and Sienese bankers are pure invention, betraying considerable ignorance of the names of the leading business families in Genoa and Tuscany, and even of the names of the real Genoese and Tuscan participants in the crusades – genuine families such as Doria and della Volta, active at the time of the Fifth Crusade.[41] Very occasionally, with the help of genuine documents in the Trésor des Chartes, the forgers alighted upon an acceptable name, such as the Conrado Usodimare who supposedly made a loan at Messina in 1190; but surnames such as de Rosio, de Niela, Struxio are inventions, not found in early thirteenth-century Genoa; equally, the Pisan names – de Jhota, de Boze – are apparently pure invention.[42] Baptismal names do, however, reveal a higher rate of plausibility than surnames: Lanfrancus, Conradus at Genoa, for example.[43] Since it is much easier to control Genoese names of the late twelfth and early thirteenth century than French ones of the same period, a useful, though not foolproof, check on suspected Courtois texts would be to compare the names of the merchants listed in those texts with the names to be found in the notarial registers. However, it does not follow that a document is genuine because one or two names are identifiable: the Courtois forgeries which mention Rostagnus Paynus or Paganus, *rector* of Marseilles, were inspired by a reference to the same name, borne by a notary of Marseilles, in a document from the Trésor des Chartes.[44] And because, as will be seen, documents concerned with St Louis's crusade in the Trésor des Chartes had great influence on the methods of the Courtois atelier, several genuine names are likely to appear in documents claiming a date between 1248 and 1252.

As far as the other contents of the documents are concerned, the forgers show greater learning. Nearly all the Courtois forgeries are based on simple variations on a pattern; the documents have their inspiration in the genuine charters concerned with St Louis's crusade.[45] Lacabane came to realise that there were four or five standard models for the Courtois forgeries; and St Louis's crusade provided ideal models, since there are plenty of authentic charters combining the name of a princely guarantor, of Genoese or other merchants, and of unknown or little-known knights. Not surprisingly some scholars, such as Jal, burned their fingers on Courtois documents which they used in addition to the Trésor des Chartes, in studies of Italian loans to St Louis's crusaders.[46] Scholarly use of the Courtois documents, as early as 1842, reinforced public faith in the forgers' claims. It is possible to see how close the Courtois texts were to the St Louis models by examining a genuine document of August 1249, drawn up at the siege of Damietta; William, heir to the county of Flanders, borrows £5,000 of Tours from five citizens of Genoa; the loan is guaranteed by King Louis, subject to the surrender of William's lands.[47] Exactly the same formulae appear in the plentiful Courtois

140

forgeries from the period 1248 to 1252. But the forgers also transferred back in time the methods they observed in use in the mid-thirteenth century, and decided – rightly or wrongly – that almost identical documents would also suit the reign of Philip Augustus or Louis VIII. Moreover, the model provided by the siege of Damietta under St Louis would also serve excellently for the Fifth Crusade; there too Damietta was besieged, but there was less danger that eagle-eyed critics would notice discrepancies between forged charters and genuine ones, since the latter were very few. So too the presence of Sienese moneylenders at Limassol in 1249, recorded in the Trésor des Chartes, is mirrored in the appearance of Sienese merchants in the Cabinet Courtois – though with little attention to the chronology of Sienese commercial expansion.[48] Finally, the more ambitious documents issued by the forgers, loans by ecclesiastics to crusaders made in France before the departure of the armies, were also adaptations of authentic texts from the Archives Nationales; here the reign of Philip Augustus did indeed provide models.[49] It seems likely that the forgers studied one section of the Trésor des Chartes particularly closely: carton J 441, rich in documents concerning St Louis's crusade.[50] It is therefore quite possible that they obtained parchment by trimming the charters in this and other sections.

It can be grudgingly admitted that the Courtois forgeries were brilliantly achieved. There were small touches which inspired confidence: the seals (which also cost purchasers dearly); the occasional reference to real but secondary figures such as Rostagnus Paganus, which helped convince Röhricht that the documents were, by and large, acceptable. It is some tribute to the dangerous skills of Courtois and Le Tellier that Röhricht drew up, at the end of his *Studien*, an Index Crucesignatorum which contains many names invented half a century earlier by the forgers.[51] Documents from the Cabinet Courtois continue to pose dangers through their excellence of execution, their inherent plausibility and, above all, through their wide dispersal.

NOTES

1 R. Röhricht, *Studien zur Geschichte des Fünften Kreuzzuges* (Innsbruck, 1891), iii; cf. Röhricht's *Quinti belli sacri scriptores minores* (Geneva, 1879), and *Testimonia de quinto bello sacro minora* (Geneva, 1882). The title of the *Studien* was originally to be: *Epistolarium, Cartularium, Index cruce signatorum, Delineatio geographica*.

2 Röhricht, *Studien*, §IV. Chartae Variae, pp. 57-75, nos. 1, 8, 9, 10, 12, 14, 15, 16, 18, 19, 20, 21, 22, 23, 27, 28, 29, 31, 32, 34, 35, 36, 37, 38, 39, 41, 42, 43, 44, 45. The documents concerned with Bologna have no connection with the present discussion, however.

3 Apart from instances cited infra, notes 45-50, see Joinville, *Histoire de Saint Louis*, ed. Natalis de Wailly (Paris, 1868), 91.

4 Röhricht, *Studien*, no. 35, from Paris, Bibliothèque Nationale, MS Lat. 17803, nos. 125, 204, 349.

5 Röhricht, *Studien*, no. 39, from MS 17803, nos. 59 and 423.

6 A.L. Delley de Blancmesnil, *Notice sur quelques anciens titres, suivie de considérations sur les salles des croisades au Musée de Versailles* (Paris, 1866); P. Roger, *La noblesse de France aux croisades* (Paris, 1845); H. Lavoix, *Monnaies à légendes arabes frappées en Syrie par les croisés* (Paris, 1877). Unfortunately Röhricht gives only the most meagre reference to each of these works.

7 Röhricht, *Studien*, p. iv; cf. Lavoix, p. 5.

8 For descriptions, see L. Delisle, *Manuscrits latins et français ajoutés aux fonds des nouvelles acquisitions pendant les années 1875-1891. Inventaire alphabétique*, i-ii (Paris, 1891), 690 (under the heading 'Croisades' – n.a.l. 1664-1668). MS 17803 B comprises notes and copies collected by M. Frédéric Zryd; MS 17803A contains a few 'originals'. See also L. Delisle, *Inventaire des manuscrits latins conservés à la Bibliothèque Nationale sous les nos 8823-28613* (Paris, 1863-71), Notre-Dame et d'autres fonds, p. 69.

9 List of photographs, etc., Delisle, *Nouvelles acquisitions*, p. 690.

10 Röhricht, *Studien*, nos. 15, 39, 42, etc. There is an especially fine seal in MS 17803A, document dated February, 1190.

11 In Röhricht, *Testimonia*, the editor includes references to Henri comte de Nevers from chronicle sources (Ogerio Pane, *Annales Ianuenses*) and from MS 17803, no. 128 – *Testimonia*, pp. xxxvi, 238; compare P. Pressutti, *Regesta Honorii Papae III*, vol. i (Rome, 1888), nos. 1498, 1543, 1558, 1581.

12 R-H. Bautier, 'La collection de chartes de croisade dite "Collection Courtois"', *Comptes-rendus des séances de l'Academie des Inscriptions et Belles Lettres* (1956), 382-5; A. Cartellieri, *Philipp II. August König von Frankreich*, ii, *Der Kreuzzug (1187-91)* (Leipzig and Paris, 1906), 302-24.

13 I am grateful to Professor Bautier for enlarging on the details given in his communication to the Académie des Inscriptions; it is to be hoped that a fuller account of the career of Courtois and his team will appear.

14 For a lengthy bibliography, see G. Saffroy, *Bibliographie généalogique héraldique et nobiliaire de la France dès origines à nos jours. Imprimés et manuscrits*. i. *Généralités* (Paris, 1968), 166-7, nos. 3629-44; cf. Cartellieri's excellent discussion, listing over 40 items.

15 Bautier, p. 382.

16 MS 17803A, no. 3, letter by Courtois, Paris, 28 June 1843: 'Je declare avoir reçu de madame la comtesse de Chastenay-Lanty la somme de Cinq cents francs pour le prix de la cession que je lui fais de deux titres qui font partie de mon cabinet généalogique'. 500 fr. was the normal price Courtois charged for his grander charters: Bautier, p. 382; R. de Courson de la Villeneuve, 'Authenticité des titres des croisades de la collection Courtois', extr. de la *Revue de l'histoire de l'Ouest* (1898), 32. Also, nouv. acq. lat. 1666, no. 76.

17 MS 17803A ('original'); MS 17803, f. 146r, no. 441 (lithograph); nouv. acq. lat. 1664, no. 8, transcription by Léon Lacabane, with notes on the seal. French translation: 17803A, no. 4.

18 MS 17803; also 17803A no. 5 (French translation). See Appendix I *infra*.

19 Much of Lacabane's correspondence with the court is in nouv. acq. lat. 1664, 1665, 1666, papers left to the Bibliothèque Nationale after Lacabane died. On claims of ancestry: nouv. acq. lat. 1666, no. 76.

20 Draft letter by Lacabane, critical of Le Tellier: nouv. acq. lat. 1666, f. 73 (1843): 'Je ne puis comprendre (corr. to: 'guère me rendre compte de concevoir') votre determination de ne communiquer à la fois que le nombre de pieces dont on peut trouver le placement dans les vingt-quatre heures'.

21 Courson, 'Authenticité' (1898), p. 1. Nouv. acq. lat. 1666-8 were 'tenus secrets'. But even MS 17803 was only shown with M. Delisle's approval: R. de Courson de la Villeneuve. 'Authenticité des titres des croisades de la collection Courtois', extr. de la *Revue de l'histoire de l'Ouest*, part 1 (1896), 17n.

22 Courson, 'Authenticité' (1898), p. 42. The positive conclusions of the Abbé Gazzera of Turin had considerable effect in France: Courson, p. 14.

23 Nouv. acq. lat. 1666, nos. 83, 85. Cf. no. 100: 'je les crois tous fausses'; Lacabane continues that had he had enough time to examine the charters properly when the Salles were being enlarged, 'j'eusse conseillé de ne pas en accepter une seule'. Cf. Cartellieri, *Philip II*. ii, 320.

24 Nouv. acq. lat. 1666, no. 101. But cf. no. 76, letter to Le Tellier, where the small paper documents are described as

'la partie la moins lucrative' (1843). An example is given in Appendix II.

25   Courson (1896), p. 1; Courson (1898), p. 13. The Banco di San Giorgio was surely a poor candidate, since it did not even exist until 1407.

26   See the attack by A. Borel d'Hauterive, originally printed in the *Revue historique de la noblesse*, iii (1844), and reprinted by Delley de Blancmesnil, *Notice*, pp. 132-42; for Lainé see Saffroy, p. 166-7, especially his 'Musée de Versailles, salle des croisades', *Archives de la noblesse de France*, ix (1844), and his *Discussion entre MM. Lainé et Borel d'Hauterive au sujet de la salle des croisades au musée de Versailles* (s.d.).

27   Borel d'Hauterive, in Blancmesnil, p. 133.

28   Bautier, p. 384; MS 17803 nos. 58, 205, 392; Röhricht, *Studien*, no. 27; Lavoix, p. 9.

29   Bautier, pp. 384-5; cf. the requests for information or recognition of pedigree in nouv. acq. lat. 1667, passim.

30   M. de Nieuwekerke wrote to Lacabane in 1858 saying that 'vous avez été charge d'examiner les titres des familles qui reclamaient l'adjonction de leurs armoiries dans la Salles des Croisades au Musée de Versailles' – nouv. acq. lat. 1668, f.2.

31   Nouv. acq. lat. 1666, no. 66.

32   Comments following Bautier's communication, p. 386. See further R-H. Bautier, 'Forgeries et Falsifications de documents par une officine généalogique au milieu du XIXe siècle', *Bibliothèque de l'Ecole des Chartes*, cxxxii (1974), 91-2; cf. L. Delisle, 'Procédé employé par un faussaire contemporain', *ibid.*, xlix (1888), 304-6.

33   Saffroy, *Bibliographie généalogique*, pp. 166-7.

34   Bautier, p. 383.

35   Bautier, p. 384; Lavoix, pp. 17-18 for the use of the royal seal – see MS 17803, no. 306.

36   Bautier, p. 383.

37   MS 17803, nos. 446 and 447; nouv. acq. lat. 1664, no. 11. Also transcription of no. 447 in MS 17803, no. 47; translation by Roger, *Noblesse de France*, pp. 108-9 (characteristically without stating any source).

38   Nouv. acq. lat. 1666, no. 101.

39   G. Lee, 'The oldest European account-book: a Florentine bank ledger of 1211', *Nottingham Mediaeval Studies*, xvi (1972), 28-60.

40   Roger, *Noblesse de France*, pp. 104 ('1218') and 130 ('1249'); perhaps so elegant a name was too good to abandon. Röhricht, *Studien*, no. 12, from MS 17803, no. 383; and, in very similar terms, MS 17803, no. 161. The documents attributed to the Fifth Crusade contain a learned reference to current business methods: ceteras LXXXX libras prefati mercatores nobis tradere se obligauerunt infra duos menses vel antea si navis quedam januensis vocata *Salus* ante hunc terminum ad cismarinas partes applicuerit'. Plausible though this picture (drawn here from no. 161) may be, it is simply an adaptation of the terms used in genuine charters of 1248-52.

41   Ogerio Pane in Röhricht, *Testimonia*, p. 239: 'nobiles cives Ianue Iohannem Rubeum de Volta et Petrum Aurie rectores et presides'. Guglielmo Embriaco and Lanfranco Rubeo della Volta were sent to discuss the planning of the crusade with Henri de Nevers and the comte de la Marche: Ogerio Pane, *ibid.*, p. 238.

42   'Conradum ususmaris' appears in MS 17803, no. 446; cf. Roger, p. 118. For invented names, see Roger, pp. 98-142, and the lists at the start of MS 17803 (f. 3r-4r, nos. 5 to 34). Cf Lavoix, p. 18.

43   E.g. Roger, *Noblesse de France*, pp. 124-5: 'Lanfranc de Gusulfis'.

44   *Layettes du Trésor des Chartes*, ed. M. Joseph de Laborde, i (Paris, 1863), no. 485a; cf. Röhricht, *Studien*, p. v, n. 3 and (for the forgeries) no. 10, listing 20 documents in what are mostly very brief summaries in MS 17803. Cf Lavoix, p. 11, with text.

45   A large literature here: see now W.C. Jordan, *Louis IX and the challenge of the crusade* (Princeton, 1979), for a survey of the problem of war finance (especially pp. 94-104); and, among older works, A. Sayous, 'Les mandats de saint Louis sur son trésor', *Revue historique*, clxvii (1931), 254-304; the documents from Genoese notarial registers printed on pp. 290-304 are totally different in wording and structure to the Courtois *notule*.

46   A. Jal, 'Mémoire sur quelques documents génois relatifs aux deux croisades de S. Louis', *Annales maritimes et coloniales* (1842).

47   *Layettes*, iii (Paris, 1875), no. 3800. As this document reveals, the Ceba family was indeed active in business by the mid-thirteenth century, but not, as Courtois intimated, in the years around 1200.

48   *Layettes*, iii, no. 3771.

49   On the financing of the Third Crusade, see Cartellieri, *Philipp II.*, pp. 52-74.

50   Lacabane noted that J441 no. 3 'a évidemment servi de modèle' – nouv. acq. lat. 1666, no. 83; cf. no. 85. Several other documents from J441 are listed by Lacabane, as likely models for the forgeries. Lavoix, p. 16, saw in the similarities evidence of the *authenticity* of MS 17803!

51   Röhricht, *Studien*, pp. 79-135. Röhricht provides a source reference after the names of crusaders; those names derived solely from Roger, Blancmesnil or MS 17803 must be regarded as dubious; those derived from an additional source are however 'clean'.

APPENDIX

Examples of documents from the Cabinet Courtois

I. Johannes de Chastenaio, Messina, February 1190. (Bibliothèque Nationale, MS 17803A ('original'); MS 17803, no. 441 (lithograph); nouv. acq. lat. 1664, no. 8 (Lacabane's transcription)).

Uniuersis presentes litteras inspecturis Notum sit quod nos gilo de ambleio Reginaldus de mailleio et gaufridus derf armiger mutuo recepimus a lazarino de niela angelo cauaccia et eorum sociis mercatoribus de ianua sexaginta marcas argenti eis nunc in annum reddendas pro quibus nobilis uir dominus noster Johannes de Chastenaio miles garantizore se constituit et eciam eisdem mercatoribus quedam sua iocalia obligauit licet duo bacilia seu bacinola de argento deauratos ponderis marcharum undecim et goboletum unum cum tribus pedibus ymaginatum de uno gallo sursum marcharum decem et unciarum quatuor et cuppallas duas et unam cuppinam in terminis prestator mercatori amplius declaratas. In cuius rei testimonium et sue concessionis signum predictum dominus J. de Chastenaio presentes litteras sigillo suo sigillari fecit. Actum messine anno incarnati uerbi m°. c°. nonagesimo. mense februarij.

CYROGRAPHVM

Seal (attached on parchment strip): knight on horseback; legend illegible, except letters I0....; yellow wax.

Reverse: J°. de chastenaio plegium pro Lx marc̄. arg. And in what appears as a more 'recent' hand: Sicurtà. niela. caraccia. xlv.

This is a particularly ambitious forgery, both in the elaborate contents and the attempt to imitate a chirograph.

II. Standard type of miniature documents.
(Bibliothèque Nationale, MS 17803, no. 447 ('original'); no. 47 (copy)).

These two documents refer to different individuals, but the text is identical except for the names introduced by the forgers. Both documents refer to Hugh, comte de Bar and the mythical Genoese banker L. de Nerla or Neila, whose names have been allowed to stand.

In presentia testium infra nobilis * * * * se substituit erga me L. de Nerla ianuensem ciuem loco et debito nobilis bone memorie * * quondam patris sui debentis mihi cum sex sociis suis in solidum CCCC marcas argenti et promisit pro parte sua mihi procurare loco garantizatoris illius debiti bone memorie Hugonis quendam, comitis Bavrensis, garantizatorem illius debiti H. ducem Burgundie pro dicto mutuo CCCC marcarum argenti in solidum et pro dicto novo mutuo XL marcarum argenti ipsi nobili * * personaliter factis quarum XL dictus dominus de XV contentus est et reliquum recipiet quando litteras suas patentes sigillatas et garantizatoris dicti illius debiti H. ducis Burgundie mihi tradident. In cuius rei testimonium signo suo subscripsit.

Testes sunt * * * * * * * * * * Actum accon, anno incarnationis uerbi M CXCI, mense iulii.

In no. 447: Guillelmus Cleronis miles Hugonis Cleronis quondam patris sui.

In no. 47: Herbertus de Monasterio armiger Renaldi de Monasterio quondam patris sui.

No. 447 measures only 2″ × 3″. Abbreviations are startling: i. c. for ianuensem ciuem; i. n. for ipsi nobili, etc. The lack of variety in the sums of money and other details is also startling.

ADDENDA ET CORRIGENDA

II

p. 371, lines 19–22 should state the opposite: 'Mentre, fino ai due re Martini, i re aragonesi di Sicilia non furono re d'Aragona ma rimasero independenti di Barcellona, le regioni catalane della Sardegna non ebbero mai dinastie aragonesi locali.'

VI

p. 70: The relationship between Savona and Roger II needs to be reassessed in the light of the research of Carlrichard Brühl, *Rogerii II Regis Diplomata* (*Codex diplomaticus regni Siciliae*, ser. 1, *Diplomata regum et principum e gente Normannorum*, ed. C. Brühl, F. Giunta, A. Guillou, Cologne, 1987), doc. 10, 24–8. In addition to the entries that provide the text of the three documents concerning relations with Savona in the *Registro piccolo della Catena* preserved in the Archivio di Stato at Savona, Brühl identifies the original of the second document (*Pergamene sciolte*, vol. 3, no. 3, in the same archive). Brühl's arguments concerning the dating and text of this document therefore supersede those in my *Two Italies*, 65–9. The evidence does appear trustworthy, and it may be worth laying particular stress on the links between Roger II, the Aleramico dynasty, the 'Lombard' settlers in Sicily, Savona and Genoa (see III 107).

IX

p. 127, note 8, second sentence, should read: 'Part of the Italian original was published by Persico, pp. 261–96.'

XIII

p. 547, note 53: the full reference is: D. Jacoby, 'The rise of a new emporium in the eastern Mediterranean: Famagusta in the late thirteenth century', *Méletai kai Hypomnêmata* (*Hidryma Archiepiscopou Makariou III*, Nicosia, 1984), vol. 1, 145–79; now reprinted in: David Jacoby, *Studies on the Crusader states and on Venetian expansion* (Variorum Collected Studies, 1989), no. VIII. The reference to the same item in XII, 203, note 36, in error gives the pagination twice.

INDEX

For Product Safety Concerns and Information please contact our EU representative GPSR@taylorandfrancis.com Taylor & Francis Verlag GmbH, Kaufingerstraße 24, 80331 München, Germany

T - #0027 - 230425 - C0 - 224/150/19 [21] - CB - 9780860783770 - Gloss Lamination